Praise for *The Plant-Powered Diet*

"*The Plant-Powered Diet* is a compilation of compelling arguments for the ideal nutrition plan—one that is based on whole plant foods. Palmer is welcoming to her readers as she provides solutions for eating in a more health-promoting way. I recommend this as a resource for anyone seeking a healthier diet."

—**Julieanna Hever**, MS, RD, CPT, plant-based dietitian and author of *The Complete Idiot's Guide to Plant-Based Nutrition*

"*The Plant-Powered Diet* makes the transition to a plant-powered lifestyle simple. The support tools, such as pantry lists, dining out tips, and recipes, will help anyone realistically make the leap into a plant-powered lifestyle. It's refreshing to see a focus on whole food, vegetarian recipes."

—**Dawn Jackson Blatner**, RD, author of *The Flexitarian Diet*

"In *The Plant-Powered Diet*, Sharon Palmer shares her passion for wholesome, delicious plant foods. This book, which is based on compelling scientific evidence, will help you find your own plant-based eating style that's healthy, sustainable, and delicious."

—**Cheryl Forberg**, RD, James Beard Award–winning chef, *New York Times* bestselling author, and original nutritionist for *The Biggest Loser*

"A plant-powered diet is a very powerful step in the right direction toward an all plant-based, whole-food diet. A very useful and very informative book."

—**Gene Stone**, editor of *Forks Over Knives: The Plant-Based Way to Health* and author of *The Secrets of People Who Never Get Sick*

"*The Plant-Powered Diet* is not your typical 'diet' book, but a very well-researched and practical guide to help people shift away from the typical meat-centric lifestyle. Sharon Palmer's wisdom will be invaluable in helping people embrace efforts like Meatless Monday, which can benefit their health and the health of the planet."

—**Peggy Neu**, president of The Monday Campaigns

"*The Plant Powered Diet* is a spot-on roadmap for our time. Eating deliciously, healthfully, and with a sense of our place in the world has never been easier, thanks to Sharon—I love this book!"

—**Kate Geagan**, MS, RD, author of *Go Green Get Lean:*
Trim Your Waistline with the Ultimate Low-Carbon Footprint Diet

"*The Plant-Powered Diet* is a celebration of the delicious, healthful qualities of beautiful plant foods in their natural form. Everyone can gain tremendous benefits from eating this way."

—**Patricia Bannan**, MS, RD,
nutrition expert and author of *Eat Right When Time Is Tight*

"Sharon Palmer gently guides you to a menu of healthier food choices in this well-researched and beautifully written comprehensive plan. *The Plant-Powered Diet* will educate you and motivate you to include more powerful plant foods in your diet every day."

—**Jill Weisenberger**, MS, RD, CDE,
author of *Diabetes Weight Loss—Week by Week*

The Plant-Powered Diet

The Plant-Powered Diet

THE LIFELONG EATING PLAN
FOR ACHIEVING OPTIMAL HEALTH,
BEGINNING TODAY

Sharon Palmer

HODDER

First published in the USA in 2012 by The Experiment, LLC

First published in Great Britain in 2012 by Hodder & Stoughton
An Hachette UK company

1

A CIP catalogue record for this title is available from the British Library

Trade Paperback ISBN 978 1 444 76506 9
Ebook ISBN 978 1 444 76507 6

Text design by Pauline Neuwirth, Neuwirth & Associates, Inc.

Printed and bound by CPI Group (UK) Ltd, Croydon, CR0 4YY

Hodder & Stoughton policy is to use papers that are natural, renewable and
recyclable products and made from wood grown in sustainable forests. The
logging and manufacturing processes are expected to conform to the
environmental regulations of the country of origin.

Hodder & Stoughton Ltd
338 Euston Road
London NW1 3BH

www.hodder.co.uk

This book is not intended as a substitute for the medical advice of physicians
or other clinicians. Readers should consult with a physician, dietician, or other
health care professional before beginning or making any changes to a diet,
exercise, or health program. The authors and publisher expressly disclaim
responsibility for any liability, loss, or risk – personal or otherwise – which is
incurred, directly or indirectly, as a consequence of the use and application
of any of the contents of this book.

Contents

Foreword

BY DR. DAVID L. KATZ

We actually can't say on the basis of truly conclusive evidence what specific dietary pattern is "best" for human health. There is evidence that a Mediterranean diet can be better than a low-fat diet at improving a wide array of cardiac risk factors. There is evidence that a portfolio of foods—such as whole grains, nuts, legumes, fruits, and vegetables—assembled with the specific goal of lowering cholesterol can do so better than a low-fat diet, and as well as a cholesterol-lowering drug. And yet there is also evidence that a very low-fat, plant-based diet can reverse the damaging effects of plaques that accumulate in the coronary arteries and lead to heart disease, as well as alter the way certain genes are expressed in a manner expected to reduce cancer risk.

We cannot say what specific dietary pattern is best, because definitive head-to-head comparison trials have not been done, and almost certainly won't be. Would you sign up to be randomly assigned to a specific dietary pattern for the next several decades? Only if thousands were to answer "yes" would such a trial be feasible—with the enormous costs and daunting logistics still standing in the way.

What we can agree upon, on the basis of a decisive confluence of evidence from numerous and diverse sources, is a theme of healthful eating. And perhaps none has summed it up more concisely than Michael Pollan: "Eat food, not too much, mostly plants."

The theme of healthful eating consistently emphasizes the same basic constellation of foods: vegetables, fruits, beans, legumes, nuts, seeds, and whole grains. There are several legitimate variations on the theme: Some include low- and nonfat dairy and eggs, others do not. Some include fish and seafood, others do not. Some include lean meats, others do not. All banish to the realm of rare indulgence those highly processed foods that deliver concentrated doses of refined starch, sugar, trans fat, certain saturated fats, and sodium. All start with the building blocks of actual foods that are recognizable and pronounceable, especially plant foods, and the portion control that tends to occur all but automatically when eating these foods.

That we can assert a theme of healthful eating with a confidence we lack for any specific variant is arguably a good thing. An allowance for variations on a theme is an allowance for customization. Food is a source of important pleasure in our lives, and while we should not mortgage our health for that pleasure, neither should we mortgage that pleasure for our health. The dietary sweet spot, as it were, is loving food that loves us back! Variations on the theme of healthful eating allow us each to get there in our own particular way. Several of these dietary variations have been investigated regarding their potential for health promotion.

The Mediterranean diet—more a class of diets than one *per se*—stands out as a candidate for best mixed diet laurels. Studies suggest benefits across a spectrum of health outcomes, from weight to cancer, and from cardiovascular disease to life expectancy.

A balanced, mixed diet of plant and animal foods was used in the *Diabetes Prevention Program* and produced a 58 percent reduction in the incidence of Type 2 diabetes in high-risk adults. In the various DASH diet studies, a diet including low- and nonfat dairy was more effective at lowering blood pressure than a plant-based diet without dairy.

As for the low-carb diet, this is somewhat of a misnomer—a truly low-carb diet would have to be low in vegetables, fruits, whole grains, and, to a lesser extent, beans and other legumes as well. This truly low-carb diet would not, in my view, be a reasonable consideration. A low-carb diet that does not limit vegetables or beans could more precisely be termed a "selective-carb diet," in which "good" carbs are highlighted and "bad" carbs are limited. And in fact, every "good" diet—every reasonable contender for best-diet laurels—is already a selective-carb diet, while also preserving the good sense to include fruits.

One noteworthy variation on the theme of low-carb eating is the so-called "Eco-Atkins" diet, a way to eat more protein without imposing the environmental harms attached to eating more meat (which I will discuss in more detail further on). Perhaps Eco-Atkins deserves a spot in the diet pageant, but frankly, that's debatable. There is research to show that given a choice between achieving a low dietary glycemic load by eating fewer carbohydrates or by eating better carbohydrates, eating better carbohydrates is more helpful.

For those inclined to eat only plants, a consistent body of evidence supports health benefits of a vegetarian or vegan diet, although not discernibly more than those of a Mediterranean diet. And of course, eating only plant foods does not guarantee a healthful, balanced diet. Sugar—among the more reviled of modern dietary excesses and the ultimate "bad carb"—comes from plants, after all. So the potential health benefits of veganism require that it be well practiced.

What may surprise the staunchest proponents of a vegan diet is the lack of evidence that veganism, even well practiced, is better for our personal health than well-practiced omnivorousness. There are three important considerations related to this point.

First, it stands to reason that human physiology is well adapted to certain animal foods. While paleoanthropologists may continue to debate the exact degree to which our Stone Age ancestors were gatherers versus hunters, there is consensus that they were both. Animal foods—meat, fish, and eggs—are a native part of the human diet.

Second, dietary details matter in both the animal and plant kingdoms. The category of animal foods is home to everything from wild salmon to a wide array of salamis. Some choices are likely to promote health, others to threaten it. A one-size-fits-all assessment of the health effects of eating "animal foods" is almost certain to be erroneous.

And third, what we have here is an absence of evidence, rather than evidence of absent (or present) health effects. As noted, the decades-long randomized trial of optimized vegan eating versus optimized omnivorous eating has not been conducted, and likely will not be. That said, veganism and plant-based eating are viable variations on the theme of healthy eating. And a vegan diet, when well devised, offers benefits to one's personal health and the health of the planet as well—an increasingly urgent concern.

In fact, we might do well to consider sustainability as a feature of any diet competing to be "best." Not to put too fine a point on it, but in our voracious multitudes—now roughly 7 billion of us—we can quite literally destroy the planet by the injudicious indulgence of our appetites—in particular by placing an emphasis on meat. We are fast becoming to the whole planet what locusts are to a field of wheat. And as ostensibly sentient creatures with options, we should find that hard to justify.

All of which encourages us to embrace the theme of mostly plant-based eating. But even if we do so in principle, many of us are apt to need some help putting the commitment into practice. That's where *The Plant-Powered Diet* enters the picture.

In this book, Sharon Palmer makes an impassioned and persuasive case for plant-based eating, while appropriately acknowledging the room for variations on that theme, which include plant-based vegan, vegetarian, and omnivorous diets. So much of modern health advice is about marketing a particular perspective that such a balanced and moderate approach is a truly surprising and welcome departure. Palmer highlights the destination—overall, lifelong health—but leaves you in the driver's seat to choose the route you prefer.

But *The Plant-Powered Diet* does more than point out and explain patterns of eating that will assuredly facilitate weight control and promote health—it makes the progress toward those prizes easy and incremental. Combining new insights with common sense, the book demonstrates an unintimidating, step-by-step route to improving your diet. Each chapter includes user-friendly tools and tips, and to further ease your progress, the book culminates with a 14-day suggested meal plan and 75 recipes for plant-based fare that can fit into any healthy diet. Whether these recipes mark the start of entirely plant-based eating or simply serve to incorporate more nutritious plant foods into an omnivorous diet, they will benefit all readers. *The Plant-Powered Diet* is, itself, powerful—blending good judgment, persuasive argument, balanced positions, keen insights, and empowering strategies. Sharon Palmer further seasons that mix with conviction and enthusiasm—putting on display the delight she obviously derives from loving food that loves her back. Altogether, that makes for a very enticing recipe!

So without further ado … bon appétit!

DAVID L. KATZ, MD, MPH, FACPM, FACP, is Founding Director of the Yale University Prevention Research Center. For more information on Dr. Katz, please visit his website, www.davidkatzmd.com.

Introduction

Eat more whole plants. That's the simple advice I dole out when asked about the best diet for optimal health and weight. It's a question that's come up a lot in my long career as a registered dietitian and food and nutrition journalist. You see, I live and breathe nutrition; it's my job to pore over nutrition studies, travel to nutrition research conferences, and talk to scientists in a search for strategies to help you live a longer, more vibrant life.

Recently, I've noticed a consensus growing in the nutrition world. The diet debate among dietitians and nutrition scientists has moved beyond low-fat versus low-carb versus high-protein—even beyond micronutrients like vitamins and minerals. Now we're starting to take a fresh look at diet patterns, the overall style in which people eat food. And everyone, from internationally renowned health experts to government nutrition policy–makers to food system advocates, is beginning to agree on one overarching principle: All of us can benefit from shifting to a plant-based diet.

The conversation on plant-based eating is flourishing in the mainstream, too, well outside the confines of scientific journals and conference rooms. A number of influential people in the public eye are speaking out on the benefits of eating more plants. For example, former president Bill Clinton is an often-quoted supporter of a plant-based diet, which helped him regain the physique of his youth and arrest the progression of serious heart disease.

The scientific research on the benefits of shifting away from the typical American diet—stuffed with high amounts of processed foods, meats, sugars, **saturated fats**, and sodium—and toward a whole-foods, plant-based diet has come to a crescendo. It's now clear that our current diet, referred to by researchers as the "Western diet," is leading us down a road to obesity, disease, shortened lifespan, and diminished quality of life.

Sadly, we're also exporting our diet around the world, with industrializing countries partly measuring their accomplishment by the growth of fast food chains and the increasing availability of convenience foods. Sure enough, as cultures move away from their healthy traditional diets—which are often plant based—and begin to imitate our broken-down way of eating, their rates of obesity and chronic disease soar. This phenomenon has also been clearly documented among people who have moved away from their homelands in search of greener pastures in the United States.

As our food supply has become increasingly efficient, convenient, and processed, so have our weight and chronic disease rates spiraled out of control. In this book, I pledge to introduce you to a whole new plant-based way of eating for life.

PLANT-BASED DIETS LEAD TO OPTIMAL HEALTH

A *plant-based diet* is surely becoming a buzzword, but what does it really mean? The definition of a plant-based diet isn't precise: To some it may mean a strict vegan diet that includes no animal products, and to others it may take the form of a semi-vegetarian diet. The definition of a plant-based diet is very broad and allows for your own personal spin—at its core, it's simply a diet that *emphasizes* whole plant foods, such as beans, vegetables, fruits, whole grains, nuts, and seeds. So you don't have to commit to being a strict vegetarian for life to gain the benefits of a powerful plant-based diet—anyone can do it. However, the more whole plant foods you include in your diet, the more health benefits you'll probably gain.

Scientists have discovered thousands of bioactive compounds hidden in plant foods. These plant compounds helped the living plant survive assaults from pests and UV radiation, and now we understand that they provide protection to humans, too. Researchers are only beginning to scratch the surface on how these powerful compounds squelch highly reactive **free radicals** in the body that can damage your cells, halt chronic **inflammation** levels in the body that lead to chronic disease, and more. What's interesting is that, when you isolate these compounds into single chemicals, they don't seem to possess these same protective effects. A tiny miracle happens in every plant: Hundreds of compounds and nutrients act together to protect the plant, but you need to eat the *whole plant* in order to gain these benefits, not the refined and enriched pseudo-foods you'll find lining food shelves today.

Surveys show that now people are more interested in their diet and health than ever, but unfortunately, in practice we're falling short of the mark. We live in a society in which two-thirds of adults and nearly one-third of children and teens are obese or overweight. Today, you can even find toddlers that fall into the obese category. Obesity is a downward spiral; it automatically puts a person at risk for more than twenty major diseases, including type 2 diabetes, rates of which have surged to epidemic proportions. Once called adult-onset diabetes because it was a disease reserved for the aging, type 2 diabetes now strikes people at younger and younger ages.

Now we know that chronic diseases are related to the choices that we make every day, from what we put on our plates to what we do with our feet. By adopting a healthier lifestyle that includes a plant-based diet and plenty of physical activity, you can not only look great and keep your weight in a healthy place, you can prevent life-threatening diseases from ravaging your body and stealing years from your life. You can keep your brain humming at a higher capacity, pump up your immune system, sleep better, feel more content and vibrant, and flex your muscles and joints better. You can age well, preserving your ability to remain physically, mentally, and socially active for years to come, so you'll be able to pick up your grandchildren, travel the world—and stay out of hospitals.

And that's not all. By offering this food to your family, you can ensure the health of every member, from the youngest to the oldest. The way it stands now, our future generation is set to live shorter lives hobbled by disease, disability, and a bankrupted society paying for sky-high medical bills. Do you want your children, nieces, nephews, and grandchildren to face that sort of future? You can change the course of their lives today by making changes at the dinner table and buying a pair of athletic shoes. The awesome power of prevention is in your hands.

PLANT-BASED DIETS PRESERVE THE PLANET

What you put on your plate not only affects the health of you and your family, it impacts the health of the entire planet. As our animal food consumption has soared over the past years, so have our environmental impacts. In the United States, the greenhouse gas emissions from meat production exceed those from the entire transportation sector. The more your diet centers on plants in their whole, unprocessed form, the more gently you tread on Mother Earth, preserving our natural resources for future generations to come. Ways of eating have ethical ramifications, too: Most agricultural animals are raised unsustainably and inhumanely in **concentrated animal feeding operations (CAFOs)**, where they suffer miserable lives packed together with no room to move, caked in feces, and eating an unhealthy, unsuitable diet designed to cheaply and quickly fatten them up for slaughter. A plant-based diet is healthier for us and more humane to our fellow creatures.

I believe that the twenty-first century should become marked by our evolution toward a plant-based diet. Although we certainly had a prehistorical past in which our sustenance involved both hunting animals and gathering plants, I think our future relies on "gathering" more plants and "hunting" fewer animals. The animals our ancestors hunted—an activity that involved rigorous activity that burned a lot of calories—were literally a different breed. As these animals foraged over wild expanses of the natural grasses that they evolved with, they built leaner tissues that contained healthier fat profiles than we can find today. Today, our corn-fed, CAFO-raised cattle share little resemblance to our ancestors' wild game—even today's wild game, in fact. And as our population increases and world powers banter over how to feed the global population in the coming decades, one fact remains: An acre of land planted with crops more efficiently feeds people than an acre of land dedicated to raising animals. That's not even factoring in the amount of resources such as synthetic inputs, water, and fossil fuels that are used to raise, process, and bring animal foods to the market versus plant foods. Basically, we can get most of our nutrients directly from plants, or we can get most of our nutrients indirectly—and inefficiently—from eating the animals that eat the plants.

PLANT-BASED EATING IN MY OWN LIFE AND WORK

As a child, I was lucky to grow up in the woodsy Northwest at a plant-based dinner table long before people called it that. I suppose we were known as semi-vegetarians in those days, because most of the time we ate plant proteins such as soy foods, beans, and nuts instead of animal foods. During the "crunchy" '70s, we feasted on homemade granola, dense whole wheat bread, meat substitutes made of soybeans, nut loafs, and simmered lentils and beans. At the time, I didn't think we were all that different from everyone else. (However, I'll admit I was a bit ashamed of my rough, dark slabs of homemade bread smeared with peanut butter when all the other kids had snow-white bread with bologna in their lunch boxes.)

My mother had a green thumb—having grown up on a farm in Arkansas—so in our kitchen sink there were always fresh fruits and vegetables recently plucked from the garden. But our small garden couldn't supply our family's food needs for the entire year, so every summer my family would pile into our station wagon, roll down the windows, and drive to the farms in eastern Washington, where we'd stop at local fruit and vegetable stands and buy box after box of ripe produce: green beans, salad-plate–sized tomatoes, golden peaches, succulent berries, squashes in every shape and color. I can still remember the smells swirling around in our hot car—the dusky, earthy aromas of our cache of ripe fruits and vegetables making my stomach growl all the way home. Once home, we were allowed to eat our fill of the perfectly ripe bounty—we'd make thick tomato sandwiches and eat peaches at the sink, letting the juice run down our chins—but when we were finally glutted, it was time to pull out the canner and start preserving. Eventually our garage would be lined with rows of glass jars that sparkled like colorful gems.

With all those good homemade foods filling our table, who needed to eat out? Restaurants were virtually unknown territory for me. Processed convenience foods were just beginning to enjoy their heyday in supermarkets as more women entered the workforce and the food industry graciously helped out. Still, we rarely ate out of a box, can, or bag, and we stuck to our old-fashioned, plant-based ways most of the time. I believe this lifestyle is one reason why my parents are still active in their 70s and 80s. And it certainly helped lure me into the kitchen, where I grew fascinated with the connections between the food we eat and our health. Later, as a dietitian, I continued to eat up every bit of the discovery that surrounds the complicated yet important question, *What should we eat for optimal health and enjoyment?*

Now that I've settled down in California with my own family, I've started up my own food traditions that revolve around plant foods. Visiting farmers markets, welcoming in the strawberry season, shucking fresh corn on the cob, whizzing up homemade smoothies, and stirring a bubbling pot of vegetable soup in the wintertime are all part of our family's own food culture. I'm a vegetarian, but my husband and children are plant-based omnivores, eating moderate amounts of animal foods in addition to lots of healthy, whole plants. No matter how busy we are, we find time to gather at the table to eat simple, whole foods. Sure, like other kids, my children complain about the fact that all I prepare is "organic" and "healthy" food, but they never seem to mind actually eating these foods. I'm happy to say that we all enjoy vibrant health as a reward for our plant-based eating style.

PLANT-BASED EATING IS DELICIOUS

Some people blanch at shifting to a plant-based diet because they fear it will suck the enjoyment and flavor from their meals. Have I got news for them! I've had the pleasure of speaking (and eating) with some of today's most talented chefs working in modern cuisine, from award winners like Grant Achatz to young hipsters running street food carts, and I'm happy to report that today's culinary movers and shakers appreciate a freshly picked vegetable. It's commonplace to find chefs maintaining their own vegetable gardens—even on the rooftops, if they must—in order to feature freshly harvested seasonal produce on their menus. The culinary world has come to fully appreciate just how delicious a stalk of spring asparagus or a perfect ripe peach can be, and they showcase these nutritious treasures in their menus every day. More important, home cooks are learning to see with fresh eyes the beauty of a freshly picked green bean or an apricot plucked at its peak, to notice the difference between a tomato that's been picked green and shipped around the country and one grown in their own backyard.

Fine plant foods do not only reside in expensive restaurants, hip eateries, and modern home kitchens, though. They can be found in your grandmother's red beans and rice or curried chickpeas or ratatouille. They all start with simple, fresh, seasonal plants prepared with care and thoughtfulness. And they all end with something delicious.

Consider this: When you focus on animal foods at every meal, your choices are limited to the basic beef, pork, chicken, or seafood selection. But when you plan your meals around plant foods, the sky's the limit. Just think how many greens are available in the middle of summer, from dainty microgreens to hearty kale. There are more than 150 varieties of squashes, such as yellow crookneck, tender courgette, earthy butternut, and stringy spaghetti squash. The shades and flavors of berries that grow in forests and on farms are staggering, from delicate golden salmonberries to deep purple blackberries. And don't even get me started on heirloom tomatoes. A plant-powered diet is more about what you *can* eat than what you *can't* eat. I even encourage you to enjoy the decadent flavors of dark chocolate, coffee, herbs, spices, extra virgin olive oil, and red wine—what's not to like about that! A delicious world of discovery—with an astonishing variety of flavors, textures, and aromas—awaits you.

A PLANT-POWERED DIET FOR LIFE

Remember, no matter where you are, no matter what your personal health or weight goals may be, you can gain benefits from a plant-based diet today. You may decide to move toward a vegan, vegetarian, or plant-based omnivorous diet, but whatever you choose, know that you will improve your health and reap a multitude of rewards. I have poured all of my experience in food and nutrition into the following pages to help you find your own version of a powerful, plant-based diet. I will show you how to move away from a processed, meat-obsessed diet to a simpler, more vital way of living. A plant-powered diet isn't a "diet" that you are either "on" or "off"; it's a style of eating, for life. Each chapter opens up a wide world of plant foods—whole grains, legumes, nuts, seeds, fruits, and vegetables—in new combinations and old. I'll walk you through the aisles of supermarkets and farmers markets, give you my top tips for making the best selections of foods, and share examples of positive decision making. Most of all, I will share with you the delicious wonders of eating whole plant foods.

In chapters 2 through 11, you will find daily Plant-Powered Action Alerts—activities that will help you discover your own plant-powered eating style. After completing 14 days of Plant-Powered Action Alerts, you'll be equipped with the tools to get started on your individual plant-based way of eating for life. I'll share my Daily Plant-Powered Guide, which will help you figure out what to eat every day in order to find balance, meet your nutritional needs, and attain a healthy weight. You'll also find a Plant-Powered Pantry List and a guide to Plant-Powered Kitchen Equipment Essentials that will help you assemble the tools you'll need for your new healthy eating style. My 14-Day Plant-Powered Menu Planner will start you off with great ideas for two weeks of delicious, balanced meals. And finally, the Plant-Powered Recipe Collection in chapter 14 presents seventy-five recipes that I've personally developed and tested in my own home kitchen, complete with nutritional information. Welcome to the wonderful world of powerful plants.

Eating Plants for Optimal Health

Since the beginning of time, humans have had a unique relationship with plants. From the first time our early ancestors plucked wild seeds, grasses, herbs, grains, and fruits and saved them in pouches for the future, they realized that these powerful plants had the ability to nourish and sustain them. Yet living plants tell an even older story—one that includes a long, fruitful evolutionary process of building up mighty defenses against all sorts of pestilence, from the harmful effects of UV radiation to the blights of insects and disease. How did plants create these natural defenses? They developed thousands of **antioxidant** compounds such as **flavonoids** and **phenols**, often concentrating them in the colorful outer skins of their fruits. These compounds provided a self-defense system that ensured the species survived the test of time. Scientists are learning that humans have a symbiotic relationship with plants. Not only do we grow or collect the plants and help spread their seeds, which ensures their propagation and survival, but we also gain self-protective benefits when we eat these foods filled with bioactive compounds—plant substances that provide therapeutic activities such as anticancer and anti-inflammatory action.

Thus, humans have enjoyed a long history flourishing alongside plants, collecting their leaves, roots, stems, seeds, fruits, bark, and nectar for food as well as medicine. And throughout the past centuries and millennia, we were generally lean and fit. But over recent decades we've grown disconnected from our nourishing relationship with plants. As we shop for foods in the supermarket aisles, it's becoming more and more difficult to recognize the plant or food source that these food items came from. When you pick up a box of flaked cereal, can you trace it back to a grain waving in an amber field? When you take a bite out of a cheese puff, can you imagine which plant food might produce that neon orange crunch? It's no coincidence that, as our food supply becomes further removed from whole plants and the earth in which they are grown, our rates of obesity and disease continue to increase. We've wandered away from our food roots; we don't know how our steak came to rest under the cellophane in the meat section or even how orange juice finds its way into its rectangular cartons. We've delegated the preparation of our daily meals to restaurants and food companies instead of preparing them ourselves. And all of us—especially our children and grandchildren—are paying the price in our health. It's a sad day when a dietitian takes a basket of fresh fruits and vegetables to a class she's teaching in an elementary school, only to discover that many of these bright, shining faces can't even identify the fresh potato or orange in the basket (as has been my own experience).

Our calorie intake has risen while our energy needs have fallen—it's a simple matter of math. Throughout history, humans have suffered from periodic food scarcities—for proof, just look back to the bread lines of the Great Depression. Now, a surfeit of cheap, high-calorie, nutrient-poor foods is available on almost every street corner twenty-four hours a day. When I was a child, my family packed a picnic lunch for our family road trips, because we knew food would not be available along the way. You certainly can't say that today: Food is for sale everywhere, from gas stations to bookstores. God forbid that we miss out on an opportunity to eat, or that we hear our stomachs growl from the first signs of hunger! It wouldn't be so bad if these widely available food choices were **nutrient dense** and moderate in calories, but you know exactly what foods you'll find at ubiquitous quick-stop spots: saucer-sized cookies, frosted donuts, candy bars, gargantuan sodas, and greasy hot dogs. Such a sea of calories—and yet our bodies were masterfully designed to preserve calories to survive the lean times.

Your own miraculous being possesses the genetic fingerprints that have stood the test of time over millennia, as your ancestors endured generations of food scarcity and thus acquired the ability to lower their metabolic furnaces in order to operate more efficiently on the existing food supply. This calorie efficiency helped ensure the survival of your bloodline, but unfortunately, it does little help to help you survive in today's world of processed foods plumped up with fat, sodium, sugars, and calories—foods that never existed in nature.

Along with this shift into what I call the "calories, calories everywhere" era came the rise of modern machines that have replaced nearly all of the demands we once placed on our bodies. Throughout history, our bodies required certain levels of calories—fuel, essentially—to power our high activity levels, whether we needed to run to chase that wild game (or run away from that predator!), walk for miles in our nomadic search for greener pastures, or search for plants to collect and eat. For a long time humans relied on manual labor to do everything, including moving from place to place, growing food, building shelter, and producing goods. Today, there is a machine to do virtually everything we need done—escalators to take us upstairs, vacuum cleaners to tidy our living rooms, even machines to "work out" on at the gym. Our activity levels have declined dramatically, so our bodies no longer need the concentrated calories that sodas, French fries, and chicken nuggets are offering—it simply stores all that extra fuel as fat. That's the only way your body knows how to handle those extra calories.

EATING OURSELVES TO DEATH

Our disconnections from physical activity and the nourishing, whole plant foods we evolved with lead to one thing: a lifestyle that is clearly killing us. The leading killers in our society are cardiovascular diseases (e.g., coronary artery disease, hypertension, stroke, and heart failure), type 2 diabetes, **metabolic syndrome** (a clustering of factors that increase risk of disease), and cancer.[1] What do these killer diseases have in common? According to overwhelming evidence, they are all directly related to what you eat and how much you move. And this health crisis isn't confined to the United States—it's going global. According to the World Health Organization, the leading causes of death across the world are high blood pressure, tobacco use, high blood glucose, physical inactivity, and being overweight or obese—conditions that raise the risk of chronic diseases such as heart disease, diabetes, and cancers. With the exception of tobacco use, all of these top killers are related to diet and exercise.[2]

The way we eat has changed dramatically in the past forty years. Today we're drinking more calories in sweetened beverages, eating larger portions, slurping up more added fats and oils in our foods, feasting on more refined grains like white flour, and eating more foods away from home. The number of fast food restaurants has more than doubled since the '70s.[3] This is the way we typically eat in America, also known as the Western diet. It's characterized by high intakes of animal foods—in particular, processed meats and red meats, butter, eggs, and high-fat dairy products—as well as refined grains (e.g., white flour), and low intakes of fruits, vegetables, whole grains, legumes (beans, peas, and lentils), nuts, and seeds.[4] Thus, the Western diet is stacked with calories, fat, saturated fat, sodium, and sugar but low in fiber, vitamins, minerals, and antioxidants. It really shouldn't be a surprise that our diet is literally killing us.

All you've got to do is picture some of our most iconic meals, foods that veritably scream "American food," and you'll see what I mean. A hamburger on a white bun; an 8-ounce steak and a baked potato with butter and sour cream; chicken nuggets with fries; eggs and bacon with white toast; pepperoni pizza—see what I mean? A whole lot of animal food, calories, fat, saturated fat, and salt and not many whole grains, fruits, vegetables, legumes, nuts, or seeds. Here's how we're eating ourselves to death:

1. **Eating Ourselves Fat.** You've already heard the sorry statistics on obesity: two-thirds of adults and nearly one-third of children and teens are now obese or overweight. Despite the attention placed on our burgeoning belt sizes, obesity levels don't seem to be improving much. Obesity is directly related to two things: what you put on your plate and how much you move. Unfortunately, obesity leads to a laundry list of other health problems:
   - Coronary heart disease
   - Type 2 diabetes
   - Cancers (endometrial, breast, and colon)
   - Hypertension (i.e., high blood pressure)

- **Dyslipidemia**
- Stroke
- Liver and gallbladder disease
- Sleep apnea and respiratory problems
- Osteoarthritis (i.e., a degeneration of cartilage and its underlying bone within a joint)
- Gynecological problems (abnormal menses, infertility)[5]

2. **Eating Ourselves Sick.** You may not realize it, but even if you're at a healthy weight, your diet still has the power to damage your health. Yes, even thin people can eat an unhealthful diet, suffer from high cholesterol and high blood pressure, and develop heart disease and cancer. Your daily food choices can add up to a lifestyle that increases your chances of developing disease and dying early. If you eat like the average American, you're filling up on processed foods, red meats, sweetened beverages, salt, sugar, and saturated fat and skimping on whole grains, fruits, vegetables, vitamins, minerals, and fiber. This way of eating has been linked with a number of diseases, such as coronary artery disease, hypertension, diabetes, metabolic syndrome, and several forms of cancer.[6]

3. **Eating Too Many Unhealthy Fats and Refined Carbs.** It's well established that heart disease is linked to unhealthful fats like saturated fats found in animal foods and tropical oils like coconut, palm kernel, and palm oils; **dietary cholesterol** from animal foods; and **trans fats** found in partially hydrogenated oils and used in margarines, fried foods, and baked goods. Saturated fats boost your total cholesterol levels as well as your "bad" **LDL cholesterol** levels, a major risk factor for developing heart disease. It's good to keep your saturated fat intake below 7 percent of your total calories, but most Americans are eating about 11 percent of their calories in saturated fat. Cholesterol, found only in animal foods, raises "bad" LDL cholesterol in some people, so it's still a good idea to keep your intake down. And then there's the *really* bad fat: trans fats. Although a very small amount may be found naturally in some foods, the vast majority of trans fats found their way into our diets through the process of hydrogenating vegetable oils for food production.

Trans fats not only raise LDL cholesterol levels, they also lower "good" **HDL cholesterol** levels.

Starting in the late 1980s, public health experts did begin preaching that saturated fat in the diet was dangerous, but somehow their low-saturated-fat message transformed into a general low-fat mania in the public. So dietary fat—regardless of the *type* of fat—became the bad guy, and carbs—regardless of the *type* of carbs—became the good guys. Enter the Snackwell's era, where virtually any food product that could call itself low-fat wore a health halo, and our intake of refined flours and sugars swelled as a result. Now health experts are beginning to understand that the formula of swapping out fat for highly processed carbohydrates is not a winning proposition—in fact, it may increase the risk of heart disease as well as metabolic disorders. Today, we're eating an average of six daily servings of refined grains and 16 percent of our total calories from added sugars.

The bottom line: We're eating too much saturated animal fat—high-fat dairy products, eggs, chicken, beef, pork, and processed meats like ham, cold cuts, bacon, and sausage—and too many refined carbohydrates, in foods like processed breakfast cereals, refined breads and bagels, snack crackers and crisps made of white flour, baked goods like cakes and cookies, "nutrition" bars, candy, and most of all, sugary beverages like sodas, teas, and sports and "energy" drinks.[7]

4. **Eating Too Much Salt.** The past few years have borne out a new recognition for the destructive power that high levels of sodium (or salt) can unleash on your health. And our problem is not with the salt shaker at the dining table; we're getting the vast majority of our salt from convenience, processed, and prepared foods, according to statistics. After all, we live in a world of processed foods, such as soups and rice mixes that contain 1,000 milligrams of sodium per serving (and, according to surveys, most people eat two or three times the suggested serving size), and restaurant meals that often provide more than 3,000 milligrams of sodium per serving. Our "salt tooth" is putting us at risk for high blood pressure, a serious condition that can lead to a variety of maladies such as heart disease and stroke.

According to the Institute of Medicine, if Americans were to reduce their sodium intake to recommended levels, it would save 100,000 lives each year. For most Americans, that means reducing to a sodium intake of 1,500 milligrams per day. That's pretty bad news, considering we're now taking in an average of 3,400 milligrams per day, mostly from processed foods like chicken dishes, pizza, pasta dishes, cold cuts, and condiments.[8]

5. **Eating Ourselves to Inflammation.** Certain foods that you eat every day can stoke your body's levels of inflammation, a condition that scientists now widely believe is a root of the chronic killer diseases of our time, including heart disease, metabolic syndrome, type 2 diabetes, cancer, rheumatoid arthritis, and neurodegenerative disease. Although acute inflammation (your body's natural reaction to an injury or assault such as stubbing your toe) is good, chronic inflammation is not. When your body's inflammatory reaction fails to shut off or becomes activated when there is no real trigger—sometimes lasting for days, months, or even years—chronic inflammation results.

According to growing evidence, your diet and lifestyle can either create a pro-inflammatory milieu or an anti-inflammatory one. In fact, inflammation may turn out to be one of the main reasons why healthful, plant-based diets promote health and the Western diet promotes disease. Italian researchers found that Western dietary patterns high in refined starches, sugars, saturated fats, and trans fats and low in fruits, vegetables, whole grains, and **omega-3 fatty acids** appear to turn on the inflammatory response, but a diet rich in whole foods, including healthful carbohydrate, fat, and protein sources along with regular exercise and not smoking, seems to cool down inflammation.[9]

6. **Eating Ourselves Away from the Good Stuff.** Because we fill our bellies with processed beverages, foods, and snacks such as crackers, crisps, cookies, bars, and sodas that are nearly devoid of nutrients, we don't have enough room for the good stuff. Our diets fall short in nutrient-rich fruits, vegetables, whole grains, and legumes—foods that provide a rich supply of nutrients like

vitamins, minerals, fiber, and **phytochemicals** for relatively few calories. On average, we're only getting three daily servings of fruits and vegetables combined (if you don't count potatoes) and only one daily serving of whole grains, falling way below our recommended intake for optimal health.[10] Study after study shows that, if you increase your intake of these healthy, plant-based foods, you'll weigh less and enjoy a lower chance of developing heart attack, stroke, heart disease, and certain types of cancer.

A MEAT LOVER'S SOCIETY

It's not news that Americans love their meat; just ask anyone visiting the United States for the first time. They're sure to comment on the enormous portions of steak, chicken, or even fish that fill their plates when they dine anywhere in the country. Indeed, surveys show that portion sizes in restaurants have increased significantly over the past four decades.[11] Most steakhouse menus proudly advertize a 16-ounce cut—a full pound of meat on your plate—and call their 8-ounce portion the "petite" serving. This oversized attitude toward meat also pervades backyard barbeques and home-style cooking. In fact, home cooks usually plan their entire meal around animal protein. According to the National Cancer Institute, the United States consumes meat at more than three times the global average.[12]

Our meat-loving ways have accelerated over the years. Ask any octogenarian how he ate during his youth, a period marked by economic hardship and food scarcity, and he'll probably tell you there was a lot less meat on the dinner table in those days. He might even regale you with stories about how meat was so precious it was reserved for Sunday dinners and how a small serving would be used to flavor a whole pot of beans for a meal. And he wouldn't be exaggerating. Meat consumption has definitely risen over the years—it's doubled between 1909 and 2007. Across the world, meat consumption is typically an indicator of economic wealth: As income levels rise, so does meat consumption. Despite a current shift toward higher poultry consumption in the United States, red meat is still the clear winner, representing 58 percent of the meat we consume. We're each eating an average of 225g of meat every day.[13]

A PRICE TO PAY FOR MEAT OBSESSION

So, what's the big fuss about eating so much meat? Well, it looks like a high-meat diet—especially red meat and processed meat—is likely to cause health problems down the road. The majority of scientific research points a damning finger at red meat, a category that includes beef, veal, pork, and lamb. In particular, the evidence is most compelling against processed meats such as cold cuts, ham, sausage, hot dogs, and bacon. It looks like the negative effects of this type of diet could be caused in part by the presence of carcinogenic compounds in cooked and processed meats, and in part by the absence of health-protective plants typical of this way of eating. In fact, researchers from the National Cancer Institute suggest that, given the plausible scientific evidence linking red and processed meats to cancer and chronic disease risk, it might be time for health experts in the US to start working on bringing our levels of meat intake down.[14] And the concerns about eating so much meat extend beyond our own health and into issues like environmental impacts and feeding the growing global population.

Even in the recent past, meat wasn't as plentiful or inexpensive as it is today—you can thank the advent of modern animal agriculture practices for making meat so cheap in America. We're churning out ground beef as efficiently as we fabricate clothes hangers, but we're paying a heavy toll in inhumane animal conditions and unhealthful food. As animals are confined, fed diets unsuited for them, and pumped with antibiotics to prevent diseases caused by overcrowding, they produce meat that is inferior in nutritional quality to that of pasture-raised animals. When cattle are allowed to roam in pastures and graze on wild grasses, their meat has a better fatty-acid profile than that of confined, grain-fed cattle. In addition, modern animal agriculture poses environmental concerns and food safety threats ranging from antibiotic resistance, caused by the overuse of antibiotics in farm animals, to toxic manure lagoons that pollute local waters and spread foodborne pathogens.

TOP ELEVEN REASONS TO CUT BACK ON (OR CUT OUT) MEAT

Here are my top, scientifically backed reasons why you should cut down on your meat intake for life.

1. **It can hurt your heart.** One of the first things any health expert will tell you if you have high blood cholesterol levels or a history of heart disease is to cut back on animal fats, because high intakes of saturated fats and cholesterol increase your LDL ("bad") cholesterol and total cholesterol levels, thus increasing your risk for heart disease. Animal foods such as red meat, processed meats, poultry dishes, and full-fat dairy products are heavy sources of saturated fats and cholesterol. Research reveals that people who eat red meat are more likely to have high blood pressure and high cholesterol levels. Although a number of studies have linked red meat consumption with heart disease, a recent Harvard meta-analysis of studies, including data on more than 1.2 million people, narrowed this connection to processed meats in particular. In the study, processed meats were linked to a 42 percent higher risk of coronary heart disease.[15] It's important to note that although poultry dishes can be large contributors to dangerous levels of saturated fat in the diet, research has not proven a direct connection between moderate poultry intake and heart disease, and a number of studies have found that eating two servings of fish per week is linked with heart health.

2. **It ups your risk of type 2 diabetes.** Scientists recently found another reason to cut back on red meat—particularly when it's processed: It ups your risk of developing type 2 diabetes, one of the most devastating diseases of our time. In an exhaustive study, researchers evaluated data from the Health Professionals Follow-up Study, which followed more than 37,000 men for 20 years; the Nurses' Health Study I, which followed more than 79,000 women for 28 years; the Nurses' Health Study II, which followed more than 87,000 women for 14 years; and other existing studies, adding up to a grand total of 442,101 participants who were evaluated regarding their dietary risk factors for developing type 2 diabetes. The researchers discovered that eating a daily 100-gram serving of red meat (the size of a deck of cards) was linked with a 19 percent increased risk of developing type 2 diabetes. Eating a daily 50-gram serving of processed meat—which equals one hot dog or sausage or two slices of bacon—was associated with a 51 percent increased risk of type 2 diabetes. And this

isn't the first time researchers have observed an increased risk for type 2 diabetes from red and processed meat consumption.[16]

3. **It may pump up inflammation.** Scientists have noticed that red meat is linked to higher levels of chronic inflammation, which can promote a string of chronic diseases such as heart disease, type 2 diabetes, and Alzheimer's disease. Scientists speculate that this pro-inflammatory response may be due to red meat's high saturated fat and iron content. On the other hand, fish intake has been linked to lower levels of inflammation.[17]

4. **It raises your risk of metabolic syndrome.** Metabolic syndrome has been called the scourge of our modern era. It's not a disease but rather a collection of unhealthy factors that include a large waist circumference, high triglyceride levels, low HDL ("good") cholesterol, high blood sugar, and high blood pressure. If you have three or more of these measurements, you've got metabolic syndrome, which puts you at risk for a number of diseases: People with metabolic syndrome are five times more likely to get type 2 diabetes and twice as likely to develop heart disease. Diet is one of the main factors in developing metabolic syndrome. A recent study that included 482 female teachers aged 40 to 60 found that higher intakes of red meat were linked with greater risk of metabolic syndrome.[18]

5. **It may boost your toxin load.** People love to eat their meat in shades of deep brown and black, coveting that grilled, smoked, charred flavor that comes from cooking red meat, poultry, and fish at high temperatures. And we also like our cured or salted meats, such as cold cuts, hot dogs, ham, and bacon. Yet evidence now reveals that these forms of cooking and processing meats produce dangerous, carcinogenic compounds such as **nitroso compounds, heterocyclic amines (HCAs),** and **polycyclic aromatic hydrocarbons (PAHs),** as well as **advanced glycation end products (AGEs),** which are related to inflammation and diabetes. Cooking animal proteins at high temperatures—deep-frying, pan-frying, grilling, and smoking—promotes the development of HCAs, PAHs, and AGEs, and the carcinogenic nitroso compounds in processed meats like cold cuts, ham, and bacon are formed from the nitrates and nitrites added during

processing. In fact, these toxins may be at the root of the disease risk we see among people who eat high levels of processed meats. That's why health experts routinely recommend that you avoid smoked or cured foods and charred or seared fish, meat, and poultry to reduce your exposure to food-borne carcinogens.[19]

Don't underestimate the dangerous toxins that can be found in foods as a result of foodborne pathogens. Many parasites, bacteria, and viruses such as *E. coli* and salmonella find their way into food as a result of animal agriculture, particularly contamination during meat and poultry processing and preparation. In addition, residues of the hormones rBST and rBGH, used to promote growth in dairy and beef cattle and sheep, have been linked to breast, prostate, and colorectal cancers in people, not to mention health problems in animals. Unfortunately, definitive evidence regarding human health risks from these hormones is inconclusive at this time.[20] But that doesn't mean we should use them. And then there are highly toxic environmental contaminants such as dioxins and mercury that can wind up in meat, dairy, fish, and shellfish. It's well known that many toxins are stored in the fat of animals; in general, the lower you eat on the food chain, the lower your toxic load will be.

6. **It can promote antibiotic resistance.** It's estimated that 70 percent of all antibiotics used in the United States are fed to animals such as cattle, chickens, pigs, and farmed fish for nontherapeutic purposes—essentially to get them to grow faster to get them to market more quickly. Many of the antibiotics used are identical or almost identical to those used for humans, such as penicillin and tetracycline. Antibiotics are automatically added to animal feed and water as a preventative measure to compensate for the overcrowded, unsanitary conditions in CAFOs that put animals at risk for disease. This routine use of antibiotics means that they spill into ground water, manure, and soil, as well as become airborne, threatening farm families, workers, and entire communities with antibiotic resistance. In a two-year review of more than 500 scientific studies on the human health impacts of antibiotic use in animal agriculture, researchers concluded that antibiotics should not be used nontherapeutically in agriculture.[21] A number of organizations, such as the American Medical Association and the American Public Health Association, back legislation that would require the FDA to review their list of approved antibiotics for animals, and a recent federal ruling requires the FDA to address the overuse of non-therapeutic antibiotics in livestock. In the meantime, reducing your consumption of animal foods—meat, farmed fish, poultry, milk, eggs, and cheese—means reducing the amount of antibiotics that spill into the environment and undermine the effectiveness of the antibiotics we need to treat human disease.

7. **It may escalate your risk of cancer.** The evidence on cancer risk and red meat—processed red meat in particular—is becoming quite convincing. Although the consumption of red meat has been implicated in several cancers—prostate, breast, lung, kidney, esophagus, lung, liver, and pancreatic—the most conclusive evidence relates to colorectal cancer. In a comprehensive investigation of the National Institute of Health–AARP Diet and Health Study, which included more than 500,000 men and women, a significant increased risk of cancers of the colorectum and esophagus (as well as lung and liver) was associated with red meat; an increased risk of colorectal and lung cancer was associated with higher intake of processed meat; and red and processed meat intake was associated with cancer mortality.[22] Why does red meat promote cancer? We don't know for sure yet, but we do know that large amounts can produce genetic damage to colon cells in just a few weeks. This may be due to the cancer-promoting compounds (nitroso compounds, HCAs, and PAHs) that are produced when meats are cooked and processed. The proof that eating red and processed meat increases your risk for colorectal cancer is so convincing, the American Institute for Cancer Research now reports that eating more than 365g of red meat per week—and *any* amount of processed meat at all—increases your risk of colorectal cancer.[23]

8. **It can add pounds.** Meats are much higher in calories and fat than most whole plant foods, so it shouldn't be a surprise that, in a study using National Health and Nutrition Examination Survey data, researchers found that people who consumed the

highest amounts of meat had a much higher daily caloric intake, about 700 calories more per day, than those who consumed the lowest amounts of meat. The study also found that those who consumed high amounts of meat were 27 percent more likely to be obese and were also more likely to have a larger waist size (i.e., abdominal obesity) than low-meat eaters.[24]

9. **It may cut your lifespan.** Now that surely caught your attention. But yes, that's the news that came out of the first large study to look at whether eating red meat regularly can affect lifespan. Using data on 500,000 adults who took part in the National Institute of Health–AARP Diet and Health Study over ten years, researchers found that those who consumed about 110g of red meat a day (the size of a small hamburger) were more than 30 percent more likely to die, mostly from heart disease and cancer, compared with those who ate the lowest amounts of meat. An increase in death rate was also observed in those with a higher processed meat intake. It all makes sense, when you consider that those eating more red meat have a higher risk for heart disease and colorectal cancer. Compared to the frequent red-meat eaters, those who routinely consumed fish, chicken, turkey, and other poultry had a slightly decreased risk of death.[25]

10. **It magnifies your carbon footprint.** If you cut back your animal food intake, you can make a big impact on planet Earth. Each year we eat billions of pounds of meat and drink billions of gallons of dairy products from billions of animals. In doing so, we not only contribute to inhumane animal practices, but we are responsible for the use of large amounts of chemical pesticides and fertilizers to produce animal feed, as well as large volumes of water and fuel to take animals to market. Byproducts of animal food production include greenhouse gas emissions, toxic manure lagoons, deforestation, and pollution of groundwater, rivers, streams, and oceans. According to a recent analysis conducted by CleanMetrics for the Environmental Working Group, greenhouse gas emissions generated by conventionally raising lamb, beef, cheese, pork, and farmed salmon—from growing the animals' food to disposing of the unused food—far exceed those from other food choices like lentils and beans.[26]

11. It squanders precious global food supplies. In our culture of climbing obesity rates, it should be a wake-up call to remember that one billion people around the world don't have enough food to eat right now. And just think how much tougher it will be to feed the world in 2050, when there will be nine billion people living on the planet. At the same time, our current agricultural practices and diet patterns are unsustainable. But environmental experts agree on one important principle that could increase the world sustainability of food for the long haul: Growing animal feed on prime croplands, no matter how efficiently, is a drain on the human food supply. Dedicating croplands to direct human food production could boost calories produced per person by nearly 50 percent, according to a recent report from researchers from Canada, the United States, Sweden, and Germany.[27]

MAKE AN ECO-IMPACT: EAT LESS MEAT

ACCORDING TO THE Environmental Working Group, eating less meat can significantly reduce your carbon footprint—the total greenhouse gas emissions produced from your activities. Here's how your eating less meat will measure up in climate-saving action over one year.

- If you eat one less burger a week . . . It's like driving 320 miles less.
- If your four-person family skips meat and cheese one day a week . . . It's like taking your car off the road for five weeks.
- If your four-person family takes steak off the menu one day a week . . . It's like taking your car off the road for almost three months.
- If everyone in the United States ate no meat or cheese for just one day a week . . . It would be like driving 91 billion miles less, or taking 7.6 million cars off the road.[28]

FROM TRADITION TO NUTRITION

If you travel the globe and visit undeveloped countries that still eat their traditional, native diets, you'll notice one common trait: Most of these diets center around plants. Just like here, animal foods tend to be the most expensive, and in many poor, unindustrialized countries they are precious. When growing your own food, a more common feature of indigenous societies, it requires a lot of resources, such as food and water, to feed an animal and then slaughter it for meat. It's cheaper and more efficient to eat the vegetables, fruits, legumes, and grains yourself and to raise animals, if you're lucky enough to have animals, for milk or for trade. Perhaps at a celebration—a wedding, religious holiday, or feast—an animal might be killed for food. But in everyday life only small amounts of animal foods are usually present in the diet.

Instead, most indigenous diets focus primarily on plants that are local to the region—plants that have surrounded a group of people over the centuries, forming the core of their food traditions and health. From quinoa, the staple of Peru, to beans, the cornerstone of the diet in Mexico, key plant foods arose in the diets of many cultures long ago. These plant foods were mostly eaten whole in their natural state; if they were processed at all, it was through simple techniques such as rough stone milling. Herbs and wild foods were also foraged, adding flavor and nutrition to traditional dishes. Folk healers developed an understanding that many plant foods helped to heal people, a fact that modern science is starting to confirm. When meat was available, it was used almost as a seasoning; a small amount flavored a meal for an entire extended family. Many native cultures still follow these food traditions today. You can see characteristics of the plant-based diet in cultural foods and traditions across the planet, from Vietnamese vegetable noodle soups to South American bean stews.

We can even trace this thoughtful eating style to our own society, in times and places where food scarcities have made a piece of meat a precious commodity. My mother tells stories from her Arkansas upbringing of helping my grandmother stoke the cookstove in the morning to heat several pots of food for the day. These pots typically contained simmering greens, beans, or peas—perhaps flavored with a bit of meat—and whatever other fresh vegetable—be it okra or green beans—was available on that particular day. Oh, and there was always a pan of cornbread in the wood-fired oven. It might sound like a humble meal, but for a dietitian it's a plant-based meal made in heaven. The greens are off the charts in vitamin, mineral, fiber, and phytochemical content; the beans or peas are packed with protein, fiber, calcium, potassium, folate, and slow-and-steady carbohydrates that will stick with you for hours; and the cornbread is made with whole grain polenta, rich in fiber and the eye-loving nutrients **lutein** and **zeaxanthin**. And the combination of aromas and flavors from the fresh greens, savory beans, and moist cornbread sets mouths watering. Sadly, these nutritionally ideal food traditions, once born of necessity, are now hard to find in the United States; Arkansas now suffers from one of the highest rates of obesity in the nation.

Still, in many locations that are cut off from modern society, such as Copper Canyon, Mexico, and Cameroon, Africa, people still follow their food traditions from the past. In these places bottles, cans, and boxes of food are a rarity. Instead, people rely on local grains such as corn or millet, locally cultivated and foraged fruits and vegetables such as greens, herbs, squashes, and cactus, and small amounts of animal foods. And obesity and chronic diseases are almost nonexistent. Yet when these people move to industrialized countries like the United States, they abandon their healthy indigenous diets and lose the protection of these plant-based foods. This phenomenon has been documented over and over again in several populations that have immigrated to the United States, including Mexican Americans, Arab Americans, and Indian Americans.

Take the Tarahumara Indians, featured in *The Jungle Effect* by Daphne Miller (William Morrow, 2008). Copper Canyon, Mexico, is home to more than 50,000 Tarahumara Indians who live in remote communities deep within the canyons. In the kitchens and farms of Copper Canyon you will discover a bounty of local foods, such as corn, beans, squash, eggs, chicken, chiles, herbs, spices, nuts, berries, wild greens, cactus, seeds, oranges, tomatoes, avocados, and occasional wild game or fish. Also known as the Mexican Pima, the Tarahumara are blood relatives of the Pima Indians of Arizona. The Tarahumara in Copper Canyon have some of the lowest rates of diabetes in the world, yet the Pima Indians of Arizona have some of the highest. As immigrant populations move to the States and consume highly refined carbohydrates in the forms of sodas, snacks, and desserts, their obesity and type 2 diabetes rates skyrocket. The Tarahumara Indians of Copper Canyon are still protected by their plant foods, which include slow-burning carbohydrates, healing spices, and nopal cactus, which appears to have glucose-controlling benefits.[29]

IN THE SPIRIT OF TRADITION

Just because you live in the modern world doesn't mean you can't get back to your plant-based roots. I'd like to share with you two success stories of modern, plant-based food cultures that can provide measurable benefits. Both the traditional Mediterranean diet and the traditional Japanese diet have been well characterized by researchers as optimal eating styles that promote health and longevity.

THE TRADITIONAL MEDITERRANEAN DIET

More than half a century ago, scientists noticed that the countries surrounding the Mediterranean enjoyed better health than other countries. Since then, scores of studies have been published on the effects of eating a traditional Mediterranean diet, linking it to a plethora of benefits, including increased longevity, improved brain function, maintenance of healthy weight, and reduced risk of heart disease, diabetes, cancer, dental disease, and Alzheimer's disease. What's so special about the Mediterranean diet? Here's a rundown of the key features of this plant-based diet:

- **Whole Grain Bounty.** The majority of grains, such as wheat, oats, rice, rye, barley, and corn, are eaten in whole, minimally processed forms.
- **Vegetables in Abundance.** Eaten at almost every meal, vegetables are normally cooked in or drizzled with olive oil or eaten raw.
- **Fresh Fruit for Dessert.** Whole fresh fruit is consumed frequently, and sweets are eaten in small amounts.
- **Olives and Olive Oil.** Whole olives are eaten frequently, and olive oil is widely used as the principal source of dietary fat in cooking, baking, and dressing salads.
- **Nuts, Beans, Legumes, and Seeds.** These foods are eaten frequently, providing healthy, high-quality fats, protein, and fiber.
- **Emphasis on Herbs and Spices.** Adding flavor and aroma as well as disease-preventing antioxidants, these plant foods are used liberally.

- **Cheese and Yogurt in Moderation.** Although dairy products are traditional, they are consumed in low to moderate amounts.
- **Fish and Shellfish, but Little Red Meat.** A variety of fish and shellfish make up an important source of omega-3 fatty acids and protein, but only small amounts of red meat are eaten.
- **Wine with Meals.** Wine is consumed regularly but moderately (up to one 150ml glass per day by women and up to two 150ml glasses by men).
- **Active and Social Lifestyle.** Foods are enjoyed in small portions in the presence of friends and family. Physical activity is a regular part of daily life.[30]

THE TRADITIONAL JAPANESE DIET

Japan is a land of contrasts. On the one hand, Japan is leaps and bounds ahead of many countries in automation, transportation, and electronics; on the other, it tenaciously preserves an intricate system of traditions that dates back centuries. Scientific evidence is beginning to suggest that some of these traditions may be at the core of the Japanese people's curiously long lifespan, a rarity in industrialized nations. The average life expectancy in Japan is 80 years for men and 85 years for women, and the average healthy life expectancy is 75 and 80, respectively. In 2008, there were 36,000 people aged 100 and older in Japan.[31] Japanese health experts credit the traditional Japanese diet as a big factor in the population's impressive life expectancies.

What's so special about the traditional Japanese diet? Here are a few of its healthful components:

- **Small Portions of Artistic Foods.** Many foods are beautifully presented in petite portions, often served in individual containers rather than on large dinner plates.
- **Lower Fat and Calorie Load.** Traditional Japanese foods are light and don't involve many heavy sauces or oils, producing fewer daily calories than the Western diet.
- **Vegetable Bonanza.** Plenty of local, seasonal vegetables of every shape, size, and color are served at every meal—even breakfast—and in a number of ways, such as steamed, simmered, stir-fried, and pickled.

- **Healthful Spices.** Foods are never boring, thanks to traditional culinary herbs and seasonings that possess strong antioxidant properties.
- **Fish over Meat.** Japanese diets famously feature moderate portions of fish but little red meat.
- **Fermented Foods.** Many fermented foods, such as miso, soy sauce, and sake, are staples in the diet. Science is beginning to discover potential health benefits of such foods.
- **Focus on Soy Foods.** Whole soy foods such as edamame, tofu, and miso are regular features of the diet.
- **Healthful Grains and Carbs.** Sure, white rice in small portions is a staple, but there has been a resurgence of brown rice in Japan. Soba noodles made from whole buckwheat are also eaten frequently. Refined breads, snack foods, and desserts are uncommon.
- **Green Tea.** Whether served hot or cold, green tea is the beverage of choice, and it's sipped all day. Not only is green tea rich in polyphenol antioxidants, but it also takes the place of high-calorie, high-sugar drinks, which are rare in Japan.
- **Car-Free Society.** In crowded cities like Tokyo, it's not practical to own a car. Thus, walking and bike riding are de rigueur.

THE TIE THAT BINDS

What do Japanese and Mediterranean diets have in common? They are both beautiful, delicious traditional diets. In fact, if you lived in Japan or Greece, you wouldn't call your style of eating a "diet" as we typically use this word. In America, we tend to think of a diet as something you are either "on" or "off." In actuality, a diet is the way that you choose to eat for life, based on your personal and cultural values. A diet isn't a heavy restriction you cast upon yourself like chains, and eating isn't something you should feel guilty about. In fact, I want you to love eating a plant-based diet. I want you to gain a whole new sense of the word "diet." I want you to come to the table with friends and family and celebrate and savor delicious food. On a Greek island in the Mediterranean Sea, a woman might lift a glass of red wine to commemorate a wonderful meal eaten at a wide table over many hours with her favorite people. That meal might be as simple as pasta tossed with fresh tomatoes, garlic, olive oil, and herbs, sautéed wild greens, and a bowlful of pistachios and figs from a nearby tree. Do you think the people at that table in Greece set out to "go on a diet"? More than likely, they're enjoying the flavors and aromas of their meal, as well as lively conversation with their dinner guests, as part of their own simple style of eating. Eating your own interpretation of a plant-based diet can be as uncomplicated as that.

SCIENTIFIC SUPPORT FOR PLANT-POWERED EATING

A body of scientific research indicates that plant-based diets promote health in a variety of ways. And why shouldn't they? A diet emphasizing whole plants contains less calories, fat, saturated fat, cholesterol, and sodium than one focused on animal foods. But it's not just about the bad stuff plant-based diets are lacking; it's more about all the good stuff they're full of—slow-release carbohydrates, healthy fats, fiber, vitamins, minerals, and a host of phytochemicals such as **lignans**, **phytosterols**, phenols, **carotenoids**, flavonoids, **sulfur compounds, isoflavones**, and **saponins**.

A number of studies document the advantages of a plant-based approach to eating, and major health organizations are stepping up to support it. Every five years top nutrition experts and scientists convene to review the body of science related to diet and health; the culmination of this process is the publication of *The Dietary Guidelines for Americans*, a set of guidelines that aims to promote optimal health for Americans. For the first time in history, the most recent set of Dietary Guidelines encourages a plant-based diet rich in vegetables, cooked beans and peas, fruits, whole grains, nuts, and seeds with only moderate amounts of lean meats, poultry, and eggs. In addition, the Dietary Guidelines report stresses a number of advantages associated with vegetarian-style eating patterns, including lower levels of obesity, a reduced risk of cardiovascular disease, and lower total mortality.[32]

The Academy of Nutrition and Dietetics (AND; formerly the American Dietetic Association) agrees with the Dietary Guidelines. In a recent position paper published by AND in which an independent and systematic review of all the research on vegetarian diets was evaluated, the organization concluded that well-planned vegetarian diets are completely healthful and nutritionally adequate for people throughout all stages of life and that they have a number of health advantages, including lower blood cholesterol levels, lower risk of heart disease, lower blood pressure levels, and lower risk of hypertension and type 2 diabetes. Vegetarians tend to have a lower body weight and lower overall cancer rates, lower intakes of saturated fat and cholesterol, and higher levels of dietary fiber, magnesium, potassium, vitamins C and E, folate, carotenoids, flavonoids, and other phytochemicals.[33] In fact, the science supporting the health benefits of vegetarian diets is so persuasive that some health experts are now using these diets as a mainstream treatment option for their patients with conditions like heart disease.

HEALTH BENEFITS GALORE

Time and time again, history and science show us that our very health and well-being rely on falling back on the whole plant foods that sustained us throughout the centuries. The health advantages of focusing on plants over animals are many. Here are ten key benefits that you can gain from a plant-based eating style. Remember to take everyone in your family along for the ride on your journey toward plant-based eating. You're never too young or too old to reap the rewards.

Ten Rewards of a Plant-Powered Diet

1. **Live longer.** Researchers have found that diets that include more whole plant foods are linked with a longer lifespan.[34] In fact, in a study of the European Prospective Investigation into Cancer and Nutrition, the largest existing database looking at diet and longevity, researchers found that the more closely people adhered to a plant-based diet, the longer their lifespan.[35] This comes as no shock, since this eating style powers you up with all the health-protective properties found in plant foods like whole grains, fruits, vegetables, legumes, nuts, and seeds.

2. **Weigh less.** It's well documented that vegetarians weigh less than their meat-eating counterparts. In a recent study of nearly 38,000 healthy men and women, the average **body mass indexes (BMIs)** of fish eaters, vegetarians, and especially vegans were lower than the average BMI of meat eaters.[36] For example, 55-year-old male and female vegans weigh about 30 pounds (14kg) less than nonvegetarians of similar height. On average, vegetarians eat less saturated fat, more fruits and vegetables, and

more low-glycemic foods than do nonvegetarians.[37] It looks like fiber—which can fill you up and help normalize blood glucose levels—may play an important role in keeping plant-based eaters' weight down. Typically, plant-based eaters consume much higher levels of fiber than those eating a lot of meat do.

3. **Tamp down oxidative stress and inflammation.** You can go through life in an anti-inflammatory state—and you can fight **oxidative stress** caused by free radicals that can damage your body—by eating more powerful plant foods such as fruits, vegetables, whole grains, tea, coffee, red wine, and olive oil. This sets the stage for long-term disease protection against disabling conditions like rheumatoid arthritis, Alzheimer's disease, and heart disease.[38] Studies have shown that you can even block the negative effects of oxidative stress in a single meal by including plant foods such as strawberries.[39]

4. **Have a healthy heart.** Take heart—if you eat a plant-based diet you'll reduce your risk of heart disease. That's the news coming out of several studies over the past couple of decades.[40] It's probably because a plant-based diet helps to lower inflammation, oxidative stress, blood pressure, and LDL ("bad") cholesterol levels. In an analysis of five studies including more than 76,000 men and women, it was found that rates of **ischemic heart disease** (caused by reduced blood supply) were 34 percent lower in vegetarians than in nonvegetarians.[41]

5. **Stave off diabetes.** You already know that Harvard researchers discovered that people who eat more red meat—especially processed meat—have a higher chance of developing type 2 diabetes. In the same study they also found that when red meat was replaced with healthier proteins, such as low-fat dairy, nuts, and whole grains, the risks of developing this disease lowered significantly. Simply by swapping one serving of red meat for a serving of nuts every day, you can decrease your risk by 21 percent; substituting low-fat dairy for the meat results in a 17 percent lower risk, and substituting whole grains would reduce your risk of developing diabetes by 23 percent.[42]

6. **Protect against cancer.** Vegetarians tend to have lower overall rates of cancer.[43] The American Institute of Cancer Research has

long suggested that you load up at least two-thirds of your plate with vegetables, fruits, whole grains, and beans to help protect you against cancer. That's because vegetables and fruits have been linked to protection against a range of cancers, including mouth, pharynx, esophagus, stomach, lung, pancreas, and prostate. Plant foods high in fibers, such as whole grains, legumes, vegetables, and fruits, appear to prevent digestive cancers by speeding up the gut transit time—the amount of time it takes foods to move through your digestive system.[44] A recent study found that women who consumed a plant-based diet rich in fruits, vegetables, legumes, and grains had a 20 percent lower risk of developing estrogen receptor-negative breast cancer than women who were not committed to a plant-based diet.[45]

7. Protect your brain. Growing evidence suggests that chronic inflammation and oxidative stress lead to the decline of the brain, resulting in the telltale signs of Alzheimer's disease. High-antioxidant plant foods such as berries, nuts, red wine, spices, and dark chocolate—along with many others—can help block oxidative stress and cool down inflammation. Omega-3 fatty acids—found in fish as well as in plant sources like walnuts—have also been linked with reversing cognitive deficits in rats. Scientists from Columbia University found that higher adherence to a Mediterranean, plant-based diet was linked with a lower risk for Alzheimer's disease.[46]

8. Support a healthy gut and immune system. You may not realize it, but your gut plays a critical role in your overall health. Your intestinal tract is not only essential for digesting food and absorbing nutrients, it is the largest immune organ in your body, producing 25 percent of your immune cells. These cells help form an immune defense system that protects you from the invasion of harmful substances like bacteria, viruses, and chemicals. We are learning more and more about how healthful bacteria in your gut can support your immune system and fend off disease. Vital to a healthy gut is a high-fiber diet, which feeds friendly bacteria and keeps your digestion running smoothly. A whole-foods, plant-based diet is naturally rich in fiber. British researchers found that a vegetarian diet and a high intake of dietary fiber were both associated with a lower likelihood of being admitted to a hospital and a lower risk of death from diverticular disease (a condition in which pouches form in the intestines).[47]

9. **Cut your risk of metabolic syndrome.** Metabolic syndrome is the dreaded condition of our time—it sets you up for a higher risk of heart disease, diabetes, and stroke. But new research reveals that vegetarians have a 36 percent lower chance of developing metabolic syndrome than do nonvegetarians. Researchers found that vegetarians had lower triglycerides, glucose levels, blood pressure, waist circumference, and BMI than meat eaters. Semi-vegetarians also had a significantly lower BMI and waist circumference than those who ate meat more regularly.[48]

10. **Save the planet.** You can seriously reduce your carbon footprint by eating fewer animal foods, according to a number of studies. Italian researchers performed a life-cycle assessment to evaluate the cradle-to-grave environmental impact of several dietary patterns. They discovered that an organic vegan diet had the smallest environmental impact, while a conventionally farmed diet that included meat had the greatest impact on the environment—and the more meat consumed, the greater the eco-impact. They also discovered that beef was the food with the single greatest impact on the environment; other high-impacting foods included cheese, fish, and milk. In essence, animals make inefficient "food production machines," using up lots of feed, water, and fossil fuels to turn plants into protein. To produce 1 calorie from beef requires 40 calories of fossil fuels, whereas producing 1 calorie from grains requires only 2.2 calories of fuel. Plant-based diets can play an important role in preserving environmental resources and in reducing hunger in poor nations.[49]

MOVING FORWARD

When you add together all of these facts—hard earned through hundreds of studies performed by dedicated researchers all over the world—they clearly point in one direction: The optimal diet for health is a whole-foods eating style that relies on plant foods in their natural form—rich in healthy fats and carbohydrates, vitamins, minerals, fiber, and antioxidants and low in calories, unhealthful saturated fats, cholesterol, and sodium. You certainly have nothing to lose by shifting from an animal-based diet to a plant-powered diet. In the following chapter, I'll get you started on personalizing your own diet. At the end of chapters 2 through 11, I will give you daily Plant-Powered Action Alerts—fourteen days' worth of daily activities that will get you started down the path of plant-based eating—plus stories from plant-powered omnivores, vegetarians, and vegans who have made the shift themselves. At the end of two weeks, you'll be ready to plunge into your own personalized eating plan that will reveal a lighter, more vibrant you.

2

Shifting Your Focus from Animals to Powerful Plants

Now you know why eating a plant-powered diet can offer you many rewards—from improved health and vigor to a lighter footprint on the planet. This pattern of eating is not only the healthiest way to go, it's also a "clean" diet that moves away from processed foods, chemical additives, and synthetic pesticides and puts you more in harmony with your environment.

In the next several chapters, I will take you on a step-by-step journey to discover your own individualized plant-powered diet—a way of eating that you adopt for life. I will walk you down supermarket aisles, peer deep into your pantry shelves, and visit your favorite restaurant kitchens in order to guide you on your path to plant-based eating. I will reveal the scientific wonders of particularly potent plant foods, such as berries, walnuts, turmeric, and mushrooms. As we go, I will offer you daily assignments in the form of Plant-Powered Action Alerts, which will help you develop the skills you need to eat more thoughtfully and healthfully. And by the time you turn the final page of this book, you will have gained all the knowledge you need to move forward with your optimal plant-powered eating plan.

MAKING A SHIFT ON THE PLANT-POWERED DIET SPECTRUM

To gain all of the benefits linked with plants, your nutrition directive is simple: Make a partial or full shift from animal foods to plant foods. Sounds good, but how do you get started? Your first step is to take a closer look at your current eating style so that you can determine your nutritional goal. Remember, you don't necessarily have to move to a total vegan or vegetarian diet. Instead, your nutrition goal should be personal, based on what you think is reasonable and what will work best for you. Consider the plant-based diet as a spectrum of choices with a vegan diet on one side and an omnivorous diet on the other. The Plant-Powered Diet Spectrum, below, will help you plot your course.

PLANT-POWERED DIET SPECTRUM

PLANT-POWERED VEGAN	PLANT-POWERED VEGETARIAN	PLANT-POWERED OMNIVORE	
		PLANT-POWERED PESCATARIAN	PLANT-POWERED OMNIVORE
Avoid all animal products, including red meat, fish, poultry, milk, dairy products, butter, and eggs. Focus on whole plant foods, such as grains, legumes, fruits, vegetables, nuts, and seeds in their natural forms.	Avoid all red meat, fish, and poultry, but include low to moderate amounts of milk, dairy products, butter, and eggs. Focus on whole plant foods, such as grains, legumes, fruits, vegetables, nuts, and seeds in their natural forms.	Avoid all red meat and poultry, but include low to moderate amounts of fish and seafood, milk, dairy products, butter, and eggs. Focus on whole plant foods, such as grains, legumes, fruits, vegetables, nuts, and seeds in their natural forms.	Limit red and processed meats to a minimum (if you consume them at all), but include low to moderate amounts of chicken, fish, milk, dairy products, butter, and eggs. Focus on whole plant foods, such as grains, legumes, fruits, vegetables, nuts, and seeds in their natural forms.

PERSONALIZED PLANT-POWERED EATING

The plant-based lifestyle is a highly personalized way of eating. If there's one thing I've learned as a dietitian over the years, it's that vegetarianism means so many different things to so many different people. It's a fact that researchers have even picked up on as they study groups of vegetarians and find it very difficult to pin down which foods they eat and which foods they avoid. There are plenty of people who consider themselves vegetarian even though they may occasionally eat fish and/or chicken—even red meat. People have many different motivations for eating vegetarian-style diets, such as reducing inhumane conditions for animals, lowering their environmental impact, observing particular religious beliefs and cultural traditions, and seeking better health.

Even though people's ideas of vegetarian diets may be hazy, there are established definitions. A vegan diet is one that excludes all animal products, including animal flesh, dairy products, eggs, and honey. A lacto-ovo vegetarian diet (simplified to "vegetarian diet" from this point forward) excludes all animal flesh but allows dairy products and eggs. And *semi-vegetarian* is a term used to describe a person who only occasionally eats meat or fish (also called "flexitarian").

The divisions between forms of plant-based eating shift for many people, too. While some are thoroughly committed to veganism for life, others flow between a vegan and vegetarian and even semi-vegetarian diet. I have friends who are vegan at home but switch to a vegetarian or even pescatarian diet when they travel because it's much easier to manage. The most important thing is that you find a diet and lifestyle that meets your personal needs and goals. If you feel inspired to eliminate animal foods completely from your diet to make a positive impact on animal welfare, on the environment, and on your own health, then go for it. But if you believe that it's not realistic for you to completely forgo animal foods, there's still a plant-based eating style that can improve your health and reduce your eco-impact. The bottom line: There are no hard-and-fast rules about the plant-based eating style; it's up to you to decide your own.

The Plant-Powered Diet Spectrum includes three broad categories: Plant-Powered Vegan, Plant-Powered Vegetarian, and Plant-Powered Omnivore. Yet, there are many levels within these categories that you can fit into. For example, within the Plant-Powered Omnivore category you can make many choices, including whether to avoid all animal flesh except for fish or to simply limit your red meat consumption to small portions twice a month. The common denominator of all the choices along the spectrum is that they emphasize eating more whole plant foods. So, decide your goal along this spectrum, and remember that it may change over time.

I started out as a semi-vegetarian as a child—eating a lacto-ovo vegetarian diet with very occasional meat-eating forays. This pattern lasted throughout most of my adulthood, until I completely gave up meat, except for small amounts of fish, about five years ago. Recently I went back full circle to give veganism a try and found that I liked the way I felt about my impact on the earth as well as my overall health. Today, I'm eating a plant-powered vegan diet most of the time, with weekend and holiday breaks as a vegetarian. You see, it's all a very personal decision that you alone can make.

TRACK YOUR EATING STYLE

In order to create a personal goal for your plant-based eating style, first you'll need to take a close look at your current eating style. Take a moment to fill out the One-Week Food Diary, listing what you dined on during the past week to the best of your recollection. Now review this diary to see how many animal foods you consumed in the last week and, more important, how many minimally processed, whole plant foods you ate. Refer to the lists of Animal Foods Hiding in Your Diet (page 32) and Whole, Minimally Processed Plant Foods (page 33) to help you identify these foods.

ONE-WEEK FOOD DIARY

MEAL	SAMPLE	SUNDAY	MONDAY	TUESDAY	WEDNESDAY	THURSDAY	FRIDAY	SATURDAY
Breakfast	Bacon & egg sandwich, coffee, milk							
Lunch	Garden vegetable salad with baked tofu, whole grain roll, apple, iced tea							
Dinner	Meatloaf, mashed potatoes, gravy, green beans, ice cream							
Snacks	Cheese and crackers, peanuts							

Here's a list of animal foods that people commonly consume every day. Be aware of these food choices as you move toward plant-based eating.

ANIMAL FOODS HIDING IN YOUR DIET

RED MEAT	Beef, beef jerky, hamburgers, steak, hot dogs, bacon, cold cuts, ham, pork chops, pork tenderloin, ribs, sausage, lamb, game meats (Note: Animal-based substances such as gelatin and lard may be ingredients in processed foods.)
POULTRY	Chicken, chicken hot dogs, chicken nuggets, chicken salad, turkey, turkey hot dogs, cold cuts, sausage
FISH/ SEAFOOD	Fresh or frozen fish fillets, fish sticks, fish sauce, canned tuna, canned salmon, smoked salmon, caviar, sardines, anchovies, shellfish (crab, shrimp, oysters, clams, crayfish, scallops, lobster)
DAIRY	Milk, cream, buttermilk, yogurt, cheese, cottage cheese, cream cheese, sour cream, butter, pudding, ice cream (Note: Dairy-based substances such as milk solids, whey, and casein may be ingredients in processed foods.)
EGGS	Eggs, egg whites, egg yolks (Note: Egg-based substances such as albumin may be ingredients in processed foods.)

For a list of common food ingredients with animal products, see the *Vegetarian Journal's Guide to Food Ingredients* at vrg.org/ingredients/index.php.

CREATE YOUR OWN PERSONAL EATING GOAL

Now it's time to look at your food diary and see where you are. How many servings of whole plant foods did you eat every day? How many servings of animal foods did you eat every day? Now, look at the Plant-Powered Diet Spectrum and decide where you currently fit in. If you're like most people, you probably fall on the righthand side of the spectrum. Now ask yourself where you would you *like* to be on the spectrum. Whether your goal is to reduce red meat as an omnivore or to shift to a vegetarian diet, remember that the most important part of the plant-powered diet is a renewed focus on whole plant foods in their natural form. And keep in mind that the plant-powered diet is not a diet you go "on" and "off"—it's a simple, healthy way to eat for life. It is a delicious, satisfying plant-based eating style that

WHOLE, MINIMALLY PROCESSED PLANT FOODS

GRAINS	LEGUMES	NUTS AND SEEDS	FRUITS	VEGETABLES	HERBS AND SPICES	BEVERAGES
Whole grains in their natural form, such as cooked kernels of amaranth, barley, buckwheat, corn, millet, steel-cut oats, quinoa, rice, sorghum, teff, triticale, wheat (e.g., wheat berries, bulgur, farro)	Beans, lentils, peas, and soy foods in their whole natural form, such as cooked or canned beans, lentils, peas (e.g., black-eyed peas, split peas) Minimally processed soy foods such as miso, soy milk, tempeh, and tofu	Nuts such as almonds, brazil nuts, macadamia nuts, peanuts (technically legumes), pecans, pine nuts, pistachios, and walnuts Seeds including chia, flax, hemp, pumpkin, sesame, and sunflower, and butters made from these nuts and seeds (with no other added ingredients)	Whole fresh, cooked, canned (in juice), frozen (no added sugar) or dried (no added sugar) fruits, such as apples, apricots, bananas, berries, cherries, citrus, grapes, mango, melons, papaya, peaches, pears, pineapple, and plums	Whole fresh, cooked, canned (with no added salt), or frozen vegetables, such as aubergine, beetroot, broccoli, cauliflower, celery, cucumber, green beans, greens, lettuce, mushrooms, onions, potatoes, radishes, seaweed, sprouts, squash, and tomatoes	Whole fresh or dried culinary herbs such as basil, coriander, mint, oregano, parsley, rosemary, and sage Whole, dried, and ground spices such as allspice, black and red pepper, cinnamon, nutmeg, saffron, and turmeric Whole fresh or dried ginger and garlic	Coffee Green, black, white, or oolong tea Herbal tea

is personalized to be right for you while bringing you the rewards of better health, stamina, and weight.

If you're currently eating meat at every meal, perhaps you would like to take on an omnivorous diet that includes more whole plant foods and fewer servings of animal foods. Your goal might be to skip meat at every breakfast and up your servings of fruits and vegetables, or maybe to try one meatless dinner for the entire family once a week. If you already avoid red meat altogether, perhaps your goal might be to take your diet to the next level and limit your animal intake to only fish. You can even take on a longer-term approach in which you gradually reduce your animal intake over time to achieve a final goal that is optimal for you. Remember, your new eating style is not just about the number of animal products you'd like to cut out; even more important is all the foods you're going to eat *more of* at every meal: plants, from beautiful beans and lentils to delicious quinoa and oats to crunchy broccoli and apples.

A WORD ABOUT PLANT-BASED JUNK DIETS

I hear it all the time: "Just because you're a vegetarian, it doesn't mean you eat healthy." And that's absolutely right. It's completely possible to fill up on plant-based junk foods such as refined grains, prepared vegetarian meals and snacks, cookies, crackers, candy, and even soda. You might as well go back to a Western diet if that's your idea of a plant-based diet. In general, the more processed a food is—even if it's a plant-based food—the more unhealthful it becomes and the greater its toll on you and on the environment.

A perfectly good potato can be sent to a factory to be mechanically peeled, chopped into a fine mash, shot through a series of sieves to separate out some components, and flash-dried into potato starch. The potato starch is sent to another big factory so it can be mixed with artificial ingredients, shaped, and deep-fried into its final life as a "veggie" crisp. The veggie crisp will be packaged and shipped to a central warehouse, where it will await further shipment to your neighborhood market, where it can wait for weeks in an air-conditioned, brightly lit room until you buy it and take it home. Let's see: Potato or veggie crisp? They're vast worlds apart in nutrition and in their carbon footprint. You could have simply purchased a fresh potato at your farmers market or received one from your CSA ("community supported agriculture," see page 152), picked by a farmer in the morning less than 100 miles away. No packaging, no processing, little transportation—only the nutrients nature intended for the potato. This scenario can be applied to many plant-based foods. There are whole plant foods all over the supermarket—in the produce section and in the aisles, where you can find dried beans, grains, and nuts—and there are processed plant foods, too, in the snacks, desserts, and convenience foods. Don't pat yourself on the back about eating a plant-based food unless you have read the back of the ingredient list, fully understand what those ingredients mean, and feel good about them.

The plant-powered diet focuses on whole plant foods found in their natural form. In the coming chapters, you will learn how to identify whole plant foods in every category—from sources of plant proteins such as soy foods and legumes to grains like wheat and rice.

RETHINKING YOUR PLATE

One of the biggest stumbling blocks in shifting to a plant-based diet is getting past the way we think about our meals. Whether packing a lunchbox for your daughter, shopping to fill your fridge for the week, thinking about what you'll fix for dinner on your way home from work, or ordering off the menu at a restaurant, the first item most people think about is the animal protein. It's that old meat-in-the-center-of-the-plate attitude that pervades our thinking. We usually ponder whether the meal will highlight ground beef, chicken breasts, or ham, and then we decide on everything else—if we even give the other foods a thought.

Shifting to a plant-based diet means you have to start thinking the other way around. You start with the plant foods first. It might go against your nature, but that's where it all starts. Maybe the meal will highlight those colorful adzuki beans you got at the natural food store. What about that ruffled Swiss chard you picked up at the vegetable stand yesterday? Once you start focusing on plants instead of the animal foods, you'll be surprised how easy it is to start changing your diet to a more healthful balance. Even if your goal is to be a plant-based omnivore, adopting this mindset can seriously overhaul your diet for the better. If you focus on the plant foods first—from wheat berries and courgette to chickpeas and almonds—you can come up with a beautiful dinner that relies on only small amounts of animal foods to complement their flavors. Consider all of those healthful plant-based food cultures that do this on a regular basis. In Thailand, you might toss together a stir-fry of aubergine, mushrooms, chili, lemon grass, and rice noodles, then stir in a small amount of shrimp to flavor the entire meal.

Your dinner plate will start looking different as you take on a plant-based diet, no matter where you fall along the spectrum. The current American dinner plate all too often looks like this: In the center rests a big hunk of meat, such as a steak, burger, chicken breast, turkey slice, pork chop, or fish fillet; on the side is a petite portion of cooked veggies like peas or green beans, plus a hefty blob of mashed potatoes, white rice, or noodles from a mix. The new American dinner plate should look like this: No "center of the plate" anything. Instead, at least three-fourths of the plate is filled with whole grains like quinoa or farro, cooked or fresh veggies, and fruit; the other fourth is filled with a healthy protein food such as beans, nuts, tofu, or, if you're an omnivore, sometimes fish. What this really means is that it's the end of compartmentalized thinking at meal time. No more considering your dinner plate as a sort of cafeteria tray with little compartments that need to be filled with meat, potatoes, and vegetables. Instead, your plate should be chock full of a variety of plant foods. Who says you have to cook only one kind of plant food at each meal? Why not cook two or three vegetables for dinner? Why not have salad *and* sautéed green beans for dinner tonight? Why not have brown rice *and* black-eyed peas at the same meal? And why not showcase a seasonal fruit bowl on the dinner table every single night? It's a whole new eating revolution—and I'll show you how you can do it simply, quickly, and healthfully every day of the week.

TOP TIPS FOR TRIMMING ANIMAL FOODS FROM YOUR DIET

No matter where you fall on the plant-powered spectrum, your goal will mean some changes in your diet that add up to eating fewer animal foods and more plant foods. Here are my top tips for making simple, easy adjustments to cut down on animal foods in your diet.

1. Start the day right. Going veggie at breakfast is one of the easiest ways to cut back on meat. You can make a significant difference in your animal intake if you go meatless seven mornings a week. With so many delicious vegetarian breakfast options, who needs meat? Try steel-cut oatmeal topped with walnuts and berries (and sometimes maple syrup, if you want a touch of sweetness); buckwheat pancakes or waffles (try Buckwheat Hazelnut Waffles with Ginger Peach Sauce, page 353); or a breakfast burrito with beans and veggies.

2. **Join the Meatless Monday bandwagon.** No matter what your goal, going meatless one day a week is an easy fix. And why not start out the work week right by doing it on Monday? That's why the Meatless Monday movement is such a huge success, and a flood of celebrities and health experts are supporting it. Visit the Web site at meatlessmonday.com for tips, recipes, and inspiration to get started.

3. **Shop for plants first.** Don't fall back into the "meat is the center of the plate" mindset. Instead of planning your menu around what meat you will serve for dinner, plan it around what plant foods you will serve. Just start your shopping in the produce aisle or at the farmers market, or use your CSA for inspiration. Which vegetables are in season, appear freshest, and look the most appealing to you? Throw them in your cart and begin your menu planning there, working backward. For example, if kale is fresh and beautiful, stir-fry it with garlic, herbs, and tofu and pile it over quinoa for dinner.

4. **If you eat meat, use it as a seasoning.** If your goal is to take on a plant-powered omnivorous diet, you can cut down on your animal food intake while upping the plants if you use meat as a flavoring in dishes instead of as the main event. This eating style can be seen in many ethnic dishes, such as curries, stir-fries, stews, and pasta dishes that consist of a pile of vegetables and grains flavored with a small amount of beef, pork, chicken, or fish. Buy a single portion of meat—one chicken breast or a serving of seafood—and turn it into a whole meal.

5. **Switch your supermarket.** Some supermarkets—with most of their real estate dedicated to processed foods, frozen pizzas, and their meat and dairy cases—make plant-based shopping tough. Instead, track down markets in your area, such as natural food stores and ethnic supermarkets, that offer more whole plant foods such as a variety of dried and canned beans and lentils, whole grains, nuts,

seeds, fruits, and vegetables. Stores that host bulk bins of grains, legumes, nuts, and seeds can offer a wider variety of eclectic and economic choices.

6. **Stock a plant-based pantry.** If you have it on hand, you will cook it. But if you have to constantly run out to the store because you don't have an ingredient, your plant-based diet won't take root and flourish. The good news is that many plant-based foods are shelf-stable, convenient, and economical. Follow my Plant-Powered Pantry List (see page 260) to equip your pantry with the essentials.

7. **Get cooking!** Don't be afraid to get creative in the kitchen. Even if you're busy, plan on one night a week to try a new vegetarian recipe. Let vegetarian magazines, cookbooks, apps, or Web sites lead the way to delicious, meatless meals. Try to perfect some new classic recipes that will become your "go-to" meals in the future. Check out chapter 13 for menu-planning ideas and chapter 14 for my own favorite collection of plant-powered recipes.

8. **Keep it simple.** You might think that plant-based cooking is very difficult to take on, but it doesn't have to be complicated. Not every meal has to involve cookbooks and chopping boards. Meatless meals can be as easy as black bean burritos, vegetarian chili and cornbread, or an avocado and hummus pita sandwich (check out my recipe for Home-Style Hummus on page 276). My helpful kitchen tips in chapter 12 will steer you in the right direction.

9. **Try ethnic flair.** Some cultures know how to do vegetarian meals right! The combination of vegetables, spices, and flavorful sauces in ethnic cuisines can make meatless meals shine. Take home tricks from your favorite ethnic restaurants, such as Mexican, Indian, Thai, and Vietnamese, and observe how the plant-based dishes are prepared so you can make similar recipes at home. (Try my recipe for Orange-Peanut Tempeh Stir-Fry with Red Rice on page 328.)

10. **Convert your favorite dishes.** Don't forget this simple trick: For an easy dinner solution, turn your favorite meat-based recipe veggie. All you've got to do is skip the meat and load up the veggies. Love pizza? Top it with broccoli, cashews, onions, and basil (see Spicy Broccoli Cashew Pizza, page 302). Skip the meat in your lasagna

and pile extra servings of veggies between the layers of noodles (see Vegetable Medley Lasagna, page 307—my family's favorite lasagna recipe). You can still put tacos on the menu once a week, just trade in the taco meat for seasoned beans.

11. **Dust off your slow cooker.** Inside the depths of your slow cooker is the seed of many delicious, meatless meals. Throw in veggies, herbs, a vegetable broth base, canned tomatoes, whole grains like barley or bulgur, and dried beans, then turn the dial. When you get home, a fragrant, hearty meal will await you. See, for example, Slow-Cooked Butter Beans with Root Vegetables (page 317).

12. **Try plant-based dairy products.** Want to cut out animal products the easy way? Try using more plant-based alternatives for milk, yogurt, and cheese. Plenty of people love the taste of soy milk in coffee (just ask Starbucks!), and the quality of plant-based cheeses—especially for cooking—has improved dramatically. Your family won't even be able to tell when you use plant-based cheeses for foods like pizza and quesadillas and plant-based milks in baking or cooking.

13. **Think "yes."** Don't dwell on what you *can't* have, think about what you *can* have! When you're focused on eating plants, there are hundreds of varieties, flavors, colors, and textures awaiting you. How many choices do you have when you eat meat? Take a trip to the produce section of your supermarket or visit a farmers market and feast your eyes on the rainbow of plant foods you can pile onto your plate.

PLANT-POWERED DIET PRINCIPLES

No matter where your individualized plant-based diet falls along the Plant-Powered Diet Spectrum (see page 28), there are several important principles for achieving the optimal health benefits of a plant-based diet. In the next several chapters, you will learn more about making these important choices in your diet for life.

- Eat fewer animal foods, especially red and processed meats. If you choose to eat animal foods, prioritize organic milk and dairy products, cage-free poultry and egg products, and wild-caught or sustainably farmed fish/seafood species that are not endangered and that are lower on the food chain (and thus lower in mercury contaminants). (Check out blueocean.org or seafoodwatch.com for the best seafood recommendations.)

- Eat more legumes, including beans, lentils, peas, and whole soy foods (see chapter 3).
- Eat moderate amounts of nuts and seeds daily (see chapter 3).
- Eat more whole grains in their natural form, including amaranth, barley, buckwheat, corn, millet, oats, quinoa, rice, sorghum, teff, triticale, and wheat (see chapter 4).
- Eat few refined grains in the form of refined flours, white rice, and products made of refined flours (see chapter 4).
- Focus on carbohydrates with a low **glycemic index (GI)**, such as most high-fiber plant foods found in their natural form (see chapter 4).
- Avoid highly processed and refined breads, cereals, side dishes, soups, snack foods, fried foods, and baked goods (see chapter 4).
- Eat more local and seasonal vegetables in a greater variety and in their natural form (see chapter 5).
- Make it a priority to purchase organic foods—foods produced without the use of most synthetic fertilizers and pesticides (see chapter 5).
- Eat more local and seasonal fruits in a greater variety in their whole form and instead of juice (see chapter 6).
- Eat few added sugars, such as high-fructose corn syrup, corn syrup, white or brown cane sugar, raw sugar, malt syrup, fructose, honey, molasses, and maple syrup (see chapter 6).
- Choose moderate amounts of healthy plant fats, such as those from olives and olive oil, nuts, seeds, and avocados (see chapter 7).
- Increase your intake of omega-3 fatty acids. If you don't eat fish, consume more omega-3s through foods like walnuts, flaxseeds, and soy, and consider a marine algae supplement (see chapter 7).
- Avoid saturated fats and cholesterol found in animal foods. Keep your intake of tropical oils such as palm, palm seed, and coconut oils to a low to moderate level (see chapter 7).
- Include flavorful culinary herbs and spices in their fresh or dried form at as many meals as possible (see chapter 8).

- Savor up to 30g of dark chocolate (minimum 70% cocoa) daily (see chapter 8).
- Enjoy unsweetened coffee or tea throughout the day (see chapter 9).
- Avoid sugar-sweetened beverages, including sports and energy drinks, fruit drinks, sodas, and iced teas (see chapter 9).
- If you drink, enjoy a daily glass of red wine with your dinner (see chapter 9).
- Engage in physical activity most days of the week (see chapter 10).
- Use caution with portion sizes. Eat mindfully, always engaged in the act of eating. When you can, enjoy your meals in the company of others (see chapter 12).
- Cook most of your meals at home and limit dining out. Create your own food traditions that celebrate simple, beautiful, plant-based meals (see chapter 12).

SEVEN PLANT-POWERED FOOD CATEGORIES

The Plant-Powered Diet is based on seven categories of plant foods in their most whole, healthful, and natural form.

- Plant proteins
- Whole grains
- Vegetables
- Fruits
- Healthy fats
- Spices, herbs, and chocolate
- Coffee, tea, and wine

In each of the following chapters, I take on a new plant-powered food category and answer all your questions about how to choose the most healthful foods within each category in order to create a balanced diet that can protect you from chronic diseases, promote a healthy weight, and help you feel more vibrant for years to come. I dig into the details of each food category, from whole grains to healthy fats, so that you can learn more about the special nutritional powers particular plant foods hold and thus feel confident about eating a plant-based diet that will meet your individual nutritional needs.

"Although I pride myself on eating nearly everything—including meat—more often than not, you'll find my fridge stuffed with kale, tofu, beans, whole grains, fruits, nuts, sardines, and dark chocolate. Simply choosing to eat a plant-based diet is what my body prefers. It's extremely affordable and convenient. When the temperature hits 110, I know that my beans and rice are safe and still delicious tucked away in my bag. My on-the-go life requires high-octane fuel that is convenient and safe. I am blessed with good genes—thanks, Mom and Dad!—however, I strongly believe that I'm making the best of what I've got by choosing the healthiest, freshest, and most wholesome foods I can get my hands on. I can compete at a high level in the sports I love, and I sleep like a baby! Do you want to be healthy? Do you want to improve the environment? Do you want to look and feel younger? Do you want to raise healthy eaters? Choose to eat fruits and vegetables at every meal."

—BARBARA, a plant-powered omnivore in Phoenix, Arizona

Here are your assignments for Day 1 and Day 2. You're already on your way to a plant-powered diet for life.

❦ PLANT-POWERED ACTION ALERT **DAY 1**

Complete a diary of your current eating style for a week (see One-Week Food Diary, page 31). Review how many animal foods and whole plant foods you are eating in an average week.

❦ PLANT-POWERED ACTION ALERT **DAY 2**

Create your own personal diet goal based on the Plant-Powered Diet Spectrum (page 28).

Unleashing Plant-Powered Proteins

There's a common misperception that I hear time and time again: It's difficult to get enough high-quality protein if you don't eat animal foods. And I'm here to prove that urban legend wrong, once and for all. Actually, it's quite simple to get adequate protein in your diet by eating plant foods, because protein is found to some degree in the makeup of virtually every plant. Whether you're eating corn, quinoa, chickpeas, squash, peanuts, or avocados, you're raking in protein. And certain plant foods, such as legumes and nuts, are particularly rich sources of protein. If you plan your diet right—with a variety of whole plant foods—you'll have no trouble meeting your body's needs for this essential nutrient.

PROTEIN 101

The reason that so many people get tripped up on protein is that there are a lot of fallacies out there regarding how much protein your body needs. You can thank the low-carb, high-protein diet craze for fueling our confusion over protein. So you can understand how to stoke your body with healthy, plant-based proteins, let's start with the basics.

Protein, fat, and carbohydrates are the three major groups of nutrients in the foods that you eat every day to provide you with energy as well as the building materials your body needs to maintain its tissues. Proteins make up many of your body's structures, including muscle, bone, skin, and hair, and they play a role in the creation of enzymes, hormones, vitamins, and **neurotransmitters** that your body requires to go about its everyday business of living. You've probably seen photos of protein-malnourished kids with swollen bellies in countries suffering from famine. Indeed, protein malnutrition (called kwashiorkor) can cause growth failure, loss of muscle mass, decreased immunity, weakening of the heart and respiratory system, and death. There's no underestimating how important dietary protein is to your body.

Protein is made up of amino acids—the building blocks needed to build the proteins in your body. Animal and soy sources of protein tend to be "complete," which means that they contain all of the nine essential amino acids your body needs to build proteins. Most plant foods, with the exception of soy, quinoa, and spinach, are low in one or two of the essential amino acids, so they are referred to as "incomplete" proteins. In the past, a complicated theory circulated that vegetarians need to "combine" certain foods to get the full range of amino acids within a single meal, assembling a "complete" protein from "incomplete" ones. This philosophy is no longer considered valid; now we know that if you simply eat a variety of plant foods—especially those that are rich in protein—you can meet your essential amino acid needs without fussing over pairing particular foods.

It's completely doable to eat a healthy plant-based diet that meets your protein—as well as carbohydrate, fat, vitamin, and mineral—needs every day. In fact, research shows that vegetarian diets are even more nutrient dense and consistent with the government's recommendations for nutritional needs than nonvegetarian ones.[1]

HOW MUCH PROTEIN IS ENOUGH?

Most people think they need oodles of protein—they're off by a long shot. The established daily protein requirement for men and women 19 years and older is 0.8 grams of protein per kilogram of body weight.[2] That means a person who weighs 150 pounds (68kg) needs 54 grams of protein per day. (See Calculate Your Protein Needs, below, to do the math on your own.) However, there are indications for slightly higher protein needs. Vegans may need to consume about 0.9 grams per kilogram of body weight, due to the lower digestibility of whole plant food sources of protein. Some research suggests that eating a bit more protein—about 1 gram per kilogram of body weight—may offer some benefits, such as reduced risk of type 2 diabetes, osteoporosis, and heart disease, as well as lower blood pressure and better weight management. If you're a competitive athlete or body builder, you may require even more protein. Even at the higher recommended level of protein (1 gram/kilogram), a 150-pound person (68kg) would only need 68 grams per day. Keep in mind that eating too much protein is an inefficient way to fuel your body with energy, and it's been linked with osteoporosis and kidney disease.[3] Another way to determine whether you're meeting your protein needs is to look at the balance of your diet: You should be getting 10 to 35 percent of your total daily calories in the form of protein.[4] If you follow the Daily Plant-Powered Protein Guide (see page 77), your protein intake should be about 14 to 18 percent of your total daily calories.

CALCULATE YOUR PROTEIN NEEDS

THE INSTITUTE OF Medicine set the daily Recommended Dietary Allowance for protein at 0.8 grams of protein per kilogram of body weight.[5] In order to calculate your protein needs, divide your weight in pounds by 2.2 to determine your weight in kilograms. Then multiply your weight in kilograms by 0.8. This number is the number of grams of protein you need every day.

For example, if you weigh 150 pounds:

150 ÷ 2.2 = 68 (your weight in kilograms)
68 × 0.8 = 54 (the amount of protein you need in grams)

Consider that a tiny 3-ounce cooked sirloin steak has 24 grams of protein (and who eats a 3-ounce steak!), and it's easy to see why most people

PLANT-POWERED PROTEIN LIST

PLANT-POWERED PROTEIN	SERVING SIZE	CALORIES	PROTEIN	FAT	SAT FAT	STAR NUTRIENTS* (AT LEAST 10% DV PER SERVING)
Almonds	25g (23 nuts)	169	6 g	15 g	1 g	Fiber, vitamin E, riboflavin, magnesium, manganese, phosphorus, copper
Black beans, cooked	85g cup	114	8 g	0.5 g	0 g	Fiber, thiamin, folate, iron, magnesium, phosphorus, manganese
Black-eyed peas, cooked	85g cup	100	7 g	0.5 g	0 g	Fiber, thiamin, folate, iron, magnesium, phosphorus, copper, manganese
Brazil nuts	25g (6–8 nuts)	190	4 g	19 g	5 g	Thiamin, magnesium, phosphorus, copper, manganese, selenium
Broad beans, cooked	85g	94	7 g	0.5 g	0 g	Fiber, folate, phosphorus, copper, manganese
Cashews	25g (18 nuts)	160	4 g	13 g	3 g	Vitamin K, iron, magnesium, phosphorus, zinc, copper, manganese
Chia seeds	25g (2½ tbsp)	137	4 g	9 g	1 g	Fiber, calcium, phosphorus, manganese
Chickpeas (garbanzo beans), cooked	85g cup	135	8 g	2 g	0 g	Fiber, folate, iron, magnesium, phosphorus, copper, manganese
Flaxseeds	25g (3 tbsp)	150	5 g	12 g	1 g	Fiber, thiamin, magnesium, phosphorus, copper, manganese, selenium
Hazelnuts	25g (21 nuts)	181	4 g	17 g	1 g	Fiber, vitamin E, magnesium, copper, manganese

PLANT-POWERED PROTEIN	SERVING SIZE	CALORIES	PROTEIN	FAT	SAT FAT	STAR NUTRIENTS* (AT LEAST 10% DV PER SERVING)
Hemp seeds, shelled	25g (3 tbsp)	157	9 g	12 g	1 g	Iron, magnesium, zinc
Kidney beans, cooked	85g cup	113	8 g	0.5	0 g	Fiber, folate, iron, phosphorus, potassium, manganese
Lentils, cooked	100g cup	115	9 g	0.5 g	0 g	Fiber, thiamin, folate, iron, phosphorus, potassium, magnesium, zinc, copper, manganese
Macadamia nuts	25g (10-12 nuts)	203	2 g	21 g	3 g	Thiamin, copper, manganese
Peanut butter	2 tbsp	188	8 g	16 g	3 g	Fiber, vitamin E, niacin, magnesium, phosphorus, manganese
Peanuts	25g (28 "nuts")	164	7 g	14 g	2 g	Vitamin E, niacin, folate, magnesium, phosphorus, manganese
Pecans	25g (19 halves)	199	3 g	21 g	2 g	Fiber, copper, manganese
Pine nuts	25g (3 tbsp)	190	4 g	19 g	1 g	Vitamins E and K, magnesium, phosphorus, zinc, copper, manganese
Pinto beans, cooked	85g cup	123	8 g	0.5 g	0 g	Fiber, thiamin, vitamin B_6, folate, iron, magnesium, phosphorus, potassium, manganese
Pistachios	25g (3½ tbsp)	160	6 g	13 g	2 g	Fiber, thiamin, vitamin B_6, phosphorus, copper, manganese

PLANT-POWERED PROTEIN	SERVING SIZE	CALORIES	PROTEIN	FAT	SAT FAT	STAR NUTRIENTS* (AT LEAST 10% DV PER SERVING)
Pumpkin seeds, hulled	25g (3 tbsp)	153	7 g	13 g	2 g	Vitamin K, iron, magnesium, phosphorus, zinc, copper, manganese
Sesame seeds	25g (3 tbsp)	160	5 g	14 g	2 g	Fiber, thiamin, vitamin B_6, calcium, iron, magnesium, phosphorus, zinc, copper, manganese
Soybeans, cooked	85g cup	149	15 g	8 g	1 g	Fiber, vitamins K and B_6, riboflavin, folate, iron, magnesium, phosphorus, potassium, copper, manganese
Split peas, cooked	100g cup	116	8 g	0.5 g	0 g	Fiber, thiamin, folate, potassium, manganese
Sunflower seeds, hulled	25g (3½ tbsp)	163	5 g	14 g	1 g	Fiber, vitamins E and B_6, niacin, folate, pantothenic acid, phosphorus, zinc, copper, manganese, selenium
Tofu, regular, with added calcium	100g	94	10 g	6 g	1 g	Calcium, iron, phosphorus, copper, manganese, selenium
Walnuts	25g (14 halves)	185	4 g	18 g	2 g	Magnesium, phosphorus, copper, manganese,
White beans, cooked	85 cup	127	8 g	0.5 g	0 g	Fiber, thiamin, folate, iron, magnesium, phosphorus, potassium, manganese

Source: Data from USDA National Nutrient Database for Standard Reference, http://ndb.nal.usda.gov

Sat Fat = saturated fat; DV = Daily Value, nutritional requirements according to the Food and Drug Administration, based on 2,000 calories per day; g = gram; tbsp = tablespoon

*Refer to the appendix (page 393) to learn how these nutrients contribute to overall health.

don't need to worry about getting enough protein. Even if you're on a completely vegan diet, it's not difficult to obtain this level of protein. You have to remember that virtually every plant food—except for refined sugars, oils, and alcohol—contains some protein, and it adds up quickly. If you make sure to include plant foods that are particularly high in protein—legumes, nuts, seeds, and soy foods—you'll be just fine. For proof, just check out the protein values of the foods in the Plant-Powered Protein List. Beyond these foods, whole grains contain their fair share of protein—cooked Kamut wheat contains 11 grams per 150g (the amount in 45g of tuna)—and even vegetables contain varying levels of protein: Cooked broccoli contains 6 grams per 150g and cooked green leafy vegetables contain 5 grams per 100g.

IT'S ALL ABOUT THE PROTEIN PACKAGE

The thing that's so unique about plant proteins—from beans to lentils to soy—is that they have an excellent "protein package," which means that the protein comes packed with other beneficial nutrients like fiber, vitamins, minerals, healthy fats, and phytochemicals and very little of the "bad stuff," like saturated fat and sodium. Take a look at that little 3-ounce sirloin steak we talked about: To get 24 grams of protein, the steak "package" has 266 calories, 7 grams of saturated fat (35 percent of your daily budget), and some good stuff like vitamin B_{12}, zinc, iron, and selenium. Now look up cooked soybeans on the Plant-Powered Protein List: If you eat a serving, you'll gain similar levels of protein (29 grams) and calories (298), but only 2 grams of saturated fat, in addition to a bevy of health-protective nutrients such as omega-3 fatty acids, fiber, thiamin, riboflavin, folate, calcium, iron, magnesium, phosphorus, potassium, manganese, isoflavones, saponins, and **phytic acid**. All these nutrients in the soybean work together to provide health benefits, in particular, reduced risks of heart disease and osteoporosis, which have been documented in hundreds of studies.

If you scan the Plant-Powered Protein List, you'll notice that most plant proteins have common attributes, such as low saturated-fat levels and plenty of fiber (a serving of beans can provide about two-thirds of your hard-to-get fiber recommendation for the whole day!). However, their nutrient strengths vary. For example, walnuts and flaxseeds are omega-3 superstars (2,565 milligrams and 6,388 milligrams per 30g, respectively). Sunflower seeds are off the charts in vitamin E, with 60g containing 101 percent of your **Daily Value (DV)**, the standard daily requirement based on a 2,000-calorie diet, and lentils are high in folate (90% DV in 200g cooked). This just serves to illustrate how important variety is in achieving a health-protective, optimal diet. When you sprinkle flaxseeds over your oatmeal, spread almond butter on whole wheat bread for lunch, and cook up a lentil vegetable stew for dinner, you're taking full advantage of all the nutrient combinations in plant foods to make your diet more nutritionally balanced and strong. So remember: Variety is the rule when it comes to choosing plant proteins—don't just stick to peanut butter sandwiches every afternoon and tofu every night.

Plant-based proteins may be one of the main reasons that vegetarians enjoy a longer lifespan, healthier weight, and lower risk of disease. By choosing plant proteins, which come "packaged" with healthy fats and lots of fiber, vitamins, minerals, and phytochemicals, you're using a double-whammy approach. You're powering up on healthful nutrients and compounds linked with better health, *and* you're replacing animal proteins that may contribute more calories, fat, saturated fat, and—depending on how it's prepared—sodium and toxins such as nitroso compounds, AGEs, HCAs, and PAHs. For every meal in which you swap animal proteins for plant proteins, you're gaining these magnified benefits.

Another bonus with many plant proteins like beans, lentils, and soybeans is that, because of their high-fiber profile, it's not easy to overeat them—which is why they are frequently linked with healthy weight maintenance in research studies. Most people who choose no-fiber steak for dinner usually double up (if not triple up) on the 3-ounce portion size from the earlier example, thus downing 532 calories and 14 grams of saturated fat—70 percent of the suggested upper limit for saturated fat. This is true for many animal food choices, whether it's cheese, steak, chicken nuggets, ribs, or even fish fingers.

If you really want to see some meat dishes that are on portion, calorie, saturated fat, and sodium overdrive, just visit your nearby family or steak restaurant. Here's a sampling of disastrous nutrition lineups—due to portion size as well as preparation style—you might find:

- Chicken wings can contain more than 1,800 calories, 50 grams of saturated fat, 4,400 milligrams of sodium, and 100 grams of protein per order.

- A full stack of beef ribs can contribute more than 2,200 calories, 80 grams of saturated fat, 2,800 milligrams of sodium, and 75 grams of protein per order (without the sides!).
- A deluxe burger can add up to more than 1,000 calories, 24 grams of saturated fat, 1,700 milligrams of sodium, and 55 grams of protein (without the fries).
- A breakfast meat-and-egg scramble can contain more than 1,100 calories, 25 grams of saturated fat, 3,400 milligrams of sodium, and 45 grams of protein (not counting toast and hash browns).
- An order of prime rib can carry more than 950 calories, 18 grams of saturated fat, 3,400 milligrams of sodium, and 125 grams of protein (not counting that loaded baked potato on the side).[6]

In contrast, try stewing up a big pot of pinto beans, black-eyed peas, or lentils with onions, garlic, and fresh herbs. You'll probably find that a typical serving—containing about 225 calories, 15 grams of protein (equivalent to the amount in 60g of fish), 1 gram of fat, and a whopping 15 grams of fiber—is a completely satisfying portion size. These plant proteins contain a wonderful nutrient balance—protein, slow-burning carbohydrates, and loads of fiber—that is highly satiating, which means they fill you up and keep you satisfied for longer.

FALLING IN LOVE WITH LEGUMES

From pinto beans in Mexico to lentils in India, legumes—a class of vegetables, also referred to as pulses, that also includes peas—have been the nutrition cornerstone of many cultures for thousands of years. In fact, dried peas dating back 11,000 years have been found in caves in Thailand, and lentils were packed away in Egyptian tombs to provide sustenance in the afterlife. Legumes are even part of our own rich American culture. They were part of a pre-Columbian South, Central, and North American agricultural tradition known as "the Three Sisters." The tribal women created mounds on which they planted corn, beans, and squash together—the climbing beans used the corn stalks for support and provided nitrogen to the soil, and the squash covered the ground, discouraging pests and weeds.

Grown throughout the world, legumes are essentially the fruit (or seeds) of certain flowering plants. Legumes are planted in the field, harvested from their pods, and sun dried before they are packaged—that's pretty much it. But legumes also have a wonderful environmental benefit beyond replacing eco-intensive animal foods: They have a unique ability to "fix nitrogen," or transfer nitrogen from the air into the soil, which reduces the need for synthetic fertilizers for growing other crops. Farmers discovered long ago that if they rotated their crops with legumes, their soil would be replenished.

It's no wonder that legumes were so treasured; they are as near to a perfect food as you can find. A portion, on average, contains at least 20% DV of fiber, folate, and manganese; 10% DV of protein, potassium, iron, magnesium, and copper; and 6–8% DV of selenium and zinc. To top it off, legumes are rich in a variety of phytochemicals, such as **alkaloids**, flavonoids, saponins, **tannins**, and **phenolic compounds**.[7]

Factor in that legumes are easy to cook, economical, and shelf stable and suit a number of culinary styles, and it's easy to see why they have been such a reliable food for centuries. And now modern science points out that eating legumes regularly can offer a number of health benefits, including lower blood cholesterol levels, lower body weight, higher intakes of dietary fiber, and lower rates of heart disease, hypertension, some types of cancer, and diabetes.[8] That's why I recommend that you eat at least one serving of legumes every day in order to promote optimal health.

You can take a new spin on legumes by trying them in alternative forms. Flours such as those made of beans, chickpeas, or lentils are becoming a more popular replacement for wheat flour. This practice is nothing new; people have been grinding legumes into flour for centuries. These high-protein, nutritious flours carry the advantage that they do not contain wheat or gluten, so they make a wonderful option for people suffering from wheat allergies or celiac disease, in which wheat and gluten must be avoided entirely. Even if you are not allergic to gluten or wheat, you can still enjoy the nutritious qualities of legume flours in baked goods: Just replace a small amount of the wheat flour in your favorite recipes with legume flour. And sprouted legumes are another delicious, nutritious way to power up on legumes. For example, sprouted lentils—lentils that have been germinated so that the seed is still intact but the nutritional profile has been boosted by the germination process—are increasingly popular. These sprouted legumes are cooked just like the nonsprouted variety, and they can be included in side dishes, salads, soups, and stews.

No matter whether you're a plant-powered vegan, vegetarian, or omnivore, it's time to include more luscious legumes in your diet. Thousands of years' worth of cultivation has led to thousands of varieties of legumes, so there's no end to the flavors, colors, sizes, and textures available. Did you know that lentils come in shades of white, yellow, pink, red, green, tan, brown, and black? And there is a resurgence of heirloom varieties of legumes, such as Mayflower, Petaluma Gold Rush, and Cherokee Trail of Tears beans, that were nearly lost to extinction. Canned beans and peas are an easy solution to including more legumes in your diet, and now you can even find refrigerated and vacuum-packed ones—just look for those without added salt. You'll find an even wider variety in dry form at natural food markets and online purveyors, and the quality of freshly cooked dried legumes is generally better than you'll find in canned products.

A whole world of legumes awaits your discovery. Try as many varieties as you can; here's a sampling of some of the most popular.

GETTING TO KNOW LEGUMES

LEGUME	DESCRIPTION	CULINARY SUGGESTIONS
Adzuki beans	Appearance: Small, reddish brown Flavor: Nutty, sweet	Use in Asian cuisine, such as Japanese desserts; sprinkle in salads; use in soups, stews, and side dishes.
Baby butter beans	Appearance: Flattened, creamy white Flavor: Rich, buttery	Use in soups, stews, and casseroles or cooked simply, with herbs and spices.
Black beans	Appearance: Small ovals with deep black skins, dark cream to gray flesh Flavor: Mild, sweet, earthy with soft texture	Use in classic Latin American, Caribbean, and Southwestern dishes, such as soups, stews, sauces, salads, burritos, and salsas.
Black-eyed peas	Appearance: Kidney shaped, white with a small black eye, very fine wrinkles Flavor: Scented aroma, distinctive taste with creamy texture	Use in Southern dishes, simply stewed and served with greens; sprinkle into salads, soups, stews, casseroles, and side dishes.

LEGUME	DESCRIPTION	CULINARY SUGGESTIONS
Cranberry beans	Appearance: Small and rounded, ivory color with red markings that disappear during cooking Flavor: Subtle, nut-like taste with creamy texture	Suits northern Italian, Spanish, and Portuguese cuisine; stew for a side dish or add to soups and stews.
Dark red kidney beans	Appearance: Large, kidney shaped, deep reddish brown Flavor: Robust, full-bodied with soft texture	Very good in chili, salads, wraps, and burritos and with rice.
Chickpeas (garbanzo beans)	Appearance: Beige to pale yellow Flavor: Nutty taste with buttery texture	A key ingredient in traditional ethnic dishes such as dal, hummus, and falafel; wonderful in salads, soups, stews, and side dishes.
Great Northern beans	Appearance: Flat, kidney-shaped, medium-size, white Flavor: Mild, delicate, taking on flavors of foods with which they're cooked	Traditionally prepared as Boston baked beans, but great in white bean chili, soups, and stews.
Haricot beans	Appearance: Small white ovals Flavor: Mild flavor with powdery texture	Use in baked beans, soups, chili, and stews.
Large butter beans	Appearance: Flat shape, ivory color Flavor: Smooth, sweet with creamy texture	Use in American succotash or simply stewed as a side dish; excellent in soups or casseroles.
Light red kidney beans	Appearance: Large, kidney shaped Flavor: Robust, full-bodied with soft, mealy texture	Use in chili, salads, soups, and stews, and with rice.

LEGUME	DESCRIPTION	CULINARY SUGGESTIONS
Pink beans	Appearance: Small, pale pink; reddish brown after cooking Flavor: Rich, meaty with slightly powdery texture	Use in chili, soups, stews, and side dishes.
Pinto beans	Appearance: Medium ovals, mottled beige and brown Flavor: Earthy flavor with powdery texture	Use in vegetarian refried beans, in Tex-Mex and Mexican dishes, or as a side dish.
Small red beans	Appearance: Dark red color; similar to red kidney but smaller Flavor: Similar to red kidney	Use in soups, salads, chili, and Creole dishes.
Lentils	Appearance: Small discs, varieties range from yellow to pink to dark green (known as French or Puy) Flavor: Earthy, slightly sweet with soft texture	Delicious in dal, soups, stews, and veggie burgers; serve as a side dish or salad.
Split peas	Appearance: Small half spheres available in yellow or green varieties Flavor: Earthy flavor with soft texture	Traditionally used in split-pea soup; add to stews and side dishes.

Source: Information from U.S. Dried Beans Council (usdrybeans.com), Northern Pulse Growers Association (northernpulse.com)

So you won't be afraid to experiment with legumes, I've included the following "Introduce Legumes into Your Kitchen" section (see page 56) and a Cooking Up Legumes Guide (see page 57). After all, some of the best culinary creations around the world feature legumes, from Indian dal to Middle Eastern hummus to the classic black-eyed peas with greens of the southern United States. In the Plant-Powered Recipe Collection in chapter 14, you'll find some of my favorite recipes starring legumes, including Three-Bean Cowboy Chili (page 321), Southwestern Black Bean, Quinoa, and Mango Medley (page 318), and Green and Gold Lentil Pot (page 316). Discover a new family-favorite meal you'll return to over and over again.

INTRODUCE LEGUMES INTO YOUR KITCHEN

Start putting legumes on your menu every day with my favorite tips.

1. Stock your pantry with a variety of canned beans, such as chickpeas and adzuki, kidney, black, cannellini, and pinto beans, for a quick addition to your menu any day of the week.
2. Bring home a new variety of dried legumes from every shopping trip to star in chilies, stews, or casseroles that week.
3. Toss chickpeas or black or kidney beans into salads for an earthy, nutritious addition.
4. Keep a batch of my Home-Style Hummus (page 276) in the fridge as your go-to spread for whole grain crackers, pita, sandwiches, and wraps all week long.
5. Start your meal with a delicious bean, lentil, or split-pea soup.
6. Make a French lentil salad by tossing cooked lentils—which can be cooked up without soaking in 20 minutes—with an olive oil and herb vinaigrette.
7. Substitute cooked, stewed, or mashed beans for potatoes or rice as a side dish twice a week.
8. Stir red beans or peas into rice for a zesty Cajun or Latin-inspired dish (see New Orleans Red Beans and Rice, page 320).
9. Stir black beans into salsa for a tasty dip.
10. Fill a whole grain tortilla with refried vegetarian beans for breakfast or lunch (check out Bean and Grilled Veggie Burritos, page 300).
11. Cook up a thick, Tuscan-style white bean soup, such as Italian Cannellini Spinach Soup (page 280).
12. Visit an online purveyor such as Bob's Red Mill (bobsredmill.com), Local Harvest (localharvest.org), Rancho Gordo (ranchogordo.com), or Purcell Mountain Farms (purcellmountainfarms.com) to find a wide variety of eclectic legumes such as Yellow Indian Woman bean or Goat's Eye bean.
13. Put Southern black-eyed peas with greens on your dinner menu rotation.

14. Remember how good baked beans—either homemade or canned—are at picnics and family meals? Put them on your menu this week!

15. Try a simple Italian classic: pasta tossed with cooked white beans, tomatoes, olive oil, and garlic.

16. For a delicious snack, roast cooked (or canned) chickpeas—drizzled with a small amount of extra virgin olive oil and seasoned to your liking—in a hot oven for about 30 minutes.

COOKING UP LEGUMES GUIDE

LEGUME	COOKING METHOD
Dried beans, chickpeas, whole dried peas	Rinse and drain the legumes. Discard any damaged legumes and any foreign material. Use one of two methods to rehydrate: Quick Hot Soak—Cover with water and boil for 2 minutes. Cover the pot and soak for 1 to 4 hours. Discard the soaking water and cover with fresh water. Overnight Cold Soak—Cover with water and soak overnight (12 hours or more). Discard the soaking water and cover with fresh water. Bring the beans and water to a boil, reduce the heat, and simmer. Most bean varieties take 1½ to 2 hours to cook, and peas take up to 40 minutes. Stir occasionally and test for tenderness. 500g yields about 550–600g cups cooked.
Split peas	Split peas do not require soaking. Rinse and drain the peas. Discard any damaged peas and any foreign material. Put the peas into a pot and add 2 parts water for each part dried peas. Bring to a boil, reduce the heat, and simmer until they reach desired tenderness, about 30 minutes. 500g yields about 600g cooked.
Lentils	Lentils do not require soaking. Rinse and drain the lentils. Discard any damaged lentils and any foreign material. Put the lentils into a pot and add 2½ parts water to each part lentils. Bring to a boil, reduce the heat, and simmer to desired tenderness, 15 to 20 minutes. 500g yields about 550g cooked.

Source: Information from U.S. Dried Beans Council (usdrybeans.com), Northern Pulse Growers Association (northernpulse.com)

|||||||||||||||||||||||||||||||||||||||||||||||||||||||||||||||||||||||||||||||||||||||||||||||||||||||||

A GASSY ISSUE

LEGUMES—ESPECIALLY BEANS—have been the "butt" of jokes about their gas-producing effects for decades. And it's true—if you're not used to them, the natural ferment-able carbohydrates contained in these ultra high-fiber foods can produce gastrointestinal discomfort in the form of tempo-rary cramping and flatulence. But, research shows, if you add them to your diet on a regular basis over time—at least once or twice a week—you can avoid gas. If you're not used to beans in your diet, start with one serving a week and gradually work your way up to at least three servings a week.

The cooking method can also reduce the naturally occurring compounds in beans that are linked with flatulence. Try using the quick hot-soak method in the Cooking Up Legumes Guide (see page 57) to soften the beans, and then drain off the soak-ing water and start with fresh water for cooking.

|||||||||||||||||||||||||||||||||||||||||||||||||||||||||||||||||||||||||||||||||||||||||||||||||||||||||

SOY, THE SUPERFOOD

Soy is a category of legumes all to itself. First cultivated in 1100 BC China, this magical bean has a rich culinary history as well as a unique nutritional profile. One of the most widely studied food sources on the planet, the soybean plant has even been shot into space, on a research mission to help answer the question of how human life might be sustained in space over the long term. Part of soy's allure is that it provides quality protein comparable to that of animal foods, leading it to be looked at as the ideal food to feed the world's hungry. A plot of land growing soy can produce ten times the amount of protein than the same plot of land dedicated to producing beef from cattle.

The buzz about soy is all about its cache of important nutrients. One serving of soybeans, adding up to less than 300 calories, provides 57% DV of protein, 41% DV of fiber, 49% DV of iron, and 18% DV of calcium, as well as at least 18% DV of ten other essential vitamins and minerals. And that's not all: Soybeans contain health-protective phytochemicals such as phytic acid, saponins, phytosterols, **protease inhibitors**, and isoflavones, which have been of particular interest to researchers. Isoflavones are **phytoestrogens** (that is, plant estrogens) that possess antifungal, antimicrobial, and antioxidant properties—traits that help the soybean plant to thrive and seem to confer similar benefits to humans.

An impressive body of scientific research has accumulated on soy's health benefits over the past twenty years. Soy has been linked with bone health, reduced cholesterol levels, lower risk of heart disease, reduction of hot flashes, and reduced prostate cancer risk and tumor metastasis. However, soy isoflavones' estrogen-like activities have led to concern about whether eating soy can raise the risk of breast cancer. The research on soy and breast cancer has been conflicting—some studies have suggested soy isoflavones possibly stimulate the growth of estrogen-sensitive tumors, but others have found no increase in breast cancer risk with soy intake. Asian populations that consume large amounts of soy foods throughout life suffer lower risks of breast cancer compared with Western nations. However, some experts believe that this may be because they tend to consume mostly unprocessed soy foods such as soybeans, tempeh, and tofu, while Americans tend to consume soy in highly processed forms like protein bars, shakes, and vegetarian meat alternatives. Newer studies have revealed an interesting finding: Soy exposure during childhood and adolescence may even reduce breast cancer risk later in life.[9] The American Institute for Cancer Research's position is that soy foods are safe in moderate amounts—up to two or three servings per day. For breast cancer survivors, the American Cancer Society reports that current evidence suggests no adverse effects on recurrence or survival from consuming soy foods.[10]

My recommendation on soy? Feel free to include up to three servings per day in your diet. But choose soy products in their least processed forms, such as whole soybeans, edamame, tofu, tempeh, and soy milk (see the Plant-Powered Whole Soy Foods Guide, page 62). I also suggest that you purchase organic soy foods, because 93 percent of soy grown in the United States is **genetically modified**.[11] Although the jury is still out on whether genetically modified foods pose health risks, a number of studies raise both human health concerns and environmental concerns over the consumption and cultivation of genetically modified foods. And organic foods are produced in a more sustainable fashion without the use of most synthetic inputs (see Go Organic, page 126).

A WORD ABOUT SOY MEAT ALTERNATIVES

Veggie burgers, soy meat crumbles, vegetarian hot dogs—it seems like soy meat alternatives are everywhere. When I was a vegetarian as a child, we had to drive long distances to seek out special stores that carried such meat alternatives; today they're at most every supermarket. And if you visit a natural food store, you're likely to find a whole section dedicated to faux meats. Although many plant-based eaters find mock meats an easy way to transition away from animal foods, I encourage you to use these products in moderation. Why? Just read the ingredient list and you'll see what I'm talking about.

Many mock meats contain a long list of processed ingredients, such as isolated soy protein, textured soy protein concentrate, hydrolyzed vegetable protein, sodium citrate, sodium phosphate, and many other multisyllabic chemicals you won't find growing in any garden or farm. Although the calorie and fat profiles may look good, they often contain high sodium levels that can negatively impact your health. Thankfully, a new generation of meat alternatives boasts cleaner labels, featuring ingredients such as peas, beans, brown rice, and carrots—ingredients that you can recognize on the label as well as see in the food product itself. But it's still important to check out the nutrition facts label when you're perusing meat alternatives: For example, some garden burgers contain as little as 3 grams of protein each, making them a skimpy replacement. Shoot for meat analogues with at least 20% DV of protein and less than 15% DV of saturated fat and sodium; check the labels before you toss any into your shopping cart (see Understanding Food Labels, page 253).

Sure, it's not a bad idea to stow away a few of your favorite faux meats in the freezer for a quick meal on a busy night, or to keep a bag of **texturized vegetable protein (TVP)** in your pantry to throw into chili or a casserole. But I encourage you to eat more whole plant proteins—beans, lentils, nuts, and seeds—that are as simple and as close to their natural form as possible. So when you select soy foods, choose them as minimally processed as possible. Refer to the Plant-Powered Whole Soy Foods Guide (page 62) to learn more about using foods like tofu and tempeh. And keep in mind that all those servings of soy can really add up. If you're drinking soy milk a couple of times a day and eating veggie bacon for breakfast, soy yogurt for a snack, soy sandwich "meat" for lunch, and a processed soy meat alternative for dinner, obviously you're far exceeding three servings a day. When it comes to plant proteins, always remember to diversify to gain a variety of nutrients! With so many beans, nuts, lentils, and seeds—not to mention non–soy-based meat and dairy alternatives—it's easy to do.

GETTING TO KNOW SEITAN

IF YOU'RE LOOKING for a fresh alternative to meat, you might want to give seitan a spin. According to legend, this wheat-based product was discovered by Buddhist monks in seventh-century China when a batch of wheat dough went awry: The starch portion had been washed away, revealing the gluten protein. Since then, seitan has been a fixed element in Asian cuisine. Traditionally, this wheat gluten is simmered in a broth of soy sauce, ginger, garlic, and seaweed. Seitan takes on the flavors it is cooked with, so it's great in stews, pilafs, and casseroles or seasoned and sautéed as you would meat. Although you can make seitan yourself by mixing up a flour dough and rinsing out the starch, it's a laborious process. Fortunately, seitan is available at some natural food stores and online purveyors in convenient mixes and in prepared and flavored products. Try my recipe for Bok Choy Seitan Pho on page 326.

FROM NUTS TO SEEDS

GET A LITTLE NUTTY

When I first studied nutrition, nuts were widely bashed among the health community because of their high fat content. We used to tell our patients to avoid them, especially if they were at risk for heart disease. But now our opinion of nuts has come full circle. A large volume of research now finds that if you consume a handful of tree nuts—about 30 to 60g—a day, including almonds, walnuts, pistachios, pine nuts, cashews, macadamias, brazil nuts, pecans, and hazelnuts, or a handful of peanuts, which are actually in the legume family, you can gain a plethora of health benefits. These

PLANT-POWERED WHOLE SOY FOODS GUIDE

SOY FOOD	SERVING SIZE	CALORIES	PROTEIN	FAT / SAT FAT	DESCRIPTION	CULINARY SUGGESTIONS
Soy milk	225ml	80-110	5-9 g	3-5 g / 0-1 g	A milk alternative produced by soaking dried soybeans and then grinding and straining them. Comes in a variety of flavors and has a milky, nutty taste.	Use in place of milk as a beverage, with coffee or cereal, or in smoothies, cooking, or baking.
Soy nuts	1½ tbsp (15 g)	78	5 g	4 g / 1 g	Whole soybeans that have been soaked in water and baked until brown. With a taste reminiscent of peanuts, soynuts come in a variety of flavors. May be made into soy nut butter.	Eat out of hand as a snack. Use as an ingredient in granola, baked goods, salads, pilafs, or stir-fries. Use soy nut butter as spread on bread or in baking.
Tofu, extra firm, firm, soft, silken, or baked	100g	65-185 g	6-20 g	4-11 g / 0-2 g	Soft, cheeselike product (also referred to as soybean curd) made by curdling fresh soymilk with a coagulant. High in calcium if calcium is used as the curdling agent. Tofu goes from low in calories, fat, and protein to higher as the texture goes from silken to extra firm.	Firm or extra firm (with a more concentrated nutrition profile) may be diced into stir-fries, soups, salads, side dishes, and entrées. Pressing (i.e., squeezing out excess liquid) and freezing out tofu produces a "meatier" texture. Soft or silken may be used in smoothies, dips, desserts, or soups. Baked may be sliced into sandwiches, salads, or stir-fries.

SOY FOOD	SERVING SIZE	CALORIES	PROTEIN	FAT / SAT FAT	DESCRIPTION	CULINARY SUGGESTIONS
Tempeh	100g	160	15 g	9 g / 2 g	Soybeans combined with a grain and fermented into a traditional Indonesian cake with a nutty flavor.	Marinate and grill; slice into stir-fries, soups, salads, casseroles, side dishes, and stews.
Edamame, cooked, shelled	85g	188	17 g	8 g / 1 g	Large soybeans harvested while sweet and green.	Boil or steam whole, then remove from the pod to enjoy as an appetizer or snack. Add shelled edamame to soups, salads, stir-fries, side dishes, and stews.
Soybeans, cooked	85g	149	15 g	8 g / 1 g	Cooked whole, dried soybeans	Stir into soups, salads, stir-fries, side dishes, chili, and stews.

Sources: USDA National Nutrient Database for Standard Reference (see Chapter 9, note 32, page 389) and nutrition facts labels; values may differ based on brand.

Sat Fat = saturated fat, oz = ounce, g = gram, tbsp = tablespoon benefits include reduced risk for heart disease, diabetes, metabolic syndrome, and some cancers. And new research pops up on nuts' health potential all the time, from improved cognitive function after eating walnuts to better erectile function linked with pistachios.[12]

What's so special about these little kernels of joy? They're full of health-protective nutrients, including protein, fiber, folic acid, niacin, vitamins E and B$_6$, magnesium, copper, zinc, selenium, phosphorus, and potassium. Tree nuts, essentially hard-shelled fruits, contain healthy monounsaturated fats that have been shown to lower LDL ("bad") cholesterol levels. Walnuts in particular contain omega-3 fatty acids that are especially good for your heart. Almonds are rich in calcium, contributing about 75 mg (8% DV) in every 30g, which can help you meet your needs if you're a vegan. And nuts also contain phytochemicals such as flavonoids, phenolic compounds, isoflavones, **ellagic acid**, and phytosterols. When you put them all together into one tiny kernel, you end up with a highly functional, health-promoting food.

All nuts are not created equal; some, such as pistachios, walnuts, almonds, and peanuts, have garnered much attention from researchers for their growing list of nutritional advantages. These nuts tend to have better fat and protein profiles than brazil nuts, cashews, and macadamias. Yet, all nuts contain measurable amounts of protein, fiber, healthy fats, vitamins, minerals, and phytochemicals that arm them with antioxidant and anti-inflammatory properties. So try to include a variety in your diet, but prioritize the superstar nuts, particularly if you're following a plant-powered vegan diet and need the rich protein and healthy fat profiles. Check out the nutritional profile of a variety of nuts on the Plant-Powered Protein List (see page 46).

Nuts have been treasured by humans—as well as birds and animals—since prehistoric times, for their sustenance as well as delicious taste and culinary features. They turn up in traditional foods around the globe—from peanuts in Thai satay sauce to pine nuts in Italian pesto. Store a wide variety in your freezer to keep them from going rancid; defrost them in minutes in order to sprinkle nuts into salads, side dishes, pilafs, cereals, breads, and baked goods. You can try just as many types of nut butters—there is a nut butter available for every nut, if you look for it—to diversify your nutrient intake. Spread nut butters on whole grain bread or crackers, use them in baked goods to replace refined oils (see chapter 7), and stir them into sauces and marinades for rich, earthy flavor.

EAT LIKE A BIRD—TURN TO SEEDS

Plants produce a remarkable object: a tiny embryonic plant covered up by a coating with some stored food to provide for its growth—a seed. The bearing of seeds completes the miraculous reproductive cycle of a plant. So, when you munch on an edible seed, you are gaining all of those nutrients—protein, fats, carbohydrates, fiber, vitamins, minerals, and phytochemicals—that the plant packed away in order to help that little seed sprout and grow. There is a long list of edible seeds that humans have been eating since the dawn of time. In fact, anthropologists believe that prehistoric humans, in their constant search for sustenance, probably collected and ate virtually every seed that didn't kill them. Although grains, legumes, and nuts are technically seeds, today we tend to separate these plant foods into their own culinary categories, and enlist into the seed group things like flaxseeds and sesame, sunflower, pumpkin, chia, and hemp seeds. Believe me—there are plenty of other edible seeds out there, such as papaya seeds and lotus seeds, but here we'll look at the seeds that are most widely available.

Each different type of seed provides a unique variety of nutrients (see the Plant-Powered Protein List, page 46). For example, sunflower seeds are high in vitamin E. Hemp seeds and flaxseeds are very high in omega-3 fatty acids, which have been linked with a number of health benefits, including heart health. And hemp even contains the more rare fatty acids **gamma-linolenic acid** and **stearidonic acid**, both linked with additional health advantages in recent research, such as improving pain in arthritis and lowering blood pressure levels. Most are rich in protein, fiber, healthy fats, vitamins, and minerals. Like some nuts, many seeds contain phytosterols, which are cholesterol-like compounds that lower blood cholesterol levels. Seeds also contain lignans, a special group of fibers that also lower cholesterol as well as blood pressure (see Fiber Sense, page 92). No wonder studies have found that certain seeds can reduce cholesterol and blood pressure levels as well as provide anticancer effects and bone protection.

As you can see, there are plenty of good reasons to include seeds in your diet. Check out the Plant-Powered Seeds Guide on the following page and get started including these crunchy gems in your diet every day. Remember that most seeds are available as butter or paste, more options for bread spreads and useful fat alternatives in cooking.

PLANT-POWERED SEEDS GUIDE

SEEDS	DESCRIPTION	CULINARY SUGGESTIONS
Hemp	The hemp plant produces seeds that are soft, with a mild, nutty flavor. You can buy them shelled or as "hemp nuts" or hemp butter.	Sprinkle onto cereals, salads, yogurt, side dishes, and grains and add to smoothies and baked goods. Use hemp butter as a spread or substitute for oils in baked goods. (Warning: It's green!)
Chia	Known as the "running food" of the Aztecs and Mayans, these tiny seeds have a mild, nutty flavor.	Sprinkle onto cereals, salads, yogurt, side dishes, and grains and add to smoothies and baked goods. Chia gel (made by soaking 2 tablespoons of chia seeds in 50–150ml of water for 10 to 15 minutes) can be used to replace up to 25 percent of the fat, oil, or eggs in a baking recipe.
Sesame	One of the oldest culinary seasonings, these tiny, soft beige seeds are mild in flavor and range in color from pale to brown to black. Also available as a paste known as tahini.	Well suited for Asian dishes, such as stir-fries, and good sprinkled onto slaws, salads, cereals, and side dishes and added to baked goods. Tahini is a key ingredient in Mediterranean dishes such as hummus (see Home-Style Hummus, page 276), but it is also delicious as a spread.
Pumpkin	Straight from your Halloween pumpkin come these large, chewy green seeds with a white hull, also known as pepitas when they are hulled. A celebrated food of the Native Americans, they can be roasted at home or purchased in their dry form.	Sprinkle onto cereals, salads, side-dishes, and stir-fries and add to smoothies. Grind into meal to add to baked goods or homemade veggie burgers.
Flax	Ranging in color from amber to reddish-brown, flaxseeds offer a mildly nutty flavor. It's best to buy them ground (or buy seeds and grind them in a blender), since they may pass through your gastrointestinal tract undigested when they are eaten whole.	Sprinkle onto cereals, salads, side-dishes, pilafs, and stir-fries and add to breads, baked goods, and smoothies.

SEEDS	DESCRIPTION	CULINARY SUGGESTIONS
Sunflower	The seeds from the lovely sunflower plant, which develop in an artistic spiral within the head of the flower, produce crunchy kernels that are gray-green or black and encased in thin shells. Also available hulled or as butter.	Best eaten by hand as a snack, but shelled seeds are excellent in cereals, breads, baked goods, trail mix, and salads. The butter is a delicious alternative to peanut butter on sandwiches.

KEEP PORTIONS PETITE

Although nuts and seeds are packed with goodness, they are very calorie dense. They contain a high number of calories for a tiny serving because of their high fat content; just 30g of them (or about 2 tablespoons of nut or seed butter) contains 140 to 200 calories. This is why I caution you to use discretion when you're munching on nuts and seeds, limiting your number of servings to a total of one or two a day (see the Daily Plant-Powered Protein Guide, page 77). If you down an entire 250g tin of mixed nuts, it could add up to more than 1,500 calories. To make sure you're not overdoing your portion of nuts or seeds, measure or count them out by referring to the serving sizes listed in the Plant-Powered Protein List (see page 46). Place individual portions into resealable bags to throw into your tote for a healthy snack on the go, or count them into a dish before you nibble on them during your day.

Although it's best to use caution to keep your calorie count in check when you eat nuts, new intriguing research suggests that nuts may not be the diet downfall we once thought. In a review of the research on nut consumption and weight using two large study cohorts, scientists found that consumption of nuts was not associated with higher risk of weight gain.[13] This may be related to the facts that people tend to replace other problematic foods in their diets with nuts and that the unique nutrient package of nuts offers higher satiety, encouraging people to feel full for longer.

A PLANT-POWERED APPROACH TO DAIRY

If your goal is to cut back on animal foods in favor of more plant foods, you've also got to take on the issue of dairy products, including milk, yogurt, cream, sour cream, cheese, cottage cheese, and butter. Although these foods are kinder than meats because they don't directly involve the slaughtering of animals, most dairy products are still produced within the modern animal agriculture system of CAFOs, in which animals are confined and typically treated inhumanely. And the eco-impact of dairy products is much higher than that of plant foods: Dairy animals are large producers of methane gas and waste, and raising them is resource-intensive, requiring large amounts of food, water, and fossil fuels. The Environmental Working Group found that cheese has an especially high carbon footprint but also reported that dairy products that are certified organic are generally less environmentally damaging than those produced conventionally.[14]

Dairy products may seem as American as apple pie, but there has been controversy surrounding their place in an optimal diet. Even though they hold a prominent role in North American and European diets, in other parts of the world people find the whole idea of drinking cow's milk—better suited for a calf than a human—downright gross. In fact, an estimated 60 percent of the world's population is lactose intolerant (that is, unable to digest the sugar found in milk). Scientists traced Europeans' ability to tolerate milk to a genetic mutation that occurred about 7,500 years ago.[15]

Sure, dairy products are recommended in the USDA's Dietary Guidelines because they contain some important nutrients—vitamin D (which is added), calcium, and vitamin B_{12} in particular—that people may have a hard time getting. And dairy products can be an important food source for plant-powered vegetarians. But are they healthy overall? There's evidence that dairy products protect bone health, but remember that full-fat dairy products—especially cheese—also contribute saturated fat and cholesterol to your diet. According to the Harvard School of Public Health, high intakes of dairy foods are linked with increased risk of prostate cancer and possibly ovarian cancer; thus, the organization suggests limiting dairy products to one to two servings per day.[16]

Whether you decide to include moderate amounts of low-fat dairy products in your plant-powered diet is completely up to you, based on your own preferences and personal health goals. Even if you choose to consume some dairy products, you can replace others with plant-based alternatives. Perhaps you'd like to start with plant-based milks in smoothies, cooking, and baking. Here again you can gain from the double-whammy approach: By swapping dairy products for plant-powered products, you can cut the amount of saturated fat and cholesterol in your diet *and* amp up on protective nutrients like fiber, vitamins, minerals, and phytochemicals.

The availability of milk alternatives has soared; today nearly every grocery store offers a plant-based milk option—or two or three—and natural food stores stock entire rows of the stuff. Companies are making plant-based milks, yogurts, cheeses, ice cream, and creamer out of a variety of foods, including soy, rice, oats, hemp, sunflower seeds, almonds, and coconut. When it comes to plant-based milks, each product offers its own distinctive flavor, texture, and nutritional lineup. Look for those that are organic, unsweetened, and good tasting. And if you're vegan or near vegan, you'll need to rely on these alternatives to provide you with rich sources of calcium, vitamin D, and protein—so know that some plant-based milks are too low in protein to qualify as a plant-based protein serving. Look for products that provide about 7 grams of protein and at least 25% DV of calcium and vitamin D per 225g serving—about the same amount found in a glass of low-fat milk. Try a few brands until you find your favorite.

Plant-based yogurts can contain a fair amount of sugar, but choose unsweetened, plain varieties and add your own fruit as a natural sweetener. The new varieties of plant-based cheeses are so delightful, especially in cooking, that you can trick almost anybody into thinking they're the real thing! Some stores carry other plant-based dairy products, such as plant-based cream cheese, that are excellent options for replacing dairy in your favorite recipes. Keep in mind that even though most plant-based milks boast pretty clean labels, some plant-based dairy products like cheese are highly processed. Keep an eye on food labels to discover the best of the bunch. A side note: Plant-based milk should never take the place of breast milk or infant formula for infant feedings.

Don't be afraid to experiment! But also remember to diversify your plant-based dairy products so that you're not always turning to soy. I like to keep a few varieties of plant-based, shelf-stable milk alternatives in my pantry to pull out as I need them. Try plant-based milks in your morning coffee, over cereal, and in cream soups, sauces, and baked goods. Use plant-based cheeses (in moderation) in pizzas, sandwiches, and casseroles, and plant-based yogurt in smoothies and desserts. My Plant-Based Dairy Alternatives Guide (page 72) will get you going in the right direction.

REPLACE IMPORTANT NUTRIENTS

IF YOU'RE AIMING for a plant-powered vegan diet—or even a nearly vegan diet—you must be careful to replace important nutrients found in animal foods, such as calcium, vitamin D, zinc, iron, and vitamin B$_{12}$.

- **Calcium:** Try to include calcium-rich plant-based foods, such as green leafy vegetables (shoot for one serving per day), almonds, and broccoli. In addition, I suggest choosing a total of two servings per day of calcium-fortified foods, such as plant-based milk alternatives, tofu, or orange juice. You may consider taking a calcium supplement to help make sure you meet your total daily calcium needs (1,000 mg for most adults; 1,200 mg a day for women over 50 and men over 70).

- **Vitamin D:** If you're not drinking milk, which is fortified with vitamin D, you might have a hard time meeting your vitamin D requirement (600 mg/day for everyone 1 to 70 years of age), so shoot for ten minutes of sunlight exposure a day, consume vitamin-D-fortified foods, such as soy milk and orange juice, and consider taking a vitamin D supplement to help meet your needs.

- **Vitamin B$_{12}$:** Don't underestimate your body's needs for vitamin B$_{12}$, available only in animal foods: meat, fish, poultry, eggs, and dairy products. You can also get vitamin B$_{12}$ in some **nutritional yeasts**, which are available at natural food stores and may be added to savory dishes, as well as from fortified products, such as cereal and soy milk. Make sure to check the label of nutritional yeasts and fortified foods to see how much vitamin B$_{12}$ they contain before purchasing them. A vitamin B$_{12}$ deficiency can result in anemia and nerve damage. That's why I recommend that *all* *plant-powered vegans take a vitamin B$_{12}$ supplement daily.* The recommended dietary allowance for adults ages 14 and up is 2.4 micrograms per day.

- **Iron and zinc:** You don't need to eat animal products to get enough iron or zinc in your diet; just consume a diet rich in a variety of whole grains, legumes, green vegetables, and nuts and you'll be good to go.[17]

TO POP A VITAMIN PILL OR NOT? While the best way to get your vitamins and minerals is through whole foods, it may be necessary to supplement your diet with particular nutrients you may be lacking in your diet, such as calcium and vitamins B$_{12}$ and D. However, it's important to take vitamin and mineral supplements at levels that don't exceed your daily requirements (see Nutrients in Action, page 393), as research hasn't yet proven any benefits related to taking excessive amounts. When you eat nutrients in foods, you really don't need to worry about overdoing a particular vitamin or mineral, but when you're popping pills, it's easy to take double or triple the amount you need.

SHOOT FOR YOUR DAILY PROTEIN SERVINGS

Follow my guide to make sure that you get enough plant-powered protein in your diet. Remember to choose minimally processed foods first, and diversify your plant proteins. For additional serving size information, refer to the Plant-Powered Proteins List at the end of this chapter (page 77).

PLANT-BASED DAIRY ALTERNATIVES GUIDE

PLANT-BASED DAIRY ALTERNATIVE	SERVING SIZE	CALORIES	PROTEIN	FAT / SAT FAT	SUGAR	FLAVOR
PLANT-BASED MILKS						
7-grain milk (from oats, rice, wheat, barley, triticale, spelt, and millet), original	250ml	140	3 g	2 g / 0 g	16 g	Mild, sweet
Almond milk, chocolate	250ml	100–120	1 g	3 g / 0 g	16–20 g	Mild, sweet, nutty, chocolate
Almond milk, plain or original	250ml	50–60	1 g	2.5 g / 0 g	5–7 g	Mild, sweet, nutty
Almond milk, unsweetened	250ml	35–50	1 g	2.5-3.5 g / 0 g	0 g	Mildly sweet, nutty
Almond milk, vanilla	250ml	70–90	1 g	2.5 g / 0 g	9–15 g	Mild, sweet, nutty, vanilla
Coconut milk, unsweetened	250ml	50	1 g	5 g / 5 g	0 g	Mild, sweet, coconut, thick
Hazelnut milk, original	250ml	110	2 g	3.5 g / 0 g	14 g	Mild, sweet, nutty
Hemp milk, original	250ml	100	2 g	6 g / .5 g	6 g	Mildly sweet
Oat milk, original	250ml	130	4 g	2.5 g / 0 g	19 g	Mild, sweet

PLANT-BASED DAIRY ALTERNATIVE	SERVING SIZE	CALORIES	PROTEIN	FAT / SAT FAT	SUGAR	FLAVOR
PLANT-BASED MILKS						
Rice milk, chocolate	250ml	160	2 g	3 g / 0 g	28 g	Mild, sweet, watery, chocolate
Rice milk, plain or original	250ml	120–130	1 g	2-2.5 g / 0 g	10-14 g	Mild, sweet, watery
Rice milk, vanilla	250ml	130	1 g	2-2.5 g / 0 g	12-14 g	Mild, sweet, watery, vanilla
Soy milk, chocolate	250ml	130–180	5-8 g	2.5-3.5 g / .5-1 g	14-19 g	Sweet, nutty, chocolate
Soy milk, lite	250ml	60	4 g	2 g / 0 g	5 g	Mild, sweet, nutty
Soy milk, low-fat	250ml	90	4 g	1.5 g / 0 g	7 g	Mild, sweet, nutty
Soy milk, non-fat	250ml	70	6 g	0 g / 0 g	9 g	Mild, sweet, nutty
Soy milk, plain or original	250ml	80–110	5-7 g	3-4 g / 0-.5 g	6-7 g	Mild, sweet, nutty
Soy Milk, Unsweetened	250ml	80-90	7-9 g	4-4.5 g / 0-.5 g	1 g	Mildly sweet, nutty

PLANT-BASED DAIRY ALTERNATIVE	SERVING SIZE	CALORIES	PROTEIN	FAT / SAT FAT	SUGAR	FLAVOR
PLANT-BASED MILKS						
Soy milk, vanilla	250ml	80–110	5–6 g	2.5 g / 0–.5 g	8–10 g	Sweet, nutty, vanilla
Sunflower milk, original	250ml	80	2 g	3.5 g / .5 g	6 g	Mild, sweet, nutty
PLANT-BASED YOGURTS						
Almond milk yogurt, vanilla	250ml	220	3 g	8 g / n/a	26 g	Mild, sweet, vanilla
Coconut milk yogurt, vanilla	175ml	140	1 g	6 g / 6 g	19 g	Mild, sweet, coconut, vanilla
Rice milk yogurt, vanilla	175ml	180	3 g	1 g / 0 g	20 g	Mild, sweet, vanilla
Soy milk yogurt, plain, unsweetened	250ml	130	10 g	6 g / 1 g	2 g	Mild, nutty
Soy milk yogurt, vanilla	175ml	150–160	5–7 g	3–4 g / 0–.5 g	18–21 g	Mild, sweet, nutty, vanilla
PLANT-BASED CREAMERS, SOUR CREAM						
Soy milk creamer, original	1 tbsp	15	0 g	1 g / 0 g	0 g	Mild, creamy
Soy sour cream	2 tbsp	85	1 g	5 g / 2 g	2 g	Mild, creamy

PLANT-BASED DAIRY ALTERNATIVE	SERVING SIZE	CALORIES	PROTEIN	FAT / SAT FAT	SUGAR	FLAVOR
PLANT-BASED CHEESE						
Plant-based Parmesan	2 tsp	15	2 g	.5 g / 0 g	0 g	Mild, good in pasta and baked dishes
Rice cheese, variety of flavors	30g	60	6 g	3 g / 0 g	0 g	Mild, good melted
Soy cheese, grated	30g	60–90	7 g	3–4 g / 0–.5 g	0 g	Mild, good melted
Soy cheese, slices	1 slice (17–19 g)	40–70	1–3 g	2–2.5 g / 0–3 g	0 g	Mild, good melted in sandwiches
Soy cream cheese	2 tbsp	85	1 g	5 g / 2 g	2 g	Mild, creamy
PLANT-BASED ICE CREAMS						
Almond milk ice cream, vanilla	50g	140	1 g	7 g / 1 g	12 g	Mild, sweet, vanilla, creamy
Coconut milk ice cream, vanilla	50g	130	1 g	6 g / 5 g	10 g	Mild, sweet, coconut, vanilla, creamy

PLANT-BASED DAIRY ALTERNATIVE	SERVING SIZE	CALORIES	PROTEIN	FAT / SAT FAT	SUGAR	FLAVOR
PLANT-BASED ICE CREAMS						
Hemp milk ice cream, vanilla	50g	140	0 g	7 g / .5 g	9 g	Mild, sweet, vanilla, creamy
Soy ice cream, vanilla	50g	110–140	1–2 g	1.5–8 g / 0–1 g	9–13 g	Mild, sweet, vanilla, creamy

Source: Nutrition information from nutrition facts labels and company Web sites of a survey of popular brands, but may not include all brands available. Includes a range of nutrition information available for several products made by various brands.

Sat Fat = saturated fat, oz = ounce, g = gram, tbsp = tablespoon, tsp = teaspoon

FOODS	SERVING SIZES	PLANT-POWERED VEGAN	PLANT-POWERED VEGETARIAN	PLANT-POWERED OMNIVORE
Legumes and Soy Foods	85g cup beans, lentils, dried peas, tofu, tempeh, seitan, or meat alternative 250ml protein-rich plant-based milk alternative or yogurt	3–5 servings, including two calcium- and vitamin D-fortified foods; consider a calcium and vitamin D supplement to meet needs Vitamin B_{12}-fortified foods or supplement to meet needs	2–4 servings	1–2 servings
Nuts and Seeds	30g nuts or seeds 2 tablespoons nut or seed butter	2 servings	1–2 servings	1–2 servings
OPTIONAL PROTEIN CHOICES FOR PLANT-POWERED VEGETARIANS OR OMNIVORES				
Dairy (fat-free or low-fat products)	250ml milk or yogurt 125ml cottage cheese 45g ounces cheese	0 servings	2 servings*	2 servings*
Egg	1 egg (30g)	0 servings	1 serving†	(included in Lean Animal Protein Servings)
Lean Animal Protein	Seafood or skinless poultry, limiting red and processed meat to occasional use	0 servings	0 servings	3–5 ounces†

Source: See Chapter 1, note 3 (page 369), and Chapter 3 notes 16, 17, and 18 (pages 373–74).

Servings are based on a daily intake of 1,500 to 2,500 calories, which is the appropriate range for weight loss and weight maintenance for most adults, depending on age, sex, and activity level.

*May replace Dairy servings with calcium- and vitamin D-fortified Legume and Soy Foods servings.

†May replace Egg or Animal Protein servings with Legumes and Soy Foods servings (1 serving Legume and Soy Foods replaces 1 ounce animal protein)

"At the age of 55, I was changing my granddaughter's diaper and I thought, 'If I remain diabetic, I'm going to lose ten or twelve years of my grandbaby's life.' Being from Oklahoma, deciding to become a vegan was a stretch. I imagine I doubled that demographic. It's remarkable: After thirteen days my type 2 diabetes was reversed—my doctor was astounded. I started with losing weight, then my doctor took me off all diabetes, cholesterol, and blood pressure meds and my energy skyrocketed. I started hiking six miles—I felt like it, because it didn't hurt anymore due to all the anti-inflammatory foods I was eating. I lost 41 pounds in 14 weeks—I went from a size 40 waist to 28 or 30 waist. Before, I had never eaten cauliflower, cabbage, or kale. My vegetables were limited to beans, corn, and fried potatoes. Now the list of vegetables I eat is lengthy—I use lots of spices to flavor them. Moving to a plant-based diet has been the most intelligent and healthy thing I have ever done. I am planning to walk all the way across the United States as a testament to my new lifestyle."

—RANDY, a plant-powered vegan in Oklahoma

"I went vegetarian for animal-rights reasons. I consume eggs and dairy only if they are organic and sustainably produced. My plant-based diet is rich in antioxidants, to which I attribute my youthful skin, great eyesight, and bountiful energy. The thrill I get from knowing I am helping animals and the planet was the impetus to make me go vegetarian, and I am committed to staying vegetarian—and helping others to become semi- or total vegetarians—for the duration of my life."

—DENISE, a plant-powered vegetarian in
San Francisco, California

❦ PLANT-POWERED ACTION ALERT **DAY 3**

Visit a natural food store (or your local grocery store if you can't find one) and peruse these aisles: bulk bins, dried foods, nuts and nut butters, soy foods, and plant-based dairy. Purchase at least one dried legume, one seed (such as chia, flax, sesame, sunflower, or hemp), and one nut or nut butter that you are less familiar with. Put them on the menu for tomorrow. Read the labels of all of the plant-based milk products to see if you can find one that is unsweetened and rich in protein, calcium, and vitamin D. Take a few varieties home and see which you like best.

The Wholesome Goodness of Grains

The secret of a plant-based diet that leads to weight loss, better health, and longevity lies in healthy plant carbohydrates such as those found in whole grains. Healthy whole grains—rich in long-lasting energy as well as fiber, protein, vitamins, minerals, and phytochemicals—form the foundation for entire traditional diets, from quinoa in Peru to millet in Africa. In every culture, you can trace indigenous grains, such as maize in the Americas and rice in China, to the sustenance and very survival of people over the generations. These grains were cultivated, harvested, and stored away to be used daily, along with whatever other local, seasonal plants like herbs, fruits, vegetables, nuts, and seeds were available. In many indigenous societies, animal foods were used sparingly. Instead, a particular grain—often used in combination with a legume—formed the core of the diet. These food practices still take place around the world, from the pot of rice accompanying a Filipino vegetable stew to the bubbling millet porridge served for breakfast in Nigeria. Keeping the silos filled with grains in order to safeguard a community from starvation goes way back in history to ancient Egyptian times. And now we know that grains offer much more than mere sustenance: They can empower you with a number of unique health benefits that range from disease prevention to weight loss.

Why are whole grains so special? It all starts with a seed. Essentially that's what a whole grain kernel is—the seed for a brand new plant. When grain grasses such as wheat or rice grow in a field, they produce seeds, or whole grain kernels, that have three parts: the bran, the germ, and the endosperm. Each seed contains all the nutrients and protection that it needs to begin growing into a mighty new plant. The germ, basically the embryo for the new plant, is filled with rich nourishment such as antioxidants and vitamins to foster its growth; the endosperm is packed with starches and protein that provide fuel for the seedling to grow; and the bran forms the outer coating that protects the seed from potential threats from the outside world. Every time you eat a whole grain kernel in its pure, simple form, as nature designed it, you gain special nutritional advantages powerful enough to bring fruitful life to a small kernel of grain.

PEERING INSIDE A WHOLE GRAIN KERNEL

Technically, a whole grain is defined as an intact grain or seed from the grass family that has an outer layer of bran, an endosperm layer, and an inner germ layer—though some grains included in the culinary whole grain family, such as buckwheat, are not true grains in a botanical sense. If you scoop up a handful of barley and take a good look at it, you see a clear example of whole grains: Each barley kernel is covered in an outer bran coating that protects the starchy endosperm and nutrient-dense germ layer. That barley is as close to nature as you can find a grain; it's simply harvested from the barley plant, dried, packaged, and transported to your local market. All you have to do is cook it in water and eat it. There are a number of simple whole grains just like barley that can be eaten in their pure, whole form. Check out my Plant-Powered Whole Grains Guide (see page 97) for a list of whole grains as well as tips for enjoying them.

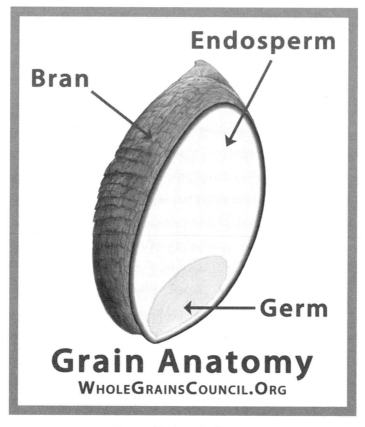

Bran

Endosperm

Germ

Grain Anatomy

WHOLEGRAINSCOUNCIL.ORG

Source: Whole Grains Council

HEALTH BENEFITS APLENTY

The scientific literature is bulging with evidence on whole grain benefits. Here's a snapshot of what you stand to gain by including these powerful plant foods in your diet every day:

- Reduced risk of stroke
- Decreased chance of type 2 diabetes
- Reduced risk of heart disease
- Increased satiety, or sense of fullness
- Better weight maintenance
- Lower risk of asthma

- Healthier carotid arteries, which supply blood and oxygen to the brain
- Lower rate of inflammation and inflammatory diseases
- Reduced chance of colorectal cancer
- Healthier blood pressure levels
- Less gum disease and tooth loss [1]

WHOLE GRAIN NUTRIENTS UP CLOSE

Every kernel of whole grain, from tiny teff to plump Kamut, contains a symphony of powerful nutrients that stokes its health benefits. These nutrients include the following:

- **Carbohydrates.** And not just any carbs—whole grain kernels are rich in low-glycemic carbs that promote slow, steady rises in glucose levels (see Getting to Know the Glycemic Index, page 94).
- **Vitamins.** Whole grains contain a bounty of vitamins, such as vitamins B_6 and E, niacin, pantothenic acid, riboflavin, thiamin, and folate, which are essential for healthy body function.
  - **Minerals.** You'll find almost every mineral essential to human health in the whole grain family, including calcium, iron, magnesium, phosphorus, zinc, copper, manganese, selenium, and potassium.
- **Fiber.** You probably know that whole grains are rich in fiber. But did you know they contain different kinds of fibers—such as **soluble fiber, insoluble fiber, oligosaccharides, resistant starch, beta-glucans**, and lignans—that all hold their own health advantages? (See Fiber Sense, page 92, to learn more about how fiber works in your body.)
- **Protein.** Most people don't realize that whole grains can contribute a significant share of protein to the diet—which is important if you're following a plant-powered vegan diet. Given that whole grains can contain up to 6 grams of protein per serving, getting 5 or more servings a day can make a serious dent in your protein goals.
- **Antioxidants.** Whole grains contain very high levels of antioxidants, amounts comparable to and sometimes even higher than

those in many fruits and vegetables. Some of these antioxidants are unique and are not even found in other plant foods. So eating more whole grains is an easy way to power up on antioxidants, which can protect you from the damaging effects of free radicals associated with the development of chronic disease.

- **Phytochemicals.** In order to protect their seeds and future offspring from pests, sunlight damage, disease, and water shortage, grain plants built up a powerful defense system in the outer skin, as well as germ, of their seeds in the form of phytochemicals. Many types of health-protective phytochemicals, linked to particular health benefits from eye protection to brain health, have been identified in grains, such as phenolic compounds, including **ferulic acid**, **vanillic acid**, anthocyanidins, and flavonols, and carotenoids such as lutein, zeaxanthin, **beta-cryptoxanthin**, **beta-carotene**, and **alpha-carotene**.

- **Healthy fats.** Whole grains also contain healthy unsaturated fats that improve blood cholesterol levels, as well as plant sterols and stanols (also known as phytosterols) that also can lower LDL cholesterol levels by helping your body to excrete it.[2]

When you add up all of the mighty nutrients found in the whole grain, it's no wonder that study after study has linked them with meaningful health benefits. All of whole grains' nutrients appear to work together in unison within the grain, providing a far greater benefit than if you were to extract the nutrients and eat them individually. And scientists have found that when you combine whole grains with other plant foods like fruits and vegetables, you simply magnify all of the nutrients contained in all of the plant foods. For example, scientists studying the antioxidant content of plant foods found that the levels of antioxidant activity in individual plant foods—as well as plant foods in combination—are much greater than the combined antioxidant activity of the isolated antioxidant compounds. This phenomenon is called synergy—all of the nutrients and phytochemicals within the plant foods work together to create an effect that is far greater than the sum of their isolated effects.[3]

In the Whole Grains Nutritional Lineup (page 86), you'll see that although all whole grains are generally rich in fiber and healthy carbohydrates, each one has a own unique nutritional profile. For example, dark rye is very high in manganese, an important mineral for a healthy nervous system; 60g of dark rye flour contains 4.3 mg, or 216% DV. And with 8 grams (16% DV) of protein in 185g cooked, quinoa is very high in complete protein; that is, it contains all the essential amino acids.[4] That's why it's so important to choose your grains with diversity in mind in order to maximize the benefits you gain from them. Don't stop at whole wheat—include an array of whole grains such as those listed in the Whole Grains Nutritional Lineup that contribute a wide variety of additional vitamins, minerals, amino acids, fibers, and phytochemicals. Check out the powerful nutritional content in some of the most commonly found whole grains.

IN SEARCH OF WHOLE GRAINS

If you ask most people what their idea of a whole grain is, they mention whole wheat bread—and technically they are right. The definition of "whole grain" also includes products made from the entire grain kernel that contain amounts of the bran, endosperm, and germ in their original proportions. That's why some whole grain flours, breads, and breakfast cereals meet the criteria for being called whole grain, even though they're ground up and you can no longer see the kernel. So, if a bread or cereal is made with 100 percent whole grain flour, it falls into the whole grain category.

Many food companies know how appealing healthy whole grains are to people, so they're plastering terms like "made with whole grain" or "multi-grain" on food labels to help sell their products—terms that may not mean much. It can be very tough to tell how much whole grain is in a product like cereal, bread, crackers, or muffins, despite clever labels suggesting their whole grain content. The only way you can really tell is to flip over the package and read the ingredients list. If the first ingredient listed is a whole grain, then the product in your hands is a good source of whole grains. Don't be fooled by ingredients like "enriched" or "wheat flour"—this is just refined white flour. Instead, look for "whole wheat," "whole oats," "whole-grain rye," "whole-grain barley," and the names of other grains or whole grain flours in the ingredient list. (See page 88 to learn about deciphering whole grain label claims, and page 253 for more on how to read nutrition labels.)

WHOLE GRAINS NUTRITIONAL LINEUP

WHOLE GRAIN	CALORIES	PROTEIN	FAT	SAT FAT	CARBOHYDRATES	FIBER	STAR NUTRIENTS* (AT LEAST 10% DV PER SERVING)
Amaranth, 75g cooked	126	5 g	2 g	0 g	23 g	3 g	Fiber, iron, magnesium, phosphorus, manganese
Barley, 80g cooked	97	2 g	0.5 g	0 g	22 g	3 g	Manganese, selenium
Brown rice, 100g cooked	108	3 g	1 g	0 g	23 g	2 g	Magnesium, manganese, selenium
Buckwheat, 65g cooked	78	3 g	0.5 g	0 g	17 g	3 g	Magnesium, manganese
Bulgur, 90g cooked	76	3 g	0 g	0 g	17 g	4 g	Fiber, manganese
Corn, 80g cooked	89	3 g	1 g	0 g	21 g	2 g	Thiamin
Millet, 85g cooked	104	3 g	1 g	0 g	21 g	1 g	Manganese
Oats, 100g cooked	83	3 g	2 g	0.5 g	16 g	2 g	Manganese
Quinoa, 90g cooked	111	4 g	2 g	0 g	20 g	3 g	Magnesium, phosphorus, manganese
Teff, 125g cooked	127	5 g	1 g	0 g	25 g	4 g	Fiber, iron, magnesium, phosphorus

WHOLE GRAIN	CALORIES	PROTEIN	FAT	SAT FAT	CARBOHYDRATES	FIBER	STAR NUTRIENTS* (AT LEAST 10% DV PER SERVING)
Wheat (emmer, farro, Kamut, spelt, wheat berries), 85g cooked	123	6 g	1 g	0 g	26 g	4 g	Fiber, niacin, magnesium, phosphorus, copper, manganese
Wild rice, 80g cooked	83	4 g	1 g	0 g	18 g	2 g	Manganese

Source: USDA National Nutrient Database for Standard Reference, http://ndb.nal.usda.gov

Sat Fat = saturated fat; DV = Daily Value, nutritional requirements according to the Food and Drug Administration, based on 2,000 calories per day; g = grams

*Refer to the appendix (page 393) to learn how these nutrients contribute to overall health.

DECIPHERING WHOLE GRAIN LABELS

BE ON THE LOOKOUT for labeling terms on breads, cereals, and snack foods that signal the presence of whole or refined grains. Here's a primer on what those labels really mean.

THIS CLAIM ON THE FOOD LABEL OR INGREDIENTS LIST:	MEANS *THIS* IN THE FOOD PRODUCT:
"Made with Whole Grains"	The product contains *some* whole grain, but it may not be a good source of whole grains.
"Wheat Bread"	There's no guarantee that the wheat is whole wheat—in fact, it's probably refined.
"Enriched," "Wheat," or "Durum" flour	It doesn't mean that the flour is whole wheat—it's probably refined.
"Multi-Grain"	The product contains more than one type of grain, but they are not necessarily whole grains.
"100% Whole Grain"	The predominant flour is 100 percent whole grain.
"Oats" or "Brown Rice"	These are whole grain ingredients.
"Whole" followed by a grain name (e.g., "Whole Quinoa," "Whole Millet")	The ingredient is whole grain.

STRIPPING GRAINS, STRIPPING HEALTH

When you strip a whole grain of its outer bran coating and germ, all you're left with is the starchy endosperm—essentially rapidly absorbed carbs minus their nutrient package of fiber, phytochemicals, vitamins, and minerals. Corn can be degerminated and rice can be refined, but the most common example of a refined grain product is white flour. During the refinement and milling process both the bran and germ are stripped away from the grain kernel, and the starchy endosperm is ground into a fine powder. Although it's true that humans have been grinding grains into flour for thousands of years, the process of refining wheat flour down to its starchy endosperm became the cultural norm over only the past two centuries. We have fallen in love with soft, white flour and all of the tender products, such as white breads and cakes, that can be made out of it. Up through the twentieth century, it was well accepted in many societies that the whiter your bread, the higher your status. Fortunately, this trend has come full circle in the last decade; artisanal breads made with grains other than refined white flour have become all the rage.

In the 1940s, the government started a grain-fortification program to replace nutrients lost when flour is refined, such as riboflavin, niacin, thiamin, iron, and as of 1998, folate. Even though fortification replaces some lost vitamins and minerals in refined grains, it can't possibly replace the multitude of other nutrients the whole grain contains. White flour has about 30 percent less protein, 80 percent less fiber, and 80 percent fewer **phenolic acids**, or phytochemical antioxidants, than whole wheat flour.[5] And remember, we now know that nutrients work together in synergy within the plant. We know that nature created these nutrients together in perfect balance to promote life for an embryonic plant and, lucky for us, humans. When we start extracting nutrients and then adding nutrients back, we don't create the same balance, and many of them also fall by the wayside. You've got to eat the whole grain—just as it was produced by the grass plant that pushed its roots deep into the rich soil for nourishment and reached its leaves into the sky for light.

And that's not all. When you strip away nutrients in grains, you compact their calories into a smaller amount of space: White flour has 10 percent more calories than whole wheat flour. We have become more and more reliant on refined grains such as white flour; we have a surplus of low-nutrient and easily absorbed carbohydrates constantly available to us. And more and more research is showing that all these highly refined carbs are increasing our risk of diseases such as type 2 diabetes.[6]

Compared with thirty years ago, our portion sizes of refined grain products have grown to immense proportions.[7] Saucer-sized cookies, bloated bagels, and mega-muffins made primarily of white flour are now the standard. Many people are tricked into thinking floury foods like blueberry muffins, fish crackers, and pretzel sticks are "healthier" snacks, but in reality, they are typically packed with empty calories—calories that come with few nutrients and do little for your health. Quickly absorbed into the bloodstream, a steady intake of such refined carbohydrates spurs your pancreas to produce the additional **insulin** needed to transport those high levels of glucose into your body tissues. High levels of insulin have insidious effects on the body, promoting damage to the brain and even increasing cancer risk.[8] See examples of foods filled with refined wheat flour in the White Flour Bonanza list.

WHITE FLOUR BONANZA

Many foods in supermarkets and restaurants are on white flour overload. Here are just a few examples. Keep in mind that the suggested serving of whole grains (see the Daily Plant-Powered Whole Grains Guide, page 104) is 75–90g of cooked whole grains or pasta or one slice of whole grain bread, each of which provides about *80 calories* and *15 grams of carbohydrates*. This will help you find more petite portions of refined grains when you scan the nutrition labels of prepared foods.

FOOD	SERVING SIZE	CALORIES	CARBOHYDRATES
Bagel, plain	125g	360	71 g
Biscuit, large	90g	280	34 g
Cake donut, plain	50g	210	27 g
Ciabatta roll	115g	250	48 g
Flour tortilla	70 g	210	35 g
Fish crackers, single-serving package	70g	350	45 g
Muffin, blueberry	165g	610	71 g
Pancakes, restaurant, no syrup	3 pancakes 150g	540	104 g
Scone, blueberry	120g	460	61 g
Soft pretzel	155g	488	101 g

Source: Nutrition information from product nutrition labels; may vary depending on manufacturer.

Total calorie and carbohydrate amounts may reflect other ingredients in the products in addition to white flour.

oz = ounce; g = grams

WHITE WHOLE WHEAT FLOUR: NOT AN OXYMORON

YOU MIGHT THINK it's just another deceptive marketing campaign, but white whole wheat flour is indeed a true whole grain flour—and it's gaining in popularity as people's interest in whole grains soars. There are six different classes of whole wheat: hard red winter, hard red spring, soft red winter, hard white, soft white, and durum. Traditional whole wheat flour is made from red wheat, which produces a darker, stronger flavor, but flour made from white wheat produces a softer, milder flavor that is similar to that of refined wheat flour. Researchers have found that even children find whole wheat products more palatable when flour from white wheat is used. Just watch out for food products that say they use white whole wheat flour but actually use it only in small amounts. (Try my recipe for Corn Muffins with Apples and Walnuts, which features white whole wheat flour, on page 352.)

EATING GRAINS WHOLE

Even whole grain flours are not the absolute best choice of healthy whole grains. It depends on how finely ground the grains are. Research shows that your body has a step-wise reaction to grains, dependent on how finely they have been ground. Your insulin and glucose response rises in the following order: whole grains, cracked grains, coarse flour, and fine flour. The biggest insulin-response increase occurs between coarse flour and fine flour. The larger the grain particle, the less easily it's absorbed by your body, and the lower its insulin and glucose response.[9] That's why the glycemic index of bread—even whole wheat bread—is typically higher than grains in their whole form.

I suggest that you focus most of your daily grain intake on those in their whole, intact form, such as cooked wheat berries, farro, barley, oats, quinoa, and brown rice, rather in their processed, pulverized form in flour products like bread, tortillas, bagels, and muffins and in many ready-to-eat breakfast cereals. The advantages of eating whole grains in their natural form go beyond glycemic benefits; these crunchy whole grains are linked with satiety, or fullness. When you are at an Italian restaurant and there is a basket of white bread on the table, before you know it you've eaten a few slices of bread but still have room for your meal. Even if you are lucky enough to be served a basket of whole grain bread, it's still easy to snack on a couple of slices before dinner. But when you eat whole grains in their natural form it's a different story. These crunchy, intact grains require much more chewing, and the more you have to chew your food, the more it makes you feel full—it's pretty hard to overeat them. In fact, studies find that high-fiber whole grains work to fill you up in many ways: They displace high-calorie foods in your diet, increase the amount of chewing you do, increase the flow of saliva and stomach juices, thus making your stomach actually expand, and slow down the absorption of foods in the small intestine.[10] See how satisfying ancient grains can be by sampling some of my favorite recipes, including Baked Farro Herb Pilaf (see page 314) and Ruby Quinoa Breakfast Bowl (see page 350).

FIBER SENSE

One of the most important contributions that only plant foods, including whole grains, can offer is dietary fiber, a group of carbohydrates that cannot be digested in your intestinal tract. Research has shown that a high-fiber diet from whole grains, legumes, fruits, and vegetables can help you feel fuller and keep your weight down, lower your cholesterol, blood pressure, and inflammation levels, protect your heart, prevent type 2 diabetes, promote a healthy digestive tract, and possibly fend off colorectal cancer.[11] **Fermentable fibers** from whole grains can even act as **prebiotics** by feeding healthy gut bacteria, offering immune support and improving digestive health.

An average woman 50 years of age or younger should get 25 grams of fiber per day; an average man in that age range should aim for 38 grams a day.[12] Most people in the United States are woefully short on fiber, eating about half that amount. But if you follow the plant-powered eating guidelines in this book, you'll find it's easy to get these levels of fiber in your diet.

There are many types of dietary fiber that are linked with amazing health benefits. Try to get all of the following fibers by increasing the variety of plant foods you eat every day.

- **Soluble fiber.** This type of fiber dissolves in water, often forming a viscous gel that is fermented in the colon. It's found in foods like legumes, oats, barley, nuts, some fruits and vegetables, and **psyllium**. Pectin in fruits and berries and gums in oatmeal, barley, and legumes are also types of soluble fiber. Research links this type of fiber with lowering cholesterol levels and preventing heart disease.
- **Insoluble fiber.** This fiber does not dissolve in water and acts like a sponge, passing through the intestines mostly unchanged. It's found in foods like wheat bran, some whole grains, nuts, seeds, some vegetables, and the skins of some fruits. **Cellulose** and **hemicellulose** in plant cell walls are types of insoluble fibers. Insoluble fiber keeps your bowels moving nicely and may protect you against colon cancer.
- **Nondigestible oligosaccharides and resistant starches.** Found in some fruits, veggies, seeds, and grains, these fibers resist digestion and feed friendly bacteria. Resistant starches, found in bananas and potatoes, may also increase the rate at which you burn calories, as well as help to lower blood glucose, or blood sugar, levels.
- **Lignans.** Technically polyphenolic compounds, lignans form part of the cell wall in some plants, such as root vegetables, wheat, and berries. Lignans offer strong antioxidant and phytoestrogenic effects that may protect against chronic diseases, such as heart disease and diabetes, and hormone-related cancers.
- **Beta-glucans.** Found in oats and barley, beta-glucans are a type of soluble fiber that can reduce cholesterol and blood sugar levels, as well as boost immune function.
- **Inulin and oligofructose.** This fiber is not digested in the upper gastrointestinal tract and stimulates the growth of friendly gut bacteria. It occurs naturally in artichokes, chicory, onions, and wheat, but it is also commonly added to foods as an isolated ingredient. Have you ever wondered how fiber finds its way into orange juice, yogurt, and some nutrition bars? Those high-fiber counts in typically low-fiber foods are due to a food science development by which fibers, such as inulin, are either isolated from foods in which they occur naturally or synthesized, then added to processed foods. Although there's no reason to think that such isolated fibers are harmful, they have not yet been proved to provide the same benefits as the many naturally occurring fibers found in whole plant

foods. So, don't be tricked by mega amounts of fiber on the food label; instead, aim for eating more plant foods in their natural form to gain the benefits of naturally occurring fiber.

If you're new to a high-fiber diet, start off slowly to avoid potential gastrointestinal symptoms, increasing the fiber in your diet gradually until you reach your goal. And drink at least 2 litres of water a day on your high-fiber diet to help keep your digestive tract running smoothly.

GETTING TO KNOW THE GLYCEMIC INDEX

Carbohydrates, including breads, cereals, fruits, and sugars provide energy for your body in the form of glucose. When you eat a carbohydrate-containing food, it raises your blood glucose levels. The glycemic index (GI) is a system that ranks different carbohydrate foods on a scale from 0 to 100 according to their effect on your blood glucose levels. Low-GI foods contain slowly digested carbohydrates and produce gradual, low rises in blood glucose, but high-GI foods contain rapidly digested carbs and prompt large, rapid rises and drops in blood glucose. As a rule of thumb, high-GI foods, such as white bread and corn flakes, are more processed and refined and low-GI foods, like barley and beans, are less refined and higher in fiber. If you'd like to look up the GI value of some popular foods, check out the Glycemic Index for Common Foods (see page 96).

When you eat a high-GI food, it's like getting to the crest of a roller coaster ride: Your blood glucose quickly rises, your insulin levels spike, and glucose is transported to your muscle tissue or into fat storage. Then, the roller coaster plummets and your blood glucose levels fall to below normal levels, stimulating your appetite to get those glucose levels up again. But when you eat a low-GI food, there's no roller coaster ride; instead, your blood glucose rises slowly, insulin is released moderately, your blood glucose levels don't fall so drastically, and you feel satisfied longer.

The GI tells only how *rapidly* a type of carbohydrate turns into sugar in the bloodstream; it doesn't take into account the *amount* of carbohydrate found in a typical serving of that food. For example, some plant foods, such as watermelon, may be high-GI (because their carbohydrates turn quickly into sugar) but contain low amounts of carbs. In practice, they have a small overall effect on blood glucose. The **glycemic load (GL)** takes into account both the GI *and* the amount of carbohydrate in a particular food and how both impact blood glucose. You can find out the GI and GL of many popular foods at the GI database (http://glycemicindex.com) created by the Human Nutrition Unit of the University of Sydney.

Promoting a low-GI diet has been gaining traction in the scientific world: The diet has been linked with improved glucose control for people with diabetes as well as reduced cholesterol levels and weight loss.[13] It's easy to eat a low-GI diet if you're consuming whole plant foods in their natural form. You may notice some healthy whole foods like potatoes fall on the high-GI list, but that doesn't mean that you have to give them up completely. Just eat smaller portions and combine them with other foods that are low-GI. Check out my top tips for eating the low-GI way:

Tips for Low-GI Plant-Powered Eating

1. The GI applies only to carb-containing foods, so don't worry about the GI of pure proteins and fats, or about nuts and nonstarchy vegetables that contain low levels of carbohydrates.

2. Don't focus so much on GI that you lose sight of the nutrient qualities of whole foods; it's not a contest to see how low you can go with GI.

3. Pile half your dinner plate with nonstarchy veggies or salads to fill up on low-GI plant carbs. (Try one of my favorite salads, such as Chinese Cabbage Slaw, page 289.)

4. Include healthy fats and proteins at each meal to lower the meal's overall GI.

5. Sure, some plant foods like watermelon and potatoes are higher on the GI scale, but don't completely eliminate them; just eat a smaller portion and combine them with low-GI foods.

6. Switch from high-GI breads made of finely ground flours to whole grain breads made with roughly ground whole grain flours, which are lower-GI.

7. Swap refined breakfast cereals, such as corn flakes, for a lower-GI choice like oats. Cook up a pot of Apple Pie Oatmeal Bowl (page 347) to see how delicious whole grain cereals can be.

8. Eat more of your grains in the form of whole, intact kernels, such as quinoa, bulgur, and barley. See the Plant-Powered Whole Grains Guide (page 97) for culinary tips.

GLYCEMIC INDEX FOR COMMON FOODS

LOW GI (55 OR LESS) CHOOSE MOST OFTEN	MEDIUM GI (56–69) CHOOSE MORE OFTEN	HIGH GI (70 OR MORE) CHOOSE LESS OFTEN
Breads: English muffin, whole grain Pumpernickel bread Seeded bread Wheat tortilla	**Breads:** Muffin, oatmeal Pita bread, white Whole wheat bread	**Breads:** Bagel, white English muffin, white French bread Waffles, white White bread
Cereals/Grains/Pasta: All-Bran™ breakfast cereal Barley Brown and wild rice Oat porridge Pasta, white or whole wheat, al dente Quinoa	**Cereals/Grains/Pasta:** Arborio rice Basmati rice Buckwheat noodles Couscous Cream of Wheat™ Mini-Wheats™ Pasta, white, cooked 10 minutes Raisin Bran™ Rice, long-grain white or brown	**Cereals/Grains/Pasta:** Corn Flakes™ Puffed wheat Rice Chex™ Rice, short or medium-grain white
Fruits: Apple Apricot Banana Grapefruit Orange Pear Strawberries	**Fruits:** Apricots, canned in light syrup Cantaloupe Cranberry juice cocktail Mango Papaya Pineapple Raisins	**Fruit:** Watermelon
Vegetables: Beans (white, black, soy, etc.) Carrot juice Carrots, raw Peas (black-eyed peas, chickpeas, split peas) Parsnips Squash Tomato juice	**Vegetables:** Beetroot Carrots, boiled Corn Sweet potato, boiled White potato, roasted	**Vegetables:** Russet potato, baked Rutabaga
Other: Cheese Chocolate Milk Nuts (peanuts, almonds, etc.) Soy milk Yogurt	**Other:** Popcorn Potato crisps Rye or wheat crackers	**Other:** Corn chips Gatorade™ Jelly beans Pop-Tarts™ Rice cakes Skittles™ Soda crackers

Source: **University of Sydney glycemic index database, glycemicindex.com/ foodSearch.php**

GLUTEN-FREE GRAINS

GOING GLUTEN-FREE may be the next "it" diet, but there's little evidence to support that healthy people should avoid gluten, a protein found in wheat and related grains such as barley, rye, spelt, Kamut, and triticale.

However, if you're one of the nearly three million people with celiac disease, an autoimmune disorder in which gluten in the diet damages the lining of the intestine, you must completely avoid gluten. Here's a list of gluten-free whole grains you can enjoy:

Amaranth

Buckwheat

Corn

Millet

PLANT-POWERED WHOLE GRAINS GUIDE

WHOLE GRAIN	DESCRIPTION	COOKING INSTRUCTIONS	CULINARY TIPS
Amaranth	A staple in ancient Aztec countries, this tiny beige seed with a light nutty to peppery taste is not a true grain in the botanical sense.	Add 190g amaranth to 500ml boiling water or broth and simmer for 20–25 minutes; makes approx 450g.	Traditionally used as a breakfast porridge, it can be cooked and stirred into grain salads or muffins; amaranth flour can be used in pancakes and whole grain breads.
Barley	This ancient grain kernel is light brown with a nutty, chewy taste.	Add 200g barley to 750ml boiling water or broth and simmer for 45–60 minutes; makes approx 500g.	Add barley to soups (see Country French Barley Vegetable Potage, page 283) or cook with herbs as a side dish; barley flour can be used in breads and baked goods.

WHOLE GRAIN	DESCRIPTION	COOKING INSTRUCTIONS	CULINARY TIPS
Buckwheat	Originating in the Balkans and moving to the East, this pseudo-grain (it's not even a form of wheat) is brown in color and nutty in taste.	Add 170g buckwheat to 500ml boiling water or broth and simmer for 20 minutes; makes approx 500g.	A star in pancakes, soba noodles, and Russian dishes, buckwheat can be featured in soups (see Winter Buckwheat Vegetable Soup, page 287) and grain pilafs; buckwheat flour is excellent in muffins, breads, pancakes, and waffles (see Buckwheat Hazelnut Waffles with Ginger Peach Sauce, page 353).
Bulgur	Known as "Middle Eastern pasta," bulgur is wheat kernels that have been boiled, dried, and cracked.	Add 140g bulgur to 500ml boiling water or broth and simmer for 10-12 minutes; makes approx 500g.	Excellent in side dishes (see Bulgur Risotto with Yellow Squash, Peas, and Pine Nuts, page 312) and in salads like tabbouleh.
Corn	Native to the Americas, whole corn, cornmeal, polenta, grits, and popcorn count as whole grains, as long as they are made from the whole kernel.	Add 120g polenta to 1 litre boiling water or broth and simmer for 25–30 minutes; makes approx 300g. To make popcorn, heat 1 tablespoon canola oil in a heavy pot. Add 15g popcorn kernels, cover with a lid, and shake until the kernels are popped.	Steam whole corn and add to salads (see South of the Border Taco Salad, page 292) and chowders; mix polenta into quick breads (see Corn Muffins with Apples and Walnuts, page 352); cook polenta with herbs and tomatoes; cook grits as a porridge; and cook popcorn as a snack.

WHOLE GRAIN	DESCRIPTION	COOKING INSTRUCTIONS	CULINARY TIPS
Couscous, whole wheat	Made from hard wheat, couscous is a staple grain product of North Africa that has a mild taste.	Add 175g couscous to 500ml boiling water or broth and allow to sit for 10 minutes (off the heat); makes approx 500g.	Serve as a side dish (see Antipasto Couscous with Chickpeas, page 310) or as a grain-based salad with grilled vegetables.
Kamut® (khorasan wheat)	An ancient variety of wheat, this plump, nutty grain has a rich, chewy taste.	Cover 185g Kamut with water and soak overnight. Drain, add 1 litre water or broth, and simmer for 45–60 minutes; makes approx 500g.	Add Kamut to vegetable soups; cook with broth and herbs to serve as a pilaf.
Millet	This longtime staple in Africa, Asia, and India is not just for the birds. The nutritious tiny yellow grain has a mild flavor.	Add 200g millet to 600ml boiling water or broth and simmer for 25–35 minutes; makes approx 700g.	Typically used in breakfast porridge (see Ancient Grain Porridge with Figs and Dates, page 349), it can also be added to vegetable soups.
Oats	Flattened to produce rolled or quick oats, or steel cut to produce a chewier texture, the mild, sweet flavor of oats is a traditional component of English and Scottish food traditions.	Add 95g steel-cut oats to 1 litre boiling water and simmer for 20 minutes; makes approx 800g.	Excellent as a porridge or mixed into muesli or granola (see Plant-Powered Granola, page 345), oats are also good in veggie burgers. Oat flour can be used in breads and baked goods.

WHOLE GRAIN	DESCRIPTION	COOKING INSTRUCTIONS	CULINARY TIPS
Pasta, whole grain	Made of various grains, such as whole wheat and brown rice, this product is a favorite in Italian cuisine.	Add 100g pasta to 1.5 litre boiling water and simmer for 8–12 minutes, then drain; yield depends on variety.	Combine with tomato sauce, olive oil, vegetables, herbs, and/ or garlic to create side dishes, entrées (see California Tofu and Vegetable Penne Toss, page 305), or salads.
Quinoa	Not a true grain in the botanical sense, quinoa was a staple of the Incan culture. The tiny kernel comes in shades of ivory, red, and black and has a tender, mildly nutty taste.	Add 170g rinsed quinoa to 600ml boiling water or broth and simmer for 25–35 minutes; makes approx 700g.	Excellent in porridges (see Ruby Quinoa Breakfast Bowl, page 350), as well as a simple side dish to replace rice.
Rice, brown	Although it's synonymous with Asia, whole grain rice (also called brown rice) varieties grow in many parts of the world and come in shades of red, black, and purple.	Add 185g rice to 600ml boiling water or broth and simmer for 25–40 minutes; makes 600–800g (depends on variety).	Cook as a breakfast porridge; serve as a side dish with curry or stir-fry (see Saffron Brown Basmati Rice, page 311); add to vegetarian sushi rolls (see Vegetable Brown Rice Sushi, page 278), and use in pudding.
Rye	The principal grain in Scandinavia, the hearty flavor of rye can be enjoyed in rye berries or rye flour.	Cover 170g rye berries with water and soak overnight. Add 1 litre water or broth, and simmer for 45–60 minutes.	Cook rye berries as a simple side dish; use rye flour in breads, pancakes, and muffins.

WHOLE GRAIN	DESCRIPTION	COOKING INSTRUCTIONS	CULINARY TIPS
Sorghum	An ancient grain from Africa, mild-tasting sorghum can be cooked as a whole grain, ground into flour, or popped like popcorn.	Add 190g sorghum to 1 litre boiling water or broth and simmer for 25–40 minutes.	Cook as a porridge; use sorghum flour in bread, pancakes, muffins, cookies, and pies.
Spelt	A variety of wheat; the whole grain kernels are sometimes referred to as "berries."	Cover 175g spelt with water and soak overnight. Drain, add 1 litre water or broth, and simmer for 45–60 minutes; makes approx 600g.	Cook as a simple side dish to accompany stir-fries (see Shiitake and Kale Spelt Bowl, page 330) and add to vegetable stews.
Teff	This tiny grain resembling a brown poppy seed is mild in flavor and is available in whole grains or as flour.	Add 195g teff to 1 litre water and simmer for 15–20 minutes; makes 750g.	Cook as a porridge (see Ancient Grain Porridge with Figs and Dates, page 349); use teff flour in breads, pancakes, and muffins.
Wheat berries	These whole wheat kernels have a chewy, nutty flavor.	Cover 185g wheat berries with water and soak overnight. Drain, add 1 litre water or broth, and simmer for 45–60 minutes; makes approx 500g.	Cook as a simple side dish; add to grain-based salads; stir into vegetable soups and stews.
Wild rice	This native American grass seed is not a true rice, and it boasts a crunchy, nutty flavor.	Add 160g wild rice to 750ml boiling water or broth and simmer for 45–55 minutes; makes approx 550g.	Cook as a side dish or breakfast cereal (see Exotic Fruit and Rice Hot Cereal, page 348).

Source: Information from the Whole Grains Council, wholegrainscouncil.org

PUMP UP THE VOLUME ON WHOLE GRAINS!

If you're not used to the whole grains game, it can be challenging to replace refined grains and cereals with healthy whole grains throughout the day. Here are my top tips for pushing whole grains in your diet:

1. Make every breakfast an opportunity to maximize whole grains. Try cooking up a pot of ancient grains such as quinoa, millet, or amaranth and reheating it in the morning. Revitalize your oatmeal breakfast tradition. If you're turning to ready-to-eat breakfast cereals, look for the least processed ones, such as muesli, or those that are made from 100 percent whole grain such as shredded wheat. Or make your own muesli or granola (see Plant-Powered Granola, page 345). Make all breakfast breads, from pancakes to muffins to toast, 100 percent whole grain products.

2. Buy a rice cooker, and use it every week to cook up brown rice and other whole grains, such as spelt or bulgur (see the Plant-Powered Whole Grains Guide, page 97). Just pour in the grain, add the required amount of water, set the timer, and walk away. You'll be left with a whole batch of grains you can use in pilaf, sprinkle in salads, or add to soups and casseroles.

3. Include more simple whole grains in their intact, natural form, such as brown rice, buckwheat, oats, quinoa, wheat berries, and wild rice. Shoot for at least half of your whole grain servings in this whole form to gain important glycemic and satiety benefits.

4. Read the labels in the bread aisle and discover breads, bagels, English muffins, pitas, and rolls made with 100 percent whole grain flour, preferably roughly ground, and enjoy them in sandwiches, as toast, or to accompany meals.

5. Replace refined flour with whole grain flour in your favorite recipes; if you're not used to the chewy texture of whole grains in breads, start with replacing half the flour with whole wheat or white whole wheat flour, and work your way up.

6. Look beyond whole wheat in order to diversify your nutrient supply. Don't be afraid to bring home a bag of buckwheat flour or quinoa flour from the natural food store to try in pancakes, muffins, and

baked goods. For starters, try making Buckwheat Hazelnut Waffles with Ginger Peach Sauce (page 353).

7. Remember that whole corn is a nutrient-rich whole grain; enjoy it simply cooked on the cob, or stir fresh or frozen kernels into soups, salads, and side dishes. (Check out my South of the Border Taco Salad, page 292, for a fabulous way to maximize corn.) Popcorn is the perfect whole grain snack, as long as it's not soaked in oil or butter. And don't forget to enjoy whole polenta in bread and tortillas as well as whole corn grits.

8. Give sprouted grains a try. These whole grain kernels have undergone the first stages of germination, revealing a tiny sprout emerging from the intact grain kernel, and they are growing in popularity. The germination process boosts levels of some nutrients like fiber, amino acids, and B vitamins, as well as the digestibility of the grain. Just cook them like you would any whole grain, use sprouted-grain flours in breads or baked goods, or try products, such as breads and crackers, made with sprouted grains.

9. Try alternatives to bread, such as 100 percent whole grain flatbreads or crackers, to accompany soups or salads.

10. When you go out to eat, ask for whole grains such as brown rice, whole grain bread, and ancient grains such as quinoa instead of refined grains.

11. Stir oats into cookies, breads, muffins, and even veggie burgers.

12. Throw a couple of handfuls of uncooked whole grain such as barley or quinoa into a vegetable soup while it's simmering. Or try one of my whole grain soup recipes, such as Country French Barley Vegetable Potage (page 283).

13. Put whole grain pasta on the menu—in entrées, side dishes, and salads—a few times a week. The California Tofu and Vegetable Penne Toss (page 305) is a good place to start.

14. Sprinkle muesli or granola over apple purée or plant-based yogurt for a healthy, delicious treat.

15. Toss salads with precooked whole grains, such as quinoa, bulgur, or wheat berries. Give the Southwestern Black Bean, Quinoa, and Mango Medley (page 318) a whirl.

HOW MUCH IS ENOUGH?

In order to follow a plant-powered diet, most of your grain servings should be whole grain, with an emphasis on grains found in their natural, intact form. As you move away from animal foods toward plant foods, it's even more important to make your grain choices count, as these foods can furnish you with protein, vitamins, and minerals that you might miss out on if you pile your diet high with refined grains. The number of grain servings you should choose each day depends on how many calories you need to maintain or achieve a healthy weight. Don't beat yourself up if you indulge in a slice of white French bread now and again at your favorite restaurant; it's what you do on a daily basis that counts. Stock your pantry with plenty of whole grain choices so they're at your fingertips.

DAILY PLANT-POWERED WHOLE GRAINS GUIDE

SERVING SIZES	PLANT-POWERED VEGAN	PLANT-POWERED VEGETARIAN	PLANT-POWERED OMNIVORE
75–100g cup cooked whole grains such as wheat berries, oats, brown rice, or quinoa			
50g cup cooked whole grain pasta			
1 slice whole grain bread	5–11 servings	5–8 servings	5–8 servings
55g whole grain ready-to-eat breakfast cereal			
30g whole grain crackers			
20cm whole grain or corn tortilla			

Sources: See Chapter 1, note 3 (page 369), and Chapter 3, notes 16 and 18 (pages 373–74).

Servings are based on a daily intake of 1,500 to 2,500 calories, which is the appropriate range for weight loss and weight maintenance for most adults, depending on age, sex, and activity level.

"My family has moved vegetables and whole grains to the center of the plate. We like to stir-fry kale, shallots, and bell peppers in olive oil and pile it atop quinoa or millet. We avoid red meat and eat small portions of lean protein, like fish or chicken, only a few times a week. We adopted a healthier lifestyle after a couple of major strokes hit our family a couple of years ago. Our energy seems to be higher, and my wife and I have both dropped two waist sizes. It feels great to donate away your 'fat pants.' It's fun to try new recipes that taste good, fill you up, and offer a lot of nutrition."

—MATTHEW, a plant-powered omnivore in Portland, Oregon

"Being a meat-and-potato girl from the Midwest, I did my master's research on produce consumption and disease rates. What an eye-opening experience! I saw that we could feed more people and help the environment by eating less meat. My husband and I started out with the goal of one dinner a week to be meatless and we progressed from there. I went from omnivore to vegan in three months. Really, it was all about learning to cook vegan."

—CRYSTAL, a plant-powered vegan in Las Vegas, Nevada

❧ PLANT-POWERED ACTION ALERT **DAY 4**

Go to the supermarket or natural foods store and purchase three whole grains in their intact form. Put a new grain on your menu for each of the next three days.

❧ PLANT-POWERED ACTION ALERT **DAY 5**

Start eating at least five servings of whole grains per day—more often in their natural form than as flour.

Falling in Love with Vegetables

From deep green leaves and hearty roots to tender shoots and fleshy orbs, vegetables are at the core of a plant-powered diet. They are packed with a multitude of powerful bioactive compounds—some of which scientists have yet to even identify—that promote life. The history of vegetables is quite colorful. As humans evolved, they gathered roots, leaves, stems, buds, flowers, and flesh from vegetable plants that grew around them. No matter where people lived, from the harsh climates of the north to steamy jungles to arid desserts, vegetable plants were available to supply important sources of energy and nutrients for humans. Archaeologists believe that, by throwing handfuls of wild vegetables into their food vessels, bubbling over an open fire, early humans added much-needed flavor, texture, color—and vital nutrients—to their meals.

Our ancestors slowly learned how to cultivate these local plants in order to offer food security for their community. When people moved on to different locations, they packed along their vegetable seeds to plant in their new locale. As travelers from the Old World of Europe explored the New World of the Americas, they made trades in indigenous vegetable plants and seeds that would change the world. For example, the tomato—originally a small golden fruit—was brought by the Spanish explorer Cortés from Peru to Spain, from where it spread throughout Europe as well as the Caribbean, Southeast Asia, and the Middle East. As the tomato made its way across the globe and farmers saved the seeds of their favorite plants, the varieties of tomatoes amassed, so that today they come in almost every color of the rainbow, from sunny yellow and pine green to scarlet red and deep purple. Every single vegetable has a similar story to tell: When people discovered its delicious qualities they collected, cultivated, and shared it with the world over the centuries.

The botanical definition of *vegetable* is any edible portion of a plant except the ovary of the plant; the ripened ovary is technically considered a fruit. So, botanically speaking, many plant foods on today's vegetable list are actually fruits, including tomatoes, aubergines, cucumbers, and green beans. But following nutritional and culinary logic, we tend to place these "fruits" on the vegetable list; for the sake of simplicity, I will also use the more practical classifications.

BOUNTY OF NUTRIENTS

Vegetables are packed with many important nutrients, including healthy carbohydrates, fiber, protein, vitamins, minerals, and phytochemicals, which is why eating a diet rich in vegetables is linked with optimal health. Here are some key nutrients you can gain from eating more veggies:

- **Healthy Carbs.** Although the carbohydrate levels are usually low in most vegetables, a few contain higher levels, such as winter squash, green peas, potatoes, and corn (which can also count as a grain). However, since these carbohydrates come packed with fiber, they are typically slow-burning carbs that can fuel your energy levels without rapid blood-sugar highs and lows.
- **Fiber.** Some vegetables are fiber superstars; for example, a medium, cooked artichoke contains 10 grams of fiber (40% DV). The vegetable family includes all types of fiber, including insoluble and soluble fiber, oligosaccharides, resistant starches, lignans, and inulin for a variety of heart and digestive health benefits and improved blood sugar levels. (See chapter 4 for more about fiber.)

- **Plant Protein.** Did you know that little ol' vegetables can also contribute significantly to your protein intake for the day? Many contain up to 3 grams serving when cooked, but some are protein beasts: Green peas have 8 grams of protein (equivalent to 30g of turkey), spinach and asparagus have 5 grams, and broccoli and Brussels sprouts have 4 grams (8–16% DV per 80g, cooked).
- **Vitamin Alphabet.** Almost every essential vitamin can be traced back to the vegetable family, including folate, thiamin, riboflavin, niacin, pantothenic acid, and vitamins A, B_6, C, and K (see Nutrients in Action, page 393).
- **Mineral Cache.** Since vegetables grow in the mineral-rich soil, they contain supplies of many essential minerals, such as iron, potassium, manganese, magnesium, phosphorus, calcium, zinc, copper, and selenium (see Nutrients in Action, page 393).
- **Phytochemical Rainbow.** Vegetables are extremely high in a cornucopia of phytochemicals that provide antioxidant and anti-inflammatory properties as well as documented health benefits. Many phytochemicals are the very same compounds that paint the skin and flesh of vegetables with vivid colors (see Phytochemical Produce Rainbow, page 113).

A SKINNY, NUTRIENT-RICH PACKAGE

Veggies are plump with important nutrients and light in calorie load. In fact, many common vegetables, such as broccoli, greens, and onions, provide fewer than 30 calories per serving. That's why vegetables are the epitome of a nutrient-rich food, because they give you the best nutrition bang for your calorie buck. The trick behind eating more low-calorie, nutrient-rich foods is to turn the spotlight on foods packed with nutrients, such as vegetables, fruits, whole grains, and legumes, instead of *only* focusing on calories. Don't just see how *low* you can go in the numbers game of calories, fat, and sugar—see how *high* you can go in the volume of nutrients you gain per calorie. The winners will be wholesome, natural plant foods.

If all you worry about is calories, then you might as well munch on sixteen bags of 100-calorie snack cookies, crisps, or crackers per day; you'd probably lose weight. However, those 100-calorie bags wouldn't contribute much in the way of nutrients—they're mostly just empty calories from refined white flour, oil, and sugar. When you take a nutrient-rich approach, on the other hand, you focus on foods that work the hardest at giving you a high nutritional payback for those calories. For instance, 180g of boiled spinach contains only 41 calories, but for that tiny caloric sum, you're rewarded handsomely in nutrients, including at least 20% DV of vitamins A, B_2, B_6, C, and K, as well as manganese, folate, magnesium, iron, calcium, and potassium per serving. Contrast spinach's nutrient payback with that of 30g of crisps, which provides only scant amounts of nutrients like vitamin C (10% DV), thiamin (2% DV), vitamin E (6% DV), and vitamin B_6 (6% DV) with its load of 160 calories—and a lot of fat and sodium to boot.

The high nutrient density of vegetables is why they can help keep your weight under control. Vegetables are rich in both fiber and water, so they fill you up without a lot of calories. It makes perfect sense: If you fill your plate high with low-calorie, high-nutrient veggies along with plant proteins and whole grains, you'll feel satisfied for longer than you would if you ate the same amount of calories in a much smaller, low-nutrient, high-calorie doughnut or monster cookie. Studies show that a nutrient-rich strategy not only helps people lose weight, it keeps them feeling more satisfied and less hungry while they're reducing their calorie intake. In fact, according to research, if you start your meal with a nutrient-rich, vegetable-based soup or salad, you will eat fewer calories during the meal.[1]

If you've been on a weight-loss diet, you know how hard it is to stick with it when the hunger pangs set in. The nutrient-rich plant approach counteracts hunger to help you lose weight; it's a major factor behind why plant-powered eaters weigh less than their Western diet counterparts.

LOOK BEYOND THE BASICS

There are hundreds of different vegetables available—thousands, if you include specific varieties—but in the United States the top three we consume are potatoes, tomatoes, and lettuce. These vegetables, like all vegetables, are certainly nutritious, but people who don't get past them are missing out on so much! Open your eyes to a whole world of vegetables—each with its own unique flavor, texture, and nutritional profile. Check out the Plant-Powered Vegetables Guide (page 115) to see the nutrients that come packed in every serving of commonly available vegetables. For example, 40g of cooked carrots provides 266% DV of vitamin A for eye health, and 65g of cooked kale contains 664% DV of vitamin K, important for blood clotting and bone health. That's why I encourage you to eat vegetables, like all plant foods, with diversity in mind. Try less familiar vegetables, such as rainbow-hued chard, rutabagas, bok choy (try Bok Choy Seitan Pho, page 326), and bitter melon. You'll gain a much more powerful nutrition lineup—as well as satisfied palate—from mixing it up.

While you're at it, check out heirloom vegetable varieties, which have been nurtured over the centuries by farmers and gardeners who saved the seeds of vegetable varieties that showed exceptional color, texture, shape, or flavor in order to replant them for the following year. You may already know about heirloom tomato varieties, such as Brandywine or Indigo Rose, but did you know that there are thousands of heirloom vegetable varieties available in the plant kingdom beyond the ones you can find in the grocery store? Sadly, some heirloom vegetables face extinction because people don't eat them anymore, thus farmers don't grow them anymore. Today's large vegetable growers typically produce a minimal variety of hybrids—plants that are the result of cross-breeding to produce particular traits, such as maximum yield or tough skins that can handle transportation or pesticide applications. Most of these are raised in a "monoculture" style of vegetable farming in which large acreages are planted with the exact same vegetable variety. Some heirloom varieties do still persist, though: French Breakfast radishes, Jenny Lind melon, and Kentucky Wonder green beans are just a few common examples that offer interesting taste, color, and texture—and relief from the standby collection of vegetables represented in most super-markets. Often the only way to try these varieties is to visit your local farmers market, join a CSA, or grow them yourself. In chapter 6 I'll show you how to shop at farmers markets or join a CSA (see page 152).

PHYTOCHEMICALS PARADE

Scientists know that vegetables possess thousands of bioactive compounds called phytochemicals that impart health benefits when you eat them—benefits that range from protecting the brain from the damaging effects of neurodegeneration to preventing the development of atherosclerosis, which leads to heart disease. These plant compounds are found in high levels in colorful vegetables, as well as in other plant foods, and are powered with antioxidant and anti-inflammatory properties that fight disease. For the plant, all these thousands of compounds found in the vegetable plant, often concentrated in its outer skin, formed a defense system from outside injury and insult—and eating that plant can offer you similar benefits. Many such phytochemicals are actually the pigments that give vegetables their vibrant colors, such as the red shade of tomatoes or the purple hue in cabbage—even different colors within the same species.

A BEVY OF BENEFITS

A DIET STACKED with a variety of veggies is like an all-access pass to a pharmacy of health-protective chemicals. That's why eating a diet rich in vegetables has been linked with protection against the following:

- Cancers, including breast and prostate[2]
- Cardiovascular disease, including heart attack and stroke[3]
- Type 2 diabetes[4]
- Cognitive decline[5]
- Age-related eye diseases[6]
- Bone loss[7]
- Lung diseases[8]
- Chronic inflammation[9]
- Metabolic syndrome, a clustering of risk factors that raises the risk of chronic illness[10]

We have much more to learn about how powerful these phytochemicals can be. Researchers are identifying brand-new bioactive substances in plants all the time—each with the potential for providing uncharted health benefits. And they have found that, when different vegetables are eaten together—as we do in many of our favorite foods, such as a vegetable soup (like my Country French Barley Vegetable Potage, page 283)—their positive health effects multiply. The latest science shows that phytochemicals may be converted into other bioactive compounds in the digestive tract because of unique **gut microflora**—the bacterial environment in your gastrointestinal tract. If you eat a healthy, plant-based diet instead of a typical Western diet, chances are you have a much friendlier balance of "good" gut bacteria that may allow you to gain even more benefits from phytochemicals.

Our ancestors' diets were probably extremely high in phytochemical content, as they feasted on a large supply of colorful vegetables. Sadly, today many people get most of their food colors from artificial food dyes like those in cheese puffs and yogurt—and that kind doesn't count! So, aim to eat produce in every shade of the rainbow in order to rake in as many different kinds of phytochemicals as you can. Check out the Phytochemical Produce Rainbow that follows to discover which color-coded bioactive compounds—with their own unique benefits—are found in your favorite vegetables and fruits.

POWERFUL VEGETABLES YOU SHOULD KNOW ABOUT

There's no such thing as a "bad" vegetable; I encourage you to eat them all in every shape, size, color, texture, and taste. But there are some vegetables that deserve special notice, so fit these beauties into your diet every week.

MAGIC MUSHROOMS

Nothing compares to the taste and fragrance of mushrooms freshly sautéed in olive oil and garlic. But there's a lot more to mushrooms than meets the nose and taste buds. Although I've included them in this chapter, these special specimens are in fact neither plant nor animal: They are classified in the kingdom of fungi. And beyond that, mushrooms are even more unique within the fungi kingdom, because they are the complex fruiting body of the fungal organism. Just as a tree produces fruit to bear seeds to continue the species, so does a fungal organism produce mushrooms to carry spores to continue its own species. There are thousands of mushroom species present in the world, but scientists estimate that only 10 percent of them have been identified.

For thousands of years people have treasured mushrooms for their rich flavor, as well as their therapeutic effects, in both folk healing and traditional medicine. A number of well-known drugs originated in the fungi kingdom, including penicillin and two statins (that is, the cholesterol-lowering drugs lovastatin and squalestatin). So it really shouldn't be a

(continued on page 122)

PHYTOCHEMICAL PRODUCE RAINBOW

PLANT COLOR	PLANT SOURCES	PHYTOCHEMICALS	HEALTH BENEFITS
Blue/Purple	**Fruits:** Blackberries, blueberries, black currants, Mission figs, plums, purple grapes, raisins **Vegetables:** Aubergine, purple potatoes, radicchio, red cabbage **Legumes:** Black beans	Anthocyanidins, ellagic acid, flavan-3-ols, **flavonols**, proanthocyanidins, **resveratrol**	Anticancer activity, promote urinary tract health, improve memory function and heart health
Green	**Fruits:** Bartlett pears, green apples, green grapes, honeydews, kiwifruits, limes **Vegetables:** Artichokes, asparagus, avocados, broccoli, cabbage, celery, cucumbers, green beans, green bell peppers, leafy greens, okra, peas, leeks, lettuce, squashes (green-skinned varieties), watercress	Beta-carotene, **flavanones, flavones**, flavonols, lutein, indoles, isothiocyanates, sulfur compounds, zeaxanthin	Anticancer activity, promote heart health, protect vision, anti-inflammatory properties
White	**Fruits:** Bananas, pears, dates, white peaches, white nectarines **Vegetables:** Cauliflower, garlic, ginger, Jerusalem artichokes, jicama, kohlrabi, onions, parsnips, shallots, turnips, white corn, white mushrooms, white potatoes	Flavanones, flavonols, indoles, isothiocyanates, sulfur compounds	Anticancer activity, promote heart health, reduced cholesterol levels, anti-inflammatory properties

PLANT COLOR	PLANT SOURCES	PHYTOCHEMICALS	HEALTH BENEFITS
Yellow/Orange	**Fruits:** Apples (yellow), apricots, cantaloupe, figs (yellow) golden kiwifruit, gooseberries, grapefruit, lemons, mangos, nectarines, oranges, papayas, peaches, pears (yellow), persimmons, pineapple, tangerines, watermelon (yellow) **Vegetables:** Carrots, pumpkin, rutabagas, summer squash (yellow), sweet corn, sweet potatoes, tomatoes (yellow), winter squash, yellow beetroot, yellow bell peppers, yellow potatoes	Alpha-carotene, beta-carotene, beta-cryptoxanthin, flavanones, flavonols, zeaxanthin	Anticancer activity, promote heart health, protect vision, anti-inflammatory properties
Red	**Fruits:** Apples (red), blood oranges, cherries, cranberries, grapefruit, red grapes, pears (red), pomegranates, raspberries, rhubarb, strawberries, watermelon **Vegetables:** Beetroot, radishes, radicchio, red bell peppers, red onions, red potatoes, tomatoes (red)	Anthocyanidins, ellagic acid, flavanones, flavonols, flavones, **lycopene**, proanthocyanidins, resveratrol	Anticancer activity, improve cognitive function, promote heart health, anti-inflammatory activity, promote urinary tract health

Source: Information from Produce for Better Health Foundation Phytochemical List, pbhfoundation.org/about/res/pic/phytolist

PLANT-POWERED VEGETABLES GUIDE

VEGETABLE	SERVING SIZE	DESCRIPTION	CULINARY SUGGESTIONS	STAR NUTRIENTS* (AT LEAST 10% DV PER SERVING)
Artichoke, globe	60g cooked	Perennial thistle that develops into a large edible bud. Green in color with mild taste.	Trim the thorns, then boil or steam and eat the edible fleshy portion in the center. May be grilled or used in casseroles (see Antipasto Couscous with Chickpeas, page 310) and dips.	Fiber, vitamins C and K, folate, magnesium, phosphorus, potassium
Asparagus	45g cooked	Spring perennial that produces tender green shoots with delicate flavor.	Steam, sauté, roast, or grill tender shoots as a side dish (see Roasted Lemon Asparagus with Red Peppers, page 335) or to include in salads.	Vitamins A, C, and K, folate
Avocado**	¼th fruit	Large, egg-shaped tree fruit that ripens after harvesting. Its green flesh boasts a buttery, earthy flavor and creamy texture.	Serve fresh in salads, sandwiches, or wraps; mash into guacamole; or mix into baked goods (see Spiced Banana Avocado Bread, page 351).	Fiber, vitamin K, folate
Beetroot	40g cooked	Beet roots are most commonly a red-purple color but are also available in white, golden, or striped. The colorful flesh provides a rich, sweet flavor.	Boil, steam, sauté, or roast and serve as a side dish or in salads (see Beetroot and Pomegranate Seed Salad, page 297).	Folate, manganese
Broccoli	40g cooked or fresh	This green head of flower buds on a thick stalk produces a crunchy, flavorful taste.	Boil or steam as a side dish, serve raw in salads and slaws, or add to stir-fries, soups, pasta dishes (see Vegetable Medley Lasagna, page 307), and side dishes.	Fiber, vitamins A, C, and K, folate

VEGETABLE	SERVING SIZE	DESCRIPTION	CULINARY SUGGESTIONS	STAR NUTRIENTS* (AT LEAST 10% DV PER SERVING)
Brussels sprouts	40g cooked	A wild cabbage that produces edible green buds that resemble tiny cabbage heads along a stalk and has a mild, cabbagelike flavor.	Boil, roast, or sauté as a side dish or in salads (see Brussels Sprouts Slaw, page 296).	Vitamins A, C, and K, folate
Cabbage	40g cooked or fresh	A leafy vegetable with a short stem and mass of leaves which forms a head. Its numerous varieties come in white, green, and red-purple shades as well as various leaf textures.	Used fresh in slaws or salads or preserved or fermented in sauerkraut. Cook as a side dish, add to soup (see Winter Buckwheat Vegetable Soup, page 287), or cook whole leaves and use to encase fillings or rolls.	Vitamins C and K
Carrots	40g cooked or fresh	This sweet-tasting, crunchy root vegetable is typically orange but comes in white, yellow, and purple shades, as well.	Serve raw as an appetizer or in salads or slaw (see Chinese Cabbage Slaw, page 289). Steam, boil, roast, or sauté as side dishes, soups, or entrées.	Vitamins A and K
Cauliflower	30g cooked or fresh	This mildly flavored vegetable features an edible floral head surrounded by thick green leaves on a short stalk. Although white is the most common color, it also comes in orange, green, and purple.	Roast, boil, steam, or sauté as a side dish or entrée (see Cauliflower and Pea Curry, page 342). Enjoy raw as an appetizer or in salads.	Fiber, vitamins C and K
Celery	50g cooked or fresh	Long light green stalks with edible green leaves and root and a crunchy, mild flavor.	Excellent in soups, stir-fries, and grain dishes (see Baked Farro Herb Pilaf, page 314) or raw as an appetizer or in salads.	Vitamin K, folate

VEGETABLE	SERVING SIZE	DESCRIPTION	CULINARY SUGGESTIONS	STAR NUTRIENTS* (AT LEAST 10% DV PER SERVING)
Chard	85g cooked	Leafy green vegetable, with stalks, that varies in color depending on the variety, both of which are eaten. It has a mildly bitter flavor.	Commonly used in Mediterranean cooking, may be enjoyed raw in salads or boiled, roasted, or sautéed as a side dish (see Farmers Market Greens and Garlic Sauté, page 337).	Vitamins A, C, and K, iron, magnesium, potassium, manganese
Corn, Sweet†	75g cooked	Grown on a tall plant as "ears," fresh sweet corn is considered both a vegetable and grain (see page 98).	Wonderful eaten boiled or roasted on the cob, it can also be boiled or roasted and added to salads and side dishes (see Southwestern Black Bean, Quinoa, and Mango Medley, page 318).	Thiamin, folate
Cucumber	60g fresh	A creeping vine produces these green, cylindrical fruits that have a fresh, clean flavor and crunchy texture.	Most often used fresh as an appetizer or in salads (see Greek Salad with Rosemary-Lemon Tofu, page 294) or dips and may be fermented or preserved as pickles.	Vitamin K
Aubergine	50g cooked	This deep purple fruit from a plant in the nightshade family has a mild, meaty texture and comes in a variety of sizes and shapes.	Very versatile and spongelike, it is commonly used in Italian, Middle Eastern (see Baba Ghanoush, page 277), and Indian dishes. Excellent grilled as a side dish.	†
Endive	25g fresh	A bitter-leafed vegetable in the chicory family with curly or flat leaves in pale green or white shades.	Sauté or roast as a side dish, serve raw in salads, or stuff with a filling.	Vitamins A and K, folate, manganese

VEGETABLE	SERVING SIZE	DESCRIPTION	CULINARY SUGGESTIONS	STAR NUTRIENTS* (AT LEAST 10% DV PER SERVING)
Green beans	65g cooked	These unripe fruits of any type of bean plant come in a variety of colors, patterns, and sizes and have a mild, earthy taste.	Eat raw, or boil, roast, or sauté as a side dish or to add to soups, stews, casseroles, and salads (see Nicoise-Style Salad, page 295).	Vitamin K, manganese
Kale	65g cooked	A form of cabbage that does not form a head. Leaves are usually green or purple and have a crunchy, mildly bitter taste.	Excellent steamed or sautéed as a side dish (see Shiitake and Kale Spelt Bowl, page 330), added to soups and stir-fries, or used raw in salads.	Vitamins A, C, and K, manganese
Leeks	50g cooked or fresh	This member of the onion family produces a long white bulb with large green leaves with a mildly spicy flavor.	Braise or roast whole leeks or slice into salads, soups (see Celeriac and Apple Bisque, page 282), or side dishes.	Vitamin K
Lettuce	50g fresh	A leaf vegetable that comes in a variety of textures and colors—and thus nutrient profiles—including white, pale green, deep green, and dark red.	Serve raw in salads (see Watermelon Peppercorn Salad, page 288) and sandwiches. Use to wrap fillings.	Vitamins A, C, and K
Mushrooms	75g cooked or fresh	The complex fruiting body of a fungal organism, mushrooms come in a variety of shapes, colors, and sizes, offering a savory, meaty taste and texture.	Eat fresh as an appetizer or in salads, add to soups and grain dishes, or sauté or grill as a burger replacement (see Grilled Portobello Mushroom "Steaks," page 340).	Riboflavin, niacin, pantothenic acid, copper, selenium; vitamin D (in UV-treated only)

VEGETABLE	SERVING SIZE	DESCRIPTION	CULINARY SUGGESTIONS	STAR NUTRIENTS* (AT LEAST 10% DV PER SERVING)
Okra	40g cooked	Edible green seed pods produced by a flowering plant yield bittersweet flavor and a sticky liquid that acts as a good thickening agent.	Featured in traditional Southern dishes, may be sautéed or added to soups and bean or grain dishes (see Vegetarian Hoppin' John, page 322). Overcooking may produce slimy texture.	Vitamins C and K, manganese
Onions	100g cooked or fresh	A bulb vegetable that comes in a variety of colors including white, yellow, and red. Flavor ranges from sweet to mild to pungent.	Used as a flavoring for many dishes, including salads, soups (see Classic French Onion Soup, page 284), side dishes, casseroles, sauces, and dips.	†
Parsnips	40g cooked	Root vegetable with light yellow flesh that resembles a carrot, but has a milder, sweeter taste.	Roast or cook as a side dish or slice into soups, casseroles (see Slow-Cooked Butter Beans with Root Vegetables, page 317), or stews.	Fiber, vitamin C, folate, manganese
Peas, green†	80g cooked	Round green seeds of a legume, shelled from pods while fresh. They have a sweet flavor and tender texture.	Steam or sauté as a side dish or add to stir-fries, curries, salads, soups, and casseroles (see Vegetable, Tofu, and Potato Pot Pie, page 333).	Fiber, vitamins A, C, and K, thiamin, folate, manganese
Peppers, bell	75g cooked or fresh	A large, bell-shaped fruit that has a sweet, crunchy flavor and comes in a variety of colors, including red, yellow, orange, and green.	Enjoy raw as an appetizer or in salads or sauté, grill, or roast as a flavoring in soups, sauces, side dishes (see Grilled Vegetable Skewers, page 336), and grain dishes.	Fiber, vitamins B₆, C, and K

VEGETABLE	SERVING SIZE	DESCRIPTION	CULINARY SUGGESTIONS	STAR NUTRIENTS* (AT LEAST 10% DV PER SERVING)
Potatoes‡	80g cooked	Starchy, tuberous vegetable that grows underground. Available in many shapes, textures, and colors, including white, yellow, red, and blue-purple.	Bake, steam, roast, sauté, or mash as a side dish (see Roasted Potato Vegetable Terrine, page 341). Add to soups and casseroles.	Vitamins B$_6$ and C
Radishes	60g fresh	Edible root vegetable with a crunchy, spicy flavor. Comes in a variety of sizes and colors, such as pink, red, white, gray, purple, and yellow.	Slice into salads or slaw, serve raw as an appetizer or to accompany sandwiches, or sauté as a side dish.	Vitamin C
Spinach	90g cooked or 30g fresh	Available in flat-leaf or curly-leaf varieties, spinach leaves are deep green in flavor and produce a rich, mildly bitter flavor.	Use raw in salads (see Curried Papaya Salad, page 291) or cook to reduce bitterness. Add to soups, pasta dishes, and side dishes.	Fiber, vitamins A, E, and K, folate, riboflavin, calcium, iron, magnesium, manganese
Squash, summer (e.g., crookneck, yellow, scallop, and courgette)	60g cooked or fresh	Fruits in the gourd family, a subset of squashes, that are harvested when immature while the rind is soft. Available in a variety of shapes, sizes, and colors, they provide a tender, mild flavor.	Serve fresh or cook, sauté, grill, or roast in side dishes, soups, pasta dishes, and wraps (see Bean and Grilled Veggie Burritos, page 300) or add to breads.	Manganese

VEGETABLE	SERVING SIZE	DESCRIPTION	CULINARY SUGGESTIONS	STAR NUTRIENTS* (AT LEAST 10% DV PER SERVING)
Squash, winter (e.g., butternut, acorn, and Hubbard), and pumpkins‡	100g cooked	Fruits in the gourd family with hard shells, hollow, seed-filled cavities, and sweet flesh.	Slice in half, scoop out the seeds, and boil or roast squash. Serve as a side dish or in soups (see Roasted Squash Bisque with Macadamias, page 286), casseroles, or salads.	Fiber, vitamins A and C, manganese
Sweet potatoes‡	90g cooked	This large, deep-orange root vegetable has a sweet, tender taste.	Boil, bake, or mash as a side dish (see Sweet Potato Pumpkin Seed Casserole, page 343) or to stir into desserts. Roast into baked "fries."	Fiber, vitamins A, B_6, and C, pantothenic acid, potassium, manganese
Tomatoes	100g cooked or fresh	This juicy, sweet fruit from a plant in the nightshade family comes in a variety of colors, such as yellow, green, orange, red, and purple.	Enjoy fresh in salads or sandwiches. Sauté or cook to add to soups, sauces, pasta dishes (see Orzo with Tomatoes and Fennel Seed, page 306), Mexican dishes, and curries.	Vitamin C

Source: USDA National Nutrient Database for Standard Reference, http://ndb.nal.usda.gov

DV = Daily Value, nutritional requirements according to the Food and Drug Administration, based on 2,000 calories per day

* Refer to the appendix (page 393) to learn how these nutrients contribute to overall health.

**If you're trying to lose weight, count avocado as a serving of plant fat.

† Although rich in many vitamins and minerals, a ½-cup cooked portion does not contain at least 10% DV of any single nutrient.

‡ If you're trying to lose weight, count these starchy vegetables as a grain serving (see Daily Plant-Powered Guide, page 244).

surprise that mushrooms turn out to have powerful health potential because they contain special nutritional components, including beta-glucans, proteins, carbohydrates, fats, vitamins, trace elements, sterols, phenols, and **terpenoids**, as well as unique bacteria, yeasts, and molds. Mushrooms also contain a compound that can convert sunshine into vitamin D, just like you can do in your skin. If the mushrooms are exposed to ultraviolet light while they are cultivated, they can contain significant levels of vitamin D. This is good news because vitamin D, which is not available in many food sources, is linked with many important health benefits, including cancer prevention, autoimmune disease protection, immune defense, promotion of mental health, and maintaining healthy bones, teeth, and muscles.

Studies have found that mushrooms' special nutritional profile may promote many health benefits, including anticancer activity, antioxidant action, and immune-enhancing benefits.[11] The most intriguing area for mushroom research is in cancer protection; in Japan and China, mushrooms are already widely used as a therapy for cancer treatment. At City of Hope, a National Cancer Institute–designated Comprehensive Cancer Care Center in Duarte, California, researchers are investigating mushrooms' potential in reducing breast and prostate cancer growth in human clinical studies.

Meaty and savory, mushrooms are the perfect "plant-based" food to replace animal foods in your diet. You can sauté them as a taco filling, grill them as a burger replacement, and stir them into casseroles, soups, stir-fries, and pasta dishes. Try my recipe for Shiitake and Kale Spelt Bowl (see page 330) to see how simple and delicious mushrooms can be. And don't forget to sample new varieties of mushrooms beyond the mild, white (or button) variety; try crimini, portobello, enoki, oyster, maitake, and shiitake mushrooms in your next meal. All mushrooms are beneficial, but some in particular have been studied for their anticancer potential, including maitake and shiitake.

DEEP RED TOMATOES

Painting your plate red is one way to gain the health benefits of eating more plant foods—eat more tomatoes, America's favorite nonpotato vegetable. Whether you slice them fresh into salads, sandwiches, wraps, or salsa or stir cooked tomato products such as tomato sauce or canned tomatoes into pasta dishes, soups, chili, curry, or casseroles, you can reap plenty of health rewards. Tomatoes contain a symphony of nutrients, including fiber; vitamins A, C, and K; iron and potassium; and the important antioxidant lycopene, the plant compound that gives tomatoes their rich red hue. When you cook tomatoes, the lycopene becomes even more available to your body. And it looks like lycopene may be behind the growing list of health benefits scientists have linked to eating more tomatoes, including heart health, lower inflammation and oxidation levels, improved cholesterol and blood pressure levels, antiplatelet activity that helps protect against the formation of blood clots, bone health, protection of the skin from ultraviolet damage, and prostate cancer prevention.[12] That's a lot of reasons to eat more tomatoes. (Try one of my favorite recipes, Tofu Cacciatore, page 324.)

FORAGE FOR GREEN LEAFIES

Popeye had it right about spinach. Like all green leafy vegetables, spinach is a veritable powerhouse of nutrition, containing at least nineteen essential nutrients in a cooked serving. Many green leafies (such as collard greens, turnip greens, kale, and bok choy) are also rich in calcium. In fact, 85g of cooked collard greens provides 27% DV of calcium—about the same amount as a large glass of milk. Especially if you are vegan or nearly vegan, you should include a dark green leafy vegetable in your diet every day. And that's not all: Green leafy vegetables like lettuce, spinach, beetroot greens, turnip greens, mustard greens, collard greens, kale, watercress, endive, rocket, and chard also contain a coterie of health-promoting phytochemicals, such as beta-carotene, **betalains**, **chlorophyll**, kaempferol, lutein, **quercetin**, and zeaxanthin. It's hard to believe that you can fit that much nutrition into a handful of green leaves.

The nutrients found in the green leaves of edible plants appear to work together to fend off disease. Eating green leafy vegetables has been linked with reducing inflammation and oxidation levels and with heart health, protection of the eye against age-related eye disease, anticancer activity, bone health, and protection against mental decline.[13]

Many indigenous diets foster wonderful traditions of foraging for wild greens. My mother's childhood chore in her country town in Arkansas was to gather up wild poke greens and lamb's-quarter for dinner. Today, you can still find people honoring their timeworn tradition of gathering wild greens, from *horta* in Greece to *mfumbwa* in West Africa. In fact, what you call "weeds" in your garden, such as dandelion leaves and purslane, are actually edible greens that your ancestors once collected as a food staple. Whether you forage for them in your backyard or buy them at the supermarket or farmers market, put greens on your menu at least a few times a week. By cooking greens you can tone down any bitter flavors and concentrate their nutrients—a bunch of greens can cook down to two servings. My favorite way to maximize their bold, verdant flavor is to sauté them in a bit of olive oil and garlic (see Farmers Market Greens and Garlic Sauté, page 337).

CRUCIFEROUS VEGETABLE CANCER DEFENDERS

Broccoli, Brussels sprouts, cabbage, cauliflower, collard greens, kale, kohlrabi, mustard greens, rutabaga, turnips, bok choy, Chinese cabbage, rocket, horseradish, radish, wasabi, and watercress—that's a list of pungent, flavorful plant foods known as cruciferous vegetables, according to their botanical classification. What's so special about this group of veggies? In addition to their orchestra of vitamins, such as folate and vitamin C, minerals like manganese, and fiber, cruciferous vegetables include unique sulfur-containing compounds called glucosinolates that impart the characteristic pungent aroma and spicy taste that you experience when you bite into a broccoli floret or taste a dab of wasabi on your sushi roll.

Because of glucosinolates, high intakes of cruciferous vegetables have been associated with lower risks of lung, stomach, colorectal, breast, and prostate cancer. It's thought that glucosinolates protect you against cancer by lowering inflammation levels, boosting immune function, "turning on" genes that suppress tumors, slowing cancer cell growth, and stimulating a process that signals cancer cells to self-destruct. Indeed, cancer organizations like the National Cancer Institute and American Institute for Cancer Research recognize the benefits of eating more cruciferous vegetables in order to protect against cancer.[14]

It's easy to put cruciferous veggies on the menu at least a few times a week. You probably noticed that some are also green leafy vegetables, giving you a double dose of healthiness. Chop broccoli, cabbage, cauliflower, radishes, and rocket into your salads (try Chinese Cabbage Slaw, page 289, which features cabbage). Stir-fry bok choy, Brussels sprouts, cabbage, and kale and serve with brown rice. Roast rutabaga and turnips for a delicious side dish. And enjoy the spicy flavor of wasabi and horseradish as an accompaniment to dishes such as salads, marinades, and Asian foods.

DIVE INTO SEA VEGETABLES

Look beyond the land to the ocean to reap a variety of nutritious sea vegetables, forms of algae that range from seaweed to kelp. Japanese cultures have been consuming them for more than 10,000 years, and many other countries located by the sea have relied on sea vegetables for nutritional sustenance, as well as for medicinal and beauty purposes, for centuries. And it looks like they've been on to something.

Thousands of sea vegetables have been identified and classified based on color (brown, red, or green). Popular types of seaweed include nori, arame, and sea palm. Depending on type, sea vegetables may possess many nutrients, including protein; the vitamin B group and vitamins A, C, D, E, and K; and minerals like calcium, iron, phosphorus, potassium, magnesium, and iodine. Iodine is of particular concern to vegans, who have been found to be deficient in this mineral that is most often found in seafood and milk. Seaweed is an excellent source of iodine; in fact some types have very high levels—like kelp, which can contain up to 2650 mcg of iodine per gram. However, be aware that high amounts of iodine can promote hyperthyroidism that in turn may lead to health conditions such as heart irregularities. Plan to consume only moderate amounts of seaweed that provide up to 150 mcg of iodine per day. Due to their harsh growing environment, sea vegetables produce interesting bioactive compounds, such as peptides, alkaloids, **phlorotannins**, and **fucoidans**—starchlike molecules that appear to have anti-inflammatory and antiviral benefits. In particular, research has linked sea vegetables with lowering blood pressure and to anticancer, antidiabetic, and antiallergic activities.[15]

Although their taste is unique, sea vegetables can be very versatile. Typically sun-dried or pickled and sold in packages, marine vegetable are easy to slice into dishes like soups, stir-fries, grains, dressings, and sauces. You can even find snacks made from dried, seasoned seaweed in stores; just keep an eye on sodium levels in some of these products. Make a splash by adding an exotic touch of sea vegetables to your next meal (and try my recipe for Vegetable Brown Rice Sushi, page 278).

STEM-TO-ROOT EATING

WHEN OUR ANCESTORS collected vegetable plants in the wild and harvested them from their gardens, they ate virtually every part of the vegetable that wouldn't kill them—from stem to root. Today, we've gradually lost sight of the fact that many of the best parts of the vegetable plant, such as beetroot tops and broccoli stalks, are simply tossed away (often before they ever make it to supermarket shelves, much less your kitchen), and this practice contributes to the growing amount of food waste in the west. About 40 percent of the food produced in the United States—including vegetables—will never be eaten, squandering precious resources like energy, water, and soil. Here are a few typically wasted vegetable parts worth giving a shot in your kitchen:

- Leaves and greens of Brussels sprouts, beetroot, carrots, cauliflower, celery, and radishes and of pea, cucumber, and squash plants
- Flowers of broccoli, chive, coriander, dandelion parsley, and courgette
- Stems of broccoli, cauliflower, chard, and kale

GO ORGANIC

As you shift your eating style toward a plant-powered diet, I encourage you to make another important transition by choosing organic foods first. You may feel that the higher price for organic foods isn't worth it, but there are many reasons to choose organic foods for yourself and your family: You'll naturally reduce your dietary load of the synthetic inputs in your food supply, such as pesticides and fertilizers and, in the case of animal products, antibiotics and growth hormones. But when you buy organic, you're also contributing to a better world outside your own household by promoting a method of agriculture that works *with* nature instead of against it. Every time you buy organic, you're fighting against pesticide runoff infecting waterways, dead zones in oceans caused by synthetic fertilizers, destructive soil practices, threatened wildlife species, and the exposure of farm communities to dangerous chemicals. If you think about it, organic agriculture is really the way your great-grandfather grew food, before the advent of industrial agricultural chemicals. He knew that he had to take care of the land and the soil in order to produce crops for future generations. And now science is proving that organic agriculture indeed leads to many positive results. The following evidence-based benefits are the leading reasons why you should choose organic foods first:

Organic Benefits to the Environment

- Organic farming creates healthy soils to grow food for years to come.
- Organic agriculture reduces nitrogen and phosphorus contamination of groundwater.
- Organic production conserves fossil fuel energy.
- Decreased dependence on synthetic pesticides protects ecosystems.

Organic Benefits to the Farmer

- Crop rotation and composting contribute to financial savings.
- Organic farming methods reduce exposure to pesticides by farm laborers and family members.
- In developing countries, organic farming improves community and household food security by increasing income and food availability.
- Fair prices for organic products help farmers and encourage young people to enter farming.
- Current research shows that crop yields are consistent with or better than those produced by conventional agriculture.

Organic Benefits to You

- Certain plants cultivated in an organic system contain higher levels of antioxidants.
- Children who consume organic diets have lower exposure to organophosphorous pesticides as measured by urine in studies.

- Research demonstrates improved flavor in organically grown fruit like strawberries and apples versus conventionally produced fruit.
- Promising research suggests that plants cultivated in organic systems are higher in certain nutrients, but more research on this is needed.
- Organic regulations do not allow the use of antibiotics in livestock, which has been linked to antibiotic resistance in humans.[16]

PUSH YOUR VEGGIES!

There are so many reasons to pump up the volume on veggies, but so few people are taking full advantage of them. Only 26 percent of adults eat a full serving of vegetables three or more times a day.[17] Here are my favorite tips for boosting those precious servings of vegetables to at least six servings a day.

1. Mix onions, mushrooms, and bell peppers into a morning veggie burrito, omelet, tofu scramble, or breakfast pita.
2. Try sliced tomatoes or a baked tomato half at breakfast—it's a favorite in the United Kingdom.
3. Pile lettuce, spinach, sprouts, tomatoes, cucumbers, avocado, peppers, and/or onions into your whole grain sandwich, pita, or wrap.
4. At least weekly, put vegetable stir-fry on the menu. Sauté cabbage, broccoli, celery, mangetout, bell peppers, carrots, onions, and/or mushrooms with tofu or nuts and your favorite spices and serve with brown rice or whole grains like wheat berries.
5. Make your own vegetarian pizza packed with spinach, courgette, onions, and mushrooms or try my recipe for Spicy Broccoli Cashew Pizza (see page 302).
6. Have a homemade veggie burger once a week, topped with lettuce, tomato, onions, pickles, and avocado.
7. Make a hearty chili with beans, fresh or canned tomatoes, onions, and peppers (check out Three-Bean Cowboy Chili, page 321).
8. Double up on cooked vegetable servings at dinner time.
9. Add chopped vegetables, such as mushrooms, green peas, broccoli, carrots, summer squash, green beans, and red peppers, to broth-based soups.
10. Include a garden salad or broth-based vegetable soup at every dinner.

11. Mix vegetables into your favorite casseroles—try peas or squash in your macaroni and cheese or broccoli and kale in your lasagna.

12. Use leftover chopped, cooked vegetables (broccoli, carrots, mushrooms, bell peppers, green peas) in a soup, stew, or casserole the next day.

13. Use low-sodium tomato juice as a base for soups.

14. Make a big pot of vegetable soup and freeze in individual containers for a quick, microwaveable lunch.

15. Don't just limit salad to a plate of pale greens; try a variety of leaves, from red oak to rocket, and top them with a rainbow of veggies, including cucumbers, carrots, squash, broccoli, cauliflower, peas, corn, peppers, tomatoes, and jicama.

DAILY PLANT-POWERED VEGETABLE GUIDE

SERVING SIZES	PLANT-POWERED VEGAN	PLANT-POWERED VEGETARIAN	PLANT-POWERED OMNIVORE
50g raw leafy greens, such as lettuce, spinach, kale, and watercress 40g any other raw or cooked vegetables 200ml reduced-sodium vegetable juice	6-9 servings, including at least one leafy green vegetable every day	6-9 servings	6-9 servings

Sources: See Chapter 1, note 3 (page 369), and Chapter 3, notes 16 and 18 (pages 373-74).

Servings are based on a daily intake of 1,500 to 2,500 calories, which is the appropriate range for weight loss and weight maintenance for most adults, depending on age, sex, and activity level.

"Growing up with a large vegetable garden and orchards, there were always fresh or preserved ingredients in our meals throughout the year. However, going off to college, moving to an urban area, and starting a career took me somewhat off course from the homegrown fare I was accustomed to. When my husband and I were ready to buy a house, we wanted enough space to have gardens and orchards so we could grow our own food. As both of our

careers evolved and we gained heightened awareness of the environmental, economical, social, and health impacts of the global food system, this propelled us to be more serious about growing our own food and supporting local farmers. The bottom line is, fresh food from a garden simply tastes the best, hands down. You can't beat a sugar snap pea, cherry tomato, string bean, or sun-ripened raspberry picked and eaten while standing in a garden. It makes a difference on the household food budget and it tastes better, was not sprayed with chemicals, and was not trucked in from across the country. But the biggest benefit is the satisfaction that we can grow, harvest, preserve, and savor our own food."

—ANGIE, a plant-powered omnivore in Elkhart, Iowa

"As aging baby boomers, my wife and I are concerned with being as healthy as possible, and we realize our diet contributes to our overall health and well-being. We adopted a vegan diet and both lost a significant amount of weight and feel better physically. I received the best Christmas gift when our family physician informed me that my type 2 diabetes was reversed and that I could discontinue my medication, which she attributed to my new-found diet. Our family, friends, and coworkers have seen the positive changes in us, and it has inspired them to make changes in their own lives to eat healthier, too."

—JULIAN, a plant-powered vegan from Nashville, Tennessee

❦ PLANT-POWERED ACTION ALERT **DAY 6**
Buy three new vegetables that you normally don't purchase and put them on the menu within the next two days.

❦ PLANT-POWERED ACTION ALERT **DAY 7**
Start eating at least six servings of vegetables per day (but shoot for nine!).

Fruits, Nature's Perfect Sweetener

Ahh, a perfectly sweet strawberry, fresh from the garden or a roadside stand. Nothing can beat that intoxicating aroma and juicy sweet flavor. Can you imagine what fresh fruit was like for our early ancestors, who eagerly anticipated the first warm days of summer and the first glimpse of the season's ruby and purple berries against the green, dense forest? Apart from an occasional bee hive here and there, fruits were the only sweet thing our ancestors got to experience. Just think how they must have savored that first sweet explosion in their mouths that marked the fruit-bearing season. No wonder summer fruits played such a significant role in our culinary, medicinal, and nutritional past.

Every ancient people developed traditions around these naturally sweet plant foods. For the Native Americans, blueberries—or "star berries," for the star shape of the berry's blossom end—was a gift from the Great Spirit to relieve their hunger and illness. They collected blueberries in forests and bogs and dried them in order to savor them throughout the year in soups and stews. The juice and leaves of blueberries were used for medicinal purposes, such as to soothe a sore throat or to "boost the blood." In the cold climates of Scandinavia—where fruits and vegetables flourish briefly during a summer filled with long, sunny days—old traditions of preserving the prodigious bounty of summer berries that fill the forests have been passed down through the years. Berries such as lingonberries are preserved into a jam called *silt* that will then accompany savory dishes all year long, and an assortment of berries, including elderberries, raspberries, and black currants, are cooked down into a concentrated syrup that can later be reconstituted into a drink called *saft*. These traditions not only took full advantage of the indigenous plant foods that were available, but they supplied sweet and delicious flavors—as well as potent nutrients—to people, which helped to sustain them all year long.

Just consider how tough it was for early people to migrate from warmer southern climates with abundant, yearlong plant supplies to cold terrains that boasted only a brief growing season. They learned, through knowledge handed down by elders and local folk healers, that their bodies craved these plant foods. If they didn't eat them, their gums would swell, their teeth would fall out, their skin would become scaly, and their bones wouldn't form properly. You've no doubt heard about how scurvy was common among sixteenth-century sailors and pirates who braved long trips at sea without fresh fruits or vegetables in to eat. The captains of the ships soon learned to stock them with lemons, which seemed to cure scurvy, even though there was no medical understanding at that time that scurvy was caused by vitamin C deficiency. Indeed, the science of nutrition got its start when scientists started identifying nutrients in foods that humans needed in their diets to survive; if we don't get enough essential protein, fat, carbohydrates, vitamins, and minerals in our diets, we exhibit health problems from our nutrient deficiencies as a direct result. Fruits have long been an important part of the puzzle; humans have had a direct evolutionary relationship with fruits—as with other plant foods—since the first days we walked the earth.

Did you know that fruits such as berries seem to have a unique relationship with birds and humans? Scientists at the University of Rhode Island believe that the reason both birds and humans possess trichromatic vision—the ability to distinguish the color red from green—is that we evolved this trait in order to find the berries growing hidden among dense, green leafy vines and bushes. When birds and humans ate the berries, they helped to disperse the seeds and ensure the survival of the berry plants. The plant also placed powerful phytochemicals in berries' flesh that protected them from pests and environmental damage. These compounds also have a profound impact on humans: They appear to reduce the risk of diseases like cancer, heart disease, diabetes, and age-related mental decline. And that's just the story on one type of fruit. From lemons to apples and grapes to papaya, all fruits hold nutritional powers that can help you live a longer, healthier, leaner life.

It's no wonder that fruits, like apples, have been a symbol of seduction in the Bible, as well as in fairy tales. The botanical story of fruit is about as sexy as it gets. In essence, a fruit is the method by which a plant spreads its seeds in its ongoing quest to continue the species. Botanically speaking, a fruit is the part of a flowering plant derived from one or more ovaries—the female reproductive organ of the flower located at the base of the petals. When pollen is deposited on the stigma of the flower, the ova are fertilized and develop into seeds with a fleshy, edible layer that forms the fruit. If you've ever tended a watermelon plant, you've seen this story play out before your eyes: The first showy blossoms appear on the vines, signaling the bees to come do their job of pollination, which fertilizes the ovary at the base of the flower. Slowly, the tiny baby watermelon appears, then the flesh around the seeds plumps and grows into a large, sweet melon that tempts you to pick it, bite into it, and spit out its seeds. And the story continues from there, as the cycle renews itself. Plants that bear edible fruits coevolved in a mutually beneficial dance with animals and humans over the millennia. We dispersed their seeds as we ate the fruit, which helped the plant to grow anew; in return we gained valuable nutrients that we became dependent upon. The plants didn't need to produce the sweet, edible flesh around its seeds for its own direct benefit, but by evolving to produce such tantalizing fruit, they ensured that animals and humans would pluck them, eat the flesh, and spit out or defecate the seeds.

A BUSHEL OF NUTRIENTS

Every time you bite into a piece of fruit, you send a flood of powerful nutrients into your body that can impact your health favorably. Here are some nutritional highlights of fruits:

- **A Low-Fat, Low-Calorie Package.** Most fruits contain negligible amounts of fats and are low in calories. A small piece of whole fruit contains about 60 calories and a wide range of nutrients, depending on the variety.

- **Healthy Carbs.** Whole, unsweetened fruits contain healthy carbohydrates that come packed with fiber, which means you get a source of energy that will stick with you for a longer period of time. A small piece of fruit provides you with about 15 grams of carbohydrates, depending on the variety.

- **Fiber Treasures.** Fruits are treasure troves of all different types of fiber. A single large apple can boost your fiber intake by 5 grams (20% DV). You get most of that fiber in the fruit's protective, edible skin and any seeds that come along for the ride. You may not realize it, but when you eat some fruits, such as berries and kiwi, you're also eating the tiny seeds along with the flesh. Soluble fiber can be found in fruits like berries; pectin, a particular type of soluble fiber which has been linked to immune support, is found in apples and citrus. Insoluble fiber is high in the skin of many fruits such as grapes. Nondigestible oligosaccharides, resistant starches, insulin, and oligofructose are found in fruits such as bananas; and lignans are available in berries. Refer to chapter 4 to better understand the multitude of benefits you can gain from including all types of fiber in your diet.

- **Vital Vitamins.** The fruit food family provides a wide range of essential vitamins, including vitamins A, B$_6$, C, E, and K; riboflavin, thiamin, niacin, and pantothenic acid (see Nutrients in Action, page 393). In particular, many fresh fruits provide good sources of vitamin C—vitally important in many of your body's most important functions. For example, 80g of fresh guava provides you with a whopping 314% DV of vitamin C. You need vitamin C to promote a healthy immune function, to heal wounds, and to maintain bones, teeth, muscles, skin, ligaments, and blood vessels. It also acts as a powerful antioxidant to fight damaging free radicals that can lead to cancer and disease.[1]

- **Mineral Vaults.** You can also gain a supply of minerals, such as calcium, potassium, manganese, magnesium, and copper, by eating more fruits every day. Specifically, potassium—abundant in many fruits—can help balance out the negative effects on your blood pressure of eating too much sodium.[2]

- **Phytochemicals on Display.** Fruits are exceptionally high in phytochemicals that are stocked with antioxidant and anti-inflammatory properties and contribute specific health benefits, including heart health and protection against Alzheimer's disease. You'll find a range of powerful phytochemicals in fruits, from beta-carotenes in yellow-orange fruits to **anthocyanins** in blue-purple fruits to ellagic acid in red fruits. (See Phytochemicals Parade, page 110, to discover the variety of phytochemicals you can find in colorful fruits.)

HEALTH BENEFITS IN EVERY BITE

The powerful nutrients stored in fruits means that they offer you health protection in every bite. And all these nutrients—vitamins, minerals, antioxidants, fiber, and other bioactive compounds—appear to act in synergy, producing effects that are far greater than the sum of the compounds working individually. That's why scores of studies show that people who eat more fruits have a lower risk for developing many diseases, including the following:

- High blood pressure[3]
- Heart disease[4]
- Stroke[5]
- Certain cancers, such as mouth, throat, voice box, esophagus, stomach, colorectal, and lung[6]
- Degenerative eye disease[7]
- Type 2 diabetes[8]
- Obesity, by improving satiety[9]
- Neurodegenerative diseases, such as Alzheimer's[10]
- Diverticulitis, through improved digestive health[11]
- Chronic obstructive pulmonary disease (COPD)[12]

POWERFUL FRUITS YOU CAN REALLY SINK YOUR TEETH INTO

From tiny huckleberries to plump pineapples, all fruits contain exciting health-protective potential. In the world of whole fruits, there are no bad choices, but some are special superstars in the world of researchers. Just maintain a cautious eye on exotic so-called "superfruits," such as acai, mangosteen, and baobob. Although these fruits are certainly nutritious and rich in antioxidants, many people have been taken advantage of by unscrupulous Web-based companies that promise miraculous benefits, such as curing cancer and instant weight loss, if you take their expensive daily drinks and supplements. Yet there's little evidence to support many of the hopeful claims made by such companies. Sure, there's nothing wrong with enjoying acai and mangosteen, but don't forget to eat from a whole rainbow—and alphabet—of fruits that come from closer to home, and for a fraction of the price. Get started with these super favorites, from A to C, and don't stop there!

- **An Apple a Day.** It looks like that advice might ring true after all. A slew of studies have documented just how beneficial it is to include more apples in your diet. These plump, crisp beauties cultivated and eaten around the world are filled with a class of phytochemicals called phenolic compounds that have strong antioxidant activities. In particular, quercetin, the primary phenolic in apples, has been linked with slowing down the digestion of carbohydrates and improving blood glucose control.[13] Apples are also rich in a soluble fiber called pectin, which can lower blood cholesterol and thus offers potential protection against heart disease.[14] The fiber and phenolic compounds may work together to help control your appetite: One study found that if you eat an apple fifteen minutes before your meal you'll eat 15 percent fewer calories.[15] And apple nutrients bolster your gastrointestinal tract with healthy bacteria to promote digestive health and immune function. Apples have even been singled out for their potential protection against lung cancer as well as asthma.[16]

  Most of the apple's phenolic compounds are located in the skin, where they work as a natural sunscreen for the apple, which, it turns out, is particularly sensitive to sun exposure. Depending on the color of the skin, apple peels contain different phytochemicals; red apples contain powerful anthocyanins, for example. Scientists have observed that apples that are exposed to more stress have even higher levels of polyphenolic compounds.[17] This theory applies all over the plant kingdom; winemakers know that when grapes have to struggle on the vine, they contain more bioactive compounds, which results in more complex, flavorful wines. It may be that an imperfect, wrinkled up organic apple may have more phenolic compounds than a perfect, polished apple that was pampered with plenty of water, synthetic fertilizers, and pesticides to protect it. After all, it's the struggle for survival that spurred the polyphenol defense system to develop in the first place.

- **Berry Beautiful.** I spent one hot summer as a teen picking strawberries for cash. We had an arrangement: I could eat all I wanted in the field for free and then I was paid for how many flats of strawberries I could fill. Every day, I came home gorged on strawberries—their sticky sweet smell on my hands, face, and hair. And I had few earnings to speak of because I ate more strawberries then I harvested for the poor farmer!

There's definitely something irresistible about the small, jewel-like berries of North America, which include blackberries, black raspberries, blueberries, cranberries, red raspberries, and strawberries. Over the past decade, a cascade of research studies have shown that these antioxidant-rich fruits have a profound impact on health, lowering the risks of chronic diseases such as cancer, cardiovascular disease, diabetes, and age-related mental decline. Navindra Seeram, a University of Rhode Island scientist, has observed that in nature animals naturally gravitate toward berries. Some birds trade their bug diets for berries right before the enormous physical demands of migration, and bears tend to load up on them prior to hibernation. Maybe they intuit something we have only recently confirmed: Berries offer protection against the damaging effects of physical stress on the body.

High in fiber, potassium, and vitamin C, berries also contain polyphenols—a group of phytochemicals that include anthocyanins, procyanidins, and ellagitannins—the compounds responsible for the red, blue, and purple colors you find in berries. Scientists believe that these compounds may be at the root of berries' health benefits. It's becoming clear that when you eat berries, polyphenols move into body tissues, such as those of the brain, eye, and prostate, where they get to work reducing oxidation and inflammation and boosting immune response. One fascinating new study found that, if you consume a strawberry beverage with a high-fat, refined-carb breakfast, you can blunt the oxidative effects of the meal.[18] And research now confirms that cranberries can indeed help protect you against urinary tract infections.[19] The body of research showing the protective effects of berries on cognition, memory, and age-related mental decline coming out of the USDA Human Nutrition Research Center at Tufts University in Boston is so compelling, I eat berries every day in order to stack the odds in my favor.[20]

- **Citrus Delights.** What do oranges, grapefruit, lemons, and limes have in common? If you guessed high vitamin C content, you're right. Indeed, these citrus fruits are very rich in this important nutrient—just one large orange provides 163% DV of vitamin C. Perhaps that's one reason why citrus fruits are among the most popular fruits around the world. People have long treasured the zesty flavor and health appeal of oranges, tangerines, mandarins, lemons, and other citrus fruits. They've been celebrated in many traditional foods such as North African preserved lemons and Scottish marmalade, as well as in holiday customs, such as the Christmas tradition of stuffing an orange into a stocking dangling over the fireplace.

You'll find a bevy of important nutrients besides vitamin C in citrus fruits, including potassium, folate, calcium, thiamin, niacin, vitamin B_6, phosphorus, magnesium, copper, riboflavin, pantothenic acid, and fibers such as pectin and lignan. To top it off, more than 170 different phytochemicals have been identified in citrus fruits, including **monoterpenes**, **limonoids**, flavonoids, and carotenoids, which have documented antioxidant, anti-inflammatory, immune-boosting, and anticancer effects. A large proportion of the beneficial compounds in citrus fruits are found in the peel and inner white pulp, so drinking the juice won't give you the same benefits as eating the whole fruit. These powerful substances are behind the benefits seen with eating more citrus fruits, such as protection from heart disease, stroke, arthritis, asthma, Alzheimer's disease, cognitive decline, multiple sclerosis, age-related eye disease, ulcerative colitis, and diabetes. In particular, cancer protection seems promising; high citrus-fruit intake is linked with a 40 to 50 percent reduction in risk for several cancers, such as esophageal, larynx, mouth, and stomach.[21] It looks like you just found another reason to start your day with citrus.

THE WHOLE FRUIT AND NOTHING BUT THE FRUIT

Much of the nutritional power of fruit is packed in its protective outer skin and edible seeds. You're much better off eating a whole piece of fruit, skin and all, than a peeled fruit, pureed fruit, or—worse yet—fruit juice. Fruit juice is squeezed out of its nutrient-rich package into a concentrated liquid that's quickly absorbed into the bloodstream, spiking blood glucose and insulin levels. Did you know that it takes about two whole oranges to get a small glass of orange juice? It's easy to swig down a glass of OJ in the morning, but not so easy to wolf down two whole oranges. Drinking juice takes all of the chewing and fiber out of the equation, both of which slow consumption and increase satiety. We drink juice faster than we can eat fruit, and we feel less full afterward, which can be a concern if you're watching your weight or blood glucose levels. In addition, processing fruits into juices may reduce their vitamin C content, which can be lost in oxidation. A fresh apple will fill you up and leave you more satisfied than the same amount of calories in the form of applesauce, apple purée, or even apple juice with added fiber.[22] Try to make most of your fruit choices as whole and as close to nature as you can. Check out this example of how an apple's nutritional value progressively deteriorates with each step of processing.

THE APPLE, FOUR DEGREES OF SEPARATION

	FRESH APPLE WITH SKIN (SMALL, 149 G)	FRESH APPLE, PEELED (SMALL, 132 G)	APPLE PURÉE, UNSWEETENED (125ML)	APPLE JUICE, UNSWEETENED (125ML)
Calories	77	63	51	57
Carbohydrates	21 g	17 g	14 g	14 g
Fiber	4 g	2 g	2 g	0 g
Vitamin C	11% DV	9% DV	2% DV	2% DV

Source: Information from USDA National Nutrient Database for Standard Reference, http://ndb.nal.usda.gov

DV = Daily Value, nutritional requirements according to the Food and Drug Administration, based on 2,000 calories per day; g = grams

A whole world of fruits awaits your discovery. These naturally sweet plant foods can add a delicious, nutritious touch to your day. Fruits not only provide you with powerful nutrients, but they can satisfy that sweet tooth of yours. Try to include a serving of fruit at every meal as your dessert and add an additional serving as a snack to meet your suggested three to four servings each day. Check out the following Plant-Powered Fruits Guide, which lists commonly available fruits along with their "star nutrients." Remember, there are many varieties of fruits beyond the standard staples like Fuji apples and navel oranges. Did you know that there are more than 7,500 different kinds of apples? For example, Arkansas Black apples bear a bruised-purple-colored skin, and My Jewel is a California apple with a banana flavor. You may find unusual varieties at some supermarkets and natural food stores, but you've also simply got to visit your local farmers market or join a CSA and check out the spectrum of fruits that Mother Nature has to offer in your region in season (see Experience Your Local Farmers Market, below). And remember—as with all plant foods—choose a diverse selection of fruits to maximize your enjoyment of their flavor and optimize their nutritional value.

EXPERIENCE YOUR LOCAL FARMERS MARKET

Your local farmers market is where fruits really happen—as well as vegetables, legumes, nuts, and seeds. Grab a canvas bag, walk down the aisles, and let the kaleidoscope of vibrant colors and mélange of earthy aromas wash over you. You will find seasonal vegetables in unusual varieties, such as carrots ranging from pale yellow to purple, with their spry tops still attached and earth still clinging to their roots. And you will discover ripe fruits such as nectarines, plums, and peaches, which can be difficult to find in some supermarkets, where fruits are often picked unripe and shipped over long distances and long periods before they sit in neat rows under bright lights. That's one of the main benefits of farmers markets: The produce is often picked fresh and perfectly ripe that morning by the very farmer who is waiting on you. You can ask the farmer about how the crops are grown—from the use of fertilizers to strategies for pest control. You can take home the farmstead's favorite recipe for fresh strawberry preserves. You can have a relationship with the person who grows your food.

(continued on page 150)

PLANT-POWERED FRUITS GUIDE

FRUIT	SERVING SIZE	DESCRIPTION	CULINARY SUGGESTIONS	STAR NUTRIENTS* (AT LEAST 10% DV PER SERVING)
Apple	1 small	A member of the rose family, the skin of this fruit comes in shades of red, green, or yellow, and the juicy flesh boasts a refreshing, sweet flavor.	Eat fresh, bake into desserts and breads (see Corn Muffins with Apples and Walnuts, page 352), and accompany savory dishes such as soups and stews. Available preserved as dried apples, apple purée and juice.	Fiber, vitamin C
Apricots	2	This small **stone fruit** bears smooth to fuzzy skin and sweet, juicy flesh in shades of yellow to orange to red.	Delicious fresh as a snack or sliced into cereals, yogurts,' and smoothies. Use in desserts and baked goods. Also available canned, as nectar, dried, or preserved as jam.	Vitamins A and C
Banana	1 small	This tropical fruit comes in its own packaging—a thick yellow peel that, when removed, reveals sweet, creamy white flesh. Also comes in less common colors, like red, pink, purple, and black.	Delicious fresh as a snack or sliced into yogurt' or cereal (see my recipe for Banana Peach Yogurt Parfait, page 362), blended into smoothies, and baked in desserts and breads.	Fiber, vitamins B$_6$ and C, potassium, manganese
Blackberries	70g	Grown on canes, this aggregate fruit shows off a deep black-purple color and a sweet delicious flavor.	Enjoy fresh in cereals and salads or include in puddings, fruit desserts (see Country Berry Cobbler, page 363), and other baked goods. Also available preserved as jam.	Fiber, vitamins C and K, manganese

FRUIT	SERVING SIZE	DESCRIPTION	CULINARY SUGGESTIONS	STAR NUTRIENTS* (AT LEAST 10% DV PER SERVING)
Blueberries	75g	Sweet, blue-purple berries produced by a flowering perennial plant that grows in North America.	Enjoy fresh to top cereal or yogurt,† puree into smoothies (see Blueberry Banana Power Smoothie, page 358), and include in baked desserts or breads, such as pancakes and muffins. Also available frozen, dried, and preserved as jam.	Vitamins C and K, manganese
Boysenberries	75g	A cross between a European raspberry, a common blackberry, and a loganberry, boysenberries have a deep maroon color and succulent flavor.	Eat fresh as a snack or include in baked desserts and breads. Also available frozen or preserved as jam.	Fiber, folate, manganese
Cantaloupe	80g	A relative of the gourd family, this melon has a round, light brown rind and firm orange flesh that is refreshing and fragrant.	Eat fresh as a snack or in salads or desserts (see Minted Cantaloupe with Blueberries, page 362).	Vitamins A and C
Cherries	70g	A sweet or tart stone fruit that comes in many different varieties that range from yellow to red to black in color.	Excellent eaten fresh as a snack. Also include in desserts, cereals (see Ruby Quinoa Breakfast Bowl, page 350), or breads. Available dried, frozen, or preserved as jam.	Vitamin C

FRUIT	SERVING SIZE	DESCRIPTION	CULINARY SUGGESTIONS	STAR NUTRIENTS* (AT LEAST 10% DV PER SERVING)
Cranberries	50g	A tart, deep red berry that grows in acidic bogs in the Northern hemisphere.	Typically made into juice, sauce, or relish or dried. Sprinkle over cereals, yogurt,' or salads (see Brussels Sprouts Slaw, page 294) or include in baked dessert and bread recipes.	Vitamin C
Dates	40g	A sweet, earthy fruit of varying size, texture, and color—from yellow to light or dark brown—produced by the date palm tree.	Delicious eaten fresh as a snack or sliced into cereals, yogurts,' or smoothies. Add to baked goods or desserts (see Date, Walnut, and Dark Chocolate Cookies, page 367).	Fiber
Figs	2 small	This ancient Mediterranean fruit grows on large trees and comes in several varieties that include golden, green, purple, and black colors.	Eat fresh as a snack or sliced into cereals (see Ancient Grain Porridge with Figs and Dates, page 349) or salads. Add to baked goods and desserts or sauté as an addition to savory dishes. Also available dried or preserved as jam.	Fiber
Grapefruit	½ medium	A large, round citrus fruit with yellow-orange skin and pink, white, or red flesh and a tart, acidic flavor.	Typically enjoyed fresh as is, but also excellent in salads (see Grapefruit and Avocado Ensalada, page 289) or desserts.	Vitamins A and C

FRUIT	SERVING SIZE	DESCRIPTION	CULINARY SUGGESTIONS	STAR NUTRIENTS* (AT LEAST 10% DV PER SERVING)
Grapes	16	A sweet, juicy perennial berry that grows on woody vines and is available in many varieties ranging from yellow and green to red and deep purple in color.	Excellent fresh as a snack or added to salads and desserts (see Rainbow Fruit Bowl with Orange Sauce, page 361). May also be enjoyed dried (as raisins) or as juice or wine.	Vitamins C and K
Guava	80g chopped	A small tropical fruit with a tough outer skin and sweet, fragrant white or pink flesh.	Enjoy fresh, sliced into salads or desserts, or blended into smoothies.	Fiber, vitamin C, folate, copper, potassium
Honeydew	⅛th melon	This round to oblong melon has a pale green, sweet, fragrant flesh.	Eat fresh as a snack or sliced into salads or desserts.	Vitamin C
Kiwifruit	1 medium	A small oblong fruit with rough brown skin and bright green, sweet flesh and tiny, black, edible seeds.	Excellent fresh as a snack, sliced into salads or desserts, or blended into smoothies.	Vitamins C and K
Lemon	1 medium	A bright yellow oblong citrus fruit with a sour, acidic flavor.	Use the juice, rind, and zest as a fragrant, tasty addition to salads (see Greek Salad with Rosemary-Lemon Tofu, page 294), vegetables, desserts, and baked goods.	Vitamin C
Lime	1 medium	A small green to yellow, round citrus fruit with a sour, acidic flavor.	May use the juice, rind, and zest to accent salads, vegetables, desserts, and baked goods. Commonly featured in Mexican or Southwestern foods.	Vitamin C

FRUIT	SERVING SIZE	DESCRIPTION	CULINARY SUGGESTIONS	STAR NUTRIENTS* (AT LEAST 10% DV PER SERVING)
Mango	80g chopped	A fleshy, sweet stone fruit with orange flesh common in tropical climates. Varies in size and skin color and bears a large inner pit.	Often used in Asian dishes, such as chutneys or fresh in salads (see Southwestern Black Bean, Quinoa, and Mango Medley, page 318), cereals, desserts, and smoothies. Also available dried or preserved as jam.	Vitamins A and C
Nectarine	1 medium	This smooth-skinned, round, yellowish-red fruit is part of the peach family.	Delicious served fresh, as a snack, sliced into cereals, yogurts,' or salads, or baked into desserts. Also available dried or preserved as jam.	Fiber, vitamin C
Orange	1 small	The most commonly grown tree fruit in the world, this round, juicy citrus fruit comes in many varieties.	Typically eaten fresh as a snack or as juice, it can also be added fresh to salads, desserts, and smoothies.	Vitamin C
Papaya	70g chopped	This tropical fruit, grown on a large tree-like plant, is available in red and yellow varieties. It boasts a soft, sweet flesh and edible seeds.	Enjoy fresh, sliced into cereals, salsas, dips, smoothies, or salads (see Curried Papaya Salad, page 291) or cook in curries. Also available dried.	Fiber, vitamins A and C

FRUIT	SERVING SIZE	DESCRIPTION	CULINARY SUGGESTIONS	STAR NUTRIENTS* (AT LEAST 10% DV PER SERVING)
Peach	1 medium	This fuzzy-skinned, round, yellowish orange stone fruit is available in many varieties. The flesh is juicy and sweet.	Excellent fresh, as a snack or sliced into cereals, yogurts,' and smoothies, or included in puddings, desserts, and baked goods (see Buckwheat Hazelnut Waffles with Ginger Peach Sauce, page 353). Available preserved in jams, canned and in dried forms.	Fiber, vitamins A and C, potassium
Pear	1 small	A relative of the apple, this fruit produces pale, gritted, sweet flesh encased in edible skin that varies in color from yellow to green to red.	Eat fresh as a snack or sliced over cereal, salads, and yogurts.' Pair with savory dishes, cook into a sauce, or bake into desserts (see Ginger Pear Crisp, page 364) and breads. Also available preserved in canned and dried forms.	Fiber, vitamin C
Persimmon	1 large	This small round or pumpkin-shaped fruit is typically a brilliant orange color—although green and black varieties exist—and contains sweet flesh that gets very soft as it ripens.	Enjoy fresh as a snack or sliced into cereals or salads. Include in desserts, baked goods, and breads.	Vitamin C
Pineapple	80g chopped	This large, sweet yellow fruit with rough brown skin is produced from a tropical plant with short stocky stems and rough waxy leaves.	Excellent eaten fresh, it may be sliced into salads, cereals, side dishes, desserts, smoothies, and salsas. It is also available canned, as juice, and dried.	Vitamin C and manganese

FRUIT	SERVING SIZE	DESCRIPTION	CULINARY SUGGESTIONS	STAR NUTRIENTS* (AT LEAST 10% DV PER SERVING)
Plum	1 large	A small round stone fruit with a waxy, tart skin and sweet soft flesh, this fruit comes in a variety of colors ranging from yellow to green to purple.	Delicious fresh as a snack or added to desserts. Also available dried (prunes) and preserved.	Vitamin C
Pomegranate	90g seeds	This large round fruit, technically a berry, has a thick reddish skin containing edible seeds covered in red, juicy flesh called arils.	Delicious fresh as a snack or added to cereals, yogurt,† or salads (see Beetroot and Pomegranate Seed Salad, page 297). Also available as juice.	Fiber, vitamins C and K
Raspberries	60g	This sweet, delicate fruit grows on canes and comes in several varieties, including yellow, red, purple and black colors.	Use fresh as a snack, to top cereals, yogurt,† or pudding, or to add to salads, smoothies, and spreads. Include in desserts and baked goods. Also available frozen, dried, and preserved as jam.	Fiber, vitamin C, manganese
Star fruit	1 medium	Also called carambola, this fruit has ridges running down five sides, forming a star shape when the fruit is sliced. Encased in a yellow, waxy skin, the flesh is bright and sweet.	Eat fresh, as a snack, or sliced into salads, fruit trays, and desserts.	Fiber, vitamin C

FRUIT	SERVING SIZE	DESCRIPTION	CULINARY SUGGESTIONS	STAR NUTRIENTS* (AT LEAST 10% DV PER SERVING)
Strawberries	80g	This popular bright red, heart-shaped fruit grows from small, low plants. Its characteristic aroma and flavor makes it a popular food additive around the world.	Enjoy fresh, as a snack (try Summer Fruit Skewers with Strawberry Dip, page 360), or sliced into cereals, salads, or smoothies. Include in puddings, pies, and frozen desserts. Available frozen and pre-served as jam.	Vitamin C, manganese
Watermelon	75g chopped	This large round melon usually has a smooth, thick, green-striped rind and red, sweet, juicy flesh, but there are more than 1,200 different varieties displaying various colors and sizes.	Typically eaten fresh as a snack, it may also be sliced into salads (see Watermelon Peppercorn Salad, page 288) and included in smoothies and frozen desserts.	Vitamin C

Source: Information from USDA National Nutrient Database for Standard Reference, http://ndb.nal.usda.gov

DV = Daily Value, nutritional requirements according to the Food and Drug Administration, based on 2,000 calories per day

*Refer to my Nutrients in Action appendix on page 393 to learn how these nutrients contribute to overall health.

†May choose dairy yogurt (omnivore and vegetarian plans) or plant-based yogurts.

BEYOND FRESH: PRESERVED PRODUCE IS PRECIOUS

YOU MIGHT BE convinced that the only way to eat fruits and vegetables at their best is when they are fresh. Sure, fresh produce might win taste tests, but preserved fruits and vegetables—whether they are frozen, canned, or dried—can be every bit as nutritious. Although vitamin C and the vitamin B group may be lost in the preserving process, some other nutrients fare better by being preserved. For example, the important tomato antioxidant lycopene, which has been linked with heart health and prostate cancer protection, is more available to your body when it's cooked, as it is in canned tomato products.[23]

Consider the fact that when you see fresh fruits and vegetables out of season in your supermarket, they may have been picked unripe and shipped from distant places, thus minimizing their potential nutrient content, as well as increasing the use of resources such as the fossil fuels required to transport them. Today's renaissance of canning and preserving fruits and vegetables takes its cue from the past, when people had to lay away their bountiful summer crops in order to make them last all winter long. So, honor the seasons and enjoy fresh produce during its peak, then turn to preserved fruits and vegetables when they are out of season.

Just remember to check the nutrition facts labels when choosing brands of preserved produce, as some canned, frozen, and dried fruits and vegetables may contain significant amounts of added salt and/or sugar. And keep portion size in mind when eating dried fruits, which have higher concentrations of calories and natural sugar than fresh fruits. 30g of dried fruit is roughly equivalent to 75g of fresh fruit.

Wondering where to find your nearest farmers market? Visit the U.S. Department of Agriculture's listing at http://apps.ams.usda.gov/FarmersMarkets. Keep in mind that farmers markets, which rely on seasonal produce available in a particular region, may establish varying schedules depending on your growing season. Although in the Southwest you can find farmers markets open year-round, they may be closed during the winter in other regions, such as the Midwest or Northeast.

There are so many reasons to scout out and shop at your farmers market; here are the most compelling:

- You'll enjoy delicious, ripe, nutrient-rich fruits and vegetables picked just hours ago. Studies show that ripe fruits and vegetables can contain more nutrients than unripe produce. Note that non-local fruits are often picked while unripe, to make them durable for shipping, so local fruits are a healthier choice.
- You will support a local food system in which food doesn't have to travel so far to get to your plate; thus, you'll reduce your carbon footprint.
- You and your household can eat more organic produce, which is widely available at many farmers markets. (See page 126 for more on the benefits of organic produce.)
- You'll encourage farmers to grow heirloom varieties of fruits and vegetables that are facing extinction because people don't eat them very often. If you buy them, they will grow them. (See page 109 for more on heirloom produce.)
- You will keep your dollars in your local community where they can support small farmers and your surrounding economy.
- You'll get connected with how your food is grown. Bring your children or grandchildren along so they can learn—and taste—new experiences, too.
- You will discover the true season when each type of fruit and vegetable is fresh and at its best.
- You can try samples of new varieties of fruits and vegetables—then take them home and eat more health-protective produce!

MAKE THE MOST OF YOUR FARMERS MARKET EXPERIENCE

Wondering how to do the whole farmers market thing right? You're not the only one. That's why you see so many "window shoppers" taking in the lovely views of fresh produce but departing without any purchases. Here's how you can make the most of your experience.

1. Plot out the locations of the farmers market(s) in your community. Depending on your location, you may have several options during various times of the year. Try purchasing produce at the farmers market first and then visiting the supermarket or natural food store later in the week for your staples.

2. It's easy to overbuy at a farmers market, and if it doesn't get eaten that's a shame. Remember that the produce is usually ripe and it may not last as long as you're used to. Try to purchase only what you think you will prepare for your family during the week.

3. Consider the produce that is in season each week and the basic ingredients you will need for your menu before you shop.

4. Once you're home with your produce bounty, sort it and keep it fresh:
   - Rinse all leafy greens, pat dry, and store in containers in the refrigerator.
   - Refrigerate berries, but don't wash until just before serving.
   - Sort out delicate or ripe fruits and vegetables that need to be eaten first, such as peaches, berries, tomatoes, lettuce, herbs, mushrooms, and avocados. Enjoy longer lasting produce, such as potatoes, squash, onions, apples, pears, carrots, and beetroot, later in the week.

5. Try these simple serving styles to showcase your lovely produce purchases:
   - Drizzle simple olive oil vinaigrette over greens, tomatoes, or avocados.
   - Prepare greens by boiling, steaming, or sautéing with a small amount of olive oil, herbs, and garlic.
   - Oven-roast vegetables in a shallow ovenproof dish with a drizzle of extra virgin olive oil or grill them. (Check out Grilled Vegetable Skewers, page 336.)

6. Make a big pot of farmers market vegetable soup with potatoes, summer squash, onions, mushrooms, carrots, and seasonal vegetables.
7. Bake a berry crisp or cobbler using your fresh fruit purchases. (Try Ginger Pear Crisp, page 364.)
8. If you end up with too much produce to use, share it with a friend, neighbor, or coworker.

CHECK OUT A CSA

Farmers markets aren't the only way you can enjoy farm-fresh, local, seasonal produce. Buying a share in a CSA offers yet another way to experience a better connection with delicious fruits and vegetables at the peak of their growing season. When you join a CSA (community supported agriculture) program, you are connecting with local farmers by purchasing a "share" of their bounty in the form of a box of produce. There are many variations on the CSA format. In some CSA programs, you sign up to get a weekly box of local produce with no control over what you will receive. The farmer chooses what to harvest and pack for you based on what is available and ripe that particular week, having planned the farm's planting schedule carefully to yield optimal variety within each week and over the course of the season. Thus, you might be forced to try kale for the first time or to find a purpose for a large bunch of dill that you would have passed up in the farmers market. In other CSA programs, you may have some choice as to what you will receive each week. CSA farms that also run a farm stand or sell at a farmers market might give you credit toward discounted purchases throughout the season. Many CSAs also offer flexibility so you can cancel your weekly order while you're on vacation. In my experience, the price for a weekly CSA box, overbrimming with fresh, seasonal produce, is a real bargain. And CSAs usually offer great tips and recipes for how to use your featured produce of the week. To determine which CSAs are available in your community, visit the Local Harvest Web site at localharvest.org/csa/.

A SWEET PROBLEM

I've given you plenty of incentives to crunch on more nutritious, delicious fruits every day. And now I'll give you one more: Naturally sweet

LOCO FOR LOCAL—MOST OF THE TIME

IF YOU HAVEN'T NOTICED, I'm a big fan of local foods. Foods that come from close to home are likely fresher, more nutritious, and tastier, and use up less fossil fuel to get to your plate than those shipped halfway across the country. Purchasing from farmers markets and CSAs is one way to support the local food movement. And even supermarkets and natural food stores are getting in on the local produce act, offering more and more fruits and vegetables grown on nearby farms. But sometimes local isn't the best choice. For example, if you're buying local berries grown in a heated greenhouse, they may not be any less resource intensive than those trucked in from an outdoor farm further afield. And while I applaud locavores who eat from only a 100-mile radius from home, I believe that there are many plant foods that may not be cultivated in your community because of geographic or climatic concerns but are extremely important to your health. Nuts, avocados, citrus fruit, olives, spices, soy, and quinoa may not grow in your region, but I sure hope that you don't exclude them from your diet. Here's my rule of thumb for local eating: Eat local sources of whatever is available in your community, and buy whole, unprocessed staples such as grains, nuts, spices, olive oil, and legumes from your favorite supermarket or natural food store to fill in the gaps.

fruits can help you cut back your dependency on sugar. Americans have recently been called on the carpet for eating way too much of the crystalline stuff. The adult consumption of added sugars has been on the rise: Between 1970 and 2005, the average annual availability of added sugars increased by 19 percent, and in effect this has added an average of 76 calories to each American's daily calorie intake since the '80s—this can add up to about 8 pounds (4kg) a year of weight gain. Today, an average of 16 percent of the total calories in American diets come from added sugars, from sources like soda, energy drinks, and sports drinks (composing 36% of our added-sugar intake), grain-based desserts (13%), sugar-sweetened fruit drinks (10%), dairy-based desserts (6%), and candy (6%). As you can see, most of these added sugars don't come from the sugar bowl at home: They are added to foods during processing and preparation, and they're in the prepared foods and beverages you buy at the grocery store and in restaurants.[24]

ADDED SUGARS

MOST OF THE added sugars in our diets come from prepared and processed foods and beverages. Here are some forms of "added sugar" in the foods you eat.

Corn syrup

Corn syrup solids

High fructose corn syrup

Anhydrous dextrose

Crystal dextrose

Fructose sweetener

Liquid fructose

What's wrong with eating so much sugar? The American Heart Association (AHA) recently issued a scientific statement urging Americans to reduce their sugar intake because it can help prevent obesity and cardiovascular disease. When you eat foods with lots of added sugars, you're just getting extra calories with no nutrients in return, which can lead to weight gain and its disease-related fallout. Of special concern is sugar in beverages: Studies indicate that when you ingest extra calories in beverages as opposed to in other foods, you don't compensate by cutting back on calories later in the day, which can easily add up to extra pounds. In fact, many health experts place much of the blame for our obesity problem—especially in children—on the surplus of calories we're guzzling in sugary beverages. According to the AHA statement, evidence links excessive sugar intake with several metabolic abnormalities and adverse health conditions, as well as overconsumption of calories and shortfalls of essential nutrients. Thus, they recommend an upper limit for daily added-sugar intake: no more than 100 calories (25 grams, or about 6 teaspoons) for women and 150 calories (38 grams, or about 9 teaspoons) for men.[25]

You shouldn't worry about ridding your diet of every single gram of added sugar, but it's certainly a good idea to cut back significantly. Start reading the food labels to discover how much sugar is added to your favorite cereals, condiments, snacks, yogurts, and desserts—I guarantee you'll be shocked. Purchase foods such as granola and yogurt without added sugar, and add your own fruit or small amounts of your favorite sweetener. One thing's for sure: The food company will always add more sugar to a food item than will a health-minded consumer.

SWEET ALTERNATIVES

If you're seeking to cut back on empty calories from added sugars, there are plenty of nonnutritive (or low-calorie) sweeteners on the market, such as aspartame and sucralose. Check out my Low-Calorie Sweetener Glossary on the following page to learn more about popular sweeteners you'll find in the market.

Do low-calorie or artificial sweeteners really work to help you lose weight? There has been some conflicting research in this area. Some studies show that consuming artificial sweeteners in beverages can help you lower your calorie intake and lose weight, and some studies show that they don't work or even prompt people to gain weight.[26] There is some preliminary evidence that suggests your brain associates sweetness with energy, and when you provide your body with a sweet taste without any calories, your brain gets confused and doesn't produce its normal signals that control your eating behavior. And it's also an oft-observed human behavior that when people think they've been "good"—by drinking a diet soda, for example—they feel they can splurge on a brownie or a box of cookies, making up for the approximately 150 calories in a can of regular soda and then some. I advise against consuming large amounts of artificial sweeteners, as I advocate consuming real, whole foods that come as close to nature as possible. You're better off getting most of your sweetening power from real foods, such as fruits.

A LOW-CALORIE SWEETENER GLOSSARY

Here's the rundown on what puts the "sweet" in today's popular nonnutritive sweeteners.

- **Acesulfame Potassium.** Also known as acesulfame-K, this high-intensity sweetener is a potassium salt that is 200 times sweeter than table sugar. It was approved by the FDA in 1998, despite some studies that found that rats fed acesulfame-K developed tumors. However, a separate nine-month rat study found no evidence of carcinogenic activity.
- **Aspartame (Equal® and NutraSweet®).** Aspartame is made by linking the amino acid aspartic acid to another amino acid, phenylalanine. Gram per gram, aspartame has the same amount of calories as sugar, but because it is 200 times sweeter only a very small amount is needed. Since the FDA's approval of aspartame in 1981, this low-calorie sweetener has faced its share of criticism. However, claims of its carcinogenicity have not been proved. People with the rare condition phenylketonuria (PKU) can't metabolize phenylalanine and should avoid aspartame.
- **Polyols (erythritol, hydrogenated starch hydrolysates, isomalt, lactitol, maltitol, mannitol, sorbitol, xylitol).** Polyols (also known as sugar alcohols) are a group of low-calorie, carbohydrate-based sweeteners—some occurring naturally in fruits—that are lower in calories because the body only partially absorbs them. Even though polyols are considered safe, they can produce gastrointestinal effects like bloating, gas, and diarrhea.
- **Saccharin (Sweet'N Low®).** Discovered over a century ago, saccharin is a synthetic artificial sweetener that is 300 times sweeter than sugar. Studies in the 1970s linked it to bladder cancer in rats, but some scientists concluded that these findings weren't relevant to humans because of the difference in the physiology of the rats' urinary system. Saccharin was removed from the U.S. National Toxicology Program's Report on Carcinogens in 2000.
- **Stevia (Truvia® and PureVia™).** Stevia, or rebiana, is an extract of rebaudioside A, a sweet steviol glycoside found in the leaves of

the stevia plant. This naturally occurring sweetener is about 200 times sweeter than sugar. In 2008, the FDA allowed stevia to be used as a sweetener. Although some concerns exist over studies that show high doses may cause mutations that could lead to cancer, stevia has been used safely in other countries for the past few decades.

- **Sucralose (Splenda®).** Created by replacing three hydrogen-oxygen groups on a sucrose molecule with three chlorine atoms, sucralose is a noncaloric sweetener 600 times sweeter than table sugar. Research has not revealed any significant health concerns for sucralose, approved by the FDA in 1998.

ADDED SUGARS THAT GIVE BACK A LITTLE

It's nearly impossible to completely rid your diet of added sugars, so a better question might be which ones should be your "go-to" sweeteners. I tend to favor those that come as close to nature as possible, such as honey and maple syrup, over highly processed cane sugar and high fructose corn syrup. In fact, these natural sweeteners may even have some health rebates, according to recent research. But that's not to say that you should dump these added sugars into your foods willy-nilly—as with all sweeteners, use them sparingly.

- **Honey.** The world's original sweetener, honey has long been prized as a valuable food—and "medicine"—by humans over the centuries. And today, modern science confirms that honey has many intriguing health possibilities. How do honeybees create this delectable confection we know as honey? It all starts with a colony of up to 80,000 bees that live together in a beehive. The bees collect nectar from plants in their mouths where it mixes with enzymes in their saliva. They carry back their precious cargo and deposit it into cells in walls of the beehive for future use. The fluttering of their wings reduces the moisture content of the honey. The bees from a colony may collectively visit more than two million flowers in order to make 500g of honey. Many vegans consider honey to be an animal product and avoid consuming it on ethical grounds. Studies show, however, that there are potential benefits linked with honey, such as anti-inflammatory, anticancer, antibacterial, antioxidant, and immune-boosting properties.[27] These activities seem to originate from the phenolic compounds, such as ellagic acid, that come from the nectar in the plant.

- **Maple Syrup.** Maple syrup may be as all-American as apple pie, and now it looks like this natural sweetener is full of unique phytochemicals that may possess health benefits. Given that maple syrup is a minimally processed liquid that comes from plants— namely maple trees—this discovery shouldn't be surprising. The syrup is made by first tapping through the bark of the sugar maple, which is native to the Northeast region of North America, in late winter to early spring to collect a watery, colorless sap at the rate of about 10 to 20 gallons per tree per season. Then the sap is boiled down in order to concentrate the liquids; 40 gallons of sap

IS AGAVE A BETTER ALTERNATIVE TO SUGAR?

MADE FROM A SUCCULENT that grows in Mexico and is a cousin to tequila, agave nectar is today's hot alternative to sugar. While agave is often marketed as natural, its production takes a little more processing than meets the eye. To make the nectar, juice is collected from the core of the agave plant, which is then filtered and heated in order to break down the carbohydrates into sugars. The finished product is a sweet, syrup-like liquid that's a little more processed than honey, but not nearly as processed as high fructose corn syrup. The main sweetener in agave nectar is fructose (the same sugar found in fruit) because raw agave juice is rich in inulin, a complex form of fructose. Agave nectar has about the same number of calories as table sugar (16 calories per teaspoon), but it's sweeter, so less is needed. It's been widely promoted for its low-GI and potential blood sugar benefits: The GI for agave nectar is 20 to 30, in contrast to honey's 55, and table sugar's 68. However, there is no evidence to demonstrate that agave provides any specific benefits for blood glucose control.

will become 1 gallon of syrup. This process allows the syrup to take on its characteristic flavor, color, and odor. Among the phytochemicals found in maple syrup, phenolics dominate the bunch. Scientists recently identified fifty-three phenolic compounds in maple syrup, four of which were newly discovered compounds. The phytochemical profile of maple syrup looks promising—it's been linked with antioxidant and anti-inflammatory benefits that may offer protection against chronic diseases such as type 2 diabetes.[28]

WHOLE FRUIT: THE BEST SWEET ALTERNATIVE

Natural fruits can even *replace* added sugars in your favorite foods—from cereals and yogurt to breads and cookies. It's easy to stir bananas, berries, chopped dates, and dried fruit into your favorite recipes in order to cut back—or even cut out—sugar. Just think of fruits as sweeteners with benefits, since they add a naturally sweet taste to foods and contribute fiber, minerals, vitamins, and phytochemicals as a bonus. Check out the following Guide to Whole Fruits as Sweeteners to discover how to use whole fruits to replace refined sugar in your kitchen.

Even fruits have natural sugars in them that are broken down by your body into metabolic building blocks that can be used as energy. But remember that refined sugars produce that rapid, high rise in blood glucose we're trying to avoid, and most whole fruits produce a gradual rise in blood glucose that's healthier for your body. You can eat 23 grams of carbohydrates in a fresh pear, and it may take you a good five minutes to munch through its crunchy skin and flesh before it's all done. Or you can get those same 23 grams of carbs in the form of refined sugar in one and a half ropes of red licorice in about 30 seconds. Along with a variety of vitamins, minerals, and phytochemicals, the pear comes with 5 grams of fiber to help slow the release of glucose into your bloodstream and give you a sense of fullness. The licorice sends a quick burst of glucose into your bloodstream, leaving you hungry in no time and reaching for more.

GUIDE TO WHOLE FRUITS AS SWEETENERS

FRUITS	CULINARY SUGGESTIONS
Apple purée, unsweetened	Add to hot breakfast cereals, yogurt,* and smoothies; sweeten baked goods like cakes, breads, and soft cookies.'
Bananas	Slice over cereals and yogurt,* mix into smoothies, or use mashed to replace sugar in breads, cakes, puddings, and cookies.'
Berries (e.g., blackberries, blueberries, raspberries, strawberries)	Stir into cereals, yogurt,* puddings, smoothies, pies, and breads. Puree to make a topping for pancakes and desserts.
Dates	Chop and add to cookies, cakes, pies, and desserts to replace sugar. Puree and add to dressings, marinades, and smoothies.
Dried fruit, unsweetened (e.g., apricots, berries, cherries, figs, raisins)	Stir into cereal, yogurt,* granola, trail mix, puddings, pies, cookies, breads, and cakes. Don't forget about portion control!
Prunes, canned, unsweetened	Use in cereals and yogurt.* Puree to replace sugar in baked goods like pancakes, quick breads, cakes, and cookies.'

*May choose dairy yogurt (omnivore and vegetarian plans) or plant-based yogurts.

'In recipes, you may replace half of the required sugar with this fruit, and cut the liquid amount by 50ml.

MAKE ROOM FOR FRUIT!

Replacing sweeteners with fruit isn't the only way to get in those elusive three to four servings of fruits every day. Here are some more of my favorite fruit-forward tips:

1. **Start Out Your Day with Fruit.** And I'm not talking about OJ every morning! Top cooked cereal with berries, sprinkle raisins on plant-based yogurt, or slice a banana over toast. If you're on the run, grab a piece of fruit such as an apple, pear, or nectarine and munch on it in transit.

2. **Nature's Ultimate Snack.** You don't need to slice or bag up nature's perfect portable snacks—many of them come packaged

and "prewrapped" for you. Throw a piece of fruit such as a banana, peach, apricot, or orange into your handbag or briefcase for your afternoon snack.

3. **Whiz Up a Power Smoothie.** There are plenty of smoothie shops available that can blend up a delicious, fruity concoction, but many add lots of sugar to the recipe, pushing up the calories for your seemingly healthy snack. Try making your own smoothie at home sans the sugar by using my recipe for a Blueberry Banana Power Smoothie (see page 358).

4. **Put Fruit on the Dessert Menu.** Satisfy your sweet tooth after each meal with fruit—whether it's au natural or in a delicious fruity dessert, such as Summer Fruit Skewers with Strawberry Dip (see page 360).

5. **Hidden Rewards.** Use the natural sweetness of fruits to sweeten breads, cookies, and desserts while gaining a serving of antioxidant-rich fruit (try Buckwheat Hazelnut Waffles with Ginger Peach Sauce, page 353).

6. **Dried Fruit Munchies.** Pack a single-serving bag of dried fruit, such as apples, apricots, peaches, or pineapple, in your bag or briefcase for a healthy snack during the day.

7. **Wintertime Fruit Solutions.** When the summer season wanes, don't stop eating fruit—just turn to winter staples, such as apples or oranges, and unsweetened canned or dried fruits to top cereals and to enjoy as desserts and snacks.

8. **Salad Sensations.** I love the flavorful additions of fruits to salads— just look at some of my favorite salad recipes that call on the flavors of watermelon, cranberries, pomegranate, and papaya to pack pizzazz into an ordinary bed of salad greens (see page 288).

9. **Real Fruit Toppings.** Say good-bye to the fake fruits found in many food products, such as yogurts, cereals, breads, and desserts. Sure, the package may say its blueberry flavored, but read the ingredient list and you may discover there is only blueberry flavoring or a scant amount of real fruit in the mix. Instead, stir your own real fruit into plant-based yogurts, cereals, muffins, and desserts. Try making a Banana Peach Yogurt Parfait (page 362) for starters.

10. **Savory Additions.** Fruits are also delicious additions to savory meals. Try pears or apples with fall side dishes or soups (such as

Celeriac and Apple Bisque, page 282); citrus fruit as marinades for tofu, mixed into stir-fries, or whisked into salad dressings; and tropical fruits such as papaya or mango in chutneys or curries.

11. **Feature a Fruit Basket.** The most beautiful dining room décor in the world is one that is edible. Fill a basket with beautiful, seasonal fruit for your dining room table and watch it disappear. Your family will grab it on the go, slice it over their morning cereal, and munch it as a snack or dessert—I guarantee it.

DAILY PLANT-POWERED FRUIT GUIDE

SERVING SIZES*	PLANT-POWERED VEGAN	PLANT-POWERED VEGETARIAN	PLANT-POWERED OMNIVORE
1 small apple, pear, banana, or orange 75g cup fresh or frozen berries or chopped fruit 125g canned, unsweetened fruit 30g dried fruit 125ml unsweetened juice	3–4 servings	3–4 servings	3–4 servings

Sources: See Chapter 1, note 3 (page 369), and Chapter 3, notes 16 and 18 (pages 373–74).

Servings are based on a daily intake of 1,500 to 2,500 calories, which is the appropriate range for weight loss and weight maintenance for most adults, depending on age, sex, and activity level.

*Please see the Plant-Powered Fruits Guide (page 141) for additional information on serving size.

"I began making serious changes in my diet in 1995 with my second diagnosis of breast cancer. The trick was to make changes that would give me the most bang for the buck to improve the odds for my long-term survival after cancer, plus improve my overall health and wellness. I first increased my fruit and vegetable intake from five to nine a day, every day, and began creating

my power-packed smoothies and being more intentional about including organic foods in my diet. I first became a near vegetarian, and then a near vegan, but for the past four to five years I have started adding back small amounts of organic, locally raised animal foods into my diet. My diet is still predominantly plant based, with daily intake of beans, legumes, whole grains, nuts, and seeds as my main protein sources, and nine-plus servings of produce daily. As I felt like I got my health under control, I was able to see a larger picture of how healthy soil is connected to healthy food, which is connected to healthy people and communities. I am considered 'cancer-free' as of today, though my oncologist told me much later that he had not expected me to be cancer-free at two years past my diagnosis based on the aggressive characteristics of my second breast cancer tumor. Within the first year, I also saw my weight gradually drop by ten pounds, my total cholesterol drop 50 points, and my fasting blood sugars drop from high normal to normal, and I had much more energy than I did after my first breast cancer diagnosis."

—DIANA, a plant-powered omnivore in Ann Arbor, Michigan

"I went from being a meat-and-potatoes Irish gal to vegan. It started with concerns about my health after coming home from Europe. I saw the chemicals in our beef and decided that if France didn't want our meat, neither did I. Now I realize that being vegan is the most important thing I can do for the planet and the legacy of my family. I am tired of burying people in their 50s due to heart disease. I'm over 50, but people never believe my age and think my skin is so young. I have more energy than the teens I work with, am running my first marathon, and find it so hard to explain to people what it feels like to be healthy every day. The society as a whole is shifting."

—MARTY, a plant-powered vegan in East Stroudsburg,
Pennsylvania

❧ PLANT-POWERED ACTION ALERT **DAY 8**

Buy three varieties of local, seasonal fruit at the supermarket, natural food store, or farmers market and put them on your menu. Eat at least three to four servings of unsweetened, whole fruit every day.

❧ PLANT-POWERED ACTION ALERT **DAY 9**

Try substituting whole fruit for added sugar in your favorite dessert recipe.

Plant
Fats Rule

A few decades ago we were
ushered into the "fat phobia" era. Everyone was afraid of fats—they were
thought to be responsible for making you fat, as well as prompting diseases
like cancer and heart disease. In reality, the scientific evidence didn't bear
this out. Research back then showed that replacing saturated fats found in
animal foods with unsaturated fats found in plant foods reduced the risk
of heart disease, but somehow the simplified advice that trickled down to
the public was "cut fat intake"—end of story. Soon the "eating fat makes
you fat" myth took hold, and the food industry created low-fat everything,
from pastries to crackers. The food manufacturers skimmed off the fat in
their formulations and dumped in refined carbs like white flour and sugar
to fill in the flavor gaps. People started reaching for the low-fat versions of
foods more often, patting themselves on the back for making a "healthy"
decision. And since the low-fat food was "healthy," why not eat the whole
box? This low-fat, high-refined-carb craze helped to propel the emerging
obesity epidemic.

This fear of fat turned out to be dead wrong. Now we know that it's not
so much the *amount* of total fat that clogs your arteries; it's the *type* of fat

you choose. Hundreds of studies have pointed out two important facts: (1) Animal fats that are high in saturated fatty acids can raise your blood lipids and increase your risk for heart disease. (2) Healthy polyunsaturated and monounsaturated fatty acids found in plant foods like nuts, seeds, avocados, and olives lower your blood lipids, which decreases your risk for heart disease.

The moral of the story? Make peace with fats—especially the healthy ones that come from plants. An adequate amount of fats in your diet is essential for normal health; these fats can help you absorb certain vitamins and phytochemicals more easily, increase your sense of fullness at meals in order to promote a stable weight, make your foods taste delicious, and even lower your risk for heart disease. One of the most intriguing—and delicious—facets of the traditional Mediterranean diet, linked with myriad health benefits, is its rather generous allotment of healthy, plant-based fats such as olive oil in the diet. It may be one of the chief reasons why this plant-based traditional diet offers so many health-protective advantages.

An optimal fat lineup is another one of the many rewards you'll receive from taking on a plant-powered diet. When you reduce your animal foods intake, you automatically cut down on the saturated fats and dietary cholesterol found in these foods. And when you boost your plant food intake, including sources of plant fats such as avocado, nuts, seeds, and olives, you gain supplies of unsaturated fats that come perfectly outfitted in a nutrient-rich package —with protein, vitamins, minerals, fiber, and phytochemicals that offer their own unique bioactive benefits. (Refer to the Plant-Powered Protein List, page 46, to discover the nutrient contributions you can gain from nuts and seeds.)

However, it's still important to remember that an overabundance of even healthy fats can wreak havoc on your weight. Fats are very dense in calories—one teaspoon of oil contains 4.5 grams of fat and 40 calories—so a small amount goes a long way. If you overdo your fat intake, you can end up consuming large amounts of calories that can push your weight up, which can bring on a number of health-related problems. So go ahead and cut back on saturated fats in favor of unsaturated plant fats, but remember to go easy on even the good stuff if you're watching your weight.

A PRIMER ON FATS

Here's a fresh look at what the latest research tells us about how various types of dietary fat and cholesterol impact our health.

- **Total Fat.** Dietary fats are a class of nutrients that include specific fatty acids such as **polyunsaturated fatty acids (PUFAs) and monounsaturated fatty acids (MUFAs).** Even though it's been well established that you shouldn't worry too much about lowering your total dietary fat intake for the sake of direct disease prevention, remember that keeping total fat intake in line is a key factor in maintaining calorie and weight balance, your first line of defense against developing chronic diseases. This is because fat contains nine calories per gram, in contrast to carbohydrates and protein, which contain four calories per gram. That's why 30g of nuts—rich in PUFAs and MUFAs—contains about 180 calories, but 30g of raisins, made up primarily of carbohydrates, contains about half that amount. Although science has yet to establish the perfect ratio of fat, carbohydrates, and protein that leads to the most successful weight loss, there is evidence that dietary patterns that are nutrient-rich and low in caloric density—namely diets high in vegetables, fruit, whole grains, and legumes and relatively low in total fat and added sugars—are linked with healthy body weight.

  Bottom Line: Aim for about 20 to 35 percent of your total calories from fat, which adds up to 44 to 78 grams a day for the average person. The emphasis should be on the *type* of fats you choose most often; PUFAs and MUFAs should be your top priority.[1]

- **Saturated Fat.** Found in animal foods such as meat, poultry, and full-fat dairy products like milk, cheese, yogurt, cream, ice cream, and butter and tropical oils such as coconut, palm, and palm kernel oil, saturated fats are the dangerous fats you want to limit (see Fifteen Top Saturated Fat Sources in the American Diet, page 170). There is strong evidence that saturated fats are associated with increased total and LDL ("bad") cholesterol, type 2 diabetes, risk of cardiovascular disease, and **insulin resistance**.

  Bottom Line: Keep your saturated fat intake below 10 percent of your total calories—that's 22 grams for the average person. Try to gradually bring this amount even lower—to below 7 percent of total calories or 16 grams of saturated fat—for optimal health effects.[2]

- **Monounsaturated Fats and Polyunsaturated Fats.** Compelling evidence indicates that if you reduce saturated fats in your diet and replace those calories with unsaturated fats like MUFAs or PUFAs, you can decrease your risks of cardiovascular disease and type 2 diabetes because these fats improve your blood cholesterol levels and the responsiveness of insulin in your body. MUFAs are found in food sources like avocados, peanut butter, nuts, seeds, olives, and canola, peanut, sunflower, and sesame oils. PUFAs are found in nuts, seeds, and vegetable oils such as safflower, corn, sunflower, soy, and cottonseed.

  Bottom Line: The majority of your fats should come in the form of MUFAs and PUFAs. If you're limiting your saturated fat intake to 7 percent of your total calories as recommended, it means you have room to spend 13 to 28 percent of your calorie budget on healthy unsaturated fats—that's 29 to 62 grams of fat per day for the average person. Check out the Plant-Powered Fats Guide (page 172) to see how plant fats stack up.[3]

- **Omega-3 Fatty Acids.** There's little debate that omega-3 fatty acids, a type of PUFA, fit into the healthy fat category. They have been shown to reduce inflammation, lower blood lipid levels and blood pressure, and reduce the risk of heart attacks and sudden death for people with coronary heart disease. And there's growing evidence that they may even protect the brain from neurodegenerative diseases like Alzheimer's, as well as help in the management of type 2 diabetes, depression, and arthritis. Types of omega-3 fatty acids from foods include alpha-linolenic acid (ALA) from plant foods like flax, soy, and walnuts and eicosapentaenoic acid (EPA) and docosahexaenoic acid (DHA) from seafood sources, such as salmon and herring. Although researchers have discovered heart health and immune-function benefits from plant omega-3s, most of the science showing omega-3 benefits has been pinned to EPA and DHA found in fish and fish oil. Keep in mind that your body can convert ALA into EPA and DHA, though at very low levels. Some evidence suggests that the Western diet's high ratio of **omega-6 fatty acids**—found abundantly in processed vegetable oils like soybean, corn, and safflower—to omega-3 fatty acids decreases the conversion rate of ALA into EPA/DHA, because they both compete for the same metabolic pathways. It is thought that the early human diet had a 1:1 ratio of omega-6s to omega-3s, but today in the United States it's more like 10:1 to 30:1, due to the flood of refined vegetable oils—primarily soybean oil—in our overly processed diets.

Bottom Line: If you're a plant-powered omnivore, devote most of your animal food servings to seafood (about two 115g servings per week) in order to get an average intake of 250 milligrams of combined EPA and DHA per day, and also include plant-based omega-3 fatty acids in your diet every day. The American Heart Association recommends 1 gram of combined EPA and DHA for people with documented coronary heart disease. If you're a plant-powered vegetarian or vegan, make sure you get plant sources of omega-3 fatty acids in your diet (see the Plant-Powered Fats Guide, page 172), and keep your levels of omega-6s under control by avoiding highly processed foods that contain high levels of these fats, such as crisps, snack foods, fried foods, and baked goods. Keep in mind that marine algae is a good, plant-based source of EPA and DHA—that's what fish feed on that boosts their omega-3s in the first place—and marine-algae EPA/DHA supplements are available. Just be sure to consult your health care provider to discuss whether supplements are right for you, and avoid taking very high dosages (more than 3 grams per day) which may cause bleeding in some people.[4]

- **Dietary Cholesterol.** Although it's technically not a fat, dietary cholesterol found in animal products such as egg yolks, dairy products, and meats can still have an impact on blood lipids and therefore can boost your risk for heart disease. If you're a plant-based vegan, your diet will be free of dietary cholesterol, as it's only found in animal foods. If you're a plant-based vegetarian or omnivore, you can rest a little easier about your egg intake these days. Although eggs were once bashed for their high cholesterol levels, clinical trials now suggest that eating one egg a day is not linked with a higher risk of coronary heart disease or stroke in healthy adults. However, if you're at high risk for heart disease or diabetes due to family history or preconditions like extra weight or high cholesterol levels, you may need to cut back a little more on eggs and other animal foods to achieve a stricter target of low dietary cholesterol intake.

Bottom Line: Aim for less than 300 milligrams of cholesterol per day if you're healthy and less than 200 milligrams per day if you are at high risk for cardiovascular disease or type 2 diabetes.[5]

- **Trans Fatty Acids.** There's little disagreement that artificial trans fats serve no benefit in our diet. Now we know that they are linked with poor blood lipid profiles and increased risk of cardiovascular

FIFTEEN TOP SATURATED FAT SOURCES IN THE AMERICAN DIET

RANKING	FOOD ITEM	CONTRIBUTION TO SATURATED FAT INTAKE
1	Cheese, full fat	8.5%
2	Pizza	5.9%
3	Grain-based desserts such as cakes, cookies, pies, cobblers, sweet rolls, pastries, and doughnuts	5.8%
4	Dairy desserts, including ice cream, frozen yogurt, sherbet, milk shakes, and pudding	5.6%
5	Chicken and chicken dishes	5.5%
6	Sausage, franks, bacon, and ribs	4.9%
7	Burgers	4.4%
8	Mexican dishes	4.1%
9	Beef and beef dishes	4.1%
10	Milk, reduced fat*	3.9%
11	Pasta and pasta dishes	3.7%
12	Milk, whole	3.4%
13	Eggs and egg dishes	3.2%
14	Candy	3.1%
15	Butter	2.9%

Source: See Chapter 7, note 6 (page 382).

*Contains less saturated fat than whole milk, but because people consume more of it, it is a greater source of fat in the diet.

disease. Produced by a manufactured process of partially hydrogenating PUFAs so that they become more solid, trans fats were first
developed to replace the saturated fats in products like margarine,
snacks, baked goods, and fried foods when they fell out of fashion.

Thanks to the high-profile media coverage on the dangers of
trans fats, most of them have been removed from the food supply.
However, significant amounts of trans fats are still hiding in some
processed and prepared foods. When a single serving contains less
than 0.5 grams of trans fats per serving, food companies can list
the amount of trans fats as "0 grams" on the package. Obviously, all
those small amounts can add up if you're eating several servings a
day. The only way you can know that a food has a small amount of
trans fats is to read the ingredients list and see if it lists "partially
hydrogenated oil"—this is the calling card for trans fats.

Bottom Line. Eliminate industrial trans fats from your diet altogether by reading food labels carefully and making sure your favorite restaurants do not use partially hydrogenated oils in cooking.[7]

TURNING TO WHOLE PLANT FATS

How do you introduce healthy plant fats into your diet? Instead of always
relying on highly processed, refined oils and margarine spreads, which
are generally stripped of their fiber, vitamins, minerals, and phytochemical compounds, turn to whole plant fats such as those listed in the Plant-
Powered Fats Guide. These whole plant sources of fats offer maximum
health benefits beyond their healthy fat profiles, due to the rich assortment
of nutrients, fiber, and phytochemicals they contain. A number of studies
have found benefits from including nuts in the diet, such as heart health,
bone health, cancer prevention, improved cognitive function, and diabetes
prevention and treatment. And avocados are rich in MUFAs, vitamins B_6,
C, E, and K, folate, potassium, magnesium, fiber, and carotenoid antioxidants, which have been linked with protection against certain cancers, heart
disease, and age-related eye disease.[8]

Take a look at the powerful plant foods on the following page to see how
their fats are lined up in your favor, remembering to focus more on the *kinds*
of fats included than on the total quantity, choosing more of the fats in the
shaded columns when possible.

PLANT-POWERED FATS GUIDE

PLANT FAT	SERVING SIZE	CALORIES	TOTAL FAT	SAT FAT	MUFAs	PUFAs	OMEGA-3 FA (ALA)
Almond butter	1 tbsp	101	10 g	1 g	6 g	2 g	68 mg
Almonds	1 oz	169	15 g	1 g	10 g	4 g	2 mg
Avocado	¼	81	7 g	1 g	5 g	1 g	55 mg
Brazil nuts	1 oz	185	19 g	4 g	7 g	6 g	5 mg
Cashews	1 oz	155	12 g	2 g	7 g	2 g	17 mg
Chia seeds	1 oz	137	9 g	1 g	1 g	7 g	4,915 mg
Flaxseeds	1 oz	150	12 g	1 g	2 g	8 g	6,388 mg
Hazelnuts	1 oz	181	18 g	1 g	13 g	2 g	17 mg
Hemp seeds, shelled	1 oz	160	12 g	1 g	1 g	9 g	2,264 mg
Macadamia nuts	1 oz	203	22 g	3 g	17 g	0 g	55 mg
Olives, ripe, canned	1 oz	32	3 g	0 g	2 g	0 g	18 mg
Peanut butter	1 tbsp	94	8 g	1 g	4 g	2 g	13 mg
Peanuts	1 oz	164	14 g	2 g	7 g	4 g	1 mg
Pecans	1 oz	199	21 g	2 g	12 g	6 g	278 mg
Pine nuts	1 oz	190	19 g	1 g	5 g	10 g	32 mg
Pistachios	1 oz	157	13 g	2 g	7 g	4 g	72 mg
Pumpkin seeds (pepitas), hulled	1 oz	153	13 g	3 g	4 g	6 g	51 mg
Sesame seeds	1 oz	160	14 g	2 g	5 g	6 g	105 mg
Sunflower seed butter	1 tbsp	93	8 g	1 g	2 g	5 g	11 mg
Sunflower seeds, hulled	1 oz	163	14 g	2 g	3 g	9 g	19 mg
Walnuts	1 oz	185	18 g	2 g	3 g	13 g	2,565 mg

Source: Data from USDA National Nutrient Database for Standard Reference, http://ndb.nal.usda.gov

Sat Fat = saturated fat, MUFAs = monounsaturated fatty acids, PUFAs = polyunsaturated fatty acids, FA = fatty acids, ALA = alpha-linolenic acid, tbsp = tablespoon, oz = ounce, g = gram, mg = milligram

You can simply eat these plant foods whole as nature intended them: Munch on a handful of nuts or seeds as a snack or part of your meal; stir nuts, seeds, avocados, and olives into salads, stir-fries, side dishes, and entrées; or spread nut butters or mashed avocado on your sandwich instead of refined margarine spreads. You can even replace refined oils and fats in some of your favorite recipes—from quick breads and desserts to savory sauces and dips—with nut butters, ground seeds, and mashed avocado. (Check out my recipe for Spiced Banana Avocado Bread, page 351, and see how you can replace refined oils with avocado in baking.) My Whole Plant Fats in the Kitchen guide will show you how to let the nutritional power of delicious, whole plant fats shine in your favorite foods.

WHOLE PLANT FATS IN THE KITCHEN

WHOLE PLANT FATS	CULINARY SUGGESTIONS
Avocados	Use mashed as a dip, salad dressing, spread on bread, and to replace the fat in baked goods. Slice into sandwiches, wraps, burritos (see Bean and Grilled Veggie Burritos, page 300), and salads.
Olives	Used finely chopped as a spread on breads and crackers (i.e., tapenade), a dip for vegetables, and an ingredient in entrées, side dishes, salads (see Nicoise-Style Salad, page 295), pasta dishes, and breads.
Peanuts and peanut butter	Use peanut butter as a spread on bread, wraps, or crackers; as a dip for vegetables; and an ingredient in sauces, dressings, marinades, and Asian dishes. Use peanuts in salads (see Chinese Cabbage Slaw, page 289), side dishes, stir-fries, breads, baked goods, and cereals.
Seeds (sesame, sunflower, flax, chia, pumpkin, hemp) and seed butters	Use seed butter as a spread for breads, wraps, and sandwiches; in dips for crackers and vegetables (see Home-Style Hummus, page 276); and as an ingredient in sauces, dips, dressings, and Asian dishes. Use whole seeds in salads, side dishes, stir-fries, baked goods, yogurt,* and cereals.
Tree nuts and tree nut butters (almonds, brazil nuts, cashews, hazelnuts, macadamias, pecans, pine nuts, pistachios, walnuts)	Use nut butter as a spread on bread, wraps (see Cherry Sunflower Seed Wraps, page 301), or crackers; as a dip for vegetables; and as an ingredient in sauces, vinaigrettes, marinades, and Asian dishes. Use nuts in salads, side dishes, pasta dishes, stir-fries, breads, baked goods, yogurt,* and cereals.

*Note: Plant-powered vegetarian and omnivore meal plans may include yogurt; plant-powered vegan meal plans may include plant-based yogurts.

OLIVE OIL: NUMBER ONE IN THE KITCHEN

It's all well and good to include more nuts and seeds in your diet, but you still need suitable plant fat alternatives that will work in cooking and in dressings and marinades. The plant oil that you should reach for most often is extra virgin olive oil, the least refined plant oil of the bunch, which contains healthy MUFAs and powerful antioxidants. Extra virgin olive oil is made up of high levels of oleic acid, a type of MUFA that has been linked with lower rates of heart disease and chronic diseases, as well as several antioxidant compounds, including polyphenols such as **tyrosol** and **oleuropein,** as well as vitamin E. And scientists have identified a compound in newly pressed, extra virgin olive oil called **oleocanthal**, which is responsible for that pungent, stinging sensation you get in the back of your throat when you taste a good olive oil. It turns out that oleocanthal can decrease inflammation levels in your body in the same way that nonsteroidal anti-inflammatory drugs (NSAIDs) such as ibuprofen can.[9] Studies have also found that when you include moderate amounts of fat, such as olive oil, in the preparation of vegetables, certain phytochemicals such as carotenoids are more available to your body.[10]

Olive oil's beneficial health properties are nothing new. It enjoys a long history as a health tonic. From rubbing it into the skin for a beauty treatment to sipping it for pain relief, olive oil has been part of traditional folk medicine for centuries. Although olives originated in Asia Minor around 6,000 BC, the Romans were largely responsible for spreading the olive tree through the Mediterranean, where it has been a key part of the traditional Mediterranean diet for the past 5,000 years or more. About four decades ago, scientists noticed that extra virgin olive oil in the Mediterranean diet was linked with lower rates of heart disease, and since then many studies have confirmed this observation. Olive oil also has been linked with breast cancer protection and insulin sensitivity.

Best of all, olive oil makes foods taste fabulous. A drizzle over tomatoes, in your sauté pan, or over a tender salad adds a world of robust flavor. In fact, scientists found that people will eat more vegetables when they are cooked in small amounts of olive oil than when cooked plain. Try my Mediterranean-Style Sautéed Vegetables to discover a culinary style that can transform your vegetables from boring to magnificent. Make sure you use *extra virgin* olive oil, as many of these noted health benefits have not been found in the more refined forms of olive oil. And don't use a heavy hand with the olive oil bottle—just a teaspoon or less per serving will do in many cases. If you pour on a big glug of olive oil over your pasta or veggies, you could be adding over 400 calories to your meal! Most of the recipes in the Plant-Powered Recipe Collection in chapter 14 use small amounts of olive oil to achieve maximum flavor.

MEDITERRANEAN-STYLE SAUTÉED VEGETABLES

BOILED, STEAMED, OR microwaved veggies can be so boring. Cook them the Mediterranean way, with the help of a hint of extra virgin olive oil to bring out their maximum flavor potential. You can use this technique to cook up any vegetable, from spinach to mushrooms to green beans.

MAKES 2 SERVINGS

1 teaspoon extra virgin olive oil

2 cups fresh or frozen vegetable (or a combination of vegetables)

3 tablespoons water

Preferred seasonings, such as fresh minced garlic or ginger, herbs, black pepper, or lemon juice

1. Heat the extra virgin olive oil in a sauté pan over medium heat. Add the vegetables, water, and seasonings.
2. Sauté over medium heat until the vegetables are crisp-tender. (Note: Some firmer vegetables may require additional water while cooking to avoid sticking.)

LIVING WITH EVERYDAY FATS

Your mission is to choose whole plant fats such as nuts, seeds, and avocados first, and turn to olive oil as your preferred cooking and preparation fat. But what about all your other culinary needs, such as buttering toast or baking cookies? Here's a rundown on your best fat choices:

- **Butter.** Although this animal source of fat, produced from nothing but cream and sometimes salt, is about as natural as it gets, it's relatively high in saturated fat: one tablespoon contains 100 calories, 11 grams fat, and 7 grams saturated fat. If you're a plant-powered vegetarian or omnivore, you should try to keep your intake of this animal fat as low as possible. Of course, plant-powered vegans already exclude animal foods like butter from their diets.

- **Margarine Spreads.** Made as an alternative to butter, this completely manufactured product is composed of highly processed oils. A slew of different margarine spreads are available today, with various ingredients, such as olive oil and flaxseed oil, as well as different formulations of fat. In the past, soft margarine spreads typically contained trans fats, but most have now removed trans fats from the lineup. However, some may contain amounts of partially hydrogenated oils small enough to be listed as "0 grams trans fats" on the label. If margarine spreads are a must for you, then keep your portions modest; stick to soft spreads that contain more liquid oil and thus have lower saturated fat content and better overall fat profiles; and look for products that contain no partially hydrogenated oils.

- **Stick Margarines and Shortening.** In order to obtain their solid texture, the formulation of stick margarines and shortening usually relies on partially hydrogenated oils, which provide trans fats, and/or hydrogenated oils, which provide saturated fats. These solid products can contain up to 3 grams of trans fat and/or saturated fat per serving, so try to avoid using them in your everyday diet.

- **Liquid Vegetable Oils.** I encourage you to use extra virgin olive oil as your first choice of liquid vegetable oils, but I know that sometimes its peppery, olivey flavor just doesn't suit a particular recipe. You can turn to other vegetable oils, such as those in the Plant Oils Fat Breakdown (see page 178), as an alternative. I favor canola oil as a neutral-flavored oil with a high-MUFA profile. You can also experiment with oils such as walnut oil in baking (try my recipe for Country Berry Cobbler on page 363, which features walnut oil), or sesame or peanut oil in Asian stir-fries. Just remember to keep your portions petite.

- **Palm Oil.** When trans fats became the "bad fat on the block," palm oil became the savior of the food industry. In order to provide the texture and quality consumers had come to expect in their baked and snack goods, a more solid, saturated fat was in demand. Thus, food manufacturers turned to palm oil, which is now ubiquitous in many of the prepared foods on store shelves—just turn over the label and read for yourself. So, how does palm oil rate healthwise? According to the American Heart Association, palm oil is high in saturated fats (about 50% saturated), and therefore they suggest avoiding it. Yet preliminary research suggests that "virgin," or red, palm oil, one of the earliest plant oils cultivated by humans, may protect the heart from oxidative stress because it contains carotenoids, **tocopherols**, tocotrienols, and lycopene antioxidants.[11] More research is needed to clarify the role of palm oil in human health. And it's also important to consider that the palm oil industry has faced criticism for destroying tropical rain forests in Asia to cultivate palm.[12] For now, it's probably wise to keep your palm oil intake to a moderate level within your saturated fat targets for optimal health. And don't get palm oil mixed up with palm kernel oil, which should be limited even more because it's made up of about 80 percent saturated fat.

- **Coconut Oil.** It seems like we've been going through a coconut craze in recent years; coconut is everywhere, from coconut butter to coconut water. Even though some people sip coconut oil as a medicinal cocktail, the evidence isn't quite there to support coconut's health advantages. The truth is that coconut oil is very high in saturated fats; about 86 percent of its total fat is saturated. Yet, controversy swirls around whether coconut oil is a "healthy" fat. Researchers in Asia, where coconut oil is widely consumed, share both sides of the debate. Although no significant evidence of deleterious health effects has been found in Asian countries that have relied for decades on coconut oil—which has saturated fatty acids different from animal fats—increasing rates of metabolic syndrome, diabetes, and obesity have been observed in populations like India's, where coconut oil intake is on the rise. Preliminary research indicates that coconut oil may have anti-inflammatory properties, but there's no proof that it can prevent cancer or diabetes, as some Web sites claim. I suggest you approach coconut oil with caution and use it within your saturated fat budget, if you choose to use it at all. And remember: You can get plenty of anti-inflammatory properties in fruits, vegetables, grains, and legumes that don't come packed with saturated fat.

In the Plant Oils Fat Breakdown table below, notice how popular plant oils stack up in terms of their fat profile. Remember to focus on oils with higher percentages of the shaded fats and lower percentages of saturated fat.

PLANT OILS FAT BREAKDOWN

PLANT OIL	SATURATED FAT	MUFAs	PUFAs
Canola oil	7%	63%	30%
Coconut oil	86%	7%	7%
Corn oil	14%	28%	58%
Cottonseed oil	28%	19%	53%
Olive oil	14%	75%	11%
Palm oil	51%	40%	9%
Peanut oil	19%	48%	33%
Safflower oil	7%	14%	79%
Soybean oil	16%	23%	61%
Sunflower oil	11%	20%	69%

Source: USDA National Nutrient Database for Standard Reference, http://ndb.nal.usda.gov.

MUFAs = monounsaturated fatty acids; PUFAs = polyunsaturated fatty acids

TEN TIPS FOR DISHING UP HEALTHY PLANT FATS THE RIGHT WAY

Get started including moderate amounts of healthy plant fats in your diet today with my top ten tips:

1. **Be careful with olive oil.** Sure, olive oil is the healthy plant fat you should choose most often, but that doesn't mean you should pour it onto your foods with abandon. Use a measuring spoon to portion it into your frying pan. If weight is a concern, shoot for no more than one teaspoon per serving. Try an oil mister, available in many kitchen shops, to mist your pan and favorite dishes with small amounts of olive oil.

2. **Replace fats with nut and seed butters.** In many recipes, such as quick breads, cookies, sauces, and side dishes, you can harness the flavor and nutrition of nuts and seeds by substituting refined fats, such as margarine and oils, with creamy nut butters, such as peanut butter, sunflower seed butter, or almond butter.

3. **Dress your salads right.** Instead of turning to bottled salad dressings, which are often full of added sugars, sodium, and saturated fats, dress your salads with a simple vinaigrette using a basic formula of one part extra virgin olive oil with two parts lemon juice or vinegar, plus herbs and spices as desired. Don't be afraid of using a modest amount of healthy fats on your salad: They've been shown to increase the absorption of nutrients present in your salad. Shoot for no more than one teaspoon of olive oil per serving.

4. **Make mayonnaise sense.** This popular condiment traditionally made with oil and eggs can be packed with calories and fat—"real" mayonnaise contains about 90 calories, 10 grams fat, and 1.5 grams saturated fat per tablespoon. Many brands of light mayonnaise contain at least half of those levels. Even Vegenaise, a plant-based mayonnaise product, contains a calorie and total fat profile similar to mayonnaise—thought it is lower in saturated fat and reduced fat versions are available. Today, some mayonnaise products boast olive oil in the mix, but double check the ingredients list to see how much of the fat content really comes

from olive oil. If you can't face a sandwich without mayonnaise, choose a "light" product that has an optimal fat lineup (low saturated fat and higher MUFAs and PUFAs), and remember to go easy on your portion size. Be especially mindful of the amount of mayonnaise you use in recipes, such as potato salad.

5. **Use avocados as fat.** Who needs refined oils and margarines when you can use whole avocado as your fat? If you're making a sandwich, skip the margarine and mayonnaise in lieu of a couple of slices of ripe avocado. Slice avocados onto your salad and drizzle with lemon juice instead of oil. Stir mashed avocado into quick breads such as muffins and cornbread instead of vegetable oil.

6. **Snack on nuts and seeds for healthy fats.** Munch on 30g (a small handful) of nuts or seeds a day as a protein- and nutrient-rich snack in order to reap the rewards of healthful plant fats.

7. **Do healthy stir-fries.** You don't need to fill the bottom of your wok or skillet with oil in order to stir-fry vegetables. Just a tablespoon will do for an entire family-size meal. Try some alternative oils to add more pizzazz to your stir-fry, such as sesame oil or peanut oil.

8. **Stir nuts and seeds into your cereals.** If you add a teaspoon of chia or hemp seeds or flaxseeds into your morning cereal, you're adding crunch, flavor, powerful nutrients, and a dose of healthy fats.

9. **Watch fats in processed foods.** From deep-fried onion rings and donuts to snack crackers and cookies, most processed and prepared foods come packed with fats—often the omega-6 variety—that can push up your total fat and calorie intake sky high and offset your omega-3 balance. You can find many lower-fat snack choices, such as baked crisps and reduced-fat crackers, but keep an eye on the food labels. Sometimes food products may contain added sugars and salts to make up for missing fat. Read the food label to see what kind of oils and fatty acid profiles are in your favorite food products before you drop them into your shopping cart. And remember: Keep highly processed foods to a minimum.

10. **Moderation is key.** Sure, MUFAs and PUFAs offer health-protective benefits, but only if you include them in a balanced

diet that promotes a healthy weight. If you start pouring on the vegetable oil in stir-fries, salads, pastas, and side-dishes; munching down a whole bag of nuts at a sitting; or including guacamole on every veggie burrito, you'll probably find yourself packing on a few pounds that won't do anything to help your health. Remember to keep your portions under control by checking out my Daily Plant-Powered Fat Guide, below.

DAILY PLANT-POWERED FAT GUIDE

SERVING SIZES	PLANT-POWERED VEGAN	PLANT-POWERED VEGETARIAN	PLANT-POWERED OMNIVORE
1 tablespoon vegetable oil, mayonnaise, or regular salad dressing 2 tablespoons light mayonnaise or salad dressing 23 olives ¼ avocado	1–3 servings*	1–3 servings*	1–2 servings*

Sources: See Chapter 1, note 3 (page 369), and Chapter 3, notes 16 and 18 (pages 373–74).

Servings are based on a daily intake of 1,500 to 2,500 calories, which is the appropriate range for weight loss and weight maintenance for most adults, depending on age, sex, and activity level.

*In addition to servings of nuts and seeds; see the Daily Whole Plant-Powered Protein Guide (page 77).

"I am eating meatless meals more often, and more whole grains and more beans—I'm eating them on most days of the week. I'm learning to like, prepare, and eat more vegetables, and make fruits and vegetables a part of every meal. I'm eating nuts as part of my meals, such as in salads, stir-fries, and pasta dishes. Health is a prime motivator for me that started more than 25 years ago. In recent years, realizing the benefit to the environment of eating less meat and less packaged food was an encouraging plus. I know that I have made a difference in my long-term health; my blood pressure and cholesterol remain excellent, and I have had less weight gain than many women my age experience. I also control

my grocery costs by not spending money on meat, processed snack foods, and soda. I set a goal of trying at least a few new recipes each month. I have a terrific, supportive family willing to try each new dish as a taste test and vote on whether to repeat or possibly change it. After years of clipping the winners, I now have several binders filled with healthy dishes I love."

—KAREN, a plant-powered omnivore in Jamestown, New York

"Initially I became vegetarian because it seemed to be something I could do on a personal level to help address world hunger issues. As time has gone by, I've become vegan for a combination of reasons—concern for animals, the environment, and worldwide food availability. I began eating more locally and seasonally due to concerns about the environment and to support local farmers. I feel better when I eat a whole-foods, plant-based diet. So far, I've avoided the high cholesterol that plagues many family members and I've been blessed with good health. Joining several CSAs has helped us to eat locally and seasonally, as has going to the farmers market and having a small garden."

—REED, a plant-powered vegan in Amherst, Massachusetts

PLANT-POWERED ACTION ALERT **DAY 10**

Try substituting a whole plant fat, such as nut butter or avocado, for refined oils in a favorite recipe today.

The Bold and the Beautiful:
Herbs, Spices, and Chocolate

That tingle on your tongue when you dip into a spicy salsa or that warm feeling you get when you walk into your mom's house when a pumpkin pie is baking in the oven—these moments just wouldn't be the same without the zip of herbs and spices. Since the beginning of time, people have cherished herbs and spices—parts of certain plants with particularly potent tastes and aromas—not only for their flavor but also to keep foods from spoiling and even for their health benefits, from soothing a sore throat to calming an upset stomach. A whole body of traditional medicine has risen out of little pinches of spices and herbs, which we now tend to relegate to our spice racks.

Plants—in particular herbs and spices—were the only form of medicine throughout much of human history. Folk healers passed down their knowledge of plant medicine over the generations, ever building on their knowledge about which herbs and spices proved the best treatment for specific ailments. In fact, the World Health Organization estimates that 80 percent of the world's population still uses such plants as their major source of medicine today. And now prestigious researchers are finding that these folk healers were right about the healing powers of spices and herbs, validating health benefits in modern research labs. Case in point: Research shows that ginger, historically used to improve digestion, among many other conditions, appears to be useful in treating nausea associated with travel sickness, chemotherapy, and morning sickness.[1]

Throughout history, spices and herbs were considered rare and precious, used not only for food and medicine, but in perfume, incense, and even embalming. In fact, they were used as currency, creating the early spice trade route that connected the exotic spices from the Far East through the Middle East, and into Europe, from which they eventually made it to the New World. Gradually, culinary styles cropped up in regions around the world that owed much of their unique flavor to these mighty plant flavorings. The world wouldn't know the pleasures of Moroccan couscous, classic French garlic soup, or Caribbean rice and beans without the culmination of regional food traditions based on herbs and spices.

ANTIOXIDANT MEDICINE CHEST

Not so long ago, my university nutrition education taught me that a bland diet, liberated from exciting spices and seasonings, was a calming diet for optimal health. And now we have come full circle to the realization that a spicier life can offer health rewards. Research now shows that flavorful herbs, generally considered to be the leaf of a plant such as basil or parsley, and spices, which include any other part of the plant, such as the buds, bark, roots, berries, seeds, or the stigmas of fruits, possess concentrated forms of antioxidants and anti-inflammatory, antimicrobial, anticancer, cholesterol-lowering, kidney- and liver-protective, and antiviral properties. We now know that some spices and herbs once thought to bring about gastric ulcers actually have antiulcer effects.[2] In every snip of green herbs and pinch of dried spice, you gain valuable sources of health-protective compounds that can stoke your diet with protection against a number of diseases, such as diabetes, heart disease, and Alzheimer's disease. You can significantly boost your total antioxidant intake when you include herbs and spices in your diet, according to new research.[3] Scientists analyzing more than 3,100 different foods found that culinary herbs and spices have the highest antioxidant content of all foods. For example, about a half teaspoon of cloves has a higher level of antioxidants than 80g of blueberries.[4] Studies also show that simply including herbs and spices in your salad dressing can pump up the volume of antioxidants in your salad.[5]

In the world of herbs and spices, these plants worked overtime to defend themselves from environmental threats and pests by putting this array of particularly powerful phytochemicals into their flesh. I couldn't help but think of this natural protective arsenal when I came face to face with it in my own organic kitchen garden. Because I live in the foothills of the San Gabriel Mountains bordering Los Angeles County, my backyard is home to a zoological treasure trove of critters, such as bears, mountain lions, deer, rattlesnakes, rabbits, bobcats, and coyotes. But the most destructive predator in my carefully plotted garden was the California ground squirrel, a stealthy little rodent that can scale over or burrow under any fence you might care to erect. The ground squirrels would clip down the tender shoots of my vegetable plants like a lawn mower, but they left one section of my garden completely untouched: the herb garden. Although the carrots, beetroot, lettuce, and green beans didn't stand a chance, my chives, oregano, coriander, and basil flourished. Those green herbs were packed with such powerful chemicals, the squirrely predators wanted nothing to do with them. My herbs were destined for survival. And when humans eat these herbs, it looks like we can gain protective benefits of our own.

It hasn't gone unnoticed that some countries have lower cancer rates compared to Western countries—at least, not by the National Cancer Institute. India enjoys the lowest risk of colorectal cancer in the world and has one of the lowest rates of Alzheimer's disease among adults aged 70 to 79—4.4 times lower than in the United States.[6] There are many intriguing characteristics in the Indian diet that might explain this protection, including a high rate of vegetarianism and high intake of a variety of plant foods, such as vegetables, whole grains, and legumes. But one diet feature in particular stands out: At the heart of the Indian diet is a veritable medicine chest of colorful, powerful herbs and spices, many of which have proven health benefits, including aniseed, bay leaf, black pepper, cardamom, chilies, cinnamon, clove, coriander, cumin, dill, fennel, fenugreek, garlic, ginger, mango powder, mint, mustard, nutmeg, onion seeds, parsley, poppy seeds, saffron, sesame seeds, tamarind, and turmeric. All these herbs and spices are essential in the creation of one of the most healthful, delectable cuisines on the planet. If you crave the spicy flavors of traditional Indian dishes like biryani (a rice dish), chole (chickpeas), dal (a dish made of lentils or beans), or bhaji (potato curry), you know what I'm talking about.

BEYOND ANTIOXIDANTS

Herbs and spices are not *just* about antioxidants; they contain other health properties, including anti-inflammatory compounds that can protect against the development of chronic diseases such as heart disease and cancer. Some spices and herbs provide similar effects as anti-inflammatory drugs, without any side effects. Remember, humans have been consuming these powerful plant foods—as whole foods, not as isolated supplements— safely for thousands of years. You can't say the same thing about drugs.

What's even more fascinating is that the antioxidant and anti-inflammatory effects of herbs and spices act synergistically; the benefits are magnified with the more varieties you throw into the mix. This makes sense—any good cook knows the power of using more than one herb or spice to flavor a rich dish. In many cuisines, spices are enjoyed in a mélange. For example, a sensational Indian curry dish may include up to twenty-nine spices—including turmeric, garlic, ginger, pepper, and coriander—all in one fragrant pot. And this practice has proved effective: Preliminary research shows that, when combined, curcumin from turmeric and piperine from black pepper work synergistically to decrease breast cancer stem cells.[7]

Spicing up your diet can even help you manage your weight. Research is starting to show that a zesty diet can make you feel more satisfied from eating smaller amounts and even give a slight boost to your metabolism. Scientists know that flavor-active compounds such as spices can modify your digestion, absorption of nutrients, and metabolism through activating special pathways in your body's cells.[8] This may be why studies show that when people consume spices, such as saffron, at a meal, they tend to eat less and lose weight.[9] And consuming red pepper—the spice that can make you break out into a sweat if you add too much to your chili—has been found to slightly raise the number of calories people burn.[10] But more research needs to occur in this area before we fully understand the contributions spices can make to weight control.

The good news on herbs and spices comes at an opportune time, because hot and bold on the dinner plate is in. More than ever, Americans are folding spicy, ethnic cuisine into their own food traditions. Half a century ago, the most exotic food at the dinner table might have been spaghetti, but today it's not unusual to dine on Mexican enchiladas or spicy Thai noodles any night of the week, with convenience versions of these entrées available at nearly every supermarket. Then again, despite America's love affair with flavorful foods, plenty of people find that "hot" spices, such as black or red pepper, do not agree with them for various reasons. If you are among them, I urge you to power up on the milder green herbs and spices such as cinnamon and nutmeg to add health-protective power to your meals.

TOP HERBS AND SPICES FOR HEALTH

There are a number of herbs and spices currently under investigation for health benefits, and I have included some of the most promising in the following list. It's important to note that much of the health research on spices and herbs is still in its infancy; so stay tuned as researchers further mine this field in order to elucidate the potential these plants hold to fight disease. Remember, spices—like all plant foods—offer no "silver bullet"; there's little proof that they cure conditions like cancer or Alzheimer's disease, even though some Web sites selling herb and spice supplements might suggest otherwise. Simply include these powerful plant foods in your diet to boost your natural defense system against disease:

1. **Turmeric, the Spice King.** Probably the most celebrated spice in the research world, turmeric is responsible for the characteristic yellow-gold hue in curry powder, popular in Indian cooking and traditional medicine for centuries. The spice, which comes from the rhizome of the turmeric plant, is packed with a polyphenol called curcumin that demonstrates antioxidant and anti-inflammatory activities. Studies have found that turmeric may protect against cancer, diabetes, heart disease, arthritis, and gastrointestinal problems.[11] Of particular interest is turmeric's potential in Alzheimer's disease protection. Scientists discovered that rodents fed curcumin experienced delayed accumulation of the protein fragments called **beta-amyloids** in the brain that is a hallmark in the development of Alzheimer's.[12] Not all studies have found a brain-protective effect for turmeric, and more research in this area is set to be published in coming years. Regardless, it certainly seems like a good idea to boost the color and flavor of your foods with turmeric.

2. **Beyond the Fields of Garlic.** Forget about guarding against vampires; there's some evidence that garlic may help protect you against

a real monster: heart disease. Folklore attributes a multitude of far-ranging health benefits to garlic—from wound healing to treating rheumatism—but modern studies show that this pungent bulb may have heart-healthy effects, such as lowering inflammation, oxidative stress, cholesterol levels, and blood pressure, as well as exhibiting anticlotting activity.[13] It turns out that this plant in the onion family contains bioactive substances including allicin, quercetin, and organosulfur compounds that may be behind its benefits. However, a recent National Institute of Health–funded clinical trial found that consumption of garlic did not successfully reduce cholesterol levels.

3. **Hot, Hot Pepper.** You can't beat the heat of peppers—red, black, or white—for their strong health effects. Red pepper is the dried fruit pod of the Capsicum family, which encompasses a number of spice forms, such as chili pepper, tabasco pepper, African chilies, paprika, and cayenne pepper. These spices all have one thing in common: They're a concentrated source of capsaicin, the powerful phytochemical that gives chiles their heat. Studies suggest that capsaicin has cancer-protective, anti-inflammatory, and pain-relieving effects.[14] On the other hand, black and white pepper both come from the small dried berry of the vine *Piper nigrum* and contain piperine, a bioactive compound linked with antioxidant, anti-inflammatory, and anticancer effects.[15]

4. **The Sweet Comfort of Cinnamon.** As comforting as grandma's apple pie, cinnamon—the dried inner bark of evergreen trees in the genus *Cinnamomum*—is one of our most beloved spices. But cinnamon has much more to offer than its trademark sweet aroma and flavor: It supplies antioxidant, anti-inflammatory, and antimicrobial effects. The most intriguing area of cinnamon research shows a potential blood-glucose– and insulin-regulating effect, due to cinnamon's polyphenols, which may act like insulin in the body. Studies have found modest improvements in lowering blood glucose among patients with type 2 diabetes.[16] Although it's too soon to know for sure whether it's a useful tool for diabetes management, it certainly doesn't hurt to sprinkle this sweet-smelling spice into your foods every day.

5. **Over the Moon for Oregano.** When you think about this aromatic, woodsy herb, Italian cuisine is probably the first thing that comes to mind. Indeed, many traditional Italian dishes, from lasagna to pasta sauce, owe their herbal qualities in large part to this green plant in the marjoram family. What you might not realize is that oregano, like many other fresh green herbs, boasts generous levels of phytochemicals that show antioxidant, anti-inflammatory, and anticancer activity. In one study, oregano had the highest antioxidant activity among twenty-seven culinary herbs and twelve medicinal herbs tested, ranking even higher than fruits and vegetables.[17] Oregano also possesses antimicrobial activity against common food pathogens like salmonella and *E. coli*, so alongside techniques like safe refrigeration and handwashing, eating it may contribute to food safety.[18]

6. **Soothing Ginger.** Ginger, the knobby root of a plant in the Zingiberaceae family, has an illustrious history as a traditional medicine going back at least 2,500 years. Now we know that this key flavoring in Asian foods contains a mixture of several hundred known compounds, including gingerols, beta-carotene, capsaicin, caffeic acid, curcumin, and salicylate that fuel its antioxidant, anti-inflammatory, anticancer, and antimicrobial effects.[19] Some studies have shown that ginger may be helpful in treating nausea associated with pregnancy with little risk of harm, as well as in treating motion sickness and chemotherapy-related nausea.[20]

7. **Cracking the Mysteries of Nutmeg.** Inside the apricotlike fruit of the nutmeg tree, which is in the genus *Myristica* and native to Indonesia, lies a seed which yields the enchanting spice nutmeg. We tend to think of nutmeg as the perfect accompaniment to pumpkin pie and gingerbread, but in fact it is used in many savory dishes in Greece, India, and Japan. Nutmeg displays antibacterial activity toward pathogens such as *E. coli*, and it's been linked with antidepressant activity.[21] But nutmeg lovers beware: 30–60g doses have been known to cause prolonged delirium.

8. **La Vie en Rosemary.** Native to the Mediterranean, this hardy green herb has been prized throughout history for its medicinal strengths. Rosemary's characteristic piney aroma and taste make it a popular

herb in Middle Eastern, Italian, French, and Spanish cuisine. Beyond flavor, rosemary has health potential based on antioxidant, anti-inflammatory, and antimicrobial activities linked to its polyphenol composition.[22] Animal studies have demonstrated that this fragrant herb has anticancer action and even aromatherapy effects linked to pain relief and mood improvement.[23]

9. **Ice, Cool Mint.** Mint is so much more than a fresh, aromatic herb featured in toothpaste and breath mints; powerful phenols are hidden in its leaves, and volatile compounds in its essential oil. The phenolic constituents of the leaves include rosmarinic acid and several flavonoids. The main volatile components of the essential oil of peppermint are menthol and menthone. For centuries, folk healers doled out mint to treat maladies such as colic and digestive disorders, and the ancient Romans scattered their homes with mint to freshen them. Now we know that mint has significant antimicrobial action against common food-borne pathogens, as well as antiviral, antioxidant, and antitumor actions. Some animal studies show a relaxation effect on gastrointestinal tissue and pain relief action from mint.[24]

10. **Deep Green Basil.** This freshly scented herb, made famous for its starring role in pesto, is a member of the mint family. Its historic use in traditional medicine still continues today; several countries, including Morocco, use basil as a medical plant to reduce cholesterol levels and the risk of heart disease. Bioactive compounds in basil include flavonoids, which seem to protect body cells against the damaging effects of oxidative stress. Indeed, basil has shown lipid-lowering potential, as well as anti-inflammatory, antibacterial, and anticancer activity, in preliminary research.[25]

11. **Sage Advice.** Legend has it that the silvery green herb we know as sage helps preserve memory; thus *sage* became a term for "wise man." This aromatic, woody herb in the genus *Salvia* is a staple seasoning in European as well as North American savory dishes. Three plant compounds—flavonoids, phenolic acids, and enzymes—come together in unison in the sage plant to create strong antioxidant and anti-inflammatory effects that help prevent damage to body cells. It's sage advice indeed to enjoy this herb, because folk healers have

been proved correct: Human studies show that sage may indeed enhance memory.[26]

12. **Crazy for Cloves.** Famous for its sweet, nutty aroma, this spice from the dried, nail-shaped flower buds of the evergreen *Syzygium aromaticum* is more than meets the nose. Cloves contain eugenol, an active compound that has been linked with prevention of certain types of cancer, inflammation, and toxicity from environmental pollutants, as well as antibacterial effects.[27]

13. **Nothing Ordinary About Vanilla.** One of the most popular flavorings in the world, vanilla originates from Mexico, where the Aztecs enjoyed it in a drink that they believed had magical health properties. Derived from dried, cured beans, or fruit pods, of the *Vanilla planifolia* plant—a member of the orchid family—vanilla offers its sweet-smelling fragrance and taste to many foods. And now scientists are beginning to discover that vanilla extract contains bioactive compounds that appear to be high in antioxidant activity.[28]

PLANT-POWERED HERBS AND SPICES CULINARY GUIDE

HERB OR SPICE	DESCRIPTION	CULINARY TIP
Allspice	This cured, unripe berry from a tropical evergreen tree releases sweet, nutty flavors and aromas in both whole and ground form.	Delicious in breads, desserts, cereals (see Ruby Quinoa Breakfast Bowl, page 350), and coffee, but it also pairs well with savory dishes, such as soups, sauces, grains, and vegetables.
Anise	Related to the parsley family, small, curved anise seeds are famous for their licorice scent and flavor.	Use to flavor breads, cakes, and cookies, or include in Indian and Middle Eastern stews.
Basil	This bright green leafy plant gives off a fresh, sweet, herbal taste and aroma.	Use in salads, appetizers (see Caprese-Style Tomatoes and Avocados, page 274), and side dishes, or enjoy in pesto over pasta and in sandwiches.

HERB OR SPICE	DESCRIPTION	CULINARY TIP
Bay leaf	These large leaves from the laurel tree lend a sharp, bitter taste.	A standby in soups, stews, and bean dishes (see New Orleans Red Beans and Rice, page 320), it's also good with grilled vegetables. Remember to discard the bay leaves, which have an unpleasant texture, before you serve the dish.
Caraway Seed	This seed from the parsley family has a tangy, sweet taste.	Traditionally used in rye breads, fruits, and cakes, caraway also accents cabbage dishes and soups.
Cardamom	Ground from a seed in the ginger family, this spice has a sweet, pungent flavor and smell.	Popular in Scandinavian baked breads and desserts, it's also good in coffee and Indian dishes and stars in the herb blend *garam masala* (see Cauliflower and Pea Curry, page 342).
Celery seed	This dried seed, which has a warm, slightly bitter flavor, is the very same seed that celery grows from.	Delicious in soups, potato dishes, salad dressings, and vegetable dishes.
Chervil	A lacy-leaved plant in the parsley family, this green herb has an anise-parsley flavor.	Use to flavor potatoes, grain pilafs, vinaigrettes, sauces, and sautéed vegetables.
Chives	These thin, hollow leaves from a plant in the onion family produce a garlic-onion bite.	Use to season baked potatoes, steamed whole grains, and salads, or serve as a colorful garnish.
Cinnamon	This dried, curled bark of a tree yields a sweet, woody flavor in both stick and ground forms.	Suits fruits, baked desserts (see Country Berry Cobbler, page 363), and breads, as well as Middle Eastern savory dishes.

HERB OR SPICE	DESCRIPTION	CULINARY TIP
Cloves	These nail-shaped dried buds offer a strong, sweet aroma and flavor in both whole and ground form.	Traditionally used in baked goods, breads, and fruits, it also pairs well with vegetable and bean dishes.
Coriander, leaf	A leaf of the young coriander plant, this herb offers a citrus-parsley flavor.	Use to season Southwestern, Thai, Indian, and Mexican foods (see South of the Border Taco Salad, page 292).
Coriander, seed	This seed from the cilantro plant has a mild, lemon-sage taste and aroma in ground or whole forms.	Accents fruits, baked goods, and breads, as well as chutneys, Mediterranean foods, and Asian dishes (see Bok Choy Seitan Pho, page 326).
Cumin	Ground or whole, this small seed offers a characteristic bitter yet warm flavor.	Good in Mexican, Indian, and Middle Eastern dishes, as well as with vegetables, and in chili (see Three-Bean Cowboy Chili, page 321).
Dill weed	This grassy, feathery plant yields a clean, pungent taste.	Traditionally served with Russian, German and Scandinavian foods, it also accents potato dishes, salads, and dips.
Fennel seed	Grayish oval seeds of the fennel plant offer a sweet, anise flavor and aroma.	Great in pasta (see Orzo with Tomatoes and Fennel Seed, page 306), grain, and vegetable dishes, as well as vinaigrettes.
Garlic	This bulb—available fresh, minced, or dried and granulated—provides a distinctive, earthy aroma and bite.	Suits a number of ethnic foods, such as South American, Asian, Indian, French, Italian, and Greek. Add to soups, pastas, marinades, dressings, grains, and vegetables (see Farmers Market Greens and Garlic Sauté, page 337).

HERB OR SPICE	DESCRIPTION	CULINARY TIP
Ginger	A root—available fresh, pickled, or minced and in dried or crystallized form—with a sweet, warm flavor and smell.	Popular in Asian and Indian sauces, stews and stir-fries, it also suits beverages and baked goods.
Marjoram	Ground or whole, this low-growing herb in the mint family lends a delicate, sweet quality.	Try it in stews, soups, potatoes, beans, grains, salads, and sauces.
Mint	This green herb provides a tangy, cool scent and taste.	Excellent in jams to suit savory dishes; in beverages, salads, and marinades; and with fruits.
Mustard seeds	Whether whole or ground, these seeds from the Brassica family offer a spicy kick.	Use to flavor sauces, vinaigrettes, potato salad, and soups. You can make your own mustard by grinding mustard seeds with a bit of vinegar and water.
Nutmeg	This ground spice lends a sweet, woodsy quality.	Traditional with fruits and in pies (see Apple Cranberry Tart Rustica, page 365), and baked goods, nutmeg also suits soups and vegetable dishes.
Oregano	Both whole and ground forms of this herb in the mint family supply a warm, woodsy aroma and taste.	Delicious in Italian and Mediterranean dishes (see Vegetable Medley Lasagna, page 307), it pairs with tomato, pasta, and grain dishes, as well as salads.
Parsley	A natural breath freshener, this green herb boasts a clean, fresh flavor.	Suits soups, pasta dishes, comfort foods (see Vegetable, Tofu, and Potato Pot Pie, page 333), salads, and sauces. Popular as a garnish for foods.

HERB OR SPICE	DESCRIPTION	CULINARY TIP
Pepper, black or white	Cracked, whole, or ground black or white pepper provides a sharp, hot flavor.	Seasons soups, stews, vegetable dishes, grains, pastas, beans, sauces, and salads (see Watermelon Peppercorn Salad, page 288).
Pepper, red	The catch-all term for all hot red pepper spices, such as cayenne, red pepper flakes, and paprika, which provide a strong, hot bite.	A little goes a long way in dishes such as beans (see Easy Kale and Broad Bean Ragout, page 315), chilis, curries, sauces, and marinades. A key ingredient in ethnic foods from Mexico, Thailand, and India, as well as Creole regions.
Poppy seeds	These dark, tiny seeds of the opium plant give off a nutty taste and smell.	Flavor breads, pancakes, muffins, cakes, cookies, and salad dressings, as well as noodle and vegetable dishes.
Rosemary	The needles of this herb produce an aromatic, piney quality.	Try it in vegetables (see Grilled Vegetable Skewers, page 336), salads, vinaigrettes, and pasta dishes.
Saffron	These precious red spice threads that impart a golden hue and earthy flavor and aroma are actually the stigmas of a crocus.	A small pinch flavors rice dishes (see Saffron Brown Basmati Rice, page 311), risotto, stews, and sauces, as well as breads.
Sage	These cottony leaves supply a warm, astringent flavor and aroma in both whole and ground forms.	Traditionally paired with savory meat dishes, sage also enhances grains, breads, dressings, soups, and pastas (see Butternut Squash Macaroni and "Cheese," page 308).

HERB OR SPICE	DESCRIPTION	CULINARY TIP
Tarragon	This green herb in the sunflower family provides a slightly bittersweet aroma and flavor.	Delicious in sauces and marinades, it also pairs with salads and bean dishes (see Slow-Cooked Butter Beans with Root Vegetables, page 317).
Thyme	Whether ground or whole, these tiny gray-green leaves contribute a slightly minty taste.	An ingredient in *herbes de Provence*, it's excellent in soups, tomato dishes, salads (see Nicoise-Style Salad, page 295), and vegetables.
Turmeric	The ground root boasts a bright orange-gold shade, as well as a bold, citrus-ginger flavor.	Essential in curry powder (see Curried Papaya Salad, page 291), it's most popular in Indian foods, but it can also flavor soups, beans, and vegetables.
Vanilla	Pure vanilla—with its sweet, perfumed taste and odor—comes from the long, green pods of a tropical orchid, which are cured and steeped in alcohol—unlike imitation vanilla, which is made with artificial flavoring.	Flavors beverages, plant-based dairy products, sauces, fruits, breads, and desserts (see Date, Walnut, and Dark Chocolate Cookies, page 367).

SPICE UP YOUR DIET RIGHT

Lend more spice appeal to your diet by upping your intake of flavorful, health-protective herbs and spices in your favorite foods. Check out my favorite tips:

1. Fresh herbs come first. Typically, fresh herbs and spices such as green herbs, garlic, and ginger have higher antioxidant content than dried or processed forms. For example, fresh garlic is one and a half times more powerful than dry garlic powder. So, keep bulbs of fresh garlic and roots of fresh ginger on hand. Place a fresh herb pot on your doorstep or kitchen window to keep these powerful ingredients on hand.

2. **Snip fresh herbs into everything.** Now that you've got a fresh herb pot at your beck and call, get out a pair of kitchen shears and snip herbs into everything: soups, stews, salads, dressings, pastas, beans, grains, vegetables, pizza, and sandwiches. Hint: Fresh herbs are best when you add them to a dish right before serving.

3. **Dried herbs and spices are good, too.** Just because fresh herbs may be more potent in some cases, that doesn't mean you should give up on dried alternatives. They are still packed with health-protective compounds. And some spices, such as mighty turmeric, are only available in their dry form. Remember that some whole spices, such as bay leaves and cinnamon sticks, are meant to provide aroma and flavor in a dish but then be removed before serving.

4. **Stock your medicine—I mean, spice—cabinet.** Try to accumulate all the different dried forms I suggest in Top Herbs and Spices for Health (page 187)—and even more varieties, if you feel up to it! Then you'll have them at your fingertips for use in everyday dishes.

5. **Use a heavy hand.** When you're using fresh green herbs, a spoonful is a little skimpy—instead, add basil, parsley, coriander, and chives by the handful. Even many dried herbs can be scooped by heaping spoonfuls into soups, vegetable and grain dishes, and stews. However, you may need to more carefully adjust the amount of hot spices such as black, white, or red pepper according to your tolerance and preference.

6. **Cut out sodium.** Take your favorite savory recipe and cut out the salt. Now replace it with herbs, spices, or a low-sodium herbal blend, such as Mrs. Dash or Spike. (See page 199 for Getting to Know Low-Sodium Herbal Blends.)

7. **Combination therapy.** Try a variety of spices and herbs—such as pepper, turmeric, basil, garlic, and ginger—in a single dish.

8. **Sweet spice strategy.** Let sweet, nutty spices—such as cloves, allspice, cinnamon, cardamom, nutmeg, and ginger—flavor your everyday cereals, fruits, desserts, and breads.

THE SODIUM ALTERNATIVE

There's one more important bonus you'll gain from packing your diet with flavorful herbs and spices: You can slash the amount of sodium in your diet. In the past few years, Americans' sodium intake has been pinpointed as a major contributor to our growing burden of health problems. High sodium intake can increase your risk for high blood pressure, which puts you at higher risk for stroke and heart disease. Despite government health officials nagging us year after year to cut back, we haven't been paying much attention. We're taking in an average of 3,400 milligrams of sodium per day. That's a far cry from the 2,300 milligrams per day people should aim for, and the 1,500 milligrams per day for individuals at high risk for hypertension, who make up 68 percent of the U.S. population and include individuals with a family history of hypertension, African Americans, and middle-aged and older adults.

Where's all of the salt coming from? That's easy: Processed and prepared foods account for 77 percent of all sodium consumed. As we rely more and more on prepared foods—from convenience and snack foods in supermarkets to restaurant and take-out meals—our sodium intake is rising. It's easy to find processed foods such as soups, entrées, and side dishes in the supermarket that contain 1,000 milligrams of sodium per serving—and you can find double that amount in many restaurant foods. In fact, the natural sodium content of foods adds up to only 10 percent of our average total intake, with another 5 to 10 percent coming from the salt shaker. The top sources of sodium intake in the US are yeast breads, chicken and chicken dishes, pizza, pasta and pasta dishes, cold cuts, condiments, Mexican dishes, sausage, franks, bacon, ribs, regular cheese, grain-based desserts, soups, and beef and beef dishes.[29] By adopting a plant-powered diet and focusing on whole plant foods over prepared, processed animal foods, you can reduce a lot of these sodium traps in your diet. Instead of relying on prepared foods, get into the kitchen and start cooking up delicious, plant-powered foods and rely on flavorful herbs and spices to do the seasoning. Check out the dishes in my Plant-Powered Recipe Collection in chapter 14, which contain no added salt and very low sodium levels. If you're just getting started on the path of lowering your sodium intake, it might take you a while to get accustomed to salt-free dishes. In that case, add one dash of salt to your meal just before serving, which will provide about 100 mg of sodium. You'll be surprised how easily you become accustomed to less salt in your foods.

GETTING TO KNOW LOW-SODIUM HERBAL BLENDS

IN YOUR PURSUIT of lowering sodium intake for optimal health, you simply must make friends with low-sodium herbal seasoning blends. A number of manufacturers produce creative herbal and spice blends that deliver plenty of flavor without those pesky milligrams of sodium. You will find that many of my Plant-Powered recipes in Chapter 14 call for "low-sodium herbal seasoning" in place of salt. This is your opportunity to discover your own favorite seasoning blend; try those created by Mrs. Dash, Spike, Spice Hunter, McCormick, Herbamare and Trader Joe's. While these seasoning blends come in many flavors, from lemon-pepper to spicy, look for a basic seasoning blend that can boost flavor in nearly any recipe without lending a specific flavor profile. Remember that you may need to adjust the other seasonings in a dish if you're adding a spicy blend. In addition, I recommend specific herbal blends in many of my favorite dishes, such as:

- Garam masala: An Indian spice blend that usually includes cumin, coriander, cardamom, pepper, cinnamon, cloves, and nutmeg
- Herbes de Provence: A French seasoning blend that includes basil, fennel seeds, lavender, marjoram, rosemary, sage, and thyme
- Poultry seasoning: A spice blend that usually includes thyme, sage, marjoram, rosemary, black pepper, and nutmeg

SKIM THE SODIUM

Here are my best tips for getting a grip on your sodium intake.

1. **Cook real food at home more often.** Prepare more meals from scratch—without the help of boxed, refrigerated, or frozen convenience foods and restaurant foods—to drastically reduce your

sodium intake. A serving of Three-Bean Cowboy Chili (page 321) has only 163 milligrams of sodium, but canned and restaurant chilies contain up to 1,300 milligrams per serving!

2. **Do your own sodium comparison.** You'll find a wide variety of sodium levels in food products in supermarkets. For example, a jar of pasta sauce can contain anywhere from 40 to 800 milligrams of sodium per serving, and rice mix can contain between 135 to 900 milligrams per serving. Try to use minimally processed foods as much as possible (like plain cooked rice instead of a rice mix), and check out the labels before you purchase products.

3. **Watch out for surprising sodium stashes.** Yes, the number one source of sodium in our diets is yeast bread—quite a surprising stash! That's because ingredients added to breads can push sodium levels up to 400 milligrams per serving. Not to mention that it's easy to eat multiple servings of bread during the day. Other surprising sources include salsa, salad dressings, and even cottage cheese. The moral of the story? Check out sodium levels of all foods before you drop them into your shopping cart.

4. **Push the fruits and veggies.** If you pile your plate high with simply prepared fresh, frozen, or canned fruits and vegetables (look for no salt added or reduced-sodium), you're filling up on naturally low-sodium—and healthy—foods.

5. **Meat and faux meat alert.** One of the major sources of sodium in the U.S. diet is animal foods. Processed, smoked, and cured meats are notoriously high in sodium, and even "plain" meats such as pork, poultry, and fish are often marinated and injected with high-sodium liquids. That's not to say that meat alternatives can't be packed with sodium, either. If you're a plant-powered omnivore, pay particular attention to the sodium levels of meat products, and choose to cook fresh meat instead of using smoked, cured products such as cold cuts and sausages. And if you're a plant-powered vegan or vegetarian, watch the sodium levels on prepared meat alternatives, and turn to whole plant proteins first.

6. **Check out restaurant Web sites for nutrition information.** Do a little menu planning before you dine out; check the sodium levels of your favorite entrées on the restaurant Web site first.

7. **Focus on whole-food snacks.** Processed snacks such as crackers,

cookies, and desserts can add another unwanted dash of sodium to your day. Try whole-food snacks, such as fresh fruit, unsalted popcorn, or a handful of unsalted nuts.

8. **Keep portion size in check.** Every time you double up on the suggested serving size of a food, you're doubling up on the sodium level, too. If you triple up, just do the math. Remember, when it comes to minimally processed, unsalted plant foods, such as fruits, veggies, whole grains, legumes, and nuts, you don't have to worry about sodium because they all have naturally low levels.

9. **Cut back on condiments.** From marinades and salad dressings to ketchup and soy sauce, keep an eye on how much sodium you slather on to your favorite foods via jars and bottles of condiments.

DARK CHOCOLATE, SINFUL NO MORE

The best news of the century is that chocolate is good for you—dark chocolate, that is (at least 70% cocoa). Considering that surveys have shown that 52 percent of women prefer chocolate to sex, it's easy to see why chocolate instantly won a health halo. The ultimate healthy indulgence, chocolate's buzz is all about its polyphenols, which have been linked to heart health. But we're not the first ones to discover chocolate's health potential. It originated from the Mayans, who ground the beans of the *Theobroma cacao* tree into a bitter brew they used as traditional medicine for heart problems, depression, and other ailments.

What the Mayans didn't know is that chocolate is full of strong antioxidants that make up over 10 percent of the weight of cocoa powder. These antioxidants are part of a class of polyphenols we call flavonoids. In addition, chocolate contains plant sterols, B vitamins, magnesium, copper, and potassium. If you're a chocoholic, you'll be delighted to hear that growing research supports eating small portions of dark chocolate or cocoa products—about 30g a day—for heart health benefits like preventing blood clots, improving insulin resistance, supporting healthy blood vessel function, and lowering blood pressure, inflammation, and LDL ("bad") cholesterol levels.[30]

However, keep in mind that today's chocolate contains more than the ground cacao beans the ancient Mayans consumed. A standard chocolate confection is typically a processed mix of other ingredients—chocolate liquor, cocoa butter, cocoa powder, sugar, emulsifiers, and milk—that may minimize its potential polyphenol content and up its saturated fat and calories. In finished chocolate products, the amount of cocoa can vary from 7 to 35 percent in milk chocolate to 30 to 80 percent in dark chocolate. And at about 130 calories per 30g, even dark chocolate is a calorie-dense food that should be eaten in moderation.

Here's the bottom line on chocolate: Enjoy up to 30g per day of dark chocolate with at least 70 percent cocoa content as a daily treat you can feel good about. To make portion control easier, check out the suggested serving size for your favorite bar of dark chocolate so you know exactly how to divvy it up into 30g portions. You can also include cocoa powder in recipes, such as beverages, baked goods, breads, puddings, and desserts— just be mindful of the ingredients you pair with your cocoa creations.

DAILY PLANT-POWERED HERBS/SPICES AND DARK CHOCOLATE GUIDE

FOOD	SERVING SIZES	PLANT-POWERED VEGAN	PLANT-POWERED VEGETARIAN	PLANT-POWERED OMNIVORE
Herbs and spices (fresh, dried, or ground)	1 tablespoon fresh, 1 teaspoon dried or ground	Use liberally	Use liberally	Use liberally
Dark chocolate (at least 70% cocoa)	30g	0–1 serving	0–1 serving	0–1 serving

---

"I consciously follow Meatless Monday—only allowing dairy or eggs and using vegan items as my center-of-the-plate protein, surrounded by veggies and whole grains, which keep me fuller. When I compare how I feel after a lunch of beans and rice and veggies versus the turkey, potato, gravy meal, I realize that I have a more productive afternoon with the vegetarian lunch. I made this switch about five years ago. I find that it helps me keep my weight in check, and I know that this type of diet is associated

with lower risks for some cancers and heart disease, so I figure it will help me stay healthier. I have a steady cholesterol level and my triglycerides are low. I also enjoy the flavors of many cultures that are mainly vegetarian, so I am happy to try these foods. My family also embraced Meatless Monday; it's a good conversation starter at dinner and a way to expose kids to alternate dining and understanding what their choices mean."

—ALMA, a plant-powered omnivore in Sammamish, Washington

"Around 30, for heart health reasons, I gave up beef and pork; a year later I felt strongly that I didn't want to eat flesh foods. The antibiotics, growth hormones, and arsenic driven into these animals that ultimately ends up in humans, along with the cruelty factor, drove it home. Creatively, I made some awesome vegetarian casseroles for my family—lots of cheese, oh yes, lots. That was my protein, right? A year of yumminess drove up my cholesterol 30 points! I figured out that cheese was not a heart healthy food. Ten to fifteen years later, our meals are bright, colorful, flavorful—truly mouth popping—mixtures of seitan, tempeh, tofu, beans, and veggies with lots of creatively combined spices and herbs. We're simply sinful. Dairy and eggs are limited—we're not completely vegan—but we don't rely so much on dairy like we used to."

—DIANA, a plant-powered vegetarian in Watertown, Massachusetts

❧ PLANT-POWERED ACTION ALERT **DAY 11**

Stock your spice cabinet with the herbs and spices listed in Top Herbs and Spices for Health (see page 187). Extra credit: Start growing a pot of fresh herbs on your windowsill or doorstep today.

Cheers to Your Health! Plant-Based Drinks with Benefits:
Coffee, Tea, and Wine

Today, your choice of beverage is more important than ever. It can make the difference between whether you hydrate your body with life-giving fluids that provide plant-powered health benefits or suck down high-glycemic, highly processed concoctions that promote rapid rises in your blood glucose and add extra inches to your waistline. You may remember the days when a case of the thirsties sent you to the water faucet for a glass of water. These days, mega beverages loaded up with calories and sugar are the standard thirst quenchers; and they're in your face everywhere, including gas stations, vending machines, coffee stands, airports, and even your gym. High-wattage energy, sports, tea, coffee, juice, and soft drinks tempt you with sparkling taste, as well as claims of antioxidant and performance power, making water seem about as boring and outdated as a gelatin aspic. But it's time to read beyond the beverage labels and get back to basics.

A SUGARY BEVERAGE HIGH

We're literally pouring a good percentage of our calorie allotment for the entire day straight down our throats, thanks to our rising intake of sugary sodas, sports and energy drinks, coffee beverages, and fruit juice drinks. About 50 percent of the added sugars in our diets come from these beverages, and soft drinks are the single largest contributor to calorie intake in the United States.[1]

There is more and more evidence, especially among children, that all of these sugary beverages we're sucking down may be a major culprit behind obesity and its health-related fallout. It's a simple fact that if you drink a 350ml soft drink containing about 150 calories (and 40 grams of sugar!) every day on top of your normal diet, you'll gain weight to the tune of about 15 pounds (7kg) per year. The problem is that when you sip that 150-calorie soda it doesn't produce the same sense of fullness that you get when you chew 150 calories worth of solid food, and according to research, you don't tend to cut back on calories at your meal to account for the extra calories. It's no wonder that studies have found that people who consume high amounts of sugary beverages are more likely to have higher calorie intake, as well as higher rates of weight gain, diabetes, and obesity. In fact, adults who drink one or more sodas per day are 27 percent more apt to be overweight or obese than those who do not drink soda, according to one study.[2]

One of the most important ways to clean up your diet for good is to kick the can—the sugary beverage can that is. Simply wipe out all of those cans, bottles, and jugs of sugary beverages from your life. And remember that looks can be deceiving in the beverage world. It may seem as if a juice drink, smoothie, or tea beverage is a healthy choice, but simply flip over the container to read the facts. You might be surprised to find that your green tea drink has just as much sugar and calories as a can of soda. Some coffee drinks can be as decadent in calories, sugar, and saturated fat as a milk shake. And science doesn't seem to bear out the claim that diet sodas can help you win the battle of the bulge, either.

The eco-impact of drinking billions of bottled and canned beverages is mind-blowing: Resources such as water and oil are required to produce the containers, and carbon emissions are released. Plus, additional resources are required to transport and refrigerate them. And that doesn't even take into account the carbon emissions produced from the manufacturing of these highly processed liquids, which include high fructose corn syrup and artificial flavorings that must be produced and shipped to the manufacturing plants. (At the plants they are dumped into vats of syrup that will be pumped into the beverage bottles you spot everywhere you turn.)

Every time you pull up to a convenience store, fast food restaurant, or coffee shop, those sugary beverages call out to you, tempting you to load up on unwanted calories. Here's a sample of the shocking levels of calories, saturated fat, and sugar in many popular beverages:

SWILLING SWEET MEGA DRINKS

BEVERAGE	CALORIES	SUGAR / SAT FAT
Coca-Cola soft drink, large (32 oz)	310	86 g / 0 g
Hi-C Orange Lava-Burst orange-flavored fruit drink, large (32 oz)	350	94 g / 0 g
Powerade Mountain Blast energy drink, large (32 oz)	220	46 g / 0 g
Jack in the Box Strawberry-Banana Smoothie, large (24 oz)	440	85 g / 0 g
Monster Energy Drink (16 oz)	200	54 g / 0 g
100% Natural Lipton Green Tea with Citrus (20 oz)	175	45 g / 0 g
Starbucks Double Chocolaty Chip Frappuccino (24 oz)	520	69 g / 15 g
Starbucks Caffé Mocha, whole milk/whipped cream (20 oz)	450	45 g / 13 g
Tropicana Pink Lemonade, large (30 oz)	365	98 g / 0 g

Sat Fat=saturated fat, oz=ounce, g=grams

Sources: Company Web sites; CalorieKing.com.

HYDRATE YOUR BODY WITH WATER

Naturally, your first beverage of choice should be plain old water. Water is as vital to your health as any other nutrient in your diet. You need adequate water for many body functions, including maintaining internal temperature and blood pressure, cushioning joints and organs, digestion, absorption, transporting nutrients, and ridding your body of toxins. Although you can go for weeks without any food, you can't live more than a few days without water.

You don't have to invest in fancy bottles of water to get the best quality. Your tap will do just fine. If you're concerned about potential environmental contaminants such as lead, chlorine, and asbestos in your local water supply, just install an inexpensive carbon filter that mounts to your faucet or comes in a pitcher. By kicking the bottled water habit, you can make a significant impact on your carbon footprint. Americans consume about 8.5 billion gallons of bottled water per year, an estimated 25 percent of which comes straight from the tap. Just like beverage bottles, producing and transporting water bottles can result in significant environmental impacts. And unfortunately, most of them end up in our nation's landfills.[3] If you're a fan of sparkling water—another great way to increase your sugar-free fluid intake—you might want to consider an in-home carbonated water system, which can reduce the cost and environmental toll of bottled sparkling water products.

HOW MUCH WATER IS ENOUGH?

The good news is that most of us are meeting our body's fluid needs just fine, just by letting thirst be our guide. We are getting about 80 percent of our water from beverages and another 20 percent from the foods we eat. Lots of fruits and vegetables contain high levels of fluids; melon, strawberries, cabbage, spinach, lettuce, cucumbers, and broccoli consist of at least 90 percent water.[4]

Here's a look at the latest recommendations for hydration.

- Women should consume a total of 2.7 liters (about eleven 8-ounce glasses) of water from beverages and in foods each day.
- Men should consume a total of 3.7 liters (about sixteen 8-ounce glasses) of water from beverages and in foods each day.[5]

GROUNDS FOR COFFEE BENEFITS

When consumed in simple form, the way they've been sipped by humans for centuries, plant-based beverages such as coffee and tea can hydrate your body and offer the added bonus of plant-powered health protection. Coffee, the stimulating beverage once frowned on by health experts, is starting to enjoy some perks, due to a growing body of research demonstrating its potential health benefits.

Legend has it that coffee beans were first discovered by a goatherd who noticed that his goats become high-spirited after eating a particular berry from a tree that grew in the Ethiopian highlands. Soon after, the locals discovered that a brew made from these berries helped them to stay alert. By the fifteenth century coffee—from the genus *Coffea*, which includes more than 6,000 different species—was actively cultivated and traded within the Arabian Peninsula, quickly installing itself as an important feature in social traditions. Even back then, this energizing drink had a way of bringing people together in homes and coffee houses, to share thought-provoking conversation, music, and literature over a rich, steaming cup. As coffee traveled to Europe it received a similar reception, finding a special place in public life and discourse. Coffee seeds were transported around the globe by travelers, traders, and missionaries to be cultivated in plantations, solidifying coffee's place as one of the most beloved beverages in the world.

Not that long ago, coffee faced undue criticism because it was thought to be too "exciting" for good heart and gastrointestinal health. Since then, hundreds of mostly positive health studies have been published investigating coffee's potential benefits for a variety of health conditions. Some of these benefits may be due to the coffee bean's high antioxidant status: Scientists have identified more than 1,000 volatile compounds in coffee beans, which appear to have antioxidant properties.[6] In fact, according to research, coffee is one of the leading sources of antioxidants in the U.S. diet.[7]

Scientists have investigated many potential coffee benefits, including the prevention of ailments ranging from gallstones to cavities, as well as reduced early mortality risk. However, a few key benefits seem to show the most promise:

- **Power up mental and physical performance.** It's evident that coffee can help you stay alert, focused, and energized. Studies show that it can enhance concentration, lower fatigue, increase alertness, and improve performance and endurance during both prolonged, exhaustive activity and short-term, high-intensity exercise.[8] Regular coffee consumption may also protect the brain. Several studies show a protection against Parkinson's disease,[9] and a ten-year study found a 20 percent lower risk of depression among coffee drinkers.[10]

- **Fight type 2 diabetes.** Coffee may lower your risk for type 2 diabetes because it appears to offer significant metabolic benefits, such as lowering insulin resistance and slowing the absorption of carbohydrates in the intestines. Studies show that drinking three to four cups per day may reduce your risk of developing diabetes by 25 percent.[11]
- **Protect Your Liver.** Some studies show that coffee can protect your liver. Coffee drinkers tend to have lower risks of abnormal liver function, cirrhosis, and liver cancer.[12]
- **Guard against colon cancer.** That daily cup (or two or three) of Joe may even protect you against colon cancer; regular consumption has been linked with protecting smokers from advanced colon cancer and lowering women's risk for colon cancer by half. However, not all studies have found this benefit.[13]

To be sure, more scientific investigation is needed before we can know for sure whether coffee can really offer protection from these conditions. But it certainly seems like there's no need to worry about sitting back, relaxing, and enjoying this fragrant, plant-based brew. It is important to note that, although coffee itself is an antioxidant-rich, plant-powered beverage, its positive elements can be negated by mixing in indulgent creams, sugars, toppings, and syrups that can prompt you to pack on pounds. One of the bonuses of enjoying coffee is that it can be a naturally calorie-free replacement for sugary beverages in your diet. Have your java black or with a small serving of plant-based milk to enjoy it at its finest.

MAKE IT TEA TIME

No doubt you've heard about the abundant health benefits linked to drinking tea, particularly green tea, which has developed such a health halo in recent years that you can find it in everything from candy to dog food to shampoo. Yet tea's reputation for promoting health is nothing new. Cultures have been celebrating tea since it was discovered nearly 5,000 years ago, when the dried leaf of a tea bush fell into a Chinese emperor's pot of boiling water—or so the story goes. Since then, people from all over the world have been sipping tea for its aromatic, stimulating qualities, as well as to prevent a variety of maladies, from mental conditions to liver problems.

Tea—the most widely consumed beverage in the world besides water—has woven its way into the fabric of cultural traditions around the globe, from elaborate Japanese tea ceremonies to Victorian high tea services with fine bone china to the American Southern custom of sipping iced tea on the veranda on a scorching hot day. And now it looks like these elegant customs may be steeped in more than history; there may be real health advantages waiting to be realized. Scientists have observed that tea drinking has been linked with a lower risk of heart disease and certain cancers, as well as with boosting oral health, bone health, immune function, and maybe even metabolism.

All true teas come from the leaves of the *Camellia sinensis* plant. It's how the leaves are processed and the level of oxygen to which they are exposed that determines what type of tea they'll become. Even though it's green tea that has enjoyed the most limelight for its health potential, white, oolong, and black teas have also been linked with disease prevention. What's so special about this plant-based beverage? True brewed teas contain high levels of flavonoids and thus provide a significant source of these potent phytochemicals. In fact, one cup of tea offers between 140 and 300 milligrams of flavonoids, depending on the type and amount of tea leaves used and how the tea is prepared. In particular, the tea plant and green tea contain **catechin** flavonoids, such as **epigallocatechin gallate (EGCG)**, which may be at the root of green tea benefits. During the processing of black tea, the tea catechin flavonoids are altered into other compounds, called theaflavins and thearubigins, that may also have bioactive benefits.[14]

Although red and herbal teas are not true teas because they don't come from the *Camellia sinensis* plant, they can still provide health benefits (see Top Herbs and Spices for Health, page 187). People have been brewing up fragrant pots of herbs in hot water since prehistoric times, expanding on their knowledge of flavors and medicinal qualities over the years. And now scientists are discovering that herbal teas—which are made from a wide variety of plants as diverse as hibiscus, chamomile, and mint—possess significant antimicrobial, antiviral, antioxidant, and antitumor actions that may protect us from disease.[15]

PLANT-POWERED GUIDE TO TEAS

TYPE OF TEA	DESCRIPTION	VARIETIES	BIOACTIVE INGREDIENTS
Black tea	Mature tea leaves that are oxidized for two to four hours before processing, which turns the leaves from green to brown and produces a full, intense flavor.	Assam, Ceylon, Darjeeling	Rich in theaflavins and thearubigins but relatively low in catechins such as EGCG.
Green tea	Mature tea leaves that are steamed, rolled, and dried directly after picking, without allowing oxidation. The green-colored tea tastes closest to fresh tea leaves.	Gunpowder, Matcha, Sencha	Its major flavonoids are catechins such as EGCG.
Herbal tea	Herbal teas do not come from *Camellia sinensis* but are infusions of the leaves, roots, bark, seeds, and/ or flowers of other plants.	Peppermint, chamomile, lemon, orange spice	Can contain antioxidant compounds, depending on the herbs included.
Oolong	Mature tea leaves that are partially oxidized— somewhere between green and black tea— before processing, producing a smoky, floral flavor.	Formosa oolong, Pouchong, Qing	The catechin, theaflavin, and thearubigin levels are generally between those of green and white teas.
Red tea (rooibos)	Not a true tea, this is an herbal tea from the plant *Aspalathus linearis*, which brews up red and produces a sweet, nutty flavor.	Green rooibos, red rooibos	Contains fewer antioxidants than real tea but supplies phytochemicals like orientin, rutin, and quercetin.

TYPE OF TEA	DESCRIPTION	VARIETIES	BIOACTIVE INGREDIENTS
White tea	These white, fuzzy buds of tea are picked while still young and not allowed to oxidize, furnishing a light, slightly sweet flavor.	Fujian, Silver Needle, White Peony	Contains high levels of catechins.

BREWING TEA HEALTH POTENTIAL

The health potential for tea is exciting. Hundreds of studies have linked this fragrant brew with a variety of benefits, from heart health to cancer protection. A study of Japanese adults found that drinking at least five cups of green tea a day reduced the risk of death from any cause by 16 percent.[16] Although the antioxidant and anti-inflammatory effects of tea flavonoids may be the source of these health benefits, other bioactive ingredients may also be at work, including enzymes, fluoride, and caffeine. Here's a look at the most promising areas of research on tea and health today:

- **A Healthy Ticker.** Tea drinkers tend to have a lower risk of heart disease. Research reveals that for every three cups of tea consumed per day, the risk of heart attack drops by 11 percent.[17] Tea may bring about heart health benefits through improving the function of blood vessels and reducing cholesterol levels.[18]
- **Cancer Defense.** Preliminary research suggests that tea drinking may protect you against cancers of the skin, lung, mouth, esophagus, stomach, colon, pancreas, bladder, and prostate. More research needs to be conducted in this area before we can fully understand tea's potential for cancer prevention.[19]
- **Immune Booster.** Early research indicates that tea may help boost the immune system to fight infection, bacteria, viruses, and fungi more effectively.[20]
- **A Pretty Smile.** Thanks to tea flavonoids and fluoride, this beverage may help fight plaque and promote healthy tooth enamel.[21]
- **Weight Loss Aid.** A lot of fuss has been made over tea's "fat-burning" potential, boosting the sales of weight loss supplements across the world. Yet the science is still unclear about whether tea

can definitively help you lose weight: Some research shows benefits, and some show none. However, studies have found a 3 to 4 percent increase in calorie burning with 5 cups of daily tea consumption, as well as a modest weight loss—about 5 percent over three months linked with ingestion of green tea extract.[22]

- **Bone Protection.** There are limited studies available in this area, but those available hint that tea drinkers may experience a protection of bone mass that might reduce the risk of osteoporosis.[23]

THE CAFFEINE BUZZ

The stimulating effects of caffeine—present in both coffee and tea—may be partially responsible for some of the benefits behind these plant-based brews. However, the antioxidant properties of coffee and tea extend to decaffeinated versions, as well. Keep in mind that caffeine may not work for everyone; it can aggravate conditions like gastroesophageal reflux disease, migraines, arrhythmias, sleep disturbance, and benign fibrocystic breast disease. Here's a glance at the caffeine contents of coffee and tea.

BEVERAGE (8 OZ)	CAFFEINE CONTENT
Green tea	9–50 mg
Black tea	42–72 mg
Coffee, brewed	72–130 mg

Source: See Chapter 9, note 24 (page 388).

mg = milligrams; amounts vary depending on variety and preparation method

A TOAST TO WINE AND YOUR HEALTH

The good news about plant-based beverages extends to one of our oldest pleasures—wine—which has been widely valued for its health benefits and flavor throughout history. Humans have been enjoying fermented drinks made of wild fruits and, later, cultivated grapes, for more than 10,000 years. Archaeologists recently discovered the world's oldest winery—dating back more than 6,000 years ago—in a cave in Armenia, complete with wine press, clay fermentation vat, and grape seeds. This nectar of the gods is even an integral part of the traditional Mediterranean diet, with its myriad health rewards. Yet wine—along with all alcoholic beverages—suffered a tarnished reputation throughout America's puritanical past up through the period of Prohibition, instituted less than a hundred years ago.

The health reputation of wine really kicked off in the early '90s, when researchers identified the "French Paradox"—the observation that the French enjoy relatively low rates of heart disease despite their high-saturated-fat diet. Data hinted that perhaps all that red wine they'd been enjoying was counteracting some of the negative effects of their diet. Americans were shocked and delighted that wine could be "healthy," and wine sales quickly shot up by 40 percent. Since then, dozens of studies have pointed out potential health advantages of drinking wine, including reduced risks of stroke, heart disease, diabetes, multiple sclerosis, Alzheimer's disease, obesity, osteoporosis, and infectious diseases. In fact, if you sip moderate amounts of wine regularly, you'll have a lower risk of dying from any cause than if you were to abstain.[25]

Perhaps the most promising case for sipping wine pertains to cardiovascular health: Research shows that moderate wine drinkers have half the risk of dying from coronary heart disease and stroke than do nondrinkers.[26]

What's in that glass of ruby-red wine that provides such mighty benefits?

- **Grape Polyphenols.** Just like fruits and vegetables, red wine is rich in polyphenols—about 200 unique types have been identified to date. The particular polyphenol that has captured scientists' attention is resveratrol, a naturally occurring compound found abundantly in grape skins and red wine.[27] Resveratrol furnishes the grape with a natural defense system against fungal infections, and now science reveals that this polyphenol has antioxidant, anticlotting, anti-inflammatory, and anticancer effects. It looks like you can gain the best benefit from drinking wine daily with meals, as the effects of these polyphenols seem to last 24 to 36 hours. However, the definitive effects of resveratrol in human health are not yet crystal clear.[28]
- **It's the Alcohol.** The fact is, drinking *any* kind of alcohol in moderation—spirits, beer, or wine—is linked with health benefits such as cardiovascular disease protection. In fact, studies show that moderate alcohol consumption can reduce the risk of heart

attack, stroke, peripheral vascular disease, sudden cardiac death, and death from all cardiovascular causes by 25 to 40 percent. This protection may be attributed to the fact that moderate drinking can improve insulin sensitivity and blood cholesterol levels and prevent blood clots. In fact, moderate drinkers live longer and carry a lower overall risk of disease than those who don't imbibe.[29]

- **The Dark Side of the Wine Glass.** If you already enjoy a glass of wine with meals here or there, it comes as good news that you may be protecting your health. But it's important to put things into perspective. Remember that alcohol is the most abused drug in the United States, and that excessive drinking (according to research, more than two drinks per day for men and more than one drink per day for women) cancels out any potential positive effects of alcohol consumption. In fact, disease and death rates are highest among heavy drinkers: There are 79,000 deaths in the United States each year due to excessive drinking, which has been linked with violence, injuries, miscarriage, alcohol poisoning, neurological disorders, cardiovascular problems, psychological conditions, social problems, cancer, liver disease, and gastrointestinal disorders.[30] Even moderate amounts of alcohol may increase your risk for cancer, including breast and colorectal cancer (however, studies show that adequate daily intake of folate—at least 600 micrograms per day—may protect women from an increased risk of breast cancer).[31] And if you push up your calorie intake by overdoing wine (containing 95 to 120 calories per 150ml glass) or overindulging in extra treats due to lowered inhibitions, the resulting weight gain is certainly not going to do your health any favors. Finally, don't forget that drinking during pregnancy is discouraged, as excessive maternal alcohol intake is linked with severe developmental problems in the fetus.

Here's my bottom-line recommendation for a healthy bottoms-up: If you drink, enjoy a glass of antioxidant-rich red wine once a day with meals (up to two if you're a guy). However, if you don't drink, there's no need to start drinking to gain any potential benefits. If you prefer beer, white wine, or liquor to red wine, you may not get as many polyphenols, but research indicates you can still gain potential heart health protection—as long as you imbibe in moderation. And if you have a family history of these cancers, you may want to further restrict your alcohol intake.

||||||||||||||||||||||||||||||||||||||||||||||||||||||||||||||||||||||||||||||||||||||||||||||||||||||||||||||

WHAT COUNTS AS A DRINK?

 A STANDARD DRINK is equal to 14 grams (0.6 ounces) of pure alcohol, which is found in:

- 350ml of beer (110–170 calories)
- 150ml of wine (95–120 calories)
- 45ml, or a "shot," of 80-proof distilled spirits or liquor, such as gin, rum, vodka, or whiskey (about 100 calories)[32]

||||||||||||||||||||||||||||||||||||||||||||||||||||||||||||||||||||||||||||||||||||||||||||||||||||||||||||||

TOP TIPS FOR WISE DRINKING

From tea and coffee to water and wine, here are my top tips for sipping health-giving fluids wisely:

1. Water is number one. So fill up a pitcher or reusable container to keep on your desk or in your work space and portion out water all day long.

2. Who needs plastic bottles of water for day trips? Fill a reusable aluminum bottle with filtered tap water when you're on the go.

3. Start your day with a coffee or tea perk—sans the rich creams, sugars, and toppings. It will also steer you away from drinking sugary beverages.

4. Enjoy a cup of herbal tea in the evenings, when caffeine might interrupt your sleep schedule.

5. Make a gallon jar of sun tea as a cool, refreshing alternative during the summer. Simply fill a clean gallon jar or pitcher with fresh water, add four to six tea bags, clean fresh mint if you like it, and sliced lemon, and place it in the sun for a couple hours until the tea is "brewed." Then store it in the refrigerator.

6. Make iced herbal tea as an alternative to traditional tea in the summer. You'll find that fruity teas based on pomegranate, berry, or citrus flavors add a zesty kick to your chilled tea experience, helping you to skip added sweeteners.

7. Enjoy herbal waters by floating slices of citrus fruit and cucumbers, and fresh herbs like rosemary, mint, and basil, in gallon jars of iced water.

8. Do you need an afternoon pickup? Don't confuse thirst with hunger. Instead of hitting the vending machine for a candy bar, try a cup of coffee or tea to boost your mental and physical performance.

9. Beware of bottled teas. Maybe some look like a healthier solution to sodas and energy drinks, but keep in mind that they may contain fewer flavonoids than traditional brewed tea because they lose some during the bottling process and because they may contain fewer constituents of real tea to begin with.

10. Enjoy wine the right way. Pour yourself a small glass and enjoy it the Mediterranean way: Slowly over a meal along with good conversation; savor the way its flavors and aromas pair with the foods on your plate.

DAILY PLANT-POWERED BEVERAGE GUIDE

BEVERAGE	SERVING SIZES	PLANT-POWERED VEGAN	PLANT-POWERED VEGETARIAN	PLANT-POWERED OMNIVORE
Water and Plant-Based Beverages	230ml water, unsweetened tea or coffee	8-13 servings	8-13 servings	8-13 servings
Optional	150ml red wine (may substitute 150ml white wine; 350ml beer; or 45ml spirits)	0-1 serving women 0-2 servings men	0-1 serving women 0-2 servings men	0-1 serving women 0-2 servings men

Source: See Chapter 9, note 33 (page 389).

Servings are based on a daily intake of 1,500 to 2,500 calories, which is the appropriate range for weight loss and weight maintenance for most adults, depending on age, sex, and activity level.

"I originally followed a vegan diet out of vanity—I wanted to stay slim. My drive then spread to disease prevention and overall health. I now applaud myself on the decision because of the added benefits of being both humane and environmentally friendly. The whole lifestyle is much more kind to all things, be it yourself, the Earth, or animals. I have found benefits like easier weight management, clear skin, more energy, a better connection and relationship with my food, and a stronger sense of compassion. I stay away from sugary sodas, juice-flavored beverages, and diet sodas. While eating out I stick to water and unsweetened tea or the occasional glass of wine."

—KRISTA, a plant-powered vegan in Manhattan Beach, California

---

PLANT-POWERED ACTION ALERT **DAY 12**

Fill a pitcher with water—2 liters for women and 3 liters for men—and finish it today. Repeat daily.

Don't Forget the Power of Exercise

A plant-powered diet won't do you much good if you leave exercise out of the equation—it's just as essential to your health as what you eat. Study after study illustrates how vital physical activity is to nearly every aspect of your well-being; it's as if every cell in your body evolved to perform in an environment rich with activity. You might say that exercise is in your DNA, because activity can even help protect your DNA from signs of aging.[1]

Your early ancestors wouldn't have lived long if they weren't physically fit. They required the physical ability to run away from danger, walk for miles in search of food and shelter, and even squat before the fire to cook their meals. Even in your parents' or grandparents' time, people's lives depended on physical activity, from toiling on farms or in industry to walking or biking as a means of transportation. Our genetic makeup is based on the close relationship between our physical activity and survival.

Today, we're increasingly accustomed to performing our labor while sitting on our butts in air-conditioned offices, then climbing into vehicles to get where we want to go. Now only 25 percent of jobs are physically active—50 percent fewer than in 1950.[2] And we have modern-day machines to do virtually every activity, from washing clothes to mowing the lawn. Even in our free time, we dedicate little energy to physical activity: An estimated 40 percent of Americans do no leisure-time exercise at all.[3] In today's convenient world, you can go through an entire day without moving many muscles.

This lack of activity is fueling our rise in obesity and chronic diseases. You probably already know that exercise is essential for weight management because it not only helps you increase the number of calories you burn up, but it also builds muscle that boosts your metabolism all day long. And regular physical activity can do much more than help you control your weight. Physical activity gets your heart pumping more efficiently, bathing your whole body in oxygen and nutrients, and it reduces the low-grade levels of inflammation at the root of so many modern health conditions. Here's a look at some of the key benefits you can gain from regular exercise:

1. **Lower your chance of heart disease.** Let me count the ways that exercise is good for your heart:
   - Makes your heart become a stronger, more efficient organ, resulting in less strain.
   - Decreases your resting heart rate, because less effort is needed to pump blood.
   - Reduces your blood pressure levels, because the force on your arteries decreases.
   - Increases your HDL ("good") cholesterol and decreases your LDL ("bad") cholesterol and triglyceride levels by transporting the bad lipids away from the body and altering your ratios.
   - Lowers your tendency for blood clots by reducing the clumping of platelets in the blood.
   - Drops your risk of heart attack by 35 to 55 percent because of many factors, including the above.
   - Lowers your weight and reduces stress.[4]
2. **Protect against cancer.** By reducing chronic inflammation and unhealthy estrogen and insulin levels, regular exercise can lower your risk of breast, colon, and endometrial cancers by an estimated 25 to 35 percent.[5]
3. **Keep your weight under control.** Studies have found that the most

successful weight loss formula combines diet with exercise. That's because exercise can help boost your metabolic rate; improve your body composition by increasing muscle mass, decreasing body fat, and decreasing waist size; improve your self-image; and even curb your appetite.

4. **Reduce your risk of stroke.** Thanks to bonuses such as improved blood pressure levels, you can lower your risk of stroke by 20 percent if you're moderately active and by 27 percent if you're highly active.[6]

5. **Maintain healthy bones and muscles.** Your muscles and bones are living tissues that respond to exercise by getting stronger. In fact, after the age of 20 you need to do some sort of weight-bearing exercise— activity that makes you work against gravity, such as walking, hiking, jogging, or weight lifting—in order to prevent bone loss that can lead to osteoporosis and broken bones. And maintaining muscle mass can improve your balance, strength, and physical function as you age.[7]

6. **De-stress your life.** Exercise boosts your "feel-good" neurotransmitters called endorphins, can push up your energy levels, improves your quality of sleep, releases daily tensions, promotes a general feeling of well-being, and counters anxiety and depression.[8]

7. **Fend off diabetes.** Regular exercise can make your body more responsive to insulin, help you maintain normal glucose levels, and, if you have diabetes, even lower the amount of diabetes meds you need.[9]

8. **Boost your brain power.** Research finds that exercise can boost your brain functioning and even protect against dementia and Alzheimer's disease.[10] And new studies find that kids also can experience improved mental performance due to physical activity.[11]

9. **Live longer.** Research shows that physical activity can lengthen your lifespan, which comes naturally as a result of all of these positive effects on your body.[12]

EXERCISE TO CHANGE YOUR LIFE

I can't stress enough the significance of moving every day. If you fit exercise into your daily life, you can live longer, feel happier, look better, weigh less, feel less pain, think more clearly, and be more active and functional. You may not think about these overwhelming benefits as much when you're younger, but as you age they become monumental. A healthy habit of regular exercise can result in aging *better*: It can help you avoid the debilitating effects of chronic diseases such as heart disease and diabetes that can steal your breath and eyesight. It can keep you mobile enough to get up out of a chair and pick up your grandchildren. It can keep your brain active and sharp. It can even help you avoid disability, which can mean the difference between living a rich, independent life or depending on assistance for your every physical need. You're never too old—or too overweight or out of shape—to gain benefits from exercise.

Let me backtrack, though, because there's another group with a lot to gain by becoming more physically active: our youth. It's well documented that the childhood obesity epidemic has a sure footing in lack of exercise. From cutting back on physical education programs in schools to increased television viewing and video game playing, society seems to be conspiring against our kids in order to suppress their activity. Just head over to a suburban neighborhood—or even a playground—these days and see how few kids are running around, kicking balls, riding bikes, or climbing monkey bars. When you combine a rise in low-nutrient, high-calorie foods with a decline in activity, there's only one mathematic result from this equation: weight gain. That's why kids today are experiencing all sorts of advanced conditions you normally see in aging, from high cholesterol levels to full-blown type 2 diabetes, a disease once reserved for the over-40 set. And once children are obese, they are set up for disastrous health problems throughout their entire lives—using up precious government resources to treat a slew of conditions, such as diabetes and heart disease, that will complicate and shorten their lives. And obese kids are also on track to experience a lower quality of life overall. As obese children move into adulthood, they are less likely to further their education past high school, gain successful employment, and find a partner, and it is more likely that they will experience discrimination and go on welfare.[13]

When it comes down to it, physical activity should be a family affair in which children, parents, and grandparents come together to move. Every time a family exercises together, a child stores memories that support the idea that, like food and water, exercise is essential to life. Parents can model the behavior that they would like to see in their children. It should also be a community affair in which entire schools, neighborhoods, and cities unite to get active. There's nothing that makes me happier than thinking of entire extended families—sons and daughters, moms and dads, and grandmothers and grandfathers—holding hands for an evening stroll after dinner, participating in a family hike on a Saturday afternoon, or engaging in a little game of kick-the-can on a warm summer night. And it makes me giddy with hope when I hear about schools initiating the President's Challenge physical fitness test, which prompts kids to aim for a standard level of fitness in activities like running and pull-ups, and when cities install traffic-free pedestrian paths to encourage biking, running, and walking. Positive things are happening every day, and you, your family, and your community can take advantage of them to get active.

LIGHT ACTIVITY COUNTS

In addition to aerobic and strengthening activities, you should include more light activities throughout the day. You may not think of mundane tasks such as housework and gardening as "real exercise," but they can really add up. Studies show that people who exercise vigorously and frequently have the lowest risk for heart disease, but *any* amount of exercise is better than none at all. Even people with existing heart disease can benefit from light exercise, but they should discuss risk factors with their health care provider before starting an exercise program.

Studies show enormous benefits can be gained from regular moderate to intensive exercise, but research is also beginning to indicate that expending energy in short bursts followed by sitting in a chair for the rest of the day isn't the best overall plan for health. Sitting for long, uninterrupted periods of time—despite regular exercise—has been linked with increased inflammatory and metabolic factors that increase risks of heart disease and cancer.[14] It makes sense: Did our ancestors sit or lie in repose 98 percent of their day, with only one 30-minute burst of activity? No, human history is marked by slow, steady activity that lasted most of the day. Unless you're one of the declining number of people with a physically active job, it's hard to replicate this sustained, low-intensity sort of physical activity in the modern world.

Here's a look at ways you can include more light activities in your day:

- **Interrupt sitting with regular one- or two-minute breaks.** Get up and stretch, get a drink of water, pace around your office, climb a flight of stairs, or do some physical chores.
- **Don't sit while talking on the phone.** Use that opportunity to walk around, do some stretching and bending, or even just stand.
- **Rediscover chores.** It may not seem like it, but all of those little pesky household activities, such as washing dishes, sweeping, vacuuming, and dusting, can burn up to 265 calories per hour.

- **Put on your gardening gloves.** Raking, hoeing, weeding, and pushing a wheelbarrow boost your exercise (and vitamin D) levels.
- **Take the stairs.** Ban the elevator and escalator forever.
- **Use your feet.** Do you really have to circle the parking lot for five minutes in order to get the prime parking spot? The answer is no.
- **Play with your children (or grandchildren) or pets.** Squat to push a race car to your child or stretch to toss a ball to your dog—it's a lot better than sitting.
- **Get romantic.** Yes, from kissing and hugging to beyond, even sexual activity counts!

GET GOING WITH AEROBIC ACTIVITY

When you perform aerobic exercise, a flood of wonderful effects washes over your body. As you repeatedly move large muscles in your legs, hips, and arms, you breathe faster, oxygen increases in your bloodstream, and your heart rate goes up, prompting more blood to flow to your muscles. Your small blood vessels dilate to carry more oxygen to your muscles and transport waste products like carbon dioxide away. You release those "feel-good" endorphins; you may even get an athlete's high.

How much aerobic activity is enough? Here's some guidance:

- If you choose activities at a moderate level, do at least 2 hours and 30 minutes a week. If you choose vigorous activities, do at least 1 hour and 15 minutes a week.
- Slowly build up the amount of time you spend doing physical activities. The more time you spend, the more health benefits you gain. Gradually increase your activity to twice your starting amount.
- Do at least 10 minutes of exercise at a time, and gradually work up to at least 20 to 30 minutes on each occasion.
- Exercise every other day to start with, then work up to exercising most days of the week.
- Remember, the more exercise you do, the better, but any amount is good for your health. Feel free to combine moderate and vigorous activities.
- Start with a warm-up, such as stretching, and finish with a cooldown—that is, a gradual diminishing of the intensity of the exercise—as well as some more stretching.[15]

EXERCISE BY INTENSITY

Light Activity (burns fewer than 3.5 calories per minute)	Moderate Activity (burns 3.5–7 calories per minute)	Vigorous Activity (burns more than 7 calories per minute)
Bicycling less than 5 mph	Aerobics, low-impact	Aerobics, high-impact
Boating	Aqua aerobics	Aerobics, step
Dancing slowly	Badminton, competitive	Backpacking
Fishing	Bicycling 5–9 mph	Basketball, competitive
Floating	Boxing with punching bag	Bicycling more than 10 mph
Golf—using cart	Calisthenics, light	Boxing—sparring
Sitting	Canoeing	Calisthenics, vigorous
Stretching	Carrying a child weighing more than 50 pounds	Circuit weight training
Walking, casual	Dancing, moderate	Dancing, vigorous
Weight training, light	Diving, competitive	Football, competitive
Yard/house work, light	Golf—carrying clubs	Hockey, competitive
Leisurely sports (table tennis, playing catch)	Gymnastics	In-line skating, fast pace
	Hiking	Jogging
	Horseback riding	Jumping rope/jumping jacks
	Housework that involves intense scrubbing/cleaning	Kickball, competitive
	Jumping on a trampoline	Lacrosse, competitive
	Roller-skating at leisurely pace	Martial arts: Karate, judo, tae kwon do, jujitsu
	Shoveling snow	Mountain climbing
	Swimming, recreational	Pushing nonmotorized lawnmower
	Tennis, competitive	Race walking (more than 4.5 mph)
	Walking briskly (3–4.5 mph)	Rugby, competitive
	Walking uphill	Running
	Weight training	Skiing, downhill or cross country
	Yoga	Soccer, competitive

(continued)

Light Activity (burns fewer than 3.5 calories per minute)	Moderate Activity (burns 3.5–7 calories per minute)	Vigorous Activity (burns more than 7 calories per minute)
	Most aerobic machines (e.g., stair climber, elliptical, stationery bike)— moderate pace	Swimming laps or synchronized swimming
		Treading water
		Water jogging
	Occupations that require an extended amount of time standing or walking	Water polo
		Wheeling a wheelchair
		Occupations that require heavy lifting or rapid movement
		Most aerobic machines (e.g., stair climber, elliptical, stationary bike)— vigorous pace

Source: U.S. Department of Health and Human Services, Promoting Physical Activity. (Champaign, IL: Human Kinetics, 1999).

Based on intensity for an average person (defined here as 154 pounds), 20–50 years old.

DON'T FORGET MUSCLE STRENGTHENING

We used to think that aerobic activity was enough, but now we know differently. A growing body of research shows that muscle strengthening exercises can maintain bone health; improve your balance, coordination, and mobility; contribute to feelings of contentment, and even improve the symptoms of many chronic conditions, including heart disease, arthritis, diabetes, and back pain. And strength training, which increases your muscle strength and mass, can also boost your metabolic rate by 15 percent, making weight control much easier. Just about everyone, regardless of health, size, gender, or age, can safely perform strengthening exercises.[16]

Here's what counts as a muscle-strengthening activity:

- Lifting weights (Remember to start out slowly.)
- Working with resistance bands
- Doing exercises that use your body weight for resistance, such as push-ups, pull-ups, sit-ups, and squats
- Heavy gardening, such as digging and shoveling
- Yoga

How much is enough? Perform muscle-strengthening activities according to this schedule:

- Do strength training at least two days a week.
- Include all the major muscle groups such as legs, hips, back, chest, stomach, shoulders, and arms, alternating by day if you prefer
- Exercises for each muscle group should be repeated 8 to 12 times per session.[17]

GETTING STARTED ON YOUR EXERCISE PLAN

One of the biggest challenges is simply getting started on an aerobic exercise plan. I've got an answer for all your excuses:

1. **I don't like to exercise.** Choose something you *do* like to do. If you hate the treadmill, don't use one—you won't stick with it. Instead, choose something you enjoy, whether it's briskly walking in your neighborhood, going to a dance class, or playing a sport like basketball, soccer, golf (skip the cart!), tennis, or racquetball.

2. **I am not able to exercise.** Choose something you *are* able to do. Don't set up unrealistic goals for yourself. Whether it's running five miles a day with a bad knee or getting up at five every morning to hit the gym when you're not a morning person, your hopes will probably be dashed, leaving you feeling disappointed and unmotivated. Make an activity goal that is realistic and achievable.

3. **I don't have time to exercise.** Put your daily exercise on your agenda, just like you do mealtimes, shopping runs, appointments, and your work schedule. Make your type of exercise useful: Ride your bike to work, walk to the supermarket, or mow the lawn.

4. **I can't get motivated.**
   - Enlist a friend. Research shows that exercise plans are more successful when you do it with a pal, which can make you feel more committed and happy about your activity.
   - Consider group exercise programs, like boot camps, spinning and yoga classes, and running clubs.
   - If it fits into your budget, enlist a personal trainer to help you stay on track with your goals.
   - As long as you're not allergic and you like pets . . . A dog will

stand by the front door, with his leash in his mouth, reminding you it's time for a walk. And he won't take no for an answer.

- Don't take the easy way out: *Make* yourself go out for a walk or run when you're tired or moody. Chances are you'll feel better when you're done.

5. **I can't afford to join a gym.** So you don't have the budget to pay for expensive gym memberships, classes, or equipment? Exercise doesn't have to cost a thing. Just go for a walk, do some heavy gardening, or dance to your favorite music (great for a rainy day!).

6. **I don't feel like I make any progress.** Studies show that people are more successful meeting their exercise goals if they track them. You can do this using an online exercise Web site or smart phone app, or the old-fashioned way with a pen and paper. Check out my Plant-Powered Food and Exercise Journal (page 254).

7. **I have a heart condition.** Careful exercise should still be possible: Discuss your fitness plan with your health care provider and watch for warning signs. If you experience chest pain, significant breathlessness, or dizziness, you should stop exercising and consult a physician about your symptoms.

"I've been a vegetarian on and off most of my life—strictly vegetarian the past seven years. I felt better about my food choices and have been a positive role model for others who think that if you go vegetarian you will be unable to be an athlete. I've still run marathons and competed in cycling events and triathlons. My husband, who is also vegetarian, trained for and competed in his first Ironman triathlon—another good example that you don't have to eat meat to be strong."

—CHRIS, a plant-powered vegetarian in Austin, Texas

🌱 **PLANT-POWERED ACTION ALERT DAY 13**
Create an exercise plan and commit to it. Start it today.

In Search of Powerful Plants in Restaurants and on the Road

Planning plant-powered meals at home can be easy, but once you take it on the road—from eating out to traveling—it gets more difficult. Restaurants are often quagmires of unhealthful food choices that can derail your best intentions. What with saucer-sized bagels, platters of deep-fried onion rings and fries, and troughs of pasta, it's no wonder that eating at restaurants can boost your calorie, fat, saturated fat, and sodium intake. Chances are, if you forfeit home cooking for dining out frequently, it will show in your health. In fact, eating out more often is linked with higher body fat and higher body weight, including obesity, according to several studies. And dining on more fast food meals is associated with eating more calories, fat, saturated fat, and sugary soft drinks and fewer fruits and vegetables and less milk.[1] Leave it to restaurants like Claim Jumper to figure out a way to pack 710 calories, 36 grams of saturated fat, and 920 milligrams of sodium into a bowl of potato cheese soup, or 1,150 calories, 21 grams of saturated fat, and 2,600 milligrams of sodium into a burger aptly named "Widow Maker."[2]

One of the most important things you can do for your health is to get cooking and take charge of your meals. But that doesn't mean you have to sacrifice dining out altogether. It's possible to enjoy a healthy plant-powered meal without the damage. Fortunately, times are changing: Many restaurants are offering up more lean, powerful plant foods—from quinoa risotto to tofu with mangetout. Chefs have always been leaders in the food movement. Just look at Mario Batali, the celebrity chef who now embraces Meatless Mondays in all fourteen of his restaurants. By offering plant-based meals once a week, Batali believes that he can make a difference in his country's health, as well as in its environmental impact. Today, chefs are finding increasingly interesting ways to showcase plant foods, and in many cases those dishes have gone from side dishes to the star of the dinner plate. Even fast food restaurants are upping their offerings of whole grains, salads, and vegetables.

Still, it's tough to sort through the food choices available in the increasing array of establishments now serving your dining and takeout needs, including coffeehouses, bagel shops, smoothie shops, diners, delis, sandwich shops, ethnic eateries, food trucks, fast food restaurants, street food vendors, bars, clubs, food courts, and white-tablecloth establishments. The secret to managing meals in restaurants without surrendering your health goals is all in planning. It takes a little skill and preparation to safely navigate the restaurant menu to avoid too many calories, grams of saturated fat and sugar, and milligrams of sodium, especially if you enjoy eating out frequently. Follow my Dining Habits for Health, below, to safeguard your meal choices.

DINING HABITS FOR HEALTH

1. **Do your homework.** Many chain and fast food restaurants now post nutritional information on their Web site or in brochures on location. Scroll through the nutritional facts for your favorite dishes, paying close attention to calories, fat, saturated fat, and sodium, before you order.

2. **Don't order when you're starving.** If you're brunching and it's been fifteen hours since your last meal, you're setting yourself up for disaster. Chances are, you'll throw caution to the wind and order anything that sounds good. Instead, eat a piece of high-fiber, naturally sweet fruit, such as an apple or pear, before heading to the restaurant to take the edge off your hunger and help you make wise choices.

3. Load up on veggies. Take every chance you can get to order veggies—even if it's in a few different places in the meal. Starting with a vegetable-based soup, green salad, or vegetable appetizer (not deep-fried) has been shown to lower the number of calories you consume later on at the meal. Instead of a monstrous, high-fat, starchy side to accompany your entrée, such as fries, mashed potatoes (probably loaded with butter), or a pile of oily pasta, ask for an extra side of vegetables. For the main event you can even request a vegetable plate, which in many places consists of the chef's special assortment of vegetables with a small side of pasta, potatoes, rice, or grains.

4. Skip the sauces and condiments. All those little pouches, cups, and packets of sauces, dressings, and condiments can really up your calorie, fat, saturated fat, and sodium ante. And remember, when a restaurant glops on the condiments for you, they usually portion out a lot more than the petite portions I've listed below—try doubling or tripling these numbers to see the real damage. Check out the numbers on condiments:

- Creamy salad dressings can contain up to 170 calories, 18 grams of fat, 30g of saturated fat, and 480 milligrams of sodium per 30g serving.
- Soy sauce contains only about 8 calories per tablespoon but has a whopping 900 milligrams of sodium; reduced-sodium soy sauce still has 530 milligrams.
- Barbeque sauce can contain up to 120 calories, 460 milligrams of sodium, and 14 grams of sugar per 30g.
- Vinaigrettes can have up to 150 calories, 12 grams of fat, 2 grams of saturated fat, and 350 milligrams of sodium per 30g.
- Honey-mustard sauce can pack up to 140 calories, 12 grams of fat, 2 grams of saturated fat, 320 milligrams of sodium, and 9 grams of sugar per 30g.[3]

If you really love the flavor of such additions, a simple solution is to ask for them on the side, so you can add just a tiny amount to your foods for flavor. For instance, you can dip the tines of your fork into sauces and condiments then spear your salad or veggies, to kick up the flavor just a notch. Or, simply ask for olive oil and vinegar on the side and drizzle on a tiny swirl of each.

5. Cut your portions. Let's face it; the biggest problem you'll face at most restaurants, from coffee shops to delis to chain restaurants, is sheer portion size: Many serve more than double or triple the normal serving size, and according to research, when people get larger portions on their plates, they usually end up eating the whole thing. Take a look at the damage:

- Italian restaurants can put as much as 110 carb-grams worth of spaghetti on your plate, but the normal serving size of carbohydrates is about 21 grams (106 calories). Sure, treat yourself to a double portion of pasta when you go out to eat, but a fivefold serving?

- Today's shop bagels can weigh in at 130g, 370 calories, and 74 grams of carbs, before the cream cheese. (The cream cheese will set you back another 100 calories, 10 grams of fat, and 6 grams of saturated fat per 30g.) Bagels used to be just three inches wide, weigh less than 70g, and provide 192 calories and 37 grams of carbohydrates. You can bring your bagel closer to the original by eating just half and saving the rest for another meal.

- Personal pizzas can contribute 1,470 calories to your waistline, along with a heart-damaging 30 grams of saturated fat and 3,670 milligrams of sodium. How did a simple food with such a humble beginning—as rustic bread smeared with tomato sauce and sold as street food in Naples—go so wrong? You're better off limiting pizza to one or two slices topped with veggies and eaten with a big side salad.

- Those little chocolate cupcakes you used to get when you were a kid had about 130 calories, 3 grams of fat, 2 grams of saturated fat, and 10 grams of sugar (without the frosting). Now, a single-sized (supposedly) slice of ooey-gooey chocolate cake can furnish a side-splitting 850 calories, 40 grams of fat, 25 grams of saturated fat, and 89 grams of sugar.[4]

How can you get past mammoth portion sizes served at eateries? Try skipping appetizers and desserts if you're getting a main course, and order smaller portions of foods if they are available, share your meal with a dining mate, or immediately pack half of your meal in a doggy bag for lunch the next day. Don't be embarrassed: It's getting to be a common restaurant request!

6. **Beware of breakfast bonanzas.** Breakfast has become the most decadent dining-out meal of the day for many people, thanks to breakfast sandwiches that weigh in at 1,520 calories, 44 grams of saturated fat, and 3,550 milligrams of sodium; omelets that donate 1,220 calories, 29 grams of saturated fat, and 2,270 milligrams of sodium; and combination platters that pack in 1,680 calories, 29 grams of saturated fat, and 4,050 milligrams of sodium (yes, you read that right). The problem is that most breakfast menus focus on refined carbohydrates in the form of muffins, bagels, pancakes, and waffles, as well as breakfast eggs and processed meat dishes packed with sodium and saturated fat—with few high-nutrient, low-calorie fruits and veggies in sight. You can still enjoy a nice experience eating out without the gluttony. Look for whole grain breads, cereals, or pancakes; a fresh fruit bowl; or a single egg or scoop of cottage cheese if you're a plant-powered vegetarian. My favorite breakfast meal when dining out? A bowl of hot oatmeal with soy milk and raisins and walnuts or a side of fresh fruit. It may be simple, but having someone else bring it to you and do the dishes makes it well worth it![5]

7. **Pass on the bread basket.** What's the most dangerous thing the waitstaff can do at a restaurant? Bring you a brimming basket of French bread slices or breadsticks, containing up to 150 calories and 400 grams of sodium each, or freshly deep-fried tortilla chips with 130 calories and 6 grams of fat in every tiny 30g portion. Now you're sitting there, stomach growling, with nothing to do but munch on the basket's contents while you wait for your meal to arrive. Before you know it, the basket is empty and they're refilling it. There's an easy solution to this problem: Ask the waitstaff to serve you a single portion on your appetizer plate or simply decline the basket altogether when it's offered to you.

8. **Remember, preparation style counts.** So often at restaurants, the meals start off right—with healthy whole ingredients such as vegetables and grains. Where the restaurants go wrong is in the preparation style. If you were to walk into the restaurant kitchen and look around, you might be shocked. Perfectly healthy foods get tossed

into deep-fat fryers, sauté pans and woks are filled with oil, butter, and cream; salads are tossed with ladles of dressing; and salty, fatty sauces are slathered over foods. In order to avoid unwanted calories, fat, and sodium, look for foods that are more simply prepared, such as steamed, grilled, and baked dishes.

9. **Understand menu clues.** When it comes to preparation styles—and calorie and saturated-fat loads—the menu description can be your first clue. If a food is "crispy" or "breaded," that's code for deep-fried. "Deluxe" usually means extra toppings, which are often of the high-calorie variety. A "ranch" tag on a sandwich usually means fatty, salty ranch dressing has been slathered on. "Combination" plates may seem like the best bang for your buck, because they've thrown just about everything but the kitchen sink onto your plate (I mean *platter*)—but do you really need that much food and calories weighing you down?

10. **Show sandwich sense.** Who doesn't like a luscious sandwich from a deli or subway shop now and again? You could create a pretty healthy meal out of a sandwich made with whole grain bread, veggies, and plant proteins, but many sandwich shops work overtime at packing in such huge portions of meats, cheeses, and sauces, you can barely wrap your mouth around them to take a bite. Your best bet is to opt for half of a sandwich filled with plant foods and a bowl of vegetable-based soup or a hearty green salad on the side.

11. **Cut through coffeehouse conundrums.** Hey, we all have our own favorite coffee drink these days—mine's a soy latte. But if coffeehouses are a regular hangout for you, be choosy about your beverage choices as well as your menu decisions. Watch out for sugary, high-fat creamy coffee concoctions, as well as those appetizing mega-muffins (up to 600 calories), fritters (up to 450 calories), and scones (up to 450 calories) peeking out from the glass domes.

12. **Fast food fixes.** It used to be that you were hard-pressed to eat healthfully at a fast food joint—but the times, they are a changin'. Many now offer whole grain breads, veggie options, light salads, vegetable soups, and fruit. Check out the fast food places in your community to determine which ones provide the best menu choices for you.

13. **Grasp smoothie tricks of the trade.** Some smoothies—packed with fruits and even vegetables—actually do offer a nutrient-rich option for a healthful snack, but others are the nutritional equivalent

of a milk shake. If you love smoothies, choose ones that contain whole fruits and vegetables and no added sugars—and get the smallest size. Remember, a smoothie is more like a snack than a beverage to accompany your meal.

14. **Do ethnic food right.** You'll find some of the most delicious plant-powered meals awaiting you in ethnic restaurants, from Vietnamese and Mexican to Indian and Middle Eastern. Unfortunately, sometimes restaurant food doesn't meet their traditional cuisines' true potential because of their preparation (see item 8). Vegetable stir-fries can be loaded down in oil and soy sauce; Thai and Indian curries can be thick with cream, coconut milk, and butter; and refried beans can contain lard, bacon grease, or oil. Get to know your local ethnic hot spots and talk to the chef about how the food is prepared. Make a few special requests, such as no cream in the sauce, vegetarian refried beans, and brown rice instead of white.

15. **Recognize that salads aren't always light.** Sure, I want you to eat more veggies, but thanks to decadent additions, salads aren't always the healthiest choice on the menu: They can pack up to 1,300 calories, 34 grams of saturated fat and 2,300 milligrams of sodium. You don't have to skip out on salads at your favorite lunch spot altogether; just watch out for these additions that can add up to beaucoup calories:

   - Croutons, wonton strips, and tortilla chips can be high in fat and calories.
   - Ladles of salad dressings and vinaigrettes can toss in hundreds of extra calories. Always ask for dressing on the side and use only a tiny bit for flavor.
   - Frisbee-sized taco or tostada shells can contain 500 calories each because they're deep-fried.
   - A liberal serving of crumbled and grated cheeses can load up the calories, sodium, and saturated fat. If you're a plant-powered vegetarian or omnivore, ask for your salad to be "easy on the cheese."
   - Processed meats, such as ham, salami, or turkey and chicken slices, can be packed with sodium (some may be rife with saturated fat, too). If you're a plant-based omnivore, opt for poached salmon or grilled chicken slices on your salad.

- Avocado, nuts, dried fruits—they're all healthy plant foods that I recommend you include in your diet *in moderation*. A little goes a long way with these. If you have a whole avocado (322 calories), 60g of walnuts (383 calories), and 70g of raisins (247 calories) on your salad . . . just do the math.[6]

16. Support plant-based dining. Even if you're a plant-based omnivore, take the opportunity to scope out vegetarian restaurants in your community and prioritize them when you eat out. Many offer imaginative, delicious ways to serve up plant-based meals, making it easy to skip meat for the night. For a real experience of the senses, check out a raw-foods restaurant, which serves only raw, plant-based foods (that haven't been heated to over 115 degrees) in extremely imaginative preparations, such as pizza made with a crust of sprouted sunflower seeds and squash, and tacos made with real spinach "tortillas." Although I believe there's not enough science to indicate you need to eat all your foods in their raw state, I do find raw food to be downright delicious.

17. Don't be afraid to ask. The best thing you can do for yourself at a restaurant is to ask a lot of questions, and for something special. Inquire about how the dish is prepared: Is it fried? What's in the sauce? Can I get it plain? Restaurants have grown more and more accommodating over the years. You usually have many more options than just what's listed on the menu. Have it your way when you dine out. Here are a few special requests worth making:

- Ask for a soup and salad—or even two appetizers—instead of an entrée.
- Create your own vegetable platter by requesting a baked potato, small portion of pasta, grains, or beans, and assorted vegetables they have on hand.
- If you see something on the menu that appeals to you—such as a salad with fruit, vegetables, and nuts—but it includes an ingredient you're trying to avoid—such as bacon—simply ask for the menu item without that ingredient.
- If you're a plant-powered omnivore, ask for your fish to be grilled rather than fried.
- Beg the cook to leave the butter out of your vegetables.

18. **Sweet solutions.** Your entrée is finished, and you're considering the dessert menu. It may seem obvious, but it bears repeating: Most sweet choices on the dessert list are wickedly calorie-laden, and 350-calorie cookies, 1,600-calorie ice cream sundaes, and 1,000-calorie slices of cheesecake will really weigh you down. After chowing down on a full dinner, who can afford that many calories? If you want to be able to zip your pants on the way home, try skipping dessert in exchange for a nice cup of coffee or tea, splitting a dessert with the whole table, or opting for simple fruit or sorbet.

PLANT-POWERED DINING

Whether you're a plant-powered vegan, vegetarian, or omnivore, your goal is to include more plant-based meals in your lifestyle for optimal health. And you can easily achieve this goal when you dine out; vegetarian meals are becoming de rigueur in restaurants even in the meat-loving USA. In a recent National Restaurant Association survey of chefs, meatless menu options were reported as one of the hottest trends, with 25 percent of chefs reporting that vegetable meals were a "perennial favorite" in their restaurants.[7] Nearly every restaurant offers a plant-based option on the menu, but don't forget to ask for something special or create your own unique combination. Check out Plant-Powered Options on the Menu, below, for ideas on how to order at restaurants in your locale.

PLANT-POWERED OPTIONS ON THE MENU

MENU CATEGORY	EXAMPLES OF MENU ITEMS
Beverages	Fruit or vegetable juice or smoothie Soy cafe latte or soy cappuccino Soy or peanut butter smoothie Tomato juice
Breakfast	Buckwheat or whole wheat pancakes and waffles Granola or muesli Oatmeal or grits
Appetizers	Bruschetta Edamame, cooked in shell Vegetables with dip Hummus Tapenade Olives or mixed nuts

MENU CATEGORY	EXAMPLES OF MENU ITEMS
Soups	Black bean soup Miso soup Split-pea or lentil soup Tomato soup Vegetable or minestrone soup
Salads	Barley, quinoa, or pasta salad Corn salad Cucumber salad Green salad Tabbouleh Three-bean, lentil, or black-eyed pea salad
Side Dishes	Baked potato or sweet potato Corn on the cob Red beans and rice Steamed brown rice or couscous Steamed, sautéed, or grilled vegetables Vegetarian refried beans Wild rice or quinoa pilaf
Breads/Sandwiches	Corn bread Whole grain roll or crackers Peanut butter sandwich Veggie burger Whole grain vegetable sandwich, wrap, or sub
Entrées	Bean burritos or vegetarian chili Falafel Moussaka Pasta primavera Ratatouille Dal (i.e., a spicy lentil or bean stew) Curry with vegetables, tofu, and/or nuts Stir-fry with vegetables, tofu, and/or nuts Whole grain pasta with pesto or marinara Whole grain vegetable lasagna Whole grain vegetable pizza
Desserts	Fresh fruit cup Fruit pie Fruit sorbet

PLANT-POWERED EATING ON THE ROAD

When I was a girl, our car didn't roll out of the driveway without our stocked picnic box securely tucked away in the back. In those days, healthful, plant-based food options on the road were few and far between. Now, plant-based options are available almost everywhere, including supermarkets, gas stations, coffeehouses, airports, airplanes, bus stations, truck stops, food trucks, convenience stores, sports and entertainment venues, places of employment, schools, and hospitals. Whether you're spending a day at an amusement park, a weekend at the beach, or a week in Europe, you certainly won't starve to death if you're focused on plant-based eating. It just might take a little ingenuity on your part. Here are my top tips for taking your plant-based eating style on the road:

1. **Pack some goodies.** Whether you're gone for a day or a week, it helps to carry a few essentials to fall back on if you can't find healthy choices on your trip. Here are some of my favorites:

   - **Soy Milk.** Individual, shelf-stable cartons are convenient to tuck into your purse or bag when soy milk may not be available to accompany your coffee or cereal.

   - **Nuts.** Packed in individual bags, nuts are handy to throw into your purse or handbag. These protein-rich plant foods can take the edge off your appetite, as well as round out a meal if your only options are a baked potato or vegetable soup.

   - **Dried Fruits.** These hardy fruits—the ultimate backpacking staple—can be tucked into individual bags for a healthy snack or to accompany a meal. You can practically run over a bag of dried fruit with a truck and it'll still be there, ready to dole out its high-fiber, high-nutrient energy.

   - **Seaweed Snacks.** If you like the flavor of these dried seaweed treats, they make an excellent filler when healthy food choices aren't available.

   - **Granola.** A bag of good granola, such as Plant-Powered Granola (page 345), is a great fallback meal with plant-based milk, especially if all you can find for breakfast in the motel lobby is a doughnut tray.

   - **Whole Grain Crackers.** Take along packaged crackers or flatbreads that feature whole grains as their first ingredient and are moderate in sodium. In a pinch, crackers can pair with all of the above snacks for a meal on the go.

   - **Whole-Food Nutrition Bars.** I'm not a fan of most granola or nutrition bars, which are often packed with processed carbs, sugars, and artificial ingredients, making them awfully close to candy bars. But there are a few, such as Larabars and Kind Bars, that are made with real ingredients. Pack a few away in your duffel bag in case you miss a meal.

2. **Scope out the dining scene.** Take an opportunity when you travel to check out the restaurant offerings in the region. Even if you're hitting an amusement park for the day, you can visit the Web site to see what dining options are available. And if you're headed to a new city, look into the plant-based eating choices available in the area.

3. **Embrace a new food culture.** If you're traveling to a completely new territory, whether it's Asia or Mexico, take this chance to sample local plant-based cuisine. Most every country offers delicious plant-based dishes, from beans and rice to tofu and vegetable stir-fries. And with more and more vegetarians hitting the road, you'll find plenty of light, plant-based options in most countries these days.

4. **A healthy road trip.** If you're taking a cross-country road trip, truck stops, gas stations, and fast food restaurants can often leave you short on healthful food choices. You're better off packing a cooler and picnicking at a rest stop along the way. Pack wraps, sandwiches, fruits, grain salads, and plant-based yogurts to make healthy eating easy and delicious.

5. **If you're stuck.** OK, we've all been there. You're committed to healthy eating, you're tummy is growling, and the only thing for miles is a 24-hour convenience store. Look for these items to quell your growling stomach: granola bars, whole fruit, yogurt (for plant-powered vegetarians or omnivores), peanuts, sunflower seeds, and whole grain crackers.

6. **Use a supermarket as a restaurant.** More and more supermarkets, from Trader Joe's to Whole Foods, offer delicious, plant-based take-away foods that you can either stock in your hotel fridge or pack in a picnic basket for a day trip. They are one of my favorite resources for healthy food choices on the road.

7. **Airplane planning.** Long gone are the days when you placed a special vegetarian meal request at the airlines before your flight. Nowadays, you're lucky if you have any food offered to you at all. You might be able to catch a healthy, plant-based option at the airport, such as a Mediterranean grilled veggie pita. But if you're rushing to catch a connecting flight, you can go hours without eating. For your next

flight, if the airline allows it, pack your own lunch in an insulated cooler bag: A plant-powered vegetable sandwich with hummus, avocado, lettuce, and tomatoes; a piece of fresh fruit; and some carrot sticks. Everyone will be jealous of your well-planned meal.

8. Speak up! Wherever you travel, ask for help. Whether you express your nutrition requests to the hotel staff, a restaurant owner, or your friend who is hosting you on the fold-out couch, don't be afraid to enlist everyone's help (without being a pest) so that you can have a pleasant, healthy dining experience on the road.

"I went vegetarian for about five years, purely for ethical reasons, but I didn't go about it in the smartest way. I basically replaced all the meat I was eating with cheese. Naturally, I kept gaining weight. I was on my way to getting obese, and a cheese lover's pizza with extra cheese didn't help at all. By the time I was 25, I had diabetic symptoms, and I was diagnosed with it when I was 28. The next day I went vegan—rather a cheating vegan. I would go to my favorite Mexican restaurant every Wednesday and get all-you-can-eat enchiladas. After a while, the trips to the Mexican restaurant subsided, until finally I simply no longer craved it. My diabetic symptoms went away in the first three months. After switching my diet, my eyesight corrected, I lost over a hundred pounds, and I became healthier, stronger, and had more endurance in my 30s than I did when I was a high school basketball player. Going vegan exposed me to factory farming issues, and that made me even happier about being vegan. Not only did I have a clean body, but my mind and heart felt clean, too."

—JASON, a plant-powered vegan in Phoenix, Arizona

"I eat a semi-vegetarian diet, and for a few months each year, I eat a full vegan diet. I find that eating a plant-based diet naturally helps to keep my weight in check, and I feel that it's better for optimal health and healthier for the environment. My cholesterol and blood sugar are low, and markers of inflammation are low. I

have learned how to use herbs and spices and I have a backyard garden, but also shop at my local farmers market every week, year-round."

—JULIE, a plant-powered omnivore from Tiburon, California

❧ PLANT-POWERED ACTION ALERT **DAY 14**

After reading this chapter, schedule a night out at a local restaurant, and put your knowledge about healthy, plant-based eating to the test.

Take the Powerful Plants Plunge

Every day you've been building up a repertoire of nutrition and lifestyle habits that culminate in a whole plant foods eating style. Now it's time to get started with your plan in earnest. Remember, a plant-powered diet—whether you choose a vegan, vegetarian, or omnivore eating style—isn't something you go "on" and "off": it's a way of eating for life. It's not a fad diet. Plant-based eating is delicious, satisfying, and nutritionally sound. It's good for everyone in your family, from your children to your spouse to your parents.

The Daily Plant-Powered Guide that follows will lead you to choose the right number and kind of whole plant foods every day. Selecting the lowest number of servings suggested in each food category (not including the optional items) will provide you with about 1,500 calories per day; the highest number of servings provides about 2,500 calories per day; and the middle of the range provides about 2,000 calories per day. You can divide up the servings within your day as you see fit; some people like to have six small meals per day, while others prefer eating only a few times a day. For suggestions on how to plan your meals, see my 14-Day Plant-Powered Menu Planner in chapter 13 (page 266).

DAILY PLANT-POWERED GUIDE

PLANT-POWERED FOOD GROUPS	SERVING SIZES	PLANT-POWERED VEGAN	PLANT-POWERED VEGETARIAN	PLANT-POWERED OMNIVORE
Plant Proteins	**Legumes and Soy Foods:** 85g beans, lentils, dried peas, tofu, tempeh, seitan, or meat alternative 125g protein-rich, plant-based milk alternative or yogurt	3–5 servings, including two calcium- and vitamin D-fortified foods, and consider a calcium and vitamin D supplement to meet needs Vitamin B$_{12}$-fortified foods or supplement to meet needs (RDA is 2.4 mcg/day)	2–4 servings	1–2 servings
	Nuts and Seeds: 30g nuts or seeds 2 tablespoons nut or seed butter	2 servings	1–2 servings	1–2 servings
Optional Proteins for Plant-Powered Vegetarians or Omnivores	**Fat-Free or Low-Fat Dairy Products:** 250ml milk or yogurt 100g cottage cheese 45g cheese	0 servings	2 servings*	2 servings*
	Eggs: 1 egg (30g)	0 servings	1 serving†	(included in Lean Animal Protein servings†)
	Lean Animal Protein: Seafood, skinless poultry, limiting red and processed meat to occasional use	0 servings	0 servings	3–5 ounces†

PLANT-POWERED FOOD GROUPS	SERVING SIZES	PLANT-POWERED VEGAN	PLANT-POWERED VEGETARIAN	PLANT-POWERED OMNIVORE
Whole Grains	90g cooked whole grains such as wheat berries, oats, brown rice or quinoa 70g cooked whole grain pasta 1 slice whole grain bread 50g whole grain ready-to-eat breakfast cereal 30g whole grain crackers 20cm whole grain or corn tortilla	5–11 servings	5–8 servings	5–8 servings
Vegetables	30g raw leafy greens 40g other fresh or cooked vegetables 50ml reduced-sodium vegetable juice	6–9 servings, including at least one leafy green vegetable every day	6–9 servings	6–9 servings
Fruit	1 small, apple, pear, banana, or orange 80g fresh, frozen, or canned unsweetened fruit 30g dried fruit 125ml unsweetened juice	3–4 servings	3–4 servings	3–4 servings
Fats	1 tablespoon vegetable oil, mayonnaise, or regular salad dressing 2 tablespoons light mayonnaise or salad dressing 23 olives or ¼ avocado	1–3 servings‡	1–3 servings‡	1–2 servings‡
Herbs and Spices	Fresh, dried, or ground forms	Use liberally	Use liberally	Use liberally

PLANT-POWERED FOOD GROUPS	SERVING SIZES	PLANT-POWERED VEGAN	PLANT-POWERED VEGETARIAN	PLANT-POWERED OMNIVORE
Beverages	225ml water, unsweetened tea, or coffee	8-13 servings	8-13 servings	8-13 servings
	Alcohol: 150ml red wine (may substitute 150ml white wine, 350ml beer, or 45ml spirits)	0-1 serving women 0-2 servings men	0-1 serving women 0-2 servings men	0-1 serving women 0-2 servings men
Optional	**Treats (100-130 calories per serving):** 30g dark chocolate (at least 70% cocoa) 1 small cookie 50g plant-based ice cream or sorbet 30g baked crisps	0-1 serving	0-1 serving	0-1 serving
Total Macronutrient Distribution		14% protein 55% carbohydrate 31% fat	16-17% protein 51-57% carbohydrate 26-33% fat	18% protein 47-51% carbohydrate 31-35% fat
Moderate to Vigorous Physical Activity		At least 20-30 minutes, including strength training twice/week[5]	At least 20-30 minutes, including strength training twice/week[5]	At least 20-30 minutes, including strength training twice/week[5]

Notes to the Daily Plant-Powered Guide:
Sources: See Chapter 1, note 3 (page 369), and Chapter 3, notes 16, 17, and 18 (pages 373–74).

Servings are based on a daily intake of 1,500 to 2,500 calories (not including optional servings), which is the appropriate range for weight loss and weight maintenance for most adults, depending on age, sex, and activity level. Macronutrient Distribution was calculated according to lowest and highest number of servings in Vegan, Vegetarian, and Omnivore diet patterns.

*May replace Dairy servings with calcium- and vitamin D–fortified Legumes and Soy Foods servings.

†May replace Egg or Animal Protein servings with Legumes and Soy Foods Servings (30g animal protein replaces 1 serving Legumes and Soy Foods).

‡In addition to servings of nuts and seeds; see the Daily Plant-Powered Protein Guide (page 77).

§Work up to this daily goal for physical activity; include muscle-strengthening activities of all major muscle groups at least twice per week; refer to chapter 10 for more information on physical activity.

AIMING FOR WEIGHT LOSS

If your goal is to lose weight, generally you should shoot for the lowest number of servings recommended in each food group. This will provide you with a balanced diet of about 1,500 calories per day. If you add either a treat, such as dark chocolate, or a glass of red wine, the calorie level will be closer to 1,600 calories per day. Depending on their size, gender, and activity levels, this provides most people with a slow, steady weight loss of about three to five pounds per month. Check out the Estimated Calorie Requirement chart (page 248) to see how many calories you need every day. In order to lose weight, you should reduce your calorie intake by about 500 calories per day to lose about four pounds per month. When it comes to weight loss, remember to set a realistic weight-loss goal for yourself and to include daily physical activity (see chapter 10), which can significantly boost your calorie requirement levels.

The Plant-Powered Diet isn't about crash dieting or just getting "skinny." It's about achieving a way of eating that can promote a safe, healthy weight loss, as well as optimal health for life. It's about *feeling good* about what you put into your body. The real beauty of this eating style is that you don't have to obsess over your food intake and feel hungry or cheated, as with fad diet plans. Instead, this eating style fosters a healthy relationship with food, because you're making choices that nourish your mind, body, and soul, as well as the environment around you.

These plant-powered foods are so naturally rich in fiber and nutrients and low in calories, you'll find that the foods pretty much do all of the "work" of a weight-loss diet for you—they easily fill you up and satisfy you. Even on a 1,500- to 1,600-calorie meal plan, you'll find generous portions of delicious foods that won't leave you feeling hungry. I know, because it's the way I eat every day, and I never suffer from hunger pangs. I have enough energy to exercise—and I mean run, row, lift weights, and ski—as well as concentrate on my busy life and everyday activities. Our family enjoys the foods that are listed in the Daily Plant-Powered Guide every day, and we are thriving: My two teenage sons are tall, lean, fit, and active—both are in high school sports teams, such as football and cross-country. My husband and I enjoy vibrant health and a healthy weight. And most important, we love food! We enjoy shopping, preparing, savoring, and talking about delicious food. We dine out, experience food cultures as we travel, and serve fabulous, plant-based foods to our friends and family in our home. There's no starvation and suffering going on in our house: just good, wholesome food and lots of activity.

If you're like many people, switching your eating style to a plant-based approach is all you need to do to start losing weight. For others, it may take a little closer attention to serving size. No matter what, I suggest that you start your plant-based diet by following the Daily Plant-Powered Guide (see page 244). You'll get a better handle on which foods you should include every day to meet your nutritional needs and to gain maximum health benefits, as well as which foods you should keep under control, such as nuts, avocados, olive oil, and dried fruits. That's why my Daily Plant-Powered Guide limits servings for many of these foods in order to help you lose weight or maintain a healthy weight. If you can't remember which particular foods you should focus on within each food group, flip back to the chapter that reviews these foods thoroughly. Once you get the hang of a plant-powered diet, it will come as naturally to you as breathing.

ESTIMATED CALORIE REQUIREMENTS

GENDER	AGE	ACTIVITY LEVEL		
		Sedentary	Moderately Active	Active
Child, either gender	2–3	1,000	1,000–1,400	1,000–1,400
Female	4–8	1,200	1,400–1,600	1,400–1,800
Female	9–13	1,600	1,600–2,000	1,800–2,000

GENDER	AGE	ACTIVITY LEVEL		
		Sedentary	Moderately Active	Active
Female	14–18	1,800	2,000	2,400
Female	19–30	2,000	2,000–2,200	2,400
Female	31–50	1,800	2,000	2,200
Female	51+	1,600	1,800	2,000–2,200
Male	4–8	1,400	1,400–1,600	1,600–2,000
Male	9–13	1,800	1,800–2,200	2,000–2,600
Male	14–18	2,200	2,400–2,800	2,800–3,200
Male	19–30	2,400	2,600–2,800	3,000
Male	31–50	2,200	2,400–2,600	2,800–3,000
Male	51+	2,000	2,200–2,400	2,400–2,800

Source: U.S. Department of Health and Human Services, *Estimated Calorie Requirements,* *2005,* http://nhlbi.nih.gov/health/public/heart/obesity/wecan/downloads/calreqtips.pdf

These levels are based on Estimated Energy Requirements from the Institute of Medicine Dietary Reference Intakes macronutrients report, calculated by gender, age, and activity level for average-sized individuals.

Sedentary means a lifestyle that includes only the light physical activity associated with typical day-to-day life.

Moderately active means a lifestyle that includes physical activity equivalent to walking about 1.5 to 3 miles per day at 3 to 4 miles per hour, in addition to the light physical activity associated with typical day-to-day life.

Active means a lifestyle that includes physical activity equivalent to walking more than 3 miles per day at 3 to 4 miles per hour, in addition to the light physical activity associated with typical day-to-day life.

WHEN WEIGHT IS NOT AN ISSUE

If your goal is to maintain your weight and achieve optimal health, you may need to consume more servings of foods than the minimum amount listed in the guide. If you eat the maximum number of servings in the guide, you'll consume about 2,500 calories per day; and if you choose a number of servings between the lowest and highest levels, you'll be getting closer to 2,000 calories, the average calorie requirement for most adults. The Estimated Calorie Requirements chart, above, can help guide you. If you are not overweight, use the Daily Plant-Powered Guide (page 244) to steer your choices, and let hunger be your guide as to how many extra servings you need beyond the minimum. If you require a great deal of calories to maintain your weight, you may need to work a little harder at fitting a sufficient number of servings of plant foods into your diet. Your main goal is to develop a balanced, plant-based eating approach that focuses on whole, unprocessed plant foods that can provide you with proven health benefits.

TREAT YOURSELF RIGHT

Deprivation—that feeling of being denied food—is a terrible side effect of "dieting"; it can make you feel hungry and discouraged and lead to unhealthful eating binges. That's why it's important to make your diet reasonable and achievable beyond the short term. This is where many fad diets fail; they can be overly restrictive and punitive, making it difficult to follow an eating plan for the long haul. Some "diets" exclude an entire food group, such as grains, making them nearly impossible—and unhealthy— to follow for a long period of time. Fad diets can make you feel guilty for "cheating" on your diet, which is never a good way to feel about food. The Plant-Powered Diet is a lifestyle; it's not a short-term diet you "go on" for six months, only to quickly resort back to an unhealthful lifestyle that will promote weight gain and health problems later on.

Let's face it: In order to live with a diet for the long term, it needs to be reasonable and enjoyable. You're going to want to get a little perk every once in a while, such as a sweet treat after a long day or even a handful of crisps at a picnic. It's easy to become so overly concerned with eating a healthful diet that you can lose balance and steer into a fearful relationship with food—and that's not healthy! You'll notice that the Daily Plant-Powered Guide (page 244) allows for up to one treat and one glass of red wine (up to two glasses for men) per day; this flexibility can help you live a lifestyle that is *livable*. For each treat serving or glass of wine you'll add 100 to 130 calories to your daily diet. If your goal is to consume about 1,600 calories per day in order to lose weight, you can easily fit in a small treat (or a glass of red wine) by following a 1,500-calorie meal plan the rest of the day. The idea is to make your treats modest—about 100 to 130 calories per portion—and as healthful as possible.

My favorite treat is 30g of dark chocolate, which makes me feel rewarded in a healthy yet indulgent way. Other treats can include the following:

- 100-calorie bag of cookies
- Small soy ice cream sandwich (130 calories)
- Small whole grain oatmeal raisin cookie (130 calories)
- 30g bag of baked crisps (120 calories)
- 50g of soy ice cream or fruit sorbet (120 calories)
- A serving of one of my dessert recipes, such as Date, Walnut, and Dark Chocolate Cookies (122 calories; see page 367).

A treat can also be a small portion of something yummy at a special occasion—whether it's a birthday party or a fancy dinner out. Is the table sharing a slice of rich chocolate cake? Just take a couple of bites to enjoy the flavor profile as your treat. When you allow special foods like this in your diet, you don't ever have to feel cheated or guilty. If weight is not a problem for you, you can fit in these small treats and a glass of wine (if you drink) every day without a problem. But if your calorie needs are modest, you may need to trim them down to every other day or significantly boost your exercise in order to keep your weight loss on track. Remember, you've got the natural goodness of "treats" already planned into your plant-powered eating plan: fruits! They're nature's perfect sweet treat that can help you feel satisfied when you're looking for a splurge. A bowl of fresh raspberries, a crisp apple, or a serving of dried apricots is a "dessert" you can enjoy three times a day!

This same philosophy goes for the entire Plant-Powered Diet. Your goal isn't to attain perfection; you should simply focus on making the wisest food choices possible every day. For example, this way of eating calls for whole grains, most often in their whole, unprocessed form, instead of refined grains, but there will be times when you can't find whole grain bread at the sandwich shop or brown rice at a Chinese restaurant. There will be times when you're invited to a friend's house for dinner and the only thing available is white spaghetti, or when you stay overnight at a relative's house and white pancakes are on the breakfast menu. The same goes for all the food choices on your Plant-Powered Diet. Set your goal and aim for it, but don't beat yourself up if you fall short occasionally. Just get back to your healthful eating and exercise plan and you'll be fine. The most important thing you can do is set up your plant-based lifestyle within your environment—at home, work, and in your community—so that you plot a course for success.

PORTION SIZE IS KEY

One of the most difficult challenges you face when you're trying to manage your weight is portion control. If you're dishing up double or triple the suggested serving size, it can push your calorie levels up, and your weight loss can stall. Research shows that, when you're faced with large portions, chances are you'll scrape your plate clean—whether or not you're hungry. Here are a few tips to help you master serving size:

- **Use scales.** It's really tricky to eyeball certain foods and estimate the portion size accurately. For example, 80g cereal—or a 40g of granola—may not look like much in the bottom of a huge cereal bowl, and a 60g portion of pasta looks pretty petite on a large dinner plate. That's why it's a good idea to use scales for a few days in order to get a better feel for what a particular serving size looks like.
- **Use visual guides.** Sometimes it's not convenient to get out a measuring cup to measure your food, so use these handy visual guides for portions:
    80g cereal flakes = a baseball
    1 pancake = a DVD
    60g cooked pasta = a light bulb
    1 slice bread = a CD
    1 tablespoon oil = a poker chip
    1 medium fruit = a baseball
    1 baked potato = a computer mouse
- **Use small plates.** Studies show that if you dish up your foods into large bowls, plates, and platters you'll eat more. And when you use a larger serving spoon you'll end up serving yourself more food and consuming more calories.[1] So, use small bowls for cereal, and use salad plates for small meals.
- **Don't eat straight out of the container.** Unfortunately, the calories you eat directly out of a container while standing in front of an open refrigerator door *do* count. If you take little nibbles and bites here and there, they can add up to whole servings of food. If you'd like a snack, get out a plate, portion out your snack, sit down, and enjoy it.

- **Read the food label.** All packaged foods, from crackers to tofu, contain suggested serving sizes. Read the suggested serving size on the food label so you know how much you should dish up before you dine. It can make a huge difference in the amount of calories you consume.
- **Use caution with snacks.** Even if you're snacking on a healthy item, such as dried fruits, nuts, or whole grain crackers, it's possible to overdo your portion size. Instead of eating out of an open bag or box—a dangerous habit—portion out the correct amount into an individual bag or dish.

UNDERSTANDING FOOD LABELS

Does it seem like the nutrition information on the food label is written in another language? Although this may seem true, it's important that you learn the language of food labels to discover important clues about the foods you consider purchasing. The ingredient list on a food label is the listing of each ingredient found in the product in descending order of predominance. The nutrition facts panel provides information about the nutrients contained in the product. Not every nutrient you need will be listed on the label, but if you eat a balanced, whole-foods, plant-based diet, you should meet your nutrient needs just fine. The sample label below, along with the key on the following page, will help guide you toward healthier food choices:

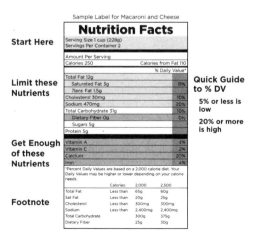

Source: See Chapter 12, note 3 (page 391).

Serving Size, Servings Per Container: Look here for the portion size and how many servings are in the container.

Calories: Check out how many calories each serving contains.

% Daily Value (DV): Indicates what percentage of your daily requirement of a particular nutrient you will get in one serving, based on the average person's daily needs; 5% or less is low, and 20% or more is high.

Total Fat: This amount includes *all* fats, whether "good" or "bad."

Saturated Fat, Sodium, Sugars: Keep these amounts as low as possible. However, in foods that contain fruit, the "sugars" listed include the natural sugars in the fruit.

Dietary Fiber, Vitamins A and C, Calcium, Iron: Boost these nutrient levels in particular, as most people's diets are short on them.

Footnote: This tells you what your daily goals for some nutrients should be on a 2,000- or 2,500-calorie diet.[2]

KEEP A RECORD TO STAY ON TRACK

One way to kick-start your new plant-powered eating plan and boost your chances for success is to keep a food and exercise journal. Studies have consistently found that recording and tracking your diet and exercise helps promote successful weight-loss outcomes.[3] Although many online services and smart-phone apps provide these services, you can do it the old-fashioned way by using the following Plant-Powered Food and Exercise Journal page. Simply reproduce this form to create a template for your own personal diary. Record all the foods and beverages that you take in all day long, as well as your physical activity, in order to stay focused on your eating, exercise and weight goals.

To learn how to fill out a daily entry, check out the sample Plant-Powered Food and Exercise Journal entry on pages 256–57. This should give you an idea of how to quickly and easily record your food intake and exercise, although feel free to write your notes in whatever way makes the most sense to you. To find recipes for the dishes noted in the sample entry, you can turn to my Plant-Powered Recipe Collection (page 270).

PLANT-POWERED FOOD AND EXERCISE JOURNAL

DATE: _____   WEIGHT: _____

MEAL	FOOD INTAKE	PROTEIN	NUTS AND SEEDS	WHOLE GRAINS	VEGGIES	FRUIT	FATS	BEVERAGES	TREATS/WINE
Breakfast									
Morning Snack									
Lunch									
Afternoon Snack									
Dinner									
Evening Snack									

Physical Activity: _____   Duration: _____

Physical Activity: _____   Duration: _____

Note: Record all foods and beverages consumed (including water), along with portion sizes. Note how many servings of each food category the portion provides in the appropriate column. Record all types of physical activity and their duration. Weigh yourself at the same time of day once a week, and record it in your journal.

A DAY OUT OF A SAMPLE PLANT-POWERED FOOD AND EXERCISE JOURNAL   DATE: MAY 12   WEIGHT: 135 POUNDS

MEAL	FOOD INTAKE	PROTEIN	NUTS AND SEEDS	WHOLE GRAINS	VEGGIES	FRUIT	FATS	BEVERAGES	TREATS/WINE
Breakfast	Ancient Grain Porridge with Figs and Dates (page 349) (small bowl)		½	1		½			
	Plant-based milk (250ml)	1						1	
	Coffee (250ml)							1	
	Vegetable juice (175ml)				1			¾	
Morning Snack	Whole grain flatbread with soy cheese (25g)	1		1					
	Water (500ml)							2	
Lunch	Grapefruit and Avocado Ensalada (page 289) (medium bowl)				1	1	1		
	Spicy Broccoli Cashew Pizza (page 302) (1 slice)	½	½	1	½				
	Fresh raspberries (125g)					1			
	Green tea (250ml)							1	

MEAL	FOOD INTAKE	PROTEIN	NUTS AND SEEDS	WHOLE GRAINS	VEGGIES	FRUIT	FATS	BEVERAGES	TREATS/WINE
Afternoon Snack	Whole grain crackers (25g)			1					
	Water (500ml)							2	
	Winter Buckwheat Vegetable Soup (page 287) (small bowl)			½	1				
Dinner	Antipasto Couscous with Chickpeas (page 310) (small bowl)	½	1	1	1		1		
	Steamed broccoli (150g)				2				
	Red wine (150ml)								1
	Water (250ml)							1	
Evening Snack	Watermelon (150g)					1			
	Water (500ml)							2	
Total Servings		3	2	5½	6½	3½	2	10¾	1

Physical Activity: Gardening **Duration:** 45 minutes

Physical Activity: Biking **Duration:** 1 hour

A PLANT-POWERED PANTRY

It's time to dig in and make your plant-powered lifestyle happen, and there's only one way to do that: Stock your kitchen with all the key elements you'll need to cook up healthy plant-based meals. If you have the right ingredients at your fingertips, it'll be a cinch to create delicious, wholesome meals every day of the week. To get started, check out my Ten-Ingredient Plant-Powered Pantry Kit.

TEN-INGREDIENT PLANT-POWERED PANTRY KIT

Do you think cooking is really difficult? If so, you're not alone. Thanks to the elimination of home economics classes in schools and an abundance of easy, convenient foods, people's cooking skills have all but vanished over the past couple of decades. But healthy cooking doesn't have to be arduous. You don't have to follow complicated recipes in order to prepare tasty meals. Have you ever wanted to be one of those cooks who simply opens the refrigerator door and whips up a fabulous meal in minutes based on the ingredients found in the kitchen? I'll show you how to be just that sort of home chef! If you have these ten items in your kitchen, along with fresh vegetables in season (or frozen vegetables) and some tofu (or seafood or chicken for you omnivores), you can create any number of meals—and I promise they will be quick, easy and delicious.

1. Garlic (fresh is best)
2. Extra virgin olive oil (EVOO) (including flavored oils such as basil, garlic and lemon)
3. Fresh lemons
4. Black pepper and red pepper flakes
5. Low-sodium herbal seasoning (see page 199)
6. Dried herbs and spices
7. Whole grains (quinoa, brown rice, barley and farro) and whole grain pasta
8. Beans, peas, and lentils (dried or canned, no salt added)
9. Canned tomatoes (no salt added)
10. Vinegars (balsamic, red wine, sherry, rice and/or flavored)

Check out these simple, one-dish combinations based on my Ten-Ingredient Plant-Powered Pantry Kit:

EASY MEAL FIXES FROM YOUR PLANT-POWERED PANTRY

TURN THIS . . . ⟶		INTO THIS:
EVOO, garlic, lemon juice, spinach, canned haricot beans, and whole grain pasta	Cook and drain the pasta and toss it with the spinach, drained beans, garlic, EVOO and lemon juice.	Italian Spinach and White Bean Whole Wheat Pasta
EVOO, garlic, ginger, lemon juice, low-sodium herbal seasoning, frozen mixed vegetables, tofu and cooked brown rice	Stir-fry the EVOO, garlic, ginger, lemon juice, herbal seasoning, frozen mixed vegetables and tofu and serve over brown rice.	Lemon Ginger Vegetable Stir-Fry with Brown Rice
Onions and garlic, canned kidney beans, canned tomatoes, and chili powder	Sauté the onions and garlic in heavy pot; add the drained beans, tomatoes, and chili powder and cook until the onions are tender.	Vegetarian Chili Bean Pot
Garlic, lemon juice, EVOO, low-sodium herbal seasoning, lettuce, canned chickpeas, fresh vegetables (e.g., broccoli, carrots, celery, cucumbers, mangetout, tomatoes)	Whisk together the garlic, lemon juice, EVOO, and low-sodium herbal seasoning; arrange the lettuce, chickpeas and assorted fresh vegetables on a platter; drizzle with vinaigrette.	Chickpea Vegetable Salad with Lemon Herb Vinaigrette

Once you're comfortable with this new cooking style, you'll be ready to branch out. Just take my Plant-Powered Pantry List for Shelf-Stable Foods on the following pages to the supermarket or natural food store and stock up on these always-handy essentials.

When your pantry is stocked, simply add fresh (and frozen) items to your refrigerator or freezer each week, using my Weekly Plant-Powered Shopping List for Fresh Foods (see page 262).

PLANT-POWERED PANTRY LIST FOR SHELF-STABLE FOODS

Plant Proteins

- [ ] Canned beans and peas, no salt added, e.g., black beans, cannellini beans, chickpeas, kidney beans

- [ ] Canned vegetarian chili (low-sodium)

- [ ] Dried beans, e.g. adzuki beans, black beans, kidney beans, haricot beans, pinto beans

- [ ] Dried lentils

- [ ] Dried peas, e.g., black-eyed peas, chickpeas (garbanzo beans), split peas

- [ ] Plant-based milk alternatives (shelf-stable)

- [ ] Nuts, e.g. almonds, hazelnuts, peanuts, pecans, pine nuts, pecans, pistachios, walnuts

- [ ] Nut and seed butters, e.g. almond butter, peanut butter, sunflower seed butter, tahini

- [ ] Seeds, e.g. chia, flax, hemp, pumpkin, sesame, sunflower

- [ ] Soy nuts

- [ ] Tofu (shelf-stable)

Whole Grains

- [ ] Polenta

- [ ] Popcorn, plain kernels or "light" microwave popcorn

- [ ] Whole grains, e.g., amaranth, barley, buckwheat (groats), millet, oats, quinoa, rice (brown or wild), rye berries, sorghum, spelt, teff, wheat (bulgur, wheat berries)

- [ ] Whole grain baking mixes, e.g. pancake mix, biscuit mix

- [ ] Whole grain crackers, flatbread (minimal added ingredients)

- [ ] Whole grain flours, e.g., amaranth, barley, buckwheat, quinoa, rice, rye, whole wheat

- [ ] Whole grain pasta or noodles, e.g., brown rice pasta, buckwheat soba noodles, multi-grain pasta, whole wheat pasta

- [ ] Whole grain pizza crust (shelf stable)

Vegetables

- [ ] Canned tomato sauce, tomato paste, or marinara sauce (low-sodium)

- [ ] Canned vegetable soup (low-sodium)

- [ ] Sea vegetables, e.g. dried seaweed or seaweed snacks

- [ ] Tomato juice (low-sodium)

- [ ] Canned vegetables (unsalted), e.g. artichokes, beets, bell peppers, corn, mushrooms, pumpkin, tomatoes (including sun-dried tomatoes)

- [ ] Vegetable juice (low-sodium)

Fruits

- [ ] Canned fruits (no sugar added), e.g apple purée, apricots, grapefruit, oranges, peaches, pears, pineapples

- [ ] Dried fruits, e.g., apples, apricots, bananas, blueberries, cherries, cranberries, dates, figs, mangoes, papaya, peaches, pears, pineapples, plums, raisins, strawberries

- [ ] Fruit spreads (no sugar added), e.g., berry, cherry, fig, peach, plum, orange

Fats

- [ ] Canola oil

- [ ] Extra virgin olive oil, including flavoured, e.g. lemon, basil, garlic

- [ ] Nut and seed oils, e.g. peanut, sesame, walnut

- [ ] Salad dressings, light (moderate in sodium, mostly monounsaturated fat)

Flavourings

- [ ] Garlic, fresh or dried

- [ ] Dried herbs, e.g. basil, bay leaf, chervil, chives, cilantro, dill weed, ginger, marjoram, mint, oregano, parsley, rosemary, sage, tarragon, thyme

- [ ] Low-sodium herbal seasoning blends, e.g, Herbamare, Mrs. Dash, Spike

- [ ] Soy sauce, reduced-sodium

- [ ] Spices, e.g. allspice, anise, cardamom, caraway seed, celery seed, cinnamon, coriander, cumin, fennel seed, mustard seeds, nutmeg, pepper (black, red), poppy seeds, saffron, turmeric, vanilla

- [ ] Vegetable broth or bouillon cubes (low-sodium)

- [ ] Vinegar, e.g. balsamic, red wine

- [ ] Wasabi paste

Beverages

- [ ] Coffee

- [ ] Red wine (optional)

- [ ] Tea, e.g. black, green, herbal, red, white

Miscellaneous

- [ ] Agave nectar

- [ ] Dark chocolate (at least 70% cocoa)

- [ ] Ener-G Egg Replacer

- [ ] Honey

- [ ] Real maple syrup

WEEKLY PLANT-POWERED SHOPPING LIST FOR FRESH FOODS

Plant Proteins

☐ Edamame (fresh or frozen)

☐ Miso (paste)

☐ Plant-based cheese, e.g. rice or soy

☐ Plant-based milk (fresh), e.g. almond, rice, soy

☐ Plant-based yogurt, e.g. almond, coconut, soy

☐ Prepared (refrigerated) beans, lentils and peas

☐ Seitan (wheat gluten)

☐ Tempeh (soy and grain cake)

☐ Tofu (fresh)

Whole Grains

☐ Whole grain breads, e.g. baguettes, bagels, muffins, rolls, sliced bread

☐ Whole grain tortillas and wraps, e.g. corn, wheat

Vegetables

☐ Fresh vegetables in season, e.g., asparagus, aubergine, avocado, beets, bell peppers, broccoli, Brussels sprouts, cabbage, carrots, cauliflower, corn, cucumber, green beans, kale, lettuce, mushrooms, okra, onions, peas, potatoes, radishes, rocket, spinach, squash (summer or winter), sweet potatoes, Swiss chard, tomatoes

☐ Frozen vegetables, such as asparagus, broccoli, Brussels sprouts, carrots, cauliflower, corn, green beans, mixed vegetable blends, okra, peas, potatoes, spinach, squash

☐ Prepared fresh vegetables, such as bagged lettuce and peeled, chopped vegetables

Fruits

☐ Fresh fruits in season, e.g. apples, apricots, bananas, blueberries, cherries, figs, grapefruit, grapes, kiwifruit, lemons, mangoes, melon, oranges, papaya, peaches, pears, pineapples, plums, pomegranates, raspberries, strawberries

☐ Frozen fruits, e.g., blueberries, cherries, raspberries, strawberries

Fats

☐ Margarine spreads (high in unsaturated fat, low in saturated fat)

Flavor

☐ Fresh herbs, e.g. basil, bay leaf, chervil, chives, coriander, dill weed, marjoram, mint, oregano, parsley, rosemary, sage, tarragon, thyme

PLANT-POWERED KITCHEN EQUIPMENT ESSENTIALS

Dress your kitchen for success by stocking it with all the gadgets you'll need to make plant-based cooking a piece of cake.

Essential:

- ☐ Spoons, including mixing spoons, slotted spoons (for serving foods in liquids), serving spoons, and a ladle for serving soup, stew or chili
- ☐ Measuring spoons for measuring ¼, ½ and 1 teaspoon, ½ tablespoon (optional) and 1 tablespoon
- ☐ Spatulas for sautéeing, pan frying, turning pancakes, removing items from a baking dish, and serving foods
- ☐ Cooking pots in small, medium and large sizes, with tightly fitting lids
- ☐ Sauté pans or frying pans in small and large sizes
- ☐ Mixi-purpose bowls in small, medium and large sizes
- ☐ Whisks for making sauces and vinaigrettes
- ☐ Multi-purpose grater for grating lemon peel on one side and larger vegetables on the other side.
- ☐ Cutting knives, including paring knife, chef's knife (8- or 9-inch), and serrated bread knife
- ☐ Metric scales, for weighing dry food
- ☐ A 1-litre measuing jug, for liquids
- ☐ Strainers for draining foods like canned beans, olives, pasta, and potatoes
- ☐ Chopping boards
- ☐ Storage containers with lids, in various sizes, to save leftovers and pack foods for lunches
- ☐ Can opener

These tools will get you started and prepare you to make all of the recipes in my Plant-Powered Recipe Collection. For some additional helpful (but optional) tools, check out the list on the following page.

Optional:

- ☐ Garlic press, to mince whole garlic
- ☐ A pastry brush, for glazing
- ☐ Potato masher, for mashing vegetables and potatoes
- ☐ Kitchen shears for slicing herbs
- ☐ Corkscrew for opening wine bottles
- ☐ Cooking timer
- ☐ Slow cooker for cooking soups, stews, bean dishes, and chili
- ☐ Small electric chopper to chop small amounts of vegetables
- ☐ Food processor to grate, shred, slice or purée fruits and vegetables
- ☐ Blender or stick blender to blend or purée fruits and vegetables
- ☐ Electric mixer (handheld or countertop) to blend batters and dough
- ☐ Waffle iron

13

14 Days of Powerful Plants

Are you having a hard time getting started with your plant-powered diet? Just take a look at my 14-day Plant-Powered Menu Planner (page 266) for ideas on how to include more plant-based meals throughout the week. This menu planner is completely plant based, so if you're shooting for a Plant-Powered Vegetarian diet, you can supplement this menu plan with dairy foods and eggs. If you're shooting for a Plant-Powered Omnivore diet, then set a goal for how many meat-free meals you'd like to eat every week and choose some of these menus for those days. The rest of the time, remember to choose moderate amounts of lean animal proteins, such as low-fat dairy products, fish, and poultry, according to the Daily Plant-Powered Guide (see page 244).

You'll find all the recipes on the menu planner in chapter 14. Each recipe has been lovingly developed and tested in my own kitchen, and my two teenage sons and husband have offered their stamp of approval. All the recipes are simple and feature whole plant foods in the most natural state possible. You won't find much added salt or sugar to speak of in these recipes, yet I think you'll find them to be shining examples of how easy and delicious it can be to eat a plant-powered diet for life.

14-DAY PLANT-POWERED MENU PLANNER
WEEK I

	SUNDAY	MONDAY	TUESDAY	WEDNESDAY	THURSDAY	FRIDAY	SATURDAY
Breakfast	Pumpkin Pecan Spice Pancakes (page 355) Fresh orange wedges Soy latte	Plant-Powered Granola (page 345) Plant-based milk Fresh pear slices	Exotic Fruit and Rice Hot Cereal (page 348) Plant-based milk	Spicy Tofu and Red Potato Hash with Salsa (page 331) Whole grain toast Grapefruit half	Ruby Quinoa Breakfast Bowl (page 350) Plant-based milk	Apple Pie Oatmeal Bowl (page 347) Plant-based milk	Buckwheat Hazelnut Waffles with Ginger Peach Sauce (page 353) Plant-based milk
Morning Snack	Plant-based yogurt with fruit	Sunflower-seed butter on whole grain crackers	Fresh plum	Corn Muffins with Apple and Walnuts (page 352)	Dark Chocolate Peanut Butter Smoothie (page 358)	Whole grain flatbread with plant-based cheese	Peanuts
Lunch	Tomato spinach soup Grilled Vegetable and Pesto Panini (page 299)	Country French Barley Vegetable Potage (page 283) Butternut Squash Macaroni and "Cheese" (page 308)	Mixed green salad Bean and Grilled Veggie Burritos (page 300) Fresh nectarine	Classic French Onion Soup (page 284) Nicoise-Style Salad (page 295) Plant-based yogurt with fruit	Mixed green salad California Tofu and Vegetable Penne Toss (page 305) Fresh raspberries	Grapefruit and Avocado Ensalada (page 289) Spicy Broccoli Cashew Pizza (page 302)	Asparagus Leek Soup with Lemon Pesto Home-Style Hummus (page 276) with whole wheat pita and fresh vegetables Summer Fruit Skewers with Strawberry Dip (page 360)
Afternoon Snack	Nuts and dried berries blend	Fresh apricots	Almonds	Sunflower seeds	Whole grain crackers Celery sticks	Banana Plant-based yogurt	Whole grain muffin

WEEK I, CONTINUED

	SUNDAY	MONDAY	TUESDAY	WEDNESDAY	THURSDAY	FRIDAY	SATURDAY
Dinner	Baked tofu Roasted Lemon Asparagus with Red Peppers (page 335) Sweet Potato Pumpkin Seed Casserole (page 343) Ginger Pear Crisp (page 364)	Chinese Cabbage Slaw (page 289) Bok Choy Seitan Pho (page 326) Mandarin orange cup	Greek Salad with Rosemary-Lemon Tofu (page 294) Aubergine Courgette Moussaka (page 338) Whole wheat pita	Beet and Pomegranate Seed Salad (page 297) Green and Gold Lentil Pot (page 316) Steamed farro	Watermelon Peppercorn Salad (page 288) Easy Kale and Broad Bean Ragout (page 315)	Winter Buckwheat Vegetable Soup (page 287) Curried Papaya Salad (page 291) Antipasto Couscous with Chickpeas (page 310)	South of the Border Taco Salad (page 292) Grilled Portobello Mushroom "Steaks" (page 340) Cooked greens Baked Farro Herb Pilaf (page 314) Country Berry Cobbler (page 363)
Evening Snack	Whole grain crackers with carrot sticks	Date, Walnut and Dark Chocolate Cookies (page 367) Plant-based milk	Minted Cantaloupe with Blueberries (page 362)	Popcorn	Apple Cranberry Tart Rustica (page 365)	Rainbow Fruit Bowl with Orange Sauce (page 361)	Banana Peach Yogurt Parfait (page 362)

WEEK 2

	SUNDAY	MONDAY	TUESDAY	WEDNESDAY	THURSDAY	FRIDAY	SATURDAY
Breakfast	Sautéed tofu with spinach Rye toast Orange wedges	Steel-cut oats with raisins and walnuts Plant-based milk	Spiced Banana Avocado Bread (page 351) Peach Soy Latte	Muesli Plant-based milk Applesauce	Ancient Grain Porridge with Figs and Dates (page 349) Plant-based milk	Bean and Grilled Veggie Burritos (page 300) Grapefruit half	Whole wheat pancakes with blueberries Vegetable Juice
Morning Snack	Soy latte Dried apricots	Seaweed snacks Almonds	Carrot sticks with almond butter	Vegetable juice Peanuts	Oatmeal raisin cookie	Bran muffin Plant-based yogurt	Brazil nuts and dried blueberries
Lunch	Orange-Peanut Tempeh Stir-Fry with Red Rice (page 328) Fresh berries	Baby greens with cherry tomatoes Vegetable Medley Lasagna (page 307) Whole grain French bread Banana	Mixed green salad Three-Bean Cowboy Chili (page 321) Corn muffin Nectarine	Tomato soup Garden burger with lettuce, avocado and tomato on whole wheat bun Pear	Carrot-raisin slaw Shiitake and Kale Spelt Bowl (page 330)	Slow-Cooked Butter Beans with Root Vegetables (page 317) Corn on the cob Cooked quinoa	Southwestern Black Bean, Quinoa, and Mango Medley (page 318) Grilled Vegetable Skewers (page 336) Baked tofu Whole grain rolls
Afternoon Snack	Pumpkin seeds and raisins	Apple purée with Plant-powered Granola (page 345)	Sugar snap peas with tahini	Radishes Plant-based milk	Tomato slices with toasted oat bread	Hazelnut butter with sprouted wheat bread	Dark chocolate Peanuts

WEEK 2, CONTINUED

	SUNDAY	MONDAY	TUESDAY	WEDNESDAY	THURSDAY	FRIDAY	SATURDAY
Dinner	Brussels Sprouts Slaw (page 296) Green and Gold Lentil Pot (page 316) Steamed farro	Bulgur Risotto with Yellow Squash, Peas, and Pine Nuts (page 312) Stewed split peas Whole grain flatbread	Cauliflower and Pea Curry (page 342) Saffron Brown Basmati Rice (page 311) Stewed lentils Plant-based milk	New Orleans Red Beans and Rice (page 320) Greens Cornbread Pineapple slices	Celery Root and Apple Bisque (page 282) Roasted Vegetable Terrine (page 341) Stewed adzuki beans Mandarin oranges	Caprese-Style Tomatoes and Avocado (see page 274) Tofu Cacciatore (see page 324) Gnocchi Sautéed greens Fresh apple	Miso tofu soup Edamame Vegetable Brown Rice Sushi (page 278) Green salad with ginger dressing Papaya slices
Evening Snack	Popcorn, light	Plant-based yogurt	Rainbow Fruit Bowl with Orange Sauce (page 361)	Dark chocolate Walnuts	Peanut butter with whole grain crackers Dried cherries	Trail mix	Banana Peach Yogurt Parfait (page 362)

Note: Snacks are included for meal-planning purposes but are optional; all plant-based milk, yogurt, and tofu products are fortified with calcium and/or vitamin D.

Plant-Powered
Recipe Collection

If you're committed to taking
on a plant-based diet, it's time to strap on an apron and get cooking! It's
really the most important way to take charge of your nutrition goals for
optimal health for your entire family. But contrary to popular opinion,
cooking doesn't have to be difficult. I promise that you can whip up many
of my recipes faster than the pizza guy can get to your front door.

Earlier, I got you started with some template recipes that work with
pantry staples and fresh produce (see Ten-Ingredient Plant-Powered
Pantry Kit, page 258). In this chapter, I will share with you some of my
favorite unique plant-based dishes, personally tested in my kitchen by
my own family. You'll find plenty of hearty pots of soup, quick and delicious salads and one-dish meals. You'll also have fun experimenting with
my zesty ethnic dishes every week. These recipes are 100 percent plant
based, so you can add them to your weekly menu whether you're a plant-
powered vegan, vegetarian, or omnivore. They are very low in sodium
and saturated fat and packed with essential nutrients that come from
whole-food ingredients, such as soy foods, pulses, whole grains, nuts,
seeds, fruits and vegetables. You should be able to find all the ingredients

for my culinary creations at most supermarkets and natural food stores. I hope these recipes will inspire you to dive into and become passionate about plant-based cooking and to share these delicious foods with your friends and family. Let's get the whole world eating a fabulous, plant-powered diet.

Note: Nutrition information for all recipes in this chapter is estimated based on information from USDA standard reference, Food Analyzer 2, and Food Processor. Star nutrients are listed for nutrients with significant levels, but may not reflect all significant sources of nutrients.

VEGETABLE AND POTATO DISHES

BREAKFASTS AND BAKED GOODS

BEVERAGES

DESSERTS

Caprese-Style Tomatoes and Avocado

Caprese—named after the Island of Capri—is a famous Italian appetizer that features mozzarella cheese. In this version I've swapped the cheese for earthy, ripe avocado slices. This is a simple, delicious starter course that can showcase a bumper crop of summer tomatoes or a beautiful heritage tomato found at the farmers market.

MAKES 6 SERVINGS

> *2 medium ripe heritage or vine-ripened tomatoes (see Note)*
> *1 avocado, ripe yet firm*
> *12 fresh basil leaves*
> *1 teaspoon extra virgin olive oil*
> *1 teaspoon balsamic vinegar*
> *Ground black pepper*
> *12 thin slices whole wheat baguette*

1. Slice each tomato into six slices. Arrange the tomato slices on a serving platter.

2. Peel the avocado and cut into 12 slices. Place one avocado slice on top of each tomato slice.

3. Place a leaf of fresh basil on top of each avocado slice.

4. Drizzle the olive oil and then the balsamic vinegar over the tomato-avocado pieces. Sprinkle with black pepper.

5. If desired, serve the platter of tomatoes and avocado with slices of whole wheat baguette on the side for creating open-faced appetizer sandwiches.

NOTE: Choose heritage tomatoes (Harmoude, Coeur de Boeuf, Golden Beef) in a variety of colors, such as red, yellow, green, and purple, for the most dramatic effect.

PER SERVING (2 TOMATO SLICES, 2 AVOCADO SLICES, AND 2 SLICES OF BREAD): Calories: 197 • Carbohydrates: 30 g • Fiber: 6 g • Protein: 6 g • Total fat: 7 g • Saturated fat: 1 g • Sodium: 303 mg • *Star nutrients:* Vitamin A (10% DV), vitamin C (12% DV), iron (11% DV)

Lemon Basil Pesto

This plant-based pesto sparkles with lemon and verdant basil tones. Serve it as a dip with a vegetable platter, whole grain pita triangles, or whole grain crackers. Or toss it into cooked pasta or salads, spread it on sandwiches, and spoon it onto soups as in Asparagus Leek Soup with Lemon Basil Pesto (page 281) to add an herbal aroma and flair. Keep a basil plant growing in your kitchen window so you can enjoy this recipe often (see chapter 8).

MAKES 10 SERVINGS

> *35g cup pine nuts*
> *35g fresh basil leaves*
> *3 garlic cloves, minced*
> *2 tablespoons fresh lemon juice*
> *1 tablespoon white balsamic vinegar (see Notes)*
> *1 tablespoon extra virgin olive oil*
> *2 tablespoons water*
> *Dash of ground black pepper*

1. Put the pine nuts into a blender or food processor and process until finely ground.

2. Add the remaining ingredients and blend until smooth, pausing periodically to scrape down the sides of the blender with a spatula.

3. Serve immediately or store in an airtight container in the refrigerator for up to 3 days.

NOTES: It may take a few minutes to purée this dense pesto. Try blending the ingredients for a bit, pausing to scrape down the sides of the blender, and blending again. Repeat these steps in order to incorporate all the ingredients into a thick pesto.

White balsamic vinegar has the rich flavor of balsamic vinegar without the dark color that can muddy the lovely green of this pesto. If you can't find white balsamic vinegar, substitute white wine vinegar.

PER SERVING (1 TABLESPOON): Calories: 33 • Carbohydrates: 1 g • Fiber: 0 g • Protein: 1 g • Total fat: 3 g • Saturated fat: 0 g • Sodium: 1 mg • *Star nutrients:* Vitamin A (5% DV), manganese (20% DV)

Home-Style Hummus

This hummus, starring nutrient-rich chickpeas, is a staple of my healthy, plant-based kitchen. Providing a rich, tasty source of plant protein, hummus offers unlimited versatility: Use it as an appetizer dip with whole grain pita bread and vegetables, spread it on sandwiches, and dollop it over salads and grains.

MAKES 8 SERVINGS

> *One 400g can chickpeas (garbanzo beans), ideally salt free, with liquid*
> *2 garlic cloves*
> *2 tablespoons lemon juice*
> *2 tablespoons tahini (sesame seed paste)*
> *¼ teaspoon ground black pepper*
> *1 teaspoon extra virgin olive oil*
> *Pinch of paprika*

1. Drain the chickpeas, reserving the liquid. Put the beans into a blender or food processor.

2. Add the garlic, lemon juice, tahini, black pepper and olive oil, as well as about half of the reserved bean liquid.

3. Purée the bean mixture, adding additional bean liquid as necessary to produce a smooth, very thick dip.

4. Pour the bean dip into a serving dish and garnish with paprika. If not serving immediately, store in an airtight container in the refrigerator for up to 3 days.

NOTE: To serve hummus as an appetizer, place a small serving dish of garnished hummus in the center of a platter. Arrange triangles of whole wheat pita bread and pieces of fresh raw vegetables, such as carrots, celery, bell peppers, mushrooms, asparagus, broccoli and mangetout, on the platter.

PER SERVING: Calories: 89 • Carbohydrates: 13 g • Fiber: 3 g • Protein: 3 g • Total fat: 3 g • Saturated fat: 0 g • Sodium: 160 mg • *Star nutrients:* Folate (10% DV), manganese (21% DV)

Baba Ghanoush

This classic Mediterranean dip owes its hearty, smoky flavor to roasted aubergine—an elegant vegetable long prized for its beauty, and now for its cache of health-protective phenolic compounds. Mix up a batch of Baba Ghanoush for a healthy party appetizer, a flavorful sandwich spread, or an accompaniment to steamed whole grains such as whole grain couscous or bulgur.

MAKES 8 SERVINGS

1 large aubergine
2 garlic cloves, minced
2 tablespoons tahini (sesame seed paste)
3 tablespoons freshly squeezed lemon juice
¼ teaspoon ground black pepper
1 teaspoon extra virgin olive oil
Pinch of ground cumin
1 tablespoon minced fresh parsley
Pinch of paprika

1. Preheat the oven to 200°C/gas 6.

2. Wash the aubergine and cut in half lengthwise. Place the halves on a baking sheet with cut sides down and bake for 30 minutes, or until the skin is dark and the aubergine is soft when pierced with a fork.

3. Transfer the cooked aubergine to a colander and run under cold water for 1 minute. Drain and allow to cool slightly. Scoop out the flesh into a small bowl and discard the skin.

4. Lightly mash the aubergine. Add the garlic, tahini, lemon juice, black pepper, olive oil and cumin, and continue to mash into a smooth dip, leaving some lumps.

5. Pour the dip into a small serving dish and garnish with the parsley and paprika.

PER SERVING: Calories: 41 • Carbohydrates: 4 g • Fiber: 2 g • Protein: 1 g • Total fat: 2 g • Saturated fat: 0 g • Sodium: 5 mg • *Star nutrients:* Vitamin C (8% DV), manganese (8% DV)

Vegetable Brown Rice Sushi

Whether you're a plant-powered omnivore or a vegetarian, I think you'll find this vegetable sushi is a real treat. And it's a lot easier to make than you might think. In this recipe I've included my favorite fillings, such as asparagus and avocados, but the sky's the limit with the plant-powered fillings you can add to your sushi rolls. You can even host a sushi-rolling party at your home and let your guests add their own vegetable combinations. Serve vegetable sushi as an appetizer, or let it star as an entrée paired with tofu miso soup, edamame and a green salad.

MAKES 8 SERVINGS (32 PIECES)

620ml water
200g uncooked short-grain brown rice
3 tablespoons reduced-sodium soy sauce
2 tablespoons rice vinegar
1 teaspoon honey or agave nectar
4 sheets nori (toasted seaweed)
2 teaspoons black or white sesame seeds
1 medium carrot, sliced into matchsticks
½ medium cucumber, sliced into matchsticks
2 thin asparagus spears
2 tablespoons micro-greens or alfalfa sprouts
½ medium avocado, thinly sliced
1 spring onion, sliced
2 medium shiitake mushrooms, sliced
½ teaspoon wasabi paste
2 tablespoons grated fresh ginger

1. If using a rice cooker, put the water and rice into the cooker and prepare according to the manufacturer's directions. If cooking on the hob, bring the water to a boil in a medium saucepan. Add the rice and reduce the heat to a simmer. Cook, covered, until all the liquid is absorbed, 45 to 50 minutes. Cool for 10 minutes.

2. In a small saucepan, heat 1 tablespoon of the soy sauce, the vinegar, and the honey, stirring occasionally, until smooth and bubbly. Pour over the rice and stir to combine.

3. Place a sushi mat or a piece of cling film on a clean chopping board.

4. Place one sheet of nori, shiny side down with the long side facing you, on the sushi mat or cling film.

5. Measure out about 150g of flavoured rice and spread it evenly with a spoon or wet hands over the sheet of nori, leaving an uncovered margin on the side closest to you of about a quarter of the length of the nori.

6. Sprinkle ½ teaspoon of the sesame seeds over the rice.

7. Arrange about a quarter of the vegetables, in any combination, horizontally over the uncovered section of the nori.

8. Starting with the vegetable side, roll up the sushi tightly, pressing with either the mat or the cling film to make a tight, cylindrical roll, being careful not to roll the plastic into the roll.

9. Using a sharp knife, slice the roll into eight slices. Repeat this process with the remaining nori, rice and vegetables. Refrigerate until ready to serve.

10. Arrange the sushi pieces on serving plates and serve with the wasabi paste, ginger and the remaining soy sauce.

NOTE: Available at kitchen shops and on the Web, sushi-rolling mats make sushi rolling a cinch. Sushi-rolling kits, which include a sushi-rolling box and a special knife, are also available. Wash thoroughly after each use.

PER SERVING: Calories: 140 • Carbohydrates: 25 g • Fiber: 4 g • Protein: 4 g • Total fat: 3 g • Saturated fat: 1 g • Sodium: 239 mg • *Star nutrients:* Vitamin A (24% DV), vitamin C (7% DV)

Italian Cannellini Spinach Soup

This recipe is a salute to Sienna, Italy, where I fell in love with a thick Tuscan bean-and-spinach soup served in a charming restaurant in a medieval square. When I came back home I created my own plant-based soup recipe, hoping to share the flavors of Tuscany with you. Its hearty yet simple characteristics are suited to an array of accompaniments, such as a toasted avocado and tomato sandwich or Nicoise-Style Salad (page 295).

MAKES 4 SERVINGS

1 teaspoon extra virgin olive oil
½ medium onion, chopped
2 celery sticks, chopped
1 garlic clove, minced
¼ teaspoon ground black pepper
½ teaspoon dried thyme
One 400g can cannellini beans, ideally salt free, with liquid (see Note)
250ml low-sodium vegetable broth
370ml water
60g fresh spinach leaves, rinsed and chopped
1 teaspoon lemon juice

1. Heat the olive oil in a large pot over medium heat.

2. Add the onion, celery, garlic, black pepper and thyme and sauté until tender, about 5 minutes.

3. Stir in the beans and liquid, broth and water and cover the pot. Bring to a slow simmer and cook for about 30 minutes.

4. Transfer about three quarters of the bean-vegetable mixture into a blender or food processor. Purée until smooth, adding liquid from the pot as needed.

5. Pour the puréed mixture back into the pot. Add the spinach and lemon juice, cover and heat until the soup is hot and the spinach is wilted, about 10 minutes.

NOTE: To substitute home-cooked cannellini beans for the canned beans, follow my instructions for cooking dried beans (page 57) and use 300g cooked beans plus 120ml water in place of the canned beans.

PER SERVING: Calories: 160 • Carbohydrates: 28 g • Fiber: 7 g • Protein: 9 g • Total fat: 2 g • Saturated fat: 0 g • Sodium: 47 mg • *Star nutrients:* Vitamin A (21% DV), vitamin C (12% DV), folate (28% DV), calcium (11% DV), iron (22% DV)

Asparagus Leek Soup with Lemon Basil Pesto

Honoring the first spring shoots of the asparagus plant, this beautiful jade soup is both light and delicious. You can serve it warm on a cool spring day or switch things up and serve it cold as a refreshing addition to a summer meal. The bright swirl of lemon pesto brings a burst of flavor and color to the soup.

MAKES 6 SERVINGS

1 teaspoon extra virgin olive oil
1 garlic clove, minced
100g sliced, well-rinsed leeks (white and green parts)
1 medium potato, peeled and diced
450g fresh asparagus, chopped
¼ teaspoon ground black pepper
1 litre low-sodium vegetable broth
35g Lemon Basil Pesto (page 275)

1. Heat the olive oil in a large pot. Add the garlic, leeks and potato and sauté for 10 minutes.
2. Add the asparagus, black pepper and broth, cover with a lid, and cook until the vegetables are tender, about 20 minutes.
3. Transfer the mixture into a blender and purée until smooth. To serve hot, pour into soup bowls and top each serving with 1 tablespoon Lemon Basil Pesto. To serve cold, refrigerate puréed soup until serving time and top with Lemon Basil Pesto just before serving.

Variations: If you're in a rush, you can substitute prepared pesto for the Lemon Basil Pesto. If fresh asparagus isn't available, you can substitute frozen: simply reduce the cooking time in step 2 to about 10 minutes.

PER SERVING: Calories: 96 • Carbohydrates: 13 g • Fiber: 3 g • Protein: 4 g • Total fat: 4 g • Saturated fat: 0 g • Sodium: 48 mg • *Star nutrients:* Vitamin A (6% DV), vitamin C (13% DV), iron (7% DV)

Celeriac and Apple Bisque

The subtle flavors of celery stems and celeriac and a hint of tart apples shine in this creamy soup. Celery may seem like a humble vegetable, but it's been linked with brain protection, thanks to powerful phytochemicals called phthalides. Serve this soup for lunch with half a rustic sandwich or as a starter course for dinner.

MAKES 6 SERVINGS

1 teaspoon extra virgin olive oil
100g sliced, well-rinsed leeks
1 medium potato, peeled and diced
1 medium celeriac, peeled and diced (see Notes)
3 medium celery sticks, chopped
1 small apple, peeled and chopped
1 teaspoon dried thyme
⅛ teaspoon ground black pepper
750ml reduced-sodium vegetable broth
370ml water
120ml unsweetened plain plant-based milk (see Notes)

1. Heat the olive oil in a large heavy pot. Add the leeks, potato, celeriac, celery sticks, apple, thyme and black pepper and sauté for 10 minutes.
2. Add the broth and water and bring to a boil. Reduce the heat, cover, and simmer for an additional 40 minutes, stirring occasionally.
3. Transfer the mixture into a blender and purée until smooth. Add the milk and process until blended. Serve immediately.

NOTES: Celeriac (also known as celery root), is a knobby bulb about the size of a large potato and is available at many supermarkets.

Choose a SUBTLE-FLAVORED PLANT-BASED milk for this recipe, such as almond, rice or hemp milk.

PER SERVING: Calories: 75 • Carbohydrates: 15 g • Fiber: 3 g • Protein: 2 g • Total fat: 1 g • Saturated fat: 0 g • Sodium: 121 mg • *Star nutrients:* Vitamin B$_6$ (10% DV), vitamin C (21% DV), manganese (12% DV)

Country French Barley Vegetable Potage

Infused with the flavors of mirepoix, the classic French culinary trifecta of onions (or leeks), carrots, and celery, this country soup is great paired with just about anything. Serve it for lunch with a salad or a sandwich such as a Grilled Vegetable and Pesto Panini (page 299) or as an accompaniment to dinner any night of the week.

MAKES 8 SERVINGS

1 teaspoon extra virgin olive oil
2 garlic cloves, minced
100g sliced, well-rinsed leeks
1 carrot, chopped
4 celery sticks, chopped
150g sliced mushrooms
1.7 litres water
2 cubes low-sodium vegetable bouillon
1½ teaspoons herbes de Provence *(see Note)*
¼ teaspoon ground black pepper
½ cup dried pearled barley

1. Heat the olive oil in a large pot over medium heat. Add the garlic, leeks, carrots and celery and sauté for 5 minutes. Stir in the mushrooms and continue to cook for an additional 2 minutes.

2. Add the water, bouillon, *herbes de Provence*, black pepper and barley. Bring to a boil, cover, and reduce the heat to simmer.

3. Simmer until the vegetables and barley are tender and the soup has thickened slightly, about 1 hour.

NOTE: *Herbes de Provence* is a French seasoning blend that is available at gourmet food or kitchen shops and includes basil, fennel seeds, lavender, marjoram, rosemary, sage and thyme.

PER SERVING: Calories: 91 • Carbohydrates: 18 g • Fiber: 4 g • Protein: 3 g • Total fat: 1 g • Saturated fat: 0 g • Sodium: 51 mg • *Star nutrients:* Vitamin A (43% DV), manganese (14% DV), selenium (10% DV)

Classic French Onion Soup

My teenage son is a connoisseur of French onion soup, the iconic French culinary masterpiece that features lots of onions cooked in a rich (usually beef) broth topped with melted cheese over bread. He orders it every chance he gets, offering his critique on how each soup measures up. In order to come up with the most authentic plant-based version possible, I scoured old French cookbooks to discover the classic elements of these soups. It's all in the onions—pound and pounds of them caramelized in the pot to create the rich flavor we have grown to cherish. My son gave this recipe a thumbs up!

MAKES 10 SERVINGS

1 tablespoon extra virgin olive oil
1.5kg yellow onions, thinly sliced
3 garlic cloves, minced
2 tablespoons flour
½ teaspoon ground black pepper
2 litres water
2 cubes low-sodium vegetable bouillon
500ml white wine
1 bay leaf
1 teaspoon dried thyme
10 small slices (25g each) whole wheat French bread
75g grated plant-based (vegetarian) Swiss cheese

1. Heat the olive oil in a large casserole dish. Add the onions and garlic and sauté for 15 minutes.
2. Preheat the oven to 200ºC/gas 6.

3. Stir in the flour and black pepper. Put the uncovered dish into the oven and bake for 15 minutes.

4. While the onion mixture is baking, place the bread on a baking sheet and add to the oven. Bake until crisp (about 5 minutes), then set aside.

5. Turn off the oven and transfer the casserole dish to the hob. Add the water, bouillon cubes, wine, bay leaf and thyme and bring to a boil. Cover, reduce the heat and simmer until the onions are tender, about 35 minutes. Remove the bay leaf.

6. Heat the oven to 250°C/gas 8. Arrange the toasted bread slices on top of the soup, either in the pot or distributed among individual oven-proof bowls. Sprinkle each slice of bread with 1 tablespoon of the shredded cheese.

7. Place the large pot or ovenproof bowls, uncovered, into the oven and bake for 10 minutes, or until the cheese is golden and the soup is bubbly. If serving out of the soup pot, scoop the soup into individual bowls and top each with one slice of cheese-covered bread.

Variation: If you'd like to omit the plant-based cheese, drizzle each slice of bread with ½ teaspoon extra virgin olive oil before baking the soup.

PER SERVING: Calories: 224 • Carbohydrates: 27 g • Fiber: 4 g • Protein: 9 g • Total fat: 5 g • Saturated fat: 0 g • Sodium: 375 mg • *Star nutrients:* Vitamin C (15% DV), folate (13% DV), selenium (14% DV)

Roasted Squash Bisque with Macadamias

As the weather cools and winter squashes—packed with health-protective carotenoids such as beta-carotene, lutein, and zeaxanthin—become widely available, be sure to put them on the menu every week. Try this creamy, golden orange soup as a delicious accompaniment to any main dish.

MAKES 4 SERVINGS

1 small winter squash, about 900g in weight
500ml reduced-sodium vegetable broth
¼ teaspoon ground black pepper
½ teaspoon ground nutmeg
175ml unsweetened plain plant-based milk (see Notes)
35g finely chopped macadamia nuts

1. Preheat the oven to 190°C/gas 5.

2. Cut the squash in half and scoop out the seeds. Place the halves on a baking sheet with cut sides down and prick the skin with a sharp knife. Bake for approximately 1 hour, or until the flesh is tender.

3. Let the squash cool slightly. Scoop out the flesh into a blender or food processor.

4. Add the broth, black pepper and nutmeg and process until smooth.

5. Pour the soup into a large saucepan and heat over low heat, stirring constantly, until it comes to a slow boil. Stir in the plant-based milk and continue to cook only until the soup bubbles and is heated through. Transfer into soup bowls and garnish with the chopped macadamia nuts.

NOTES: If you're in a rush, you can use the cubed fresh squash that is available in many supermarkets. Boil 900g of cubed squash in water until tender, about 15 minutes, and drain. Transfer the cooked squash into a blender and continue at step 4.

A NUTTY PLANT-BASED MILK, SUCH AS SOY OR HAZELNUT, SUITS THIS RECIPE WELL.

Variation: There are many winter squashes available that would suit this soup well. Try butternut or acorn.

PER SERVING: Calories: 110 • Carbohydrates: 10 g • Fiber: 3 g • Protein: 3 g • Total fat: 7 g • Saturated fat: 1 g • Sodium: 40 mg • *Star nutrients:* Vitamin A (71% DV), vitamin C (18% DV)

Winter Buckwheat Vegetable Soup

Rich in minerals and fiber, buckwheat has been a staple ingredient in Russian cuisine for centuries. Combined with other wintery staples, this filling buckwheat soup will take away the chill on a blustery day. Pair with a toasted nut-butter sandwich and fruit for an ideal, nutrient-packed meal.

MAKES 8 SERVINGS

One 400g can tomatoes, ideally salt free, with liquid
1.5 litres low-sodium vegetable broth
4 celery sticks, corsely chopped
1 medium onion, chopped
2 medium carrots, coarsely chopped
150g sliced green cabbage
2 garlic cloves, minced
½ teaspoon freshly ground black pepper
2 bay leaves
1 teaspoon low-sodium herbal seasoning
150g frozen green peas
75g uncooked buckwheat groats (kasha)

1. Pour the tomatoes and liquid and the broth into a large pot and place over high heat.
2. Add the celery, onion, carrots, cabbage, garlic, black pepper, bay leaves and herbal seasoning and cover.
3. When the mixture comes to a boil, reduce the heat to low and simmer for 35 minutes.
4. Add the green peas and buckwheat groats, cover, and cook until vegetables and grains are tender, about 20 minutes.
5. Remove the bay leaves and serve immediately.

PER SERVING: Calories: 94 • Carbohydrates: 19 g • Fiber: 4 g • Protein: 3 g • Total fat: 0 g • Saturated fat: 0 g • Sodium: 154 mg • *Star nutrients:* Vitamin A (48% DV), vitamin C (16% DV)

Watermelon Peppercorn Salad

Who knew that watermelon could pair so nicely with spicy black peppercorns and tender butterhead lettuce? This chic salad will create a summer meal to remember. And it's another delicious way to feature lycopene-rich watermelon in your diet.

MAKES 4 SERVINGS

225g torn-up butterhead lettuce
50g sliced, well-rinsed leeks
450g cubed seedless watermelon (about 2.5cm pieces)
1 tablespoon plus 1 teaspoon balsamic vinegar
1 tablespoon plus 1 teaspoon extra virgin olive oil
1 teaspoon agave nectar
¼ teaspoon whole black peppercorns
2 teaspoons chopped fresh parsley
2 tablespoons sliced almonds

1. Place the lettuce in the bottom of a salad bowl. Top with leeks and watermelon cubes.
2. Whisk together the vinegar, olive oil, and agave nectar in a small bowl. Drizzle evenly over the watermelon.
3. Roughly crush peppercorns with a mortar and pestle or rolling pin. Sprinkle over the watermelon.
4. Sprinkle the parsley and almonds over the salad and serve immediately.

NOTE: Purchase pre-cubed fresh watermelon to make this recipe in minutes.

PER SERVING: Calories: 114 • Carbohydrates: 13 g • Fiber: 2 g • Protein: 2 g • Total fat: 7 g • Saturated fat: 1 g • Sodium: 9 mg • *Star nutrients:* Vitamin A (19% DV), vitamin C (29% DV), thiamin (7% DV)

Grapefruit and Avocado Ensalada

Inspired by a dish I discovered on a sojourn to Puerto Rico, this citrus-based salad will make your next Latin meal sizzle with flavor and nutrients. Packed with vitamins C and E and healthy fats, it offers up heart-healthy nutrients in every bite. Serve it with my Bean and Grilled Veggie Burritos (page 300) or New Orleans Red Beans and Rice (page 320) to round out a wonderful meal.

MAKES 6 SERVING

> *150g, torn-up romaine lettuce*
> *2 medium grapefruits, peeled and separated into sections*
> *1 medium avocado, cut into thin wedges*
> *3 spring onions, thinly sliced*
> *1 tablespoon extra virgin olive oil*
> *1 tablespoon lemon juice*
> *⅛ teaspoon ground cumin*

1. Lightly toss together the lettuce, grapefruits, avocado, and spring onions in a salad bowl.
2. Whisk together the olive oil, lemon juice, and cumin in a small bowl. Drizzle over the salad, toss, and serve immediately.

Variation: For a sweeter salad, substitute orange segments for the grapefruit.

> **PER SERVING:** Calories: 108 • Carbohydrates: 11 g • Fiber: 3 g • Protein: 2 g • Total fat: 8 g • Saturated fat: 1 g • Sodium: 8 mg • *Star nutrients:* Vitamin A (19% DV), vitamin C (62% DV)

Chinese Cabbage Slaw

This colorful, crisp slaw does double duty as an entrée for a light lunch or a tasty side salad to accompany a meal of tofu and brown rice. Thanks to its kaleidoscope of brightly hued plant foods, such as cabbage, carrots, red onions, mangetout, edamame and peanuts, this slaw is packed with powerful phytochemicals to up your antioxidant intake for the day. Since it keeps well, you can pack this slaw in an airtight container and take it in your lunchbox the next day.

MAKES 10 SERVINGS

350g shredded Chinese cabbage (about half a head)
100g grated carrot
½ medium red onion, chopped
250g fresh mangetout, cut in half
75g frozen shelled edamame beans, thawed
75g peanuts, chopped
60ml rice wine vinegar
2 tablespoons peanut oil
1 teaspoon honey or agave nectar
2 garlic cloves, minced
½ teaspoon minced fresh ginger
1 teaspoon reduced-sodium soy sauce
¼ teaspoon red pepper flakes
1 tablespoon sesame seeds

1. Toss together the Chinese cabbage, carrot, onion, mangetout, edamame, and peanuts in a large salad bowl.

2. Whisk together the vinegar, peanut oil, honey, garlic, ginger, soy sauce and red pepper flakes in a small bowl. Drizzle over the slaw and toss until well coated.

3. Sprinkle the sesame seeds over the salad and refrigerate until serving time.

NOTE: If refrigerated in an airtight container, this slaw's crunchy texture will last a few days. If you think you'll have leftovers, just remember to hold the peanuts, which will get soggy after a few hours in the slaw. Instead, serve them on the side to be sprinkled over individual servings as desired.

PER SERVING: Calories: 120 • Carbohydrates: 10 g • Fiber: 3 g • Protein: 5 g • Total fat: 8 g • Saturated fat: 1 g • Sodium: 33 mg • *Star nutrients:* Vitamin A (69% DV), vitamin C (48% DV), niacin (10% DV), folate (18% DV)

Curried Papaya Salad

I'm addicted to the flavors and spices of Southeast Asia, so I let them inspire this salad sweetened with papaya and spiced with parsley and curry. Try it at home and you'll take your own little journey to an exotic destination. And as an added bonus, you'll be rewarded with a bounty of vitamins, minerals and antioxidants.

MAKES 4 SERVINGS

300g cubed fresh papaya
½ medium red bell pepper, sliced
75g sliced cucumber
1 tablespoon finely diced onion
2 tablespoons chopped fresh parsley
2 teaspoons lemon-flavored extra virgin olive oil
1 teaspoon rice vinegar
1 teaspoon orange juice
1 teaspoon reduced-sodium soy sauce
Pinch of ground black pepper
1 garlic clove, minced
½ teaspoon curry powder
120g baby spinach leaves
1½ tablespoons chopped macadamia nuts

1. Gently mix the papaya, bell pepper, cucumber, onion and parsley in a medium bowl.
2. Whisk together the olive oil, vinegar, orange juice, soy sauce, black pepper, garlic and curry powder in a small dish. Pour the dressing over the papaya mixture and toss.
3. Fill a salad bowl with the spinach leaves. Add the papaya mixture and toss gently.
4. Sprinkle macadamia nuts over the salad and serve.

NOTE: If you can't find lemon-flavored extra virgin olive oil, substitute extra virgin olive oil plus ¼ teaspoon lemon zest.

PER SERVING: Calories: 81 • Carbohydrates: 11 g • Fiber: 3 g • Protein: 2 g • Total fat: 4 g • Sodium: 72 mg • *Star nutrients:* Vitamin A (93% DV), vitamin C (140% DV), folate (24% DV)

South of the Border Taco Salad

A refreshing meal in a bowl, this laid-back salad is an ideal crowd pleaser for a summer barbecue or a family meal served al fresco on a pleasant day. And it's bursting with an array of disease-fighting phytochemicals, protein, and fiber—not to mention crunch and color.

MAKES 4 SERVINGS

200g chopped Romaine lettuce
175g frozen corn
170g canned kidney beans, no salt added, rinsed and drained
1 medium tomato, chopped
1 medium avocado, sliced
40g chopped onion
½ medium yellow bell pepper, chopped
2 teaspoons chopped fresh coriander
½ medium jalapeño pepper, seeded and finely chopped
2 tablespoons lemon juice
1 tablespoon extra virgin olive oil
¼ teaspoon red pepper flakes
¼ teaspoon ground cumin
1 garlic clove, minced
25g baked tortilla chips
2 tablespoons pumpkin seeds (pepitas), raw or toasted

1. Toss together the lettuce, corn, beans, tomato, avocado, onion, bell pepper, coriander and jalapeño in a large salad bowl.

2. Whisk together the lemon juice, olive oil, red pepper flakes, cumin, and garlic in a small bowl. Drizzle over the salad and toss lightly.

3. Lightly crush the tortilla chips into smaller pieces and sprinkle over the top of the salad. Sprinkle with pumpkin seeds and serve immediately.

Variation: Substitute black beans, chickpeas, black-eyed peas, soybeans, or a combination of beans for the kidney beans.

PER SERVING: Calories: 252 • Carbohydrates: 36 g • Fiber: 9 g • Protein: 9 g • Total fat: 11 g • Saturated fat: 1 g • Sodium: 279 mg • *Star nutrients:* Vitamin A (37% DV), vitamin C (114% DV), iron (12% DV), manganese (34% DV)

Tuscan White Bean and Rocket Salad

This salad contains a symphony of trademark Tuscan ingredients, such as cannellini beans, rocket, tomatoes, olives and rosemary. It's a virtuoso salad that's virtuous too—you'll get a rich dose of plant proteins, fiber, vitamins, minerals and phytochemicals in this one-dish meal. Serve it with toasted whole grain bread and fruit for a light lunch.

MAKES 4 SERVINGS (ABOUT 5 CUPS)

One 400g can cannellini beans, no salt added, rinsed and drained
50g rocket, rinsed
150g cherry tomatoes
100g pitted Kalamata olives, drained
3 tablespoons freshly squeezed lemon juice
1 tablespoon extra virgin olive oil
¼ teaspoon freshly ground black pepper
1 garlic clove, minced
½ teaspoon chopped fresh or dried rosemary

1. Toss together the cannellini beans, rocket, tomatoes and olives in a salad bowl.

2. Whisk together the lemon juice, olive oil, black pepper, garlic, and rosemary in a small bowl. Drizzle over the salad and toss. Serve immediately.

NOTE: To substitute home-cooked cannellini beans for the canned beans, follow my instructions for cooking dried beans (page 57) and use 300g cooked beans in place of the drained canned beans.

Variation: Try substituting a different type of olive for the Kalamatas, such as an Italian variety like *liguria* or *ponentine*.

PER SERVING: Calories: 190 • Carbohydrates: 27 g • Fiber: 7 g • Protein: 9 g • Total fat: 6 g • Saturated fat: 1 g • Sodium: 157 mg • *Star nutrients:* Folate (27% DV), calcium (9% DV), iron (17% DV), potassium (15% DV)

Greek Salad with Rosemary-Lemon Tofu

I planted rosemary in my garden over ten years ago, and now it's taken over with its fragrant needles and lavender blossoms that attract hummingbirds, bees and butterflies. Rosemary is the inspiration for my plant-based take on this classic Greek salad. You won't even miss the feta cheese in this salad, thanks to the marinated tofu and crunchy pistachios. Serve it with my Aubergine Courgette Moussaka (page 338) and a serving of whole grains, such as bulgur or couscous, for a memorable Greek-style meal.

MAKES 6 SERVINGS

150g firm tofu, drained and cubed
1 tablespoon extra virgin olive oil
1½ tablespoons freshly squeezed lemon juice
¼ teaspoon ground black pepper
¼ teaspoon low-sodium herbal seasoning
1 small garlic clove, minced
1 teaspoon chopped fresh rosemary
200g chopped Romaine lettuce
2 small Roma (plum) tomatoes, chopped
2 tablespoons chopped red onion
1 small yellow bell pepper, sliced
½ medium cucumber, sliced
100g pitted Kalamata olives
30g pistachios

1. Place the tofu in a small dish. In a separate bowl, whisk together the olive oil, lemon juice, black pepper, herbal seasoning, garlic and rosemary. Pour the vinaigrette over the tofu, cover and marinate in the refrigerator for at least 1 hour.
2. Toss together the lettuce, tomatoes, onion, bell pepper, cucumber, and olives in a salad bowl. Add the tofu and the vinaigrette and toss well to coat. Sprinkle with pistachios and serve immediately.

PER SERVING: Calories: 96 • Carbohydrates: 6 g • Fiber: 2 g • Protein: 4 g • Total fat: 7 g • Saturated fat: 1 g • Sodium: 106 mg • *Star nutrients:* Vitamin A (27% DV), vitamin C (28% DV), folate (17% DV), calcium (20% DV), manganese (30% DV)

Nicoise-Style Salad

I adore a classic Nicoise salad, which calls on local, traditional ingredients found in the Mediterranean region of Nice, France. Although a Nicoise salad usually features eggs and tuna, this plant-based spin-off includes other quintessential Nicoise elements, such as red potatoes, green beans, tomatoes, olives and a vinaigrette. Pair this flavorful salad with a simple soup such as Celery Root and Apple Bisque (page 282).

MAKES 6 SERVINGS

> 3 medium red-skinned potatoes, chopped into chunks
> 225g fresh green beans, trimmed
> 1 tablespoon extra virgin olive oil
> 2 tablespoons lemon juice
> 1 teaspoon Dijon mustard
> 1 teaspoon herbes de Provence
> ⅛ teaspoon ground black pepper
> 1 garlic clove, minced
> 100g pitted French olives, drained
> 150g cherry tomatoes
> 60g baby spinach leaves

1. Put the potatoes into a medium pot and cover with water. Cover the pot and bring to a boil. Reduce the heat and simmer for about 15 minutes.

2. Add the green beans and cover. Simmer until the green beans are crisp-tender and potatoes are tender yet intact, an additional 5 to 10 minutes. Drain and put the green beans and potatoes into a medium bowl.

3. Whisk together the olive oil, lemon juice, mustard, *herbes de Provence*, black pepper and garlic in a small bowl. Pour the dressing over the green beans and potatoes. Chill for about 1 hour.

4. Add the olives and cherry tomatoes to the green beans and potatoes and toss just enough to coat with the dressing.

5. Place the spinach in the bottom of a salad bowl. Add the potato mixture and lightly toss together. Serve immediately.

NOTE: If you can't find French olives, you may substitute green or Kalamata olives.

PER SERVING: Calories: 138 • Carbohydrates: 24 g • Fiber: 4 g • Protein: 3 g • Total fat: 4 g • Saturated fat: 1 g • Sodium: 120 mg • *Star nutrients:* Vitamin A (22% DV), vitamin B$_6$ (15% DV), vitamin C (52% DV)

Brussels Sprouts Slaw

Looking for a new way to enjoy Brussels sprouts? Here it is! Let this crunchy salad with a splash of sweet-tangy cranberries reintroduce you to Brussels sprouts, which are packed with sulfur compounds linked to cancer-fighting activity. In this slaw, even your kids may like them! An electric food processor or chopper really comes in handy for shredding the sprouts.

MAKES 8 SERVINGS

450g coarsely shredded Brussels sprouts
½ red onion, chopped
One 15-ounce can haricot beans, no salt added, rinsed and
    drained (see Notes)
15g sun-dried tomatoes
75g dried cranberries
60g coarsely chopped hazelnuts
2 tablespoons extra virgin olive oil
1 tablespoon lemon juice
1 tablespoon chopped fresh basil (or 1 teaspoon dried)
1 garlic clove, minced
½ teaspoon ground black pepper
1 teaspoon whole grain Dijon mustard
¼ teaspoon smoked paprika

1. Toss together the shredded sprouts, onion, beans, sun-dried tomatoes, cranberries and hazelnuts in a large bowl.
2. Whisk together the olive oil, lemon juice, basil, garlic, black pepper, mustard and paprika in a small bowl. Drizzle over the salad and toss. Refrigerate until serving time.

NOTES: This salad retains its crunchy texture for a few days in an air-tight container in the refrigerator. If you think you'll have leftovers, serve the hazelnuts on the side to be sprinkled over individual servings as desired, as they will get soggy after a few hours in the salad.

To substitute home-cooked haricot beans for the canned beans, follow my instructions for cooking dried beans (page 57) and use 300g cooked beans in place of the drained canned beans.

PER SERVING: Calories: 145 • Carbohydrates: 27 g • Fiber: 6 g • Protein: 7 g • Total fat: 2 g • Saturated fat: 0 g • Sodium: 95 mg • *Star nutrients:* Vitamin A (58% DV), vitamin C (85%), folate (22% DV)

Beetroot and Pomegranate Seed Salad

My husband's Swedish heritage has brought me an appreciation for beet-root, a somewhat undervalued vegetable that many chefs have rediscov-ered recently. This glistening ruby salad highlights beetroot and other winter plant foods. It's certainly sophisticated enough for your holiday table and beyond. The compounds responsible for beets' deep red hue, called betalains, are anti-inflammatory, too.

MAKES 4 SERVINGS (ABOUT 9 CUPS)

120g baby spinach leaves
70g assorted micro-greens
250g sliced baby beetroots, cooked and chilled
175g fresh pomegranate seeds
3 tablespoons coarsely chopped walnuts
60ml freshly squeezed orange juice
1 tablespoon plus 1 teaspoon extra virgin olive oil
⅛ teaspoon ground black pepper
1 garlic clove, minced

1. Arrange the spinach leaves in a salad bowl or on a platter. Top with the micro-greens.

2. Arrange the beetroots on top of the micro-greens and sprinkle with pomegranate seeds and walnuts.

3. Whisk together the orange juice, olive oil, black pepper and garlic in a small bowl. Drizzle the vinaigrette over the salad and serve immediately.

NOTE: If you don't have time to cook fresh beetroot for this recipe, use drained canned beetroot (preferably with no added salt) or refrigerated cooked beets, which are available in many supermarkets.

PER SERVING: Calories: 152 • Carbohydrates: 18 g • Fiber: 3 g • Protein: 3 g • Total fat: 9 g • Saturated fat: 1 g • Sodium: 160 mg • *Star nutrients:* Vitamin A (31% DV), vitamin C (34% DV), manganese (16% DV)

Grilled Vegetable and Pesto Panini

You'll think you're feasting in an Italian café when you bite into these crunchy, delicious Italian-style grilled sandwiches. Deriving their appeal from the vibrant flavors and colors of sautéed vegetables, these sandwiches are excellent paired with a refreshing salad or soup. If you're cooking for only one or two, refrigerate the extra vegetables to make up another round of panini later. If you don't have a panini machine or pan, you can press the sandwich in a frying pan under a heavy item such as another pan or even a foil-covered heavy book.

MAKES 4 SANDWICHES

2½ teaspoons extra virgin olive oil
1 garlic clove, minced
½ medium onion, sliced
½ medium yellow bell pepper, sliced
50g chopped broccoli
45g sliced portobello mushroom
2 tablespoons sliced sun-dried tomatoes
¼ teaspoon ground black pepper
¼ teaspoon low-sodium herbal seasoning
8 slices stone-ground whole wheat bread
25g Lemon Basil Pesto (page 275)
4 slices plant-based mozzarella cheese (about 17 grams each)

1. Heat 1 teaspoon of the olive oil in a frying pan.

2. Add the garlic, onion, bell pepper and broccoli and sauté for 5 minutes.

3. Add the mushroom, sun-dried tomatoes, black pepper and herbal seasoning and sauté until the vegetables are crisp yet tender, 3 to 5 minutes.

4. Heat a panini pan or panini press according to the manufacturer's directions. Pour the remaining 1½ teaspoons olive oil into a small dish. Very lightly brush one side of each slice of bread with olive oil. Place up to 4 slices of bread, oil side down, in the panini pan. Spread each slice with 1 tablespoon Lemon Basil Pesto, a quarter of the vegetable mixture, and 1 slice plant-based cheese.

5. Place another slice of bread, oil side up, on top of each sandwich. Cover with the panini press and cook 2 to 3 minutes on each side, until golden brown. Repeat with remaining ingredients, if necessary, to prepare 4 sandwiches.

NOTE: An automatic panini machine cooks the sandwich equally on both sides. A panini pan is a heavy skillet that is marked with grids and comes with a weighted press that you place on the sandwich as it cooks on each side separately.

PER SANDWICH: Calories: 275 • Carbohydrates: 34 g • Fiber: 5 g • Protein: 11 g • Total fat: 11 g • Saturated fat: 1 g • Sodium: 536 mg • *Star nutrients:* Vitamin C (21% DV), niacin (15% DV), folate (17% DV), selenium (29% DV)

Bean and Grilled Veggie Burritos

For a quick, flavorful breakfast or lunch, you can't beat this nutrient-packed burrito wrap. Take it to go, paired with a fresh salad or Thermos of soup, for a healthy lunch on the job. And if you're cooking for only one or two, you can reheat the leftover grilled vegetables for a fast, delicious meal solution later on.

MAKES 4 BURRITOS

1 teaspoon extra virgin olive oil
1 garlic clove, minced
1 small onion, sliced
1 medium green bell pepper, sliced
1 medium summer squash (about 20cm long), such as courgette or
    crookneck
½ teaspoon chili powder
1 small tomato, chopped
1 tablespoon fresh coriander (or 1 teaspoon dried)

170g canned vegetarian refried beans
Four 20cm whole wheat tortillas
25g shredded plant-based (vegetarian) cheese
1 medium avocado, cut into 8 slices

1. To make the grilled veggies, heat the olive oil in a frying pan. Add the garlic, onion, bell pepper, squash, and chili powder and sauté until tender-crisp and golden, about 10 minutes.

2. Add the tomato and coriander and sauté for an additional minute.

3. Warm the refried beans in a small pot or in the microwave.

4. To assemble the veggie burritos, spread each tortilla with 3 table-spoons refried beans, then fill with 1 tablespoon cheese, a quarter of the grilled veggies and 2 slices of avocado. Roll up and place on serving plates, seam sides down.

NOTE: If you're cooking for only one or two, assemble one or two burritos following the instructions in step 4. Reserve the extra beans, grilled vegetables, plant-based cheese, and tortillas in separate airtight containers in the refrigerator for up to 3 days. Reheat the beans and grilled veggies in the microwave in a microwave-proof dish, then prepare the burritos as directed. If you decide to assemble a burrito to warm up later in the microwave, leave out the avocado and add it after reheating.

PER BURRITO: Calories: 307 • Carbohydrates: 44 g • Fiber: 11 g • Protein: 9 g • Total fat: 12 g • Saturated fat: 1 g • Sodium: 387 mg • *Star nutrients:* Vitamin B$_6$ (15% DV), vitamin C (28% DV), folate (15% DV), thiamin (16% DV)

Cherry Sunflower Seed Wraps

Bring out the kid in everyone with this flavorful little wrap that's perfect in a bag lunch for all ages. Get a heart-healthy nutrient and antioxidant boost from the almond butter, sunflower seeds, and cherries in this crunchy wrap. Pack a Thermos of Country French Barley Vegetable Potage (page 283) to round out the meal.

Two 20cm whole wheat tortillas or wraps
2 tablespoons almond butter
4 teaspoons micro-greens
2 tablespoons sunflower seeds
2 tablespoons raisins
2 tablespoons dried cherries

1. Spread 1 tablespoon almond butter evenly over each tortilla.

2. Sprinkle 2 teaspoons micro-greens evenly over the almond butter on each tortilla, then sprinkle with 1 tablespoon sunflower seeds, 1 tablespoon raisins and 1 tablespoon dried cherries.

3. Tightly roll up each tortilla then slice in half. Serve immediately or wrap in plastic to prevent the wrap from drying out.

Variations: Substitute hemp butter, tahini, peanut butter or walnut butter for the almond butter. Try substituting dried apricot slices, dried blueberries, dried cranberries, or dried apple slices for the cherries. And you could replace the sunflower seeds with chopped walnuts, pistachios, almonds, pecans or hazelnuts. The possibilities are endless!

PER WRAP: Calories: 362 • Carbohydrates: 48 g • Fiber: 7 g • Protein: 9 g • Total fat: 17 g • Saturated fat: 1 g • Sodium: 195 mg • *Star nutrients:* Vitamin A (35% DV), vitamin E (37% DV), iron (13% DV), manganese (29% DV), zinc (12% DV)

Spicy Broccoli Cashew Pizza

Now here's a pizza—homemade, filled with veggies, on a whole wheat crust—that you can feel really good about! Use refrigerated pizza dough to cook it up faster than you could order take out. Serve a slice with Curried Papaya Salad (page 291) for the ultimate flavor explosion.

WHOLE WHEAT CRUST
180ml warm water (43°C)
1½ teaspoons active dry yeast

1 teaspoon honey
1½ teaspoons extra virgin olive oil
200g whole wheat flour
1 teaspoon polenta

TOPPINGS

6 tablespoons marinara sauce
100g plant-based grated (vegetarian) cheese
150g small broccoli florets
¼ medium onion, finely chopped
2 tablespoons whole cashews
½ teaspoon red pepper flakes
2 tablespoons chopped fresh basil (or 1 tablespoon dried)

TO MAKE THE DOUGH:

1. In a medium bowl, stir together the water, yeast and honey. Let stand for ten minutes.
2. Stir in the olive oil and flour. Tip the dough onto a lightly floured surface and knead for ten minutes.
3. Place the dough in an oiled bowl, cover with a towel, and let it rise in a warm place for about 1 hour.
4. Roll out the dough to approximately 35cm in diameter.

TO TOP AND BAKE THE PIZZA:

1. Preheat the oven to 200°C/gas 6.
2. Place the pizza dough on a pizza stone or baking sheet that has been sprinkled with polenta.
3. Spread marinara sauce evenly over the crust. Sprinkle evenly with plant-based cheese. Top with broccoli and onion then sprinkle with cashews, red pepper flakes, and fresh basil.
4. Place the pizza in the oven and bake for 20 to 25 minutes, until the cheese is melted and broccoli is crisp-tender.

Variation: Instead of broccoli, try topping your pizza with finely sliced courgettes, bell peppers, aubergines or artichoke hearts.

NOTE: You may substitute store-bought, refrigerated whole wheat pizza dough for the homemade pizza dough.

PER SERVING: Calories: 191 • Carbohydrates: 25 g • Fiber: 5 g • Protein: 12 g • Total fat: 6 g • Saturated fat: 0 g • Sodium: 214 mg • *Star nutrients:* Vitamin C (24% DV), folate (8% DV)

California Tofu and Vegetable Penne Toss

This is my favorite dish to make after a summertime trip to the farmers market. With my refrigerator stuffed with ripe, earthy vegetables, I always feel inspired to make this simple, colorful pasta and tofu medley. You can serve it hot as a main dish or cold as a pasta salad. Pair it with Italian Cannellini Spinach Soup (page 280) for a match made in heaven.

MAKES 8 SERVINGS

> 225g whole grain penne pasta, uncooked
> 1 tablespoon extra virgin olive oil
> 150g firm tofu, drained and cubed
> 1 tablespoon lemon juice
> 2 garlic cloves, minced
> ½ teaspoon ground black pepper
> 1 teaspoon low-sodium herbal seasoning
> ½ medium red bell pepper, coarsely chopped
> ½ medium yellow bell pepper, coarsely chopped
> 75g sliced spring onions
> 75g sliced button mushrooms
> 2 medium ripe tomatoes, coarsely chopped
> 1 teaspoon coarsely chopped fresh basil leaves
> 100g pitted Kalamata olives, drained
> 35g pine nuts

1. Cook the penne pasta in boiling water until al dente, about 7 to 8 minutes. Drain and set aside.
2. Heat the olive oil in a large frying pan. Add the tofu, lemon juice, garlic, black pepper, herbal seasoning and bell peppers and sauté for 5 minutes.
3. Add the spring onions and mushrooms and sauté for 2 minutes.
4. Add the tomatoes, basil, olives, cooked pasta and pine nuts. To serve

warm, sauté until heated through, about 2 minutes. To serve chilled, transfer to a bowl and allow to cool, then refrigerate.

Variations: Try shiitake, oyster, chanterelle, porcini or portobello mushrooms. Substitute Sicilian, French, or Italian olives for the Kalamata olives for a new flavor.

PER SERVING: Calories: 170 • Carbohydrates: 26 g • Fiber: 5 g • Protein: 7 g • Total fat: 6 g • Saturated fat: 1 g • Sodium: 80 mg • *Star nutrients:* Vitamin A (15% DV), vitamin C (30% DV), calcium (13% DV), iron (10% DV)

Orzo with Tomatoes and Fennel Seed

I love the anise scent and flavor of fennel, which marries with the warm flavors of the pasta and tomatoes in this simple orzo dish. Prepare more mushroom dishes like this one to pack your diet with vitamin D, which is found in UV-exposed mushrooms, and to take advantage of the anticancer and immune activity that have also been associated with mushrooms.

MAKES 4 SERVINGS

1 litre water
175g whole wheat orzo, uncooked
1½ teaspoons extra virgin olive oil
1 garlic clove, minced
1½ teaspoons fennel seeds
1½ teaspoons lemon juice
½ teaspoon low-sodium herbal seasoning
2 tablespoons sliced spring onions
150g sliced shiitake mushrooms
2 small ripe Roma (plum) tomatoes, chopped
Freshly ground black pepper

1. Bring the water to a boil in a medium pot. Add the orzo, cover, and cook for 6 to 8 minutes.

2. Meanwhile, heat the olive oil in a saucepan. Add the garlic, fennel seeds, lemon juice and herbal seasoning and sauté for 2 minutes.

3. Add the spring onions, mushrooms and tomatoes and sauté for 3 to 4 additional minutes.

4. When the orzo is done, drain off the water. Return the orzo to the pot and add the mushroom-tomato mixture. Heat, stirring occasionally, until the mixture is well combined and heated through, about 2 minutes. Season with black pepper as desired.

Variation: Don't hesitate to try enoki, oyster, portobello crimini or white mushrooms in this dish.

PER SERVING: Calories: 174 • Carbohydrates: 31 g • Fiber: 8 g • Protein: 7 g • Total fat: 3 g • Saturated fat: 0 g • Sodium: 10 mg • *Star nutrients:* Pantothenic acid (28% DV), iron (12% DV), copper (35% DV), selenium (26% DV)

Vegetable Medley Lasagna

With its kaleidoscope of colorful vegetables, this vegetable lasagna is as hearty and delicious as it is nutritious. It will quickly become a favorite of your entire family—even the omnivores! And this lasagna is even better warmed up the next day—if there's any left.

MAKES 6 SERVINGS

1 tablespoon extra virgin olive oil
1 medium onion, chopped
1 medium green bell pepper, chopped
1 medium summer squash (about 20cm long), such as courgette or crookneck, sliced
150g chopped broccoli
2 garlic cloves, minced
½ teaspoon ground black pepper
2 tablespoons chopped fresh oregano (or 2 teaspoons dried)
1 teaspoon low-sodium herbal seasoning
100g (6 sheets) whole wheat lasagna noodles, uncooked
700g reduced-sodium marinara sauce
140g packed chopped kale
150g shredded plant-based cheese

1. Heat the olive oil in a large frying pan. Add the onion, bell pepper, summer squash, broccoli, garlic, black pepper, oregano, and herbal seasoning. Sauté for about 7 minutes.
2. Preheat the oven to 180°C/gas 4.
3. Pour 130g of the marinara sauce into a deep rectangular baking dish (about 18 x 25cm) and spread it evenly over the bottom of the dish.
4. Place 3 lasagna noodles side by side on top of the sauce. In even layers, add about half of the vegetable mixture, then 70g kale, half of the remaining marinara sauce, and 75g plant-based cheese.
5. Place the remaining 3 noodles on top and repeat the layers with the remaining ingredients.
6. Cover the baking dish with a lid or foil and bake for 1 hour. Remove the cover and cook for an additional 15 minutes, or until the dish is golden and bubbly.
7. Cut the lasagna into six servings and serve immediately.

NOTE: This thick, vegetable-rich lasagna recipe is best prepared in a small, deep baking dish (about 18 x 25 x 9cm) rather than a shallow 23 x 32cm baking dish.

PER SERVING: Calories: 222 • Carbohydrates: 28 g • Fiber: 6 g • Protein: 13 g • Total fat: 7 g • Saturated fat: 1 g • Sodium: 211 mg • *Star nutrients:* Vitamin A (128% DV), vitamin B_6 (11% DV), vitamin C (77% DV), calcium (8% DV), iron (13% DV)

Butternut Squash Macaroni and "Cheese"

This plant-based macaroni and "cheese" is astonishingly rich and creamy. The butternut squash lends it a lovely golden color, as well as a sweet, earthy taste. One of my all-time favorite recipes, this scrumptious dish is perfect to tote along to your next barbecue. You'll end up winning the whole crowd over.

MAKES 6 SERVINGS

225g dry whole grain elbow macaroni
350g butternut squash, chopped (see Note)
370ml low-sodium vegetable broth

¼ teaspoon ground nutmeg

¼ teaspoon ground black pepper

¼ teaspoon smoked paprika

¼ teaspoon dry mustard

1 teaspoon dried sage

370ml unsweetened plain plant-based milk

100g plant-based grated (vegetarian) cheese

3 tablespoons bread crumbs

1 teaspoon extra virgin olive oil

1. Cook the macaroni in boiling water according to the package directions until al dente. Drain and set aside.

2. Put the squash, broth, nutmeg, black pepper, paprika, mustard and sage into a medium pot. Cover the pot and bring to a boil. Reduce the heat and simmer until the squash is tender, about 20 minutes.

3. Preheat the oven to 190°C/gas 5.

4. Lightly mash the squash mixture in the pot with a potato masher. Stir in the cooked macaroni, plant-based milk and plant-based cheese.

5. Spray a 23 x 23cm baking dish with nonstick cooking spray. Transfer the macaroni and cheese mixture into the dish.

6. Mix together the bread crumbs and olive oil in a small dish. Sprinkle over the macaroni and cheese.

7. Cover the dish with foil and bake for 15 minutes. Remove the foil and bake for an additional 15 minutes.

NOTE: To prepare cubed squash, slice the fresh butternut squash in half, scoop out the seeds, peel the outer skin, and slice the flesh into cubes. You can also purchase pre-cubed, fresh butternut squash at many supermarkets. Choose a subtle plant-based milk, such as almond, rice or hemp milk, for this dish.

PER SERVING: Calories: 238 • Carbohydrates: 39 g • Fiber: 5 g • Protein: 10 g • Total fat: 7 g • Saturated fat: 1 g • Sodium: 183 mg • *Star nutrients:* Vitamin A (91% DV), vitamin C (20% DV)

Antipasto Couscous with Chickpeas

A staple in North African cuisine, couscous is actually small pieces of semolina pasta made from whole grain flour. My whole grain couscous dish is based on a variety of flavorful preserved vegetables, such as sun-dried tomatoes, roasted peppers, and marinated artichoke hearts. You can keep these ingredients in your store cupboard and make this wholesome one-dish meal at a moment's notice. And it's just as good served cold as a salad.

MAKES 6 SERVINGS

1 tablespoon extra virgin olive oil
2 garlic cloves, minced
½ medium red onion, chopped
15g sun-dried tomatoes, sliced
175g bottled, flame-roasted red or yellow peppers, drained and chopped
75g canned marinated mushrooms, drained
175g marinated artichoke hearts, drained and sliced
175g cooked or canned chickpeas (garbanzo beans), no salt added, rinsed and drained
50g pitted green olives, drained
1 tablespoon capers
370ml water
1 teaspoon balsamic vinegar
½ teaspoon lemon pepper
½ teaspoon smoked paprika
1 teaspoon dried oregano
175g uncooked whole wheat couscous
40g chopped pistachios

1. Heat the olive oil in a large saucepan. Add the garlic and onion and sauté for 5 minutes.
2. Stir in the sun-dried tomatoes, peppers, mushrooms, artichokes, chickpeas, olives, capers, water, vinegar, lemon pepper, paprika and oregano. Cook until bubbly, about 3 minutes.

3. Pour the couscous over the vegetable mixture (do not stir) then cover the pan and remove from the heat. Let stand for 5 minutes.

4. Remove the cover and fluff the couscous with a fork. Sprinkle with the pistachios and serve immediately.

NOTE: Chill this dish to serve it as a salad. If you plan on serving it much later, reserve the pistachios to keep them from getting soggy and sprinkle them on at the last minute.

PER SERVING: Calories: 240 • Carbohydrates: 38 g • Fiber: 6 g • Protein: 8 g • Total fat: 6 g • Saturated fat: 1 g • Sodium: 252 mg • *Star nutrients:* Vitamin C (20% DV), niacin (10% DV), folate (13% DV), iron (11% DV)

Saffron Brown Basmati Rice

The cheery golden hue saffron lends to rice is a calling card for its rich antioxidant properties. Actually thread-like flower stigmas hand-collected from the purple saffron crocus, this precious spice is prized for both its flavor and health benefits. Serve this easy side dish with curries, such as Cauliflower and Pea Curry (page 342), as well as stir-fries, sautéed vegetables, and stewed beans or lentils.

MAKES 6 SERVINGS

> 200g uncooked brown basmati rice
> 250ml water
> 250ml low-sodium vegetable broth
> ½ teaspoon sesame oil
> ¼ teaspoon saffron threads

1. Put the rice, water, broth, oil and saffron into a medium saucepan with a tight-fitting lid.

2. Bring to a boil, stir once, and reduce the heat to simmer. Cook, covered, until all the liquid is absorbed and the rice is tender, about 50 minutes.

3. Remove the pot from the heat and let stand, covered, for 10 minutes. Fluff the rice with a fork and serve immediately.

NOTE: Saffron is so precious—and expensive—that some supermarkets store it in locked cabinets. If you can't find it, ask a clerk for assistance. And remember, a little goes a long way.

PER SERVING: Calories: 103 • Carbohydrates: 22 g • Fiber: 1 g • Protein: 3 g • Total fat: 1 g • Saturated fat: 0 g • Sodium: 13 mg • *Star nutrients:* Niacin (8% DV), magnesium (11% DV), manganese (44% DV)

Bulgur Risotto with Yellow Squash, Peas and Pine Nuts

Thanks to its lovely shades of gold and emerald, this straightforward whole grain dish is an attractive addition to your dinner table. For this version I've swapped out the Arborio rice traditionally featured in Italian risotto for bulgur, which offers a high-fiber boost of whole grains. Serve this one-dish meal with Tuscan White Bean and Rocket Salad (page 293) for an additional rush of protein and antioxidants.

MAKES 4 SERVINGS

1 tablespoon extra virgin olive oil
125g sliced yellow crookneck squash
150g frozen peas
75g sliced mushrooms
175g chopped onion
2 garlic cloves, minced
½ teaspoon ground black pepper
½ teaspoon low-sodium herbal seasoning
560ml low-sodium vegetable broth
120ml white wine
140g uncooked bulgur
2 teaspoons chopped fresh basil
35g pine nuts

1. Heat the olive oil in a large saucepan. Add the yellow squash, peas, mushrooms, onion, garlic, black pepper and herbal seasoning and sauté for 5 minutes.

2. Meanwhile, heat the broth and wine in a small saucepan over medium heat until warm but not boiling.

3. Stir the bulgur into the vegetable mixture. Ladle approximately 120ml of the warm broth mixture over the bulgur-vegetable mixture. Cook over medium heat, stirring constantly, until the liquid is absorbed. Add another 120ml broth mixture and continue cooking, stirring, and adding more warm broth until all the broth has been incorporated and the risotto is creamy and just tender, about 20 minutes.

4. Stir in the fresh basil and pine nuts and serve immediately.

Variation: Substitute another seasonal vegetable for the yellow squash, such as broccoli, courgette, aubergine, cauliflower, sliced Brussels sprouts or green beans.

PER SERVING: Calories: 278 • Carbohydrates: 40 g • Fiber: 11 g • Protein: 10 g • Total fat: 9 g • Saturated fat: 1 g • Sodium: 47 mg • *Star nutrients:* Vitamin C (16% DV), iron (10% DV), manganese (44% DV)

❧ Baked Farro Herb Pilaf

Featuring the ancient grain farro, my old-fashioned whole grain pilaf can complete any meal. This savory, crunchy grain dish can accompany everything from baked tofu cutlets to stewed lentils, such as Green and Gold Lentil Pot (page 316). Keep this pantry-stable ingredient on hand to add this easy dish to your menu any day of the week.

MAKES 6 SERVINGS

1 tablespoon extra virgin olive oil
2 medium carrots, sliced
2 medium celery sticks, chopped
1 small onion, sliced
2 garlic cloves, minced
1 teaspoon dried marjoram
1 teaspoon dried thyme
1 teaspoon low-sodium herbal seasoning
½ teaspoon ground black pepper
250g uncooked farro (see Note)
500ml reduced-sodium vegetable broth
250ml water

1. Heat the olive oil in a large ovenproof frying pan. Add the carrots, celery, onion and garlic and sauté for 10 minutes.

2. Preheat the oven to 180°C/gas 4.

3. Add the marjoram, thyme, herbal seasoning, black pepper, farro, broth, and water to the frying pan and stir. Cook until bubbly, about 5 minutes.

4. Cover the frying pan with a tightly fitting lid and transfer to the oven. Bake for 30 minutes.

5. Remove the lid and bake for an additional 10 minutes, or until the liquid is absorbed and the farro is tender.

NOTE: Farro, also called emmer wheat, is the forerunner, or "mother," to modern wheat. Often confused with spelt, true farro is becoming more widely available at natural food stores.

PER SERVING: Calories: 215 • Carbohydrates: 40 g • Fiber: 7 g • Protein: 7 g • Total fat: 3 g • Saturated fat: 0 g • Sodium: 46 mg • *Star nutrients:* Vitamin A (49% DV)

Easy Kale and Broad Bean Ragout

Searching for an easy one-dish meal you can whip up in minutes? Here's my simple solution: a country kale and bean ragout that won't bust your budget. It's perfect for your busiest night of the week. And you'll be all the better for tapping into its stash of protein, slow-burning carbohydrates, vitamins, minerals, and antioxidants.

MAKES 4 SERVINGS

1 tablespoon plus 2 teaspoons extra virgin olive oil
1 small onion, chopped
2 garlic cloves, minced
¼ teaspoon ground black pepper
¼ teaspoon smoked paprika
1 teaspoon low-sodium herbal seasoning
1 teaspoon dried thyme
1 bunch chopped kale
One 400g can diced tomatoes, ideally salt free, with juice
One 450g can broad beans, ideally salt free, rinsed and drained
250ml low-sodium vegetable broth
4 slices (25g) rustic whole grain bread

1. Heat 1 tablespoon of the olive oil in a large ovenproof frying pan. Add the onion, garlic, black pepper, smoked paprika, ½ teaspoon of the herbal seasoning and the thyme and sauté for 2 minutes.
2. Add the kale, tomatoes, broad beans and broth and cook, stirring occasionally, for 10 minutes.
3. Meanwhile, preheat the oven to 200°C/gas 6. Toast four slices of whole grain bread in the toaster.
4. Pour the remaining 2 teaspoons olive oil in a small dish. Brush each slice of toasted bread with oil and sprinkle with the remaining ½ teaspoon herbal seasoning. Arrange the toast slices on top of the frying pan mixture.

5. Place the frying pan in the oven and bake for 8 minutes, or until the vegetables are tender and the bread is browned and crisp.

Variation: Substitute canned (no salt added) black-eyed peas, chickpeas or pinto beans for the broad beans.

> **PER SERVING:** Calories: 280 • Carbohydrates: 45 g • Fiber: 9 g • Protein: 13 g • Total fat: 8 g • Saturated fat: 1 g • Sodium: 220 mg • *Star nutrients:* Vitamin A (130% DV), vitamin C (160% DV), folate (23% DV), calcium (19% DV), iron (22% DV), potassium (27% DV)

Green and Gold Lentil Pot

The organic green and golden-red tones of these lentils blend together with green celery and herbs to create an uncomplicated, savory dish. Simply throw all of the ingredients into a pot and it's ready to eat in 20 minutes. Serve with a salad and cooked whole grains such as quinoa, brown rice, or spelt for a hearty, high-fiber meal that will satisfy your body and soul.

MAKES 4 SERVINGS

100g dried red lentils
100g dried green lentils
750ml water
1 cube low-sodium vegetable bouillon
4 celery sticks, chopped
1 medium onion, chopped
1 fresh medium tomato, chopped (or 180g canned diced tomato)
1 garlic clove, minced
¼ teaspoon ground black pepper
¼ teaspoon smoked paprika
1 teaspoon low-sodium herbal seasoning
1 teaspoon dried sage
¼ teaspoon ground turmeric

1. Combine all the ingredients in a large pot. Stir well, cover, and bring to a simmer.
2. Cook until lentils and vegetables are tender, about 20 minutes.

PER SERVING: Calories: 191 • Carbohydrates: 34 g • Fiber: 12 g • Protein: 13 g • Total fat: 1 g • Saturated fat: 0 g • Sodium: 53 mg • *Star nutrients:* Folate (66% DV), iron (28% DV), manganese (41% DV), copper (20% DV)

Slow-Cooked Butter Beans with Root Vegetables

Perfect for fall and winter, this simple dish showcases seasonal root vegetables, such as turnips, parsnips, and carrots. Just soak the butter beans overnight, fill your slow cooker with the ingredients in the morning, and turn it on before you leave for work. Dinner will be ready when you return. Serve it on a bed of steamed grains, such as quinoa or farro, for a soothing, nutrient-rich meal.

MAKES 10 SERVINGS

> 225g dried butter beans
> 1.2 litres water
> One 400g can diced tomatoes, ideally salt free, with juice
> 1 large onion, coarsely chopped
> 3 medium carrots, coarsely chopped
> 3 medium celery sticks, coarsely chopped
> ½ large turnip, cut into large cubes
> 2 medium parsnips, peeled and coarsely chopped
> 3 medium potatoes, cut into large cubes
> 1 cube low-sodium vegetable bouillon
> 2 teaspoons dried tarragon
> 1 teaspoon ground turmeric
> 1 bay leaf
> ½ teaspoon ground black pepper
> 3 garlic cloves, minced
> 1 teaspoon low-sodium herb seasoning
> ½ teaspoon celery salt

1. Rinse the butter beans. Cover with water and soak overnight.

2. Drain the butter beans and put into the slow cooker. Add the water and the remaining ingredients and stir well.

3. Set the cooker on high and cook until the beans and vegetables are tender, about 4 hours. Remove the bay leaf and serve.

NOTE: Instead of using a slow cooker in step 2, you can put all the ingredients in a large pot with a tight-fitting lid and cook over low heat, stirring occasionally, until tender, for approximately 2 hours.

PER SERVING: Calories: 167 • Carbohydrates: 35 g • Fiber: 8 g • Protein: 8 g • Total fat: 0 g • Saturated fat: 0 g • Sodium: 67 mg • *Star nutrients:* Vitamin A (46% DV), vitamin B_6 (18% DV), vitamin C (42% DV), folate (22% DV), potassium (22% DV), manganese (29% DV)

Southwestern Black Bean, Quinoa and Mango Medley

The jewel-like black beans gleam in this crunchy, zesty salad, which is packed with disease-fighting anthocyanins, vitamin C, fiber, and lutein. Serve with corn tortillas and vegetable soup for an easy, refreshing meal. And don't forget to pack up the leftovers for lunch the next day.

MAKES 6 SERVINGS

One 400g can black beans, ideally salt free, rinsed and drained (see Notes)
185g cooked quinoa (according to package directions)
175g frozen corn
1 small red bell pepper, chopped
170g chopped fresh mango
40g finely chopped red onion
2 tablespoons chopped fresh coriander (or 2 teaspoons dried)
1 small jalapeño pepper, seeded and finely diced
Juice from 1 medium lemon
1½ tablespoons extra virgin olive oil
2 garlic cloves, minced
½ teaspoon ground cumin
½ teaspoon chili powder
¼ teaspoon ground turmeric

1. Mix together the beans, quinoa, corn, bell pepper, mango, onion, coriander, and jalapeño in a mixing bowl.

2. Whisk together the lemon juice, olive oil, garlic, cumin, chili powder, and turmeric in a small bowl. Drizzle over the mixture and toss. Refrigerate until serving time.

Variations: Substitute kidney or pinto beans for the black beans, or use cooked barley, bulgur, rice or farro instead of the quinoa.

NOTES: To substitute home-cooked black beans for the canned beans, follow my instructions for cooking dried beans (page 57) and use 300g cooked beans in place of the drained canned beans.

This dish may be served warm by heating all ingredients in a saucepan for 3 to 5 minutes, only until heated through.

PER SERVING: Calories: 164 • Carbohydrates: 27 g • Fiber: 7 g • Protein: 6 g • Total fat: 4 g • Saturated fat: 1 g • Sodium: 93 mg • *Star nutrients:* Vitamin A (29% DV), vitamin C (61% DV), folate (18% DV), iron (11% DV)

New Orleans Red Beans and Rice

There's nothing better than the simplicity of red beans and rice—a staple dish I've sampled in several countries throughout Latin America and the Caribbean. A trip to New Orleans fueled my quest for an authentic, plant-based recipe that captures the dish's humble flavor and zesty heat. Serve my version with cooked greens for a powerhouse of a meal.

MAKES 8 SERVINGS

370g dried light red kidney beans
1.6 litres water
1 medium carrot, chopped
1 medium onion, chopped
1 bay leaf
½ teaspoon ground black pepper
½ teaspoon cayenne
1 cube low-sodium vegetable bouillon
245g uncooked long-grain brown rice

1. Soak the kidney beans overnight in enough cold water to cover them.

2. Drain the beans and put them into a large pot with 1 litre fresh water. Add the carrot, onion, bay leaf, black pepper, cayenne, and bouillon and bring to a boil. Cover, reduce the heat and slowly simmer until the beans are very soft, about 1 hour and 45 minutes.

3. About 1 hour into the cooking time, start to prepare the rice. If using a rice cooker, put 660ml water and the rice into the cooker and prepare according to the manufacturer's instructions. If cooking on the hob, bring 660ml water to a boil in a medium saucepan. Add the rice and reduce the heat to a simmer. Cook, covered, until all the liquid is absorbed, 45 to 50 minutes.

4. When the beans are ready, remove the bay leaf. Lightly mash the beans and serve immediately over the hot rice.

NOTE: You can adjust the "heat" of this recipe by reducing or increasing the amount of cayenne.

PER SERVING: Calories: 251 • Carbohydrates: 48 g • Fiber: 13 g • Protein:

13 g • Total fat: 1 g • Saturated fat: 0 g • Sodium: 24 mg • *Star nutrients:* Vitamin A (45% DV), folate (48% DV), calcium (8% DV), iron (22% DV), potassium (22% DV), magnesium (25% DV)

Three-Bean Cowboy Chili

Spicy and "meaty," this chili featuring three types of beans will warm your soul on a wintry day. If you want to go the slow cooker route, you can simply fill your crock with these ingredients in the morning, set it on low, and when you return at the end of the day your kitchen will welcome you with warm, savory aromas. Pair this chili with a crisp green salad and Corn Muffins with Apples and Walnuts (page 352) for an entirely satisfying meal.

MAKES 10 SERVINGS

140g dried light red kidney beans, soaked and drained

150g dried adzuki beans, soaked and drained

125g dried haricot beans, soaked and drained

1 tablespoon extra virgin olive oil

350g chopped onions

1 medium green bell pepper, chopped

1 medium jalapeño pepper, seeded and finely diced

3 garlic cloves, minced

175g frozen yellow corn

175g chopped portobello mushrooms

1 tablespoon chili powder

1 teaspoon ground cumin

½ teaspoon ground turmeric

¼ teaspoon red pepper flakes

¼ teaspoon ground black pepper

2 tablespoons chopped fresh coriander

One 400g can diced tomatoes, ideally salt free, with juice

175g tomato paste

750ml water

500ml low-sodium vegetable broth

1. Soak the kidney, adzuki, and haricot beans overnight in enough cold water to cover them.
2. Drain the beans and set aside.
3. Heat the olive oil in a large pot. Add the onions, bell pepper, jalapeño and garlic and sauté for 10 minutes.
4. Add the corn, mushrooms, chili powder, cumin, turmeric, red pepper flakes, black pepper and coriander and sauté for an additional 5 minutes.
5. Stir in the drained beans, tomatoes, tomato paste, water, and vegetable broth and bring to a boil. Reduce the heat to low, cover, and simmer until the beans are tender, about 2 hours.

NOTES: To adjust the "heat" of this recipe, reduce or increase the quantities of chili powder, red pepper flakes, and black pepper.

To cook the chili in a slow cooker, add the soaked, drained beans and all ingredients to the crock. Dial your cooker to the high setting and cook it for 4 hours, until the beans are tender.

PER SERVING: Calories: 222 • Carbohydrates: 41 g • Fiber: 12 g • Protein: 12 g • Total fat: 2 g • Saturated fat: 0 g • Sodium: 163 mg • *Star nutrients:* Vitamin A (36% DV), vitamin C (77% DV), niacin (15% DV), calcium (9% DV), iron (22% DV), potassium (28% DV)

Vegetarian Hoppin' John

In my mother's Southern tradition, black-eyed peas are served with greens for good luck on New Year's Day. My plant-based version of this dish—an homage to my mom's Southern roots—leaves out the bacon or ham hocks in favor of another Southern favorite, okra. You don't have to wait until New Year's Day to enjoy Hoppin' John and cooked greens—you can get the delicious and nutritious effect of this traditional dish any day.

MAKES 6 SERVINGS

250g dried black-eyed peas
1 tablespoon extra virgin olive oil
1 medium onion, diced
1 medium green bell pepper, diced
3 medium celery sticks, chopped

2 medium carrots, sliced
2 garlic cloves, minced
¼ teaspoon cayenne
1 teaspoon dried thyme
500ml low-sodium vegetable broth
6 cups water
1 bay leaf
½ teaspoon liquid smoke
200g sliced fresh or frozen okra
185g uncooked long-grain brown rice

1. Soak the black-eyed peas overnight in enough cold water to cover them.
2. Drain the peas and set aside.
3. Heat the olive oil in a large heavy pot. Add the onion, bell pepper, celery, carrots, garlic, cayenne and thyme and sauté for 5 minutes.
4. Add the drained peas, broth, 750ml of the water, bay leaf, and liquid smoke to the pot and bring to a boil. Reduce the heat, cover, and simmer, stirring occasionally, for 1 hour.
5. About 30 minutes into the cooking time, start to prepare the rice. If using a rice cooker, put the remaining 750ml of water and the rice into the cooker and prepare according to the manufacturer's instructions. If cooking on the hob, bring 750ml water to a boil in a medium saucepan. Add the rice and reduce the heat to a simmer. Cook, covered, until all the liquid is absorbed, 45 to 50 minutes.
6. After the peas and vegetables have cooked for an hour, add the okra to the mixture and cook for an additional 15 minutes. Remove the bay leaf.
7. Serve the pea mixture immediately over the hot rice.

Variation: Substitute cooked barley, wheat berries, or quinoa for the brown rice for an interesting flavor variation.

PER SERVING: Calories: 314 • Carbohydrates: 58 g • Fiber: 9 g • Protein: 14 g • Total fat: 4 g • Saturated fat: 0 g • Sodium: 59 mg • *Star nutrients:* Vitamin A (63% DV), vitamin C (21% DV), folate (26% DV), calcium (14% DV), manganese (36% DV)

Tofu Cacciatore

Get a lycopene rush with my super red, tofu-based cacciatore. Pair it with a spicy Italian red wine, simple green salad, and your own pick of cooked whole grain pasta, gnocchi, or ancient grains for a meal you can create in under 30 minutes. And the leftovers will be just as good the next day.

MAKES 4 SERVINGS

1 tablespoon extra virgin olive oil
1 medium onion, chopped
1 medium green bell pepper, chopped
75g sliced mushrooms
225g firm tofu, drained and cubed
2 garlic cloves, minced
2 teaspoons dried oregano
1 teaspoon dried parsley
1 teaspoon low-sodium herbal seasoning
½ teaspoon ground black pepper
Pinch of red pepper flakes
One 400g can diced tomatoes, ideally salt free, with juice
2 tablespoons tomato paste
120ml red wine
120ml water
2 tablespoons capers

1. Heat the olive oil in a large sauté pan. Add the onion and sauté for 4 minutes.
2. Add the bell pepper, mushrooms, tofu, garlic, oregano, parsley, herbal seasoning, black pepper, and red pepper flakes and sauté for an additional 4 minutes.
3. Stir in the tomatoes, tomato paste, red wine, water and capers. Cook over medium heat until thick and bubbly, about 5 minutes.

NOTE: This dish is excellent served over hot cooked pasta, gnocchi, or whole grains such as brown rice, quinoa, wheat berries, or barley.

PER SERVING: Calories: 163 • Carbohydrates: 18 g • Fiber: 3 g • Protein: 7 g • Fat: 6 g • Saturated fat: 1 g • Sodium: 390 mg • *Star Nutrients:* Vitamin A (21% DV), vitamin C (88% DV), folate (12% DV), calcium (15% DV), iron (11% DV)

Bok Choy Seitan Pho (Vietnamese Noodle Soup)

After sampling pho at a Vietnamese noodle shop in Los Angeles, I was on a mission to create a simple plant-based version of this aromatic, festive noodle dish in my own kitchen. My recipe features seitan, a wonderful plant-based protein found in many natural food stores. My whole family loves the interactive style in which this soup is served. In fact, you can plan a dinner party around this traditional meal. Simply dish up the noodles and bubbling broth into large soup bowls, set out a variety of vegetable toppings, and let your guests serve it up their way.

MAKES 4 SERVINGS

BROTH

1 litre reduced-sodium
   vegetable broth
½ medium yellow onion,
   chopped
40g sliced shiitake
   mushrooms
1 medium carrot, sliced
4 garlic cloves, minced
8 thin slices peeled fresh
   ginger root
1 tablespoon reduced-
   sodium soy sauce
1 tablespoon rice wine
   vinegar
1 tablespoon agave syrup
¼ teaspoon ground black
   pepper
2 cinnamon sticks
2 star anise pods
½ teaspoon coriander
   seeds
6 sprigs of fresh basil
6 sprigs of fresh coriander

NOODLES

300g pack flat rice noodles

TOPPINGS

225g seitan (wheat gluten)
   strips, thinly sliced
2 small bunches of fresh
   bok choy, sliced thinly
1 cup fresh bean sprouts
2 teaspoons coarsely
   chopped coriander
2 teaspoons coarsely
   chopped basil
1 small lime, cut into
   wedges
1 small jalapeño pepper,
   seeded and diced
4 spring onions, sliced

TO PREPARE THE BROTH:

1. Combine all the broth ingredients in a large pot, cover, and bring to a low boil. Reduce the heat and simmer for 30 minutes. Strain the broth, discarding the vegetables and seasonings. Return the strained broth to the pot, cover, and keep warm (broth should be bubbling right before serving time). While broth is cooking, prepare noodles and toppings.

TO PREPARE THE NOODLES:

1. Bring a medium pot of water to a boil. Add the rice noodles, cover, and cook until just tender, about 5 minutes, or according to package directions. Drain the noodles immediately and rinse with cold water. Return the drained noodles to the pot and cover.

TO PREPARE THE TOPPINGS:

1. Arrange the toppings on a large platter.

2. To serve the soup, divide the noodles among four very large soup bowls. Either garnish the noodles with desired toppings or let your guests do their own. Ladle boiling broth over the noodles and toppings, and serve immediately. Allow hot broth to wilt vegetables and cool slightly before eating it.

PER SERVING: Calories: 310 • Carbohydrates: 55 g • Fiber: 4 g • Protein: 17 g • Total fat: 2 g • Saturated fat: 0 g • Sodium: 427 mg • *Star nutrients:* Vitamin A (39% DV), vitamin C (23% DV), iron (11% DV), selenium (13% DV)

Orange-Peanut Tempeh Stir-Fry with Red Rice

A colorful feast for the eyes—and body—this Asian-inspired stir-fry is packed with flavor and the bevy of powerful phytochemicals found in these vibrant plant foods. Featuring orange- and ginger-marinated tempeh—a fermented soy and grain cake popular in Indonesia—the zestiness and crunch of this stir-fry pairs well with the delicate tones and texture of the rice.

MAKES 4 SERVINGS

225g tempeh

250ml orange juice

1 teaspoon minced fresh ginger

2 garlic cloves, minced

2 tablespoons tamari (see Notes)

¼ teaspoon red curry paste

2 tablespoons chopped fresh coriander (or 2 teaspoons coriander dried)

250ml water

125g uncooked red rice

1 tablespoon peanut oil

2 carrots, coarsely chopped

½ onion, cut into wedges

2 celery sticks, coarsely chopped

½ red bell pepper, sliced

225g fresh mangetout

75g peanuts

2 tablespoons shelled hemp seeds

2 teaspoons cornflour

1. Cut the tempeh into cubes and place in a shallow dish.

2. Whisk together the orange juice, ginger, garlic, tamari, curry paste and coriander in a small bowl and pour over the tempeh. Refrigerate the tempeh and marinade for 1 hour.

3. If using a rice cooker, put the water and the rice into the cooker and prepare according to the manufacturer's instructions. If cooking on the hob, bring the water to a boil in a medium saucepan. Add the rice and reduce the heat to a simmer. Cook, covered, until all the liquid is absorbed, about 20 minutes.

4. Meanwhile, heat the peanut oil in a wok or frying pan. Add the carrots and sauté, stirring frequently, for 3 minutes. Add the onion and celery and stir-fry for an additional 3 minutes. Add the bell pepper, mangetout, peanuts and hemp seeds and stir-fry for an additional 2 minutes.

5. Remove the tempeh from the marinade with a fork or slotted spoon and reserve the marinade. Add the tempeh to the vegetable mixture.

6. Add the cornflour to the reserved marinade and whisk until smooth. Pour into the vegetable-tempeh mixture. Cook, stirring often, until the sauce has thickened and the vegetables are crisp-tender, about 2 minutes.

7. Serve the stir-fry immediately over the hot rice.

NOTES: If you can't find red rice, you can substitute cooked brown rice, black rice, quinoa or barley for the cooked red rice.

Tamari is similar to soy sauce but is darker in color and slightly thicker. You may substitute soy sauce for tamari.

PER SERVING: Calories: 406 • Carbohydrates: 46 g • Fiber: 7 g • Protein: 19 g • Total fat: 18 g • Saturated fat: 4 g • Sodium: 555 mg • *Star nutrients:* Vitamin A (86% DV), vitamin C (50% DV), vitamin E (9% DV), folate (19% DV), niacin (35% DV), calcium (17% DV), iron (16% DV)

Shiitake and Kale Spelt Bowl

This crunchy bowl has umami—the fifth taste—written all over it, thanks to the savory flavors of shiitake mushrooms, tofu and soy sauce. And kale—rich in vitamins and more than 45 different flavonoid compounds—is a super green food everyone should eat more of. If you soak and cook the spelt in advance, this masterpiece comes together in mere minutes.

MAKES 4 SERVINGS

125g uncooked spelt
830ml water
1 tablespoon extra virgin olive oil
1 onion, chopped
2 garlic cloves, minced
2 tablespoons reduced-sodium soy sauce
1 tablespoon sesame seeds
½ teaspoon wasabi paste
½ teaspoon red pepper flakes
75g sliced shiitake mushrooms
200g firm tofu, drained and cubed
1 bunch chopped kale

1. Cover the spelt with 660ml water in a pot, soak overnight, and drain.
2. To cook the spelt on the hob, bring the spelt and 750ml of water to a boil, reduce the heat, and simmer until tender, 45 to 60 minutes. If using a rice cooker, put the spelt and water into the cooker and prepare according to the manufacturer's instructions.
3. Heat the olive oil in a large frying pan or wok. Add the onion and garlic and sauté for 3 minutes.
4. Add the soy sauce, sesame seeds, wasabi paste, red pepper flakes, mushrooms and tofu and stir well. Sauté them for an additional 5 minutes.
5. Stir in the remaining 80ml water and the kale and sauté until the kale is slightly wilted and crisp-tender, about 4 minutes.
6. Spoon 100g cooked spelt into each of four individual bowls and top with about 300g of the shiitake-kale mixture.

Variation: Replace the cooked spelt with cooked brown rice, quinoa, bulgur or farro.

PER SERVING: Calories: 264 • Carbohydrates: 40 g • Fiber: 7 g • Protein: 14 g • Total fat: 8 g • Saturated fat: 1 g • Sodium: 306 mg • *Star nutrients:* Vitamin C (12% DV), calcium (45% DV), iron (16% DV), manganese (40% DV), copper (28% DV), selenium (23% DV), zinc (10% DV)

Spicy Tofu and Red Potato Hash with Salsa

I love this zesty potato hash served with corn tortillas for a late Saturday morning breakfast. It's also delicious as a quick, filling skillet dinner with a simple soup or salad, like South of the Border Taco Salad (page 292). The spices and colorful vegetables in the hash are loaded with anti-inflammatory properties that can help protect you from disease.

MAKES 4 SERVINGS

3 medium red-skinned potatoes, unpeeled
1 small red onion, quartered
1 small courgette
½ red bell pepper
150g extra firm tofu drained
2 garlic cloves, minced
½ teaspoon ground cumin
¼ teaspoon ground turmeric
Pinch of cayenne
¾ teaspoon low-sodium herbal seasoning
2 tablespoons chopped fresh chives
250ml prepared salsa

1. Using a food processor or a grater, shred the potatoes, onion, courgette, bell pepper and tofu. Drain in a colander.
2. Spray a large nonstick frying pan with nonstick vegetable spray and heat over medium-low heat. Add the garlic, cumin, turmeric, cayenne, herbal seasoning, and the drained vegetables and tofu and stir well.

3. Cook the hash mixture over medium-low heat for 25 to 30 minutes, turning frequently with a spatula to prevent sticking.

4. When the potatoes are tender, stir in the chives. Remove from the heat and serve with salsa.

NOTES: This recipe is a breeze if you use a food processor. Simply run all the vegetables and tofu through the food processor fitted with the grater attachment, and your ingredients are ready in a couple of minutes.

Use a nonstick frying pan to keep the hash from sticking. You can adjust the "heat" in this recipe by increasing or decreasing the amount of cayenne.

PER SERVING: Calories: 182 • Carbohydrates: 36 g • Fiber: 5 g • Protein: 8 g • Total fat: 2 g • Saturated fat: 0 g • Sodium: 215 mg • *Star nutrients:* Vitamin C (79% DV), vitamin B_6 (36% DV), potassium (30% DV), calcium (9% DV), iron (17% DV), manganese (46% DV), copper (18% DV)

Vegetable, Tofu and Potato Pot Pie

A riff on an old-fashioned chicken pot pie, this savory, thick vegetable tofu stew with whipped potato topping was passed down to me from my mother's kitchen. It is a one-dish comfort meal easily made from kitchen staples you can keep on hand. It's also delicious warmed up in a lunch box the next day.

MAKES 8 SERVINGS

1.3kg (about 8 medium) potatoes, peeled and quartered
1 tablespoon extra virgin olive oil
1 medium onion, chopped
4 medium carrots, chopped
200g celery, chopped
300g frozen peas
225g firm tofu, drained and cubed
1 garlic clove, minced
1 teaspoon poultry seasoning (see Notes)
¼ teaspoon ground turmeric
1½ teaspoons low-sodium herbal seasoning
1 teaspoon dried parsley
500ml reduced-sodium vegetable broth
250ml water
30g plain flour
250ml to 270ml unsweetened plain plant-based milk
¼ teaspoon ground black pepper

1. Put the potatoes into a large pot and add enough water to cover. Bring to a boil, reduce the heat, and cook until the potatoes are tender but not crumbly, 15 to 20 minutes. Drain the potatoes, then return to the pot and set aside.
2. Meanwhile, heat the olive oil in a large heavy pot or sauté pan. Add the onion, carrots and celery and sauté for 5 minutes. Add the peas, tofu, garlic, poultry seasoning, turmeric, 1 teaspoon of the herbal seasoning and the parsley. Cook until the vegetables are crisp-tender, about 10 minutes.

3. Whisk the broth, water and flour in a small bowl until smooth, then add to the vegetable mixture. Cook until the stew is thick and bubbly, about 5 minutes.

4. Preheat the oven to 200°C/gas 6.

5. Add 250ml of the plant-based milk, the black pepper, and the remaining ½ teaspoon herbal seasoning to the pot of potatoes. Mash with a potato masher until potatoes are a creamy consistency that can be spread easily. Add more milk to the potatoes if needed.

6. Transfer the vegetable stew into a large, deep baking dish (about 18 x 28 x 9cm). Spread the mashed potatoes over the stew. Bake, uncovered, for 20 to 25 minutes, until golden. Serve immediately.

NOTES: Poultry seasoning is a vegan spice blend that usually includes thyme, sage, marjoram, rosemary, black pepper and nutmeg.

You can substitute frozen carrots for fresh carrots to make your preparation process easier.

Keep shelf-stable firm tofu on hand so you'll always have tofu readily available.

PER SERVING: Calories: 254 • Carbohydrates: 47 g • Fiber: 7 g • Protein: 10 g • Total fat: 4 g • Saturated fat: 1 g • Sodium: 71 mg • *Star nutrients:* Vitamin A (91% DV), vitamin C (76% DV), thiamin (24% DV), folate (20% DV), calcium (34% DV), iron (22% DV)

Roasted Lemon Asparagus with Red Peppers

Celebrate spring with this understated yet fabulous way to prepare asparagus. The red peppers—rich in vitamin C and heart-healthy carotenoids—set off the jade tones of the asparagus, which contains anti-inflammatory compounds called saponins. Serve this asparagus dish for brunch, on top of a bed of greens as a salad, or as an easy side dish for dinner.

MAKES 4 SERVINGS

300g fresh asparagus (about 24 medium spears), trimmed
½ medium red bell pepper, sliced
¼ medium onion, finely chopped
1 teaspoon lemon-flavored extra virgin olive oil
2 teaspoons lemon juice
1½ teaspoons water
⅛ teaspoon ground black pepper
1 garlic clove, minced

1. Preheat the grill to high.

2. Arrange the asparagus in a shallow 23 x 23cm baking dish. Sprinkle the bell pepper and diced onion over the asparagus.

3. Whisk together the olive oil, lemon juice, water, black pepper and garlic in a small bowl and pour over the asparagus.

4. Place the baking dish on the top rack of the oven. Bake for about 20 minutes, or until the vegetables are slightly browned and crisp-tender.

NOTE: If you can't find lemon-flavored extra virgin olive oil, substitute plain extra virgin olive oil plus ¼ teaspoon lemon zest.

PER SERVING: Calories: 44 • Carbohydrates: 7 g • Fiber: 3 g • Protein: 2 g • Total fat: 1 g • Saturated fat: 0 g • Sodium: 3 mg • *Star nutrients:* Vitamin A (27% DV), vitamin C (67% DV), vitamin E (9% DV), folate (29% DV)

Grilled Vegetable Skewers

If you're in the mood for an outdoor feast, throw these colorful, rosemary-scented vegetable skewers on the barbie. And if outdoor grilling isn't on the agenda, simply place them under the grill (see Note). Serve these veggie skewers with garden burgers for a light summer meal the whole family will relish.

MAKES 4 SERVINGS

1 medium onion, cut into wedges
1 medium yellow or red bell pepper, cut into wedges
1 small courgette or summer squash (about 20cm long), thickly sliced
1 small Japanese aubergine, sliced
100g whole mushrooms
4 large sprigs of fresh rosemary
2 tablespoons extra virgin olive oil
3 tablespoons lemon juice
½ teaspoon low-sodium herbal seasoning
½ teaspoon ground black pepper
1 garlic clove, minced

1. Thread the assorted vegetable pieces (onion, bell pepper, squash, aubergine, and mushrooms) on four metal or wood skewers.
2. Push the stalk of a rosemary sprig into the vegetables in the center of each skewer. Place the skewers in a shallow dish.
3. Whisk together the olive oil, lemon juice, herbal seasoning, black pepper and garlic in a small bowl and brush onto the vegetables. Cover and allow to marinate in the refrigerator for 30 to 60 minutes.
4. Meanwhile, preheat the grill.
5. Place the vegetable skewers on the hot grill. Brush the skewers with the remaining marinade as they cook.
6. Grill until the vegetables are tender-crisp and browned, about 10 minutes on each side.

NOTE: You can cook the skewers and marinade in a shallow 23 x 32.5cm baking dish under a medium grill. Grill for about 15 minutes then turn the skewers over, baste with the marinade in the pan, and cook until the vegetables are browned and tender, about 15 minutes.

PER SKEWER: Calories: 112 • Carbohydrates: 12 g • Fiber: 4 g • Protein: 3 g • Total fat: 7 g • Saturated fat: 1 g • Sodium: 6 mg • *Star nutrients:* Vitamin C (69% DV), riboflavin (9% DV), manganese (8% DV), copper (8% DV)

Farmers Market Greens and Garlic Sauté

You can take any leafy greens—whether you find them in your garden, forage for them in the wild, or pick them up at your farmers market or supermarket—and turn them into a flavorful side dish in minutes. Try this tasty preparation for spinach, collards, kale, chard, spinach, turnip greens, dandelion greens, or bok choy for a real nutritional kick. Turn these sautéed greens into a meal by stirring in tofu or nuts and serving them with whole grains or beans, such as New Orleans Red Beans and Rice (page 320).

MAKES 2 SERVINGS

> 1 tablespoon extra virgin olive oil
> 1 garlic clove, minced
> 1 tablespoon lemon juice
> 1 tablespoon water
> Pinch of ground black pepper
> 1 medium bunch of greens (about 175g), cleaned and trimmed

1. Heat a large saucepan or frying pan over medium heat. Add the olive oil, garlic, lemon juice, water and black pepper and sauté for 1 minute.

2. Add the greens and sauté, stirring often, until the leaves are wilted, 2 to 4 minutes.

Variation: Add 100g of cubed firm tofu with the greens.

PER SERVING: Calories: 83 • Carbohydrates: 5 g • Fiber: 3 g • Protein: 1 g • Total fat: 7 g • Saturated fat: 1 g • Sodium: 34 mg • *Star nutrients:* Vitamin A (91% DV), vitamin C (38% DV), iron (7% DV), calcium (4% DV)

Aubergine Courgette Moussaka

The iconic Greek dish goes vegan in my version, which features layers of aubergine, courgette, potatoes, and eclectic spices. It's a delicious dish to share at a buffet, or paired with my Greek Salad with Rosemary-Lemon Tofu (page 294) and a batch of whole grain bulgur, it can be the star of your evening meal.

MAKES 10 SERVINGS

MOUSSAKA

1 tablespoon extra virgin olive oil
1 large red onion, chopped
3 garlic cloves, minced
1 teaspoon dried oregano
¼ teaspoon ground cinnamon
¼ teaspoon ground allspice
½ teaspoon low-sodium herbal seasoning
¼ teaspoon ground black pepper
Two 400g cans diced tomatoes, ideally salt free, with juice
2 medium potatoes, peeled and thinly sliced
1 medium aubergine, thinly sliced
2 medium courgettes, thinly sliced

SAUCE

1 tablespoon extra virgin olive oil
3 tablespoons flour
¼ teaspoon ground black pepper
Dash of nutmeg
430ml unsweetened plain plant-based milk

2 tablespoons chopped fresh parsley

TO PREPARE THE MOUSSAKA:

1. Heat the olive oil in a large frying pan. Add the onion, garlic, oregano, cinnamon, allspice, herbal seasoning and black pepper and sauté until the onions are tender, about 5 minutes.
2. Add the tomatoes and heat until bubbling.

3. Preheat the oven to 180°C/gas 4.

4. Spray a 23 x 32.5cm baking dish with nonstick cooking spray and arrange the potato slices in a layer at the bottom of the dish. Spread one third of the tomato mixture over the potatoes.

5. Add the sliced courgettes in a layer. Spread another third of the tomato mixture over the courgettes.

6. Add the sliced aubergine in a layer. Spread the remaining tomato mixture over the aubergine.

7. Cover the dish with foil and bake for 1 hour.

8. About 5 minutes before removing moussaka from the oven, make the sauce.

TO PREPARE THE SAUCE:

1. Heat the olive oil in a small saucepan. Whisk in the flour, black pepper and nutmeg and cook, whisking constantly, for 30 seconds. Whisk in the plant-based milk and cook, stirring often, until thick and bubbly, about 3 minutes.

2. After the moussaka has cooked for an hour, remove from the oven and pour the sauce evenly over. Return to the oven and bake, uncovered, for an additional 30 minutes.

3. Remove the dish from the oven, sprinkle with the parsley, and slice into 10 squares.

NOTE: Try a mild, unsweetened, plain plant-based milk such as soy, hemp, or oat to provide a neutral flavor to the sauce.

PER SERVING: Calories: 121 • Carbohydrates: 20 g • Fiber: 4 g • Protein: 4 g • Total fat: 4 g • Saturated fat: 1 g • Sodium: 59 mg • *Star nutrients:* Vitamin C (21% DV), vitamin B_6 (12% DV), manganese (15% DV)

Grilled Portobello Mushroom "Steaks"

The meatiness of giant portobello mushrooms makes them scream for a good grilling. You can even serve them as "burgers" on whole wheat buns with lettuce leaves and tomato slices. Try pairing this recipe with a light, fruity green salad, such as Watermelon Peppercorn Salad (page 288).

MAKES 2 "STEAKS"

2 large (10 x 13cm) portobello mushrooms
2 teaspoons extra virgin olive oil
2 teaspoons balsamic or red wine vinegar
1 teaspoon herbes de Provence
1 garlic clove, minced
¼ teaspoon ground black pepper

1. Wash the mushrooms and drain them. Place them in a shallow dish (23 x 23cm), gills up.
2. Stir together the remaining ingredients in a small bowl and drizzle over the mushrooms. Marinate the mushrooms in the refrigerator for one hour.
3. Remove mushrooms from marinade, reserving the marinade. Place the mushrooms on a hot grill, gill side up, allowing to cook for 5 to 8 minutes, brushing with the marinade. Flip the mushrooms over and cook the other side for 5 to 8 minutes until tender, brushing with the marinade.
4. Remove the mushrooms from the grill and serve them immediately.

PER "STEAK": Calories: 60 • Carbohydrates: 4 g • Fiber: 1 g • Protein: 2 g • Total fat: 5 g • Saturated fat: 1 g • Sodium: 5 mg • *Star nutrients:* Vitamin B$_6$ (7% DV), niacin (28% DV), pantothenic acid (19% DV), riboflavin (36% DV), copper (26% DV)

Roasted Potato Vegetable Terrine

This country terrine is sophisticated enough for a dinner party yet simple enough to complement any meal. Packed with antioxidants, anise-flavored fennel boosts the subtle palate of potatoes and zucchini in this roasted vegetable dish. Serve it with cooked beans or lentils to round out a delicious dinner.

MAKES 8 SERVINGS

> 3 large baking potatoes, peeled and cut into 2.5cm chunks
> 1 medium bulb fennel, trimmed and cut into 2.5cm chunks
> 1 medium onion, thickly sliced
> 2 tablespoons extra virgin olive oil
> 2 garlic cloves, minced
> ½ teaspoon ground black pepper
> ½ teaspoon low-sodium herbal seasoning
> 1 tablespoon fresh rosemary (or 1 teaspoon dried)
> 3 medium courgettes (about 20cm long), thickly sliced
> ½ cup sun-dried tomatoes, chopped

1. Preheat the oven to 400°F.
2. Put the potatoes, fennel, and onion into a 9 x 13-inch baking dish.
3. Drizzle the olive oil over the vegetables, and sprinkle with the garlic, black pepper, herbal seasoning, and rosemary. Toss lightly to coat.
4. Bake, uncovered, for 30 minutes.
5. Remove the baking dish from the oven and add the courgette and sun-dried tomatoes, stirring to evenly coat with the oil and seasonings.
6. Return the dish to the oven and bake, uncovered, for an additional 30 minutes, or until the vegetables are lightly browned and tender.

Variations: To experience subtle differences in color, taste, and texture, try substituting unpeeled Yukon gold potatoes, red potatoes or purple potatoes for the baking potatoes.

PER SERVING: Calories: 120 • Carbohydrates: 20 g • Fiber: 4 g • Protein: 3 g • Total fat: 4 g • Saturated fat: 1 g • Sodium: 93 mg • *Star nutrients:* Vitamin C (43% DV), niacin (10% DV), potassium (24% DV)

Cauliflower and Pea Curry

Who needs take-aways when you can whip up your own healthy curry dish? This easy curry adds a blast of health-protective, anti-inflammatory Indian spices to your diet. And its rich, exotic flavor will tempt you to include it regularly on your menu, along with Saffron Brown Basmati Rice (page 311) and a side of lentils or beans to round out the meal.

MAKES 6 SERVINGS

> 1 tablespoon sesame oil
> 1 teaspoon grated fresh ginger
> 1 garlic clove, minced
> 1 teaspoon tahini (sesame seed paste)
> 1 teaspoon peanut butter
> 1 teaspoon garam masala (see Notes)
> ½ teaspoon ground turmeric
> Dash of cayenne (see Notes)
> 250ml water
> 120ml low-sodium vegetable broth
> 1 small head cauliflower, chopped into small pieces
> 250g canned diced tomatoes, ideally salt-free, with juice
> 175g frozen peas, thawed
> 2 tablespoons chopped fresh coriander
> 60g plus 1 tablespoon unsweetened plain plant-based yogurt

1. Heat the sesame oil with the ginger, garlic, tahini, peanut butter, garam masala, turmeric and cayenne in a medium saucepan over medium heat and cook, stirring constantly, for 2 minutes.
2. Add the water, broth, cauliflower and tomatoes and stir well. Bring to a boil, then reduce the heat, cover and simmer for 10 minutes.
3. Add the peas and coriander and cook until all the vegetables are tender, about 6 minutes.
4. Stir in the yogurt and serve immediately.

NOTES: Garam masala is a traditional Indian spice blend that usually includes cumin, coriander, cardamom, pepper, cinnamon, cloves and nutmeg. It is available at ethnic markets as well as some supermarkets.

You can adjust the heat of this curry by using more or less cayenne.

PER SERVING: Calories: 88 • Carbohydrates: 12 g • Fiber: 4 g • Protein: 4 g • Total fat: 4 g • Saturated fat: 1 g • Sodium: 116 mg • *Star nutrients:* Vitamin B$_6$ (12% DV), vitamin C (78% DV), folate (16% DV), calcium (5% DV)

Sweet Potato Pumpkin Seed Casserole

This sweet potato casserole is one of my favorite additions to a holiday banquet, as well as a good old-fashioned weekday meal. Jam-packed with vitamin A, the sweet potatoes in this dish are accented with spices, citrus, apricots, maple, and the crunch of pumpkin seeds, and they all culminate into a golden, sweet casserole.

MAKES 10 SERVINGS

1.3kg sweet potatoes
1 tablespoon extra virgin olive oil
1 tablespoon maple syrup
3 tablespoons orange juice
½ teaspoon ground cinnamon
½ teaspoon ground ginger
½ teaspoon ground allspice
½ teaspoon orange zest
40g chopped unsweetened dried apricots
40g chopped pumpkin seeds, raw or roasted
3 tablespoons sliced spring onions

1. Preheat the oven to 200ºC/gas 6.
2. Scrub the sweet potatoes, pierce them several times with a fork, and place them in a 23 x 32.5cm baking dish. Bake for 50 to 60 minutes, until the potatoes are tender to the touch.
3. Remove the potatoes from the oven and allow them to cool for 10 minutes.
4. Scoop out the flesh from the sweet potatoes into a mixing bowl, discarding the peels. Gently mash with a potato masher until smooth yet slightly lumpy.
5. Add the olive oil, maple syrup, orange juice, cinnamon, ginger, allspice, orange zest and apricots to the sweet potatoes and stir until well combined.

6. Transfer the sweet potato mixture into a casserole dish or 23 x 32.5cm baking dish and sprinkle with the pumpkin seeds. Bake at 200°C/gas 6 for about 20 minutes until seeds are golden.

7. Remove the dish from the oven and sprinkle with the sliced spring onions. Serve immediately.

Variations: Try substituting pecans, walnuts, hazelnuts or pistachios for the pumpkin seeds.

PER SERVING: Calories: 154 • Carbohydrates: 33 g • Fiber: 5 g • Protein: 3 g • Total fat: 2 g • Saturated fat: 0 g • Sodium: 31 mg • *Star nutrients:* Vitamin A (553% DV), vitamin C (57% DV)

Plant-Powered Granola

I dare you to find a granola in the supermarket with this much unadulterated, wholesome goodness. Make a batch each week and keep it in an airtight canister in your pantry for up to 14 days. You can sprinkle it on fruit, applesauce, hot cereal, plant-based yogurt, or salads for a crunchy nutritional boost. Vary the ingredients to come up with your own favorite blend of fruits, nuts, and seeds.

MAKES 24 SERVINGS

300g old-fashioned oats
1 tablespoon ground flaxseed
1 tablespoon sesame seeds
1 tablespoon shelled hemp seeds
1 tablespoon chia seeds
2 teaspoons sunflower seeds
40g grated unsweetened coconut
25g slivered almonds
60g coarsely chopped walnuts
30g coarsely chopped hazelnuts
75 graisins
30g sliced unsweetened dried apricots
35g dried cranberries
30g unsweetened dried blueberries
30g dried cherries
30g chopped unsweetened dried apples
1 teaspoon ground cinnamon
2 tablespoons canola oil
3 tablespoons peanut butter
2 tablespoons water
1 tablespoon vanilla extract

1. Preheat the oven to 180°C/gas 4.

2. Combine the oats, seeds, coconut, nuts, fruit and cinnamon in a large bowl and stir well.

3. Stir together the oil, peanut butter, water and vanilla in a small pot. Heat over low heat, stirring often, until hot and bubbly.

4. Remove the pot from the heat and pour the hot liquid over the oat mixture. Stir until well combined.

5. Spread the granola in a thin layer on a baking sheet and bake for about 20 minutes, stirring every 5 minutes, until golden brown.

6. Remove the baking sheet from the oven and allow the granola to cool. Transfer to an airtight container.

Variations: Substitute various nuts, such as pecans, pistachios and macadamia nuts; various dried fruits, such as dried pineapple, banana, mango, pears and figs; and various nut butters, such as almond, sunflower seed, walnut, hazelnut or hemp butter.

PER SERVING: Calories: 211 • Carbohydrates: 27 g • Fiber: 5 g • Protein: 7 g • Total fat: 9 g • Saturated fat: 2 g • Sodium: 4 mg • *Star nutrients:* Vitamin E (15% DV), iron (10% DV), manganese (23% DV), copper (10% DV)

Apple Pie Oatmeal Bowl

The whole family will scoot to the breakfast table when this fragrant whole grain cereal is bubbling on the stovetop. And the beta-glucans, a type of soluble fiber found in oats, can lower your cholesterol levels and might even boost your immune function.

MAKES 4 SERVINGS

870ml water
75g uncooked steel-cut oats
1 large apple, peeled and sliced
60g coarsely chopped walnuts
1 tablespoon ground flaxseed
½ teaspoon ground cinnamon
¼ teaspoon ground nutmeg
¼ teaspoon ground allspice
75g dried raisins or currants

1. Bring the water to a boil in a medium saucepan.
2. Stir in all the remaining ingredients, cover, and reduce the heat to a simmer. Cook, stirring occasionally, for 20 minutes.
3. Serve immediately.

NOTES: Make a big batch without the walnuts and store it in an airtight container in the refrigerator. Heat up a single portion for breakfast over the next 3 days; just add the walnuts right before serving to keep them from getting soggy.

When the oatmeal is finished cooking, stir in some plant-based milk for an extra creamy finish.

PER SERVING: Calories: 335 • Carbohydrates: 48 g • Fiber: 7 g • Protein: 10 g • Total fat: 13 g • Saturated fat: 2 g • Sodium: 4 mg • *Star nutrients:* Vitamin B$_6$ (8% DV), calcium (6% DV), iron (16% DV), manganese (30% DV), copper (17% DV)

Exotic Fruit and Rice Hot Cereal

There's a whole world of hot cereals beyond oatmeal out there. Try this wild rice porridge accented with dried tropical fruit, cashews, and Chinese five-spice, an exotic seasoning that suits grains and baked goods as well as savory dishes. When combined with plant-based milk, this cereal is a rich source of fiber, protein, minerals, vitamins, and an array of disease-busting phytochemicals.

MAKES 4 SERVINGS

> *620ml water*
> *150g uncooked brown basmati rice*
> *50g uncooked wild rice*
> *50g cashews*
> *40g chopped unsweetened dried mangos*
> *30g chopped unsweetened dried bananas*
> *½ teaspoon Chinese five-spice seasoning*

1. Bring the water to a boil in a small pot.

2. Stir in all the remaining ingredients, cover, and reduce the heat to a simmer. Cook, stirring occasionally, until the rice is tender, about 45 minutes.

3. Serve immediately.

NOTE: This cereal can be stored in the refrigerator for a few days and reheated for breakfast. Simply omit the cashews from the recipe to prevent them from getting soggy, and add them just before eating.

PER SERVING: Calories: 281 • Carbohydrates: 48 g • Fiber: 4 g • Protein: 7 g • Total fat: 6 g • Saturated fat: 1 g • Sodium: 30 mg • *Star nutrients:* Vitamin A (20% DV), niacin (15% DV), magnesium (25% DV), selenium (13% DV)

Ancient Grain Porridge with Figs and Dates

Starring the lesser known yet powerfully nutritious ancient grains millet, teff, amaranth, and quinoa, this tasty breakfast porridge really sticks to your ribs. Flavored with cardamom, dates, dried figs, and almonds, this hot cereal has an old-world feel, but its whole grain health benefits have been proved by modern science. If you can't find teff, simply increase the amount of other grains.

MAKES 4 SERVINGS

870ml water
50g uncooked teff
50g uncooked millet
50g uncooked amaranth
40g uncooked quinoa
½ teaspoon ground cinnamon
⅛ teaspoon ground cardamom
40g chopped dates
40g chopped dried figs
35g whole almonds

1. Bring the water to a boil in a small pot.
2. Stir in the teff, millet, amaranth, quinoa, cinnamon, cardamom, dates, and figs, cover, and reduce the heat to a simmer. Cook, stirring occasionally, until the grains are tender and the water is absorbed, 15 to 20 minutes.
3. Sprinkle with almonds and serve immediately.

Variation: Make a batch without the almonds and store it in the refrigerator for the next few days. Just heat up a single portion each morning, and add the almonds just before eating.

PER SERVING: Calories: 265 • Carbohydrates: 49 g • Fiber: 6 g • Protein: 8 g • Total fat: 5 g • Saturated fat: 0 g • Sodium: 7 mg • *Star nutrients:* Vitamin E (12% DV), riboflavin (27% DV), calcium (7% DV), iron (15% DV)

Ruby Quinoa Breakfast Bowl

This deep red breakfast bowl—rich in health-protective anthocyanins, as well as protein, fiber, vitamins, and minerals—will fuel you until lunchtime. It's based on an ancient Peruvian staple, quinoa, which comes in a variety of colors, such as red, white, and black. Legend has it that this hearty ancient grain gave stamina to Incan warriors long, long ago. I think you'll find its nutrient lineup does the same for you, too.

MAKES 4 SERVINGS

170g uncooked red quinoa
620ml water
35g dried cranberries
25g dried cherries
50g chopped pecans
1 tablespoon chia seeds
½ teaspoon ground allspice
½ teaspoon ground nutmeg

1. Stir together all the ingredients in a small pot, bring to a boil, reduce the heat to low, cover, and cook, stirring occasionally, until the grain is tender and the liquid is absorbed, about 15 minutes.

2. Serve this cereal with plant-based milk, as desired.

NOTES: Make a whole batch of this cereal ahead of time, store it in the refrigerator, and reheat it in small batches later. Reserve the pecans until just before reheating to avoid softening.

FOR A CREAMY FINISH, TRY STIRRING IN A LITTLE PLANT-BASED MILK AT THE END OF THE COOKING TIME.

PER SERVING: Calories: 330 • Carbohydrates: 47 g • Fiber: 5 g • Protein: 8 g • Total fat: 14 g • Saturated fat: 1 g • Sodium: 12 mg • *Star nutrients:* Pantothenic acid (10% DV), potassium (15% DV), magnesium (31% DV)

Spiced Banana Avocado Bread

You won't believe the "clean" and nutrient-rich ingredient list that makes up this dense, dark quick bread—it's sweetened with bananas and moistened with avocados. Serve it as a snack or as an accompaniment to soup, fruit, or a salad, such as Beet and Pomegranate Seed Salad (page 297).

MAKES 12 SERVINGS

1 medium ripe avocado, quartered
2 medium very ripe bananas
60ml canola oil
1 teaspoon vanilla extract
60ml plant-based milk
2 teaspoons Ener-G Egg Replacer
25g rolled oats
120g whole wheat pastry flour
1 teaspoon baking powder
1 teaspoon baking soda
1 teaspoon ground cinnamon
½ teaspoon ground allspice
½ teaspoon ground nutmeg
1 tablespoon ground flaxseed
25g chopped walnuts

1. Preheat the oven to 180°C/gas 4.

2. Put the peeled avocado and bananas into a medium mixing bowl. Blend with an electric mixer or use a potato masher to make a smooth mixture.

3. Add the canola oil, vanilla, and plant-based milk and blend until smooth.

4. Add the egg replacer, oats, flour, baking powder, baking soda, cinnamon, allspice, nutmeg, flaxseed and walnuts and blend until just smooth; be careful not to overwork the batter.

5. Line a 23 x 13cm loaf tin with foil and pour the batter into the pan. Bake for 1 hour and 20 minutes, until a toothpick inserted into the center comes out clean.

6. Allow to cool slightly then turn out onto a cooling rack. Cool completely. Store in an airtight container in the refrigerator for up to 1 week.

Tip: This recipe produces a very dense, moist bread.

> **PER SERVING:** Calories: 143 • Carbohydrates: 15 g • Fiber: 3 g • Protein: 3 g • Total fat: 9 g • Saturated fat: 1 g • Sodium: 148 mg • *Star nutrients:* Vitamin B$_6$ (11% DV), iron (6% DV), magnesium (9% DV), selenium (11% DV)

Corn Muffins with Apples and Walnuts

Packed with powerful plants, including whole grains, fruits, nuts, and spices, these tender little muffins are so versatile. Serve them with breakfast or alongside soup, salads, or stews such as Three-Bean Cowboy Chili (page 321). Make up a batch and pop them in the freezer so you can enjoy them whenever you like.

MAKES 10 MUFFINS

1 medium apple, peeled and finely diced
370ml unsweetened plain plant-based milk
60ml canola oil
1 teaspoon vanilla extract
1 teaspoon ground cinnamon
120g polenta
120g whole wheat flour
1 tablespoon baking powder
40g chopped dates
50g chopped walnuts

1. Preheat the oven to 220°C/gas 7 and spray a muffin tin with nonstick cooking spray.
2. Stir together the apple, plant-based milk, canola oil and vanilla in a medium mixing bowl.
3. Add the cinnamon, cornmeal, flour, baking powder, dates and walnuts and stir until just combined, being careful not to overwork the batter.
4. Pour the batter into the prepared muffin tin.

5. Place the muffins in the oven and bake 15 to 20 minutes, until golden brown.

NOTE: To store the muffins in the freezer, let them cool completely, then seal them in an airtight container or bag, and freeze. To serve, remove the muffins ahead of time and allow to thaw, or heat them for 30 seconds in the microwave.

PER MUFFIN: Calories: 205 • Carbohydrates: 25 g • Fiber: 4 g • Protein: 5 g • Total fat: 11 g • Saturated fat: 1 g • Sodium: 156 mg • *Star nutrients:* Calcium (12% DV), iron (11% DV), manganese (17% DV)

Buckwheat Hazelnut Waffles with Ginger Peach Sauce

These nutty waffles served with a gingery golden peach sauce are as filling as they are delicious. Plus, you can reap the benefits of buckwheat, which has been shown to lower cholesterol levels. Serve these flavorful waffles for a late weekend breakfast or evening meal or, as a treat, with vanilla soy ice cream or lemon sorbet.

MAKES 8 SERVINGS

40g raisins
170ml water
370ml unsweetened plant-based milk
2 tablespoons maple syrup
2 tablespoons canola oil
1½ teaspoons Ener-G Egg Replacer
60g buckwheat flour
150g whole wheat pastry flour
1 tablespoon baking powder
40g finely chopped hazelnuts
One 410g can sliced yellow peaches in juice
1 tablespoon cornflour
⅛ teaspoon ground ginger

1. Bring the raisins and water to a boil in a small saucepan. Reduce the heat, cover, and simmer for 5 minutes.

2. Meanwhile, put the plant-based milk, maple syrup, canola oil, and egg replacer into a blender or food processor. Add the raisins with their cooking liquid and puree until smooth.

3. In a medium mixing bowl, stir together the buckwheat flour, pastry flour, baking powder, and chopped hazelnuts.

4. Pour the pureed raisin mixture into the flour mixture and stir just until smooth.

5. Heat a waffle iron and spray both sides with nonstick cooking spray. Pour 100ml of the batter into the waffle iron and cook until golden brown. Repeat with the rest of the batter, making sure to spray both sides of the waffle iron with additional nonstick spray before each new waffle.

6. While making the waffles, strain the liquid from the can of peaches into a small saucepan. Heat the juice over medium heat. Whisk in the cornflour and ginger and cook, whisking often, until the sauce is bubbly and thick. Stir in the peaches.

7. Serve the waffles with warm ginger peach sauce.

Variations: Replace the hazelnuts with another variety of nut, such as walnuts, pecans, almonds or pistachios. You can also replace the peaches with canned mandarin oranges, pineapple, or pears in juice, but remember to watch out for syrup-packed canned fruit, which contains a lot of added sugar.

PER SERVING: Calories: 221 • Carbohydrates: 34 g • Fiber: 5 g • Protein: 6 g • Total fat: 8 g • Saturated fat: 1 g • Sodium: 21 mg • *Star nutrients:* Calcium (13% DV), iron (11% DV), magnesium (18% DV), selenium (17% DV)

Pumpkin Pecan Spice Pancakes

Destined to be a fall breakfast favorite, this pancake recipe—fragrant with pumpkin, nutmeg, and pecans—also makes excellent waffles. Who needs to wait for breakfast to enjoy pancakes? You can put them on your dinner menu, too. In Scandinavia, people eat pancakes with split-pea soup for lunch or dinner—never breakfast. Yum!

MAKES 8 PANCAKES

> 250ml unsweetened plant-based milk
> 120ml water
> 5 tablespoons canned pumpkin
> 2 tablespoons canola oil
> 2 tablespoons maple syrup
> 2 teaspoons Ener-G Egg Replacer
> 120g white whole wheat flour
> 1 tablespoon baking powder
> 1 teaspoon ground cinnamon
> ½ teaspoon ground nutmeg
> 25g chopped pecans
> 1 tablespoon ground flaxseed

1. Combine the plant-based milk, water, pumpkin, canola oil, maple syrup and egg replacer in a medium bowl.

2. Add flour, baking powder, cinnamon, nutmeg, pecans, and flaxseed, and stir just until well combined, being careful not to overwork the batter. Let stand for 10 minutes.

3. Heat a griddle pan or frying pan over a low heat and spray with nonstick cooking spray. Ladle a third of the pancake batter onto the griddle and cook until golden on both sides and cooked through, about 4 to 5 minutes on each side.

4. Repeat the process with the rest of the batter to make eight pancakes.

NOTES: These moist pancakes take a little longer to cook than traditional pancakes. To allow them to cook all the way through, set the heat to low and cook for at least 5 minutes on each side.

To make waffles instead, heat a waffle iron and spray with nonstick cooking spray. Pour 100ml of the batter into the waffle iron and cook until golden. Repeat with the rest of the batter, making sure to spray both sides of waffle iron with nonstick spray before each new waffle.

PER PANCAKE: Calories: 132 • Carbohydrates: 18 g • Fiber: 4 g • Protein: 4 g • Total fat: 6 g • Saturated fat: 1 g • Sodium: 160 mg • *Star nutrients:* Vitamin A (42% DV), calcium (12% DV), selenium (17% DV)

Iced Berry Green Tea

In Japan, green tea is the drink de rigueur—it's sipped both hot and cold all day long. Experts believe that it may be an important part of what links the traditional Japanese diet to a long life span. Sit down to this cool, refreshing beverage packed with the dynamic duo of tea catechins and berry polyphenols, both linked with reduction of damaging inflammation and oxidation in the body.

MAKES 2 SERVINGS

> *1 bag of Japanese green tea*
> *250ml boiling water*
> *Ice cubes*
> *75g fresh or frozen assorted berries (such as raspberries,*
>   *blackberries, and blueberries)*

1. Place the tea bag in a small teapot or tea cup and cover with the boiling water. Let steep for 10 to 15 minutes.
2. Fill two 350ml drinking glasses with ice. Pour ½ cup of the tea into each glass.
3. Lightly mash the berries with a spoon in a small bowl. Spoon half of the berries into each glass. Stir gently and serve immediately.

NOTE: Make a double batch of this recipe and store it in a pitcher in the refrigerator to sip all day long.

PER SERVING: Calories: 20 • Carbohydrates: 5 g • Fiber: 1 g • Protein: 0 g • Total fat: 0 g • Saturated fat: 0 g • Sodium: 5 g • *Star nutrients:* Vitamin C (14% DV)

Blueberry Banana Power Smoothie

My kids beg me to make this deep purple, nutritional rush of a smoothie for breakfast or after-school snacks. It's certainly a great start to your day, but—thanks to high-fiber fruits and plant proteins and fats—it's also the perfect power snack when your energy level drops in the afternoon.

MAKES 2 SERVINGS

1 medium very ripe banana
225g frozen blueberries
120ml orange juice
250ml unsweetened plant-based milk
1 tablespoon ground flaxseed

1. Put all the ingredients into a blender and blend until smooth. Serve immediately.

Variation: Substitute frozen peaches, mango, pineapple, or papaya for the berries.

PER SERVING: Calories: 241 • Carbohydrates: 42 g • Fiber: 11 g • Protein: 7 g • Total fat: 5 g • Saturated fat: 1 g • Sodium: 18 mg • *Star nutrients:* Vitamin B_6 (25% DV), vitamin C (43% DV), calcium (6% DV), iron (10% DV), copper (13% DV)

Dark Chocolate Peanut Butter Smoothie

Get your antioxidant fix with this classic American flavor combination. You can whip up this smoothie in seconds for a protein-rich snack.

MAKES 2 SERVINGS

250ml dark chocolate plant-based milk
3 tablespoons peanut butter
1 tablespoon shelled hemp seeds
10 ice cubes

Put all the ingredients into a blender and blend until smooth. Serve immediately.

Variation: Try substituting almond butter to create a unique flavor profile.

PER SERVING: Calories: 246 • Carbohydrates: 18 g • Fiber: 3 g • Protein: 11 g • Total fat: 16 g • Saturated fat: 3 g • Sodium: 54 mg • *Star nutrients:* Calcium (15% DV), manganese (25% DV)

Summer Fruit Skewers with Strawberry Dip

Take advantage of all the glory of fresh summertime fruits by creating these gorgeous skewers. Dipping them into luscious strawberry dip is a fun treat for all ages. Impress everyone at your next outdoor party or picnic with this dessert that's as delicious as it is healthy.

MAKES 8 SERVINGS

DIP

150g sliced fresh strawberries
250g cubed firm tofu, drained
3 tablespoons orange juice
1 teaspoon vanilla extract

SKEWERS

8 large whole fresh strawberries
8 medium chunks fresh pineapple
8 medium chunks watermelon
8 medium chunks honeydew or cantaloupe melon
1 large nectarine, cut into 8 wedges
2 large firm plums, quartered

TO MAKE THE DIP:

1. Put the sliced strawberries, tofu, orange juice, and vanilla into a blender or food processor and process until smooth. Pour into a small serving dish and refrigerate until serving time.

TO ASSEMBLE THE SKEWERS:

1. Thread 1 strawberry, 1 chunk of pineapple, 1 chunk of watermelon, 1 chunk of melon, 1 wedge of nectarine, and 1 wedge of plum onto each skewer and place on a platter.
2. Serve the skewers with the strawberry dip.

Variation: Substitute sliced peaches for the sliced strawberries to make peach dip.

PER SERVING: Calories: 69 • Carbohydrates: 12 g • Fiber: 2 g • Protein: 3 g • Total fat: 2 g • Saturated fat: 0 g • Sodium: 4 mg • *Star nutrients:* Vitamin C (48% DV), folate (6% DV), manganese (28% DV)

Rainbow Fruit Bowl with Orange Sauce

You can enjoy this tangy, vitamin-rich fruity dessert all year long—just call on the power of preserved fruits when fresh fruits aren't in season. Whether you're serving it as a colorful side at a winter potluck or as a simple summertime dessert, this fruit bowl is destined to be popular: Set it out and watch it vanish before your eyes.

MAKES 12 SERVINGS

250g pineapple chunks (or canned pineapple in juice, drained)
150g fresh or frozen blueberries
225g pink grapefruit sections, peeled and chopped (or canned grapefruit in juice, drained and chopped)
150g green or red grapes
150g sliced bananas
150g nectarine or peach slices (or canned peaches in juice, drained)
60g plain unsweetened plant-based yogurt
2 tablespoons orange juice

1. Gently toss together the pineapple, blueberries, grapefruit, grapes, bananas, and nectarine slices in a large salad bowl.
2. Whisk the yogurt and orange juice in a small mixing bowl until smooth.
3. Pour the yogurt dressing over the fruit and toss gently to coat. Serve immediately.

Variation: Substitute seasonal fruit as desired, such as melon, apricots, raspberries, strawberries, persimmon, figs and mango.

PER SERVING: Calories: 52 • Carbohydrates: 13 g • Fiber: 1 g • Protein: 1 g • Total fat: 0 g • Saturated fat: 0 g • Sodium: 3 mg • *Star nutrients:* Vitamin C (24% DV), potassium (5% DV)

Minted Cantaloupe with Blueberries

A straightforward dessert that showcases the luscious flavors and colors of summer, this fruit bowl is also a great accompaniment to sorbet, soy ice cream, or Date, Walnut, and Dark Chocolate Cookies (page 367).

MAKES 8 SERVINGS

600g cantaloupe chunks
150g fresh blueberries
2 tablespoons peach juice (may substitute orange juice)
1 tablespoon slivered almonds
1 tablespoon sliced fresh mint

1. Toss together the cantaloupe, blueberries and peach juice in a medium serving bowl.
2. Sprinkle the almonds and mint over the fruit and serve immediately.

Variation: Substitute other melon varieties that may be available to you in season, such as watermelon or honeydew.

PER SERVING (ABOUT ⅔ CUP): Calories: 46 • Carbohydrates: 10 g • Fiber: 1 g • Protein: 1 g • Total fat: 1 g • Saturated fat: 0 g • Sodium: 9 mg • *Star nutrients:* Vitamin A (52% DV), vitamin C (62% DV)

Banana Peach Yogurt Parfait

Effortless and light, this yummy, nutrient-packed dessert is one that you can really feel good about splurging on. This plant-based parfait can also do double duty as a lovely breakfast or high-powered snack that everyone in your family will enjoy, from the youngest to the oldest.

MAKES 2 SERVINGS

250g vanilla plant-based yogurt
1 medium banana, sliced
*1 small peach, sliced (or 125g canned peaches in juice, drained and
    sliced)*
20g Plant-Powered Granola (page 345)

1. Spoon 60g plant-based yogurt into each of two clear parfait glasses.
2. Divide the banana slices between the glasses to make another layer. Sprinkle 1 tablespoon granola into each glass.
3. Divide the peach slices between the glasses in a layer. Spoon ¼ cup plant-based yogurt into each glass.
4. Sprinkle each parfait with 1 tablespoon granola and serve.

Variation: Substitute colorful berries, mangos, pineapple, or melon for the peach.

PER SERVING: Calories: 246 • Carbohydrates: 44 g • Fiber: 6 g • Protein: 8 g • Total fat: 5 g • Saturated fat: 1 g • Sodium: 9 mg • *Star nutrients:* Vitamin B$_6$ (17% DV), vitamin C (13% DV), calcium (16% DV)

Country Berry Cobbler

Whip up this wholesome old-fashioned cobbler using the bountiful fresh berries available in the summer. You can switch to frozen berries during the winter months in order to enjoy this healthy dessert all year long. Serve warm with a scoop of soy ice cream for a comforting treat.

MAKES 6 SERVINGS

60ml orange juice
½ teaspoon finely grated fresh lemon zest
2 tablespoons maple syrup
1 tablespoon cornflour
600g fresh or frozen mixed berries (such as strawberries, blueberries, raspberries, or blackberries)
90g whole wheat pastry flour
25g finely ground walnuts
½ teaspoon ground cinnamon
1½ teaspoons baking powder
1 tablespoon plus 1 teaspoon walnut oil
60ml unsweetened plant-based milk

1. Preheat the oven to 180°C/gas 4.

2. Whisk together the orange juice, lemon zest, 1 tablespoon of the maple syrup, and the cornflour in a small saucepan. Heat, stirring constantly, until the sauce thickens, 1 to 2 minutes.

3. Stir in the berries and toss to coat with the sauce.

4. Pour the berry mixture into a23 x 23cm baking dish.

5. Combine the flour, walnuts, cinnamon, and baking powder in a small bowl. Stir in the walnut oil, the remaining 1 tablespoon maple syrup and the plant-based milk to make a sticky dough.

6. Drop the dough onto the berry mixture in 6 equal spoonfuls.

7. Bake for about 45 minutes, until the berries are tender and the topping is golden brown. Serve warm.

NOTES: You may replace half of the flour with a nutritious alternative flour, such as quinoa or amaranth, and substitute canola oil for the walnut oil.

PER SERVING: Calories: 184 • Carbohydrates: 31 g • Fiber: 7 g • Protein: 4 g • Total fat: 6 g • Saturated fat: 1 g • Sodium: 94 mg • *Star nutrients:* Vitamin C (40% DV), calcium (13% DV), iron (11% DV), manganese (20% DV)

Ginger Pear Crisp

The exotic aroma of pears and ginger combine in this wonderful fall dessert. Although it may taste decadent, it's anything but, thanks to a simple whole grain oat topping sprinkled over piles of nutrient-rich pears. Serve it with an icy sorbet for a real treat without the calorie damage.

MAKES 8 SERVINGS

5 medium pears, peeled and sliced
1 teaspoon chopped crystallized ginger
1½ teaspoons ground cinnamon
60ml orange juice
3 tablespoons soft dairy-free margarine spread
1 tablespoon brown sugar
50g old-fashioned rolled oats
40g whole wheat pastry flour
2 tablespoons sliced almonds

1. Preheat the oven to 180°C/gas 4.
2. Put the sliced pears into a pie dish.
3. Grind the crystallized ginger with a mortar and pestle or a rolling pin. Sprinkle the ginger and 1 teaspoon of the cinnamon over the pears. Pour the orange juice over the pears and toss gently to coat.
4. Combine the margarine and brown sugar in a small bowl. Stir in the remaining ½ teaspoon cinnamon, rolled oats, pastry flour, and almonds. Mix until it forms a crumbly topping and sprinkle over the pears.
5. Cover with foil and bake for 45 minutes. Remove foil and bake for an additional 15 minutes, until the pears are tender and the top is golden brown. Serve warm.

Variation: Simply substitute apples or peaches for the pears to make apple or peach crisp.

PER SERVING: Calories: 178 • Carbohydrates: 29 g • Fiber: 4 g • Protein: 4 g • Total fat: 6 g • Saturated fat: 1 g • Sodium: 2 mg • *Star nutrients:* Vitamin C (13% DV), magnesium (10% DV), potassium (7% DV)

Apple Cranberry Tart Rustica

This rustic artisanal-style tart is fragrant with spices, apples, walnuts, and cranberries. Serve it with a rich cup of coffee for an afternoon break or sweet treat.

MAKES 6 SERVINGS

90g whole wheat pastry flour
3 tablespoons soft dairy-free margarine spread
3 tablespoons cold water
2 medium apples, peeled and sliced (see Note)
1 tablespoon lemon juice
½ teaspoon vanilla extract
½ teaspoon ground cinnamon
¼ teaspoon ground nutmeg
2 tablespoons dried cranberries
2 tablespoons chopped walnuts

1. Preheat the oven to 200ºC/gas 6.
2. Put the flour into a small bowl. Add the margarine and cut it in with a fork until crumbly.
3. Stir in the cold water to form a soft dough.
4. Lightly flour a board and roll out the dough into a rough circle. Transfer to a pie plate.
5. Toss together the apples, lemon juice, vanilla, cinnamon, nutmeg, cranberries, and walnuts in a small bowl. Pour into the center of the dough circle, leaving a 7.5cm margin uncovered.
6. Pull the edges of the dough inward toward the center to form a rustic, irregularly shaped frame around the filling, with the apples in the center exposed. Lightly press on the folds of dough to keep the dough in place.
7. Cover with foil and bake for 20 minutes. Remove the foil and bake for an additional 20 minutes.
8. Slice into six wedges and serve warm.

NOTE: Try a tart apple variety such as Granny Smith to emphasize the apple flavor.

Variation: Substitute pears, peaches, or pitted cherries for the apples.

PER SERVING: Calories: 151 • Carbohydrates: 20 g • Fiber: 3 g • Protein: 3 g • Total fat: 8 g • Saturated fat: 1 g • Sodium: 46 mg • *Star nutrients:* Magnesium (6% DV), selenium (16% DV)

Date, Walnut and Dark Chocolate Cookies

Within the desert region of Indio, California, you'll find an oasis of date palms that has supplied most of dates the in the United States for the past century. I borrow the rich sweetness of dates to flavor my cookies, along with the flavors of walnuts and dark chocolate. Pack these cookies into a lunch box or picnic basket, or serve them with fresh fruit or sorbet the next time you host dinner guests.

MAKES 20 COOKIES

115g soft dairy-free margarine spread, at room temperature
1 teaspoon vanilla extract
2 tablespoons honey
120g white whole wheat flour
60g plain flour
½ teaspoon baking soda
1½ teaspoons Ener-G Egg Replacer
50g finely chopped walnuts
80g diced dates
50g dark chocolate chips or broken dark chocolate pieces

1. Preheat the oven to 190ºC/gas 5.
2. Mix together margarine, vanilla, and honey in a small bowl.
3. Combine the whole wheat flour, all-purpose flour, baking soda, and egg replacer in a separate bowl.
4. Add the flour mixture to the margarine mixture and mix well to form a crumbly dough.
5. Stir in the walnuts, dates, and chocolate chips.
6. Shape the dough into walnut-sized balls and place about 7.5cm apart on a baking sheet.
7. Bake for 15 minutes, or until golden brown.

NOTE: These cookies store very well in an airtight container in the freezer.

PER COOKIE: Calories: 122 • Carbohydrates: 16 g • Fiber: 2 g • Protein: 2 g • Total fat: 6 g • Saturated fat: 1 g • Sodium: 82 mg • *Star nutrients:* Magnesium (7% DV), manganese (6% DV)

Notes

CHAPTER 1

1. Christian K. Roberts and R. James Barnard, "Effects of Exercise and Diet on Chronic Disease," *Journal of Applied Physiology* 98, no. 1 (2005): 3–30.

2. World Health Organization, *Global Health Risks: Mortality and Burden of Disease Attributed to Selected Major Risks* (Geneva, Switzerland: WHO Press, 2009).

3. U.S. Department of Agriculture and U.S. Department of Health and Human Services, *Dietary Guidelines for Americans, 2010*, 7th ed. (Washington, DC: U.S. Government Printing Office, December 2010).

4. Frank B. Hu, Eric Rimm, Stephanie A. Smith-Warner, Diane Feskanich, Meir J. Stampfer, Albert Ascherio, Laura Sampson, and Walter C. Willett, "Reproducibility and Validity of Dietary Patterns Assessed with a Food-Frequency Questionnaire," *American Journal of Clinical Nutrition* 69, no. 2 (1999): 243–49.

5. Centers for Disease Control and Prevention. "Overweight and Obesity: Health Consequences," last modified March 3, 2011, http://www.cdc.gov/obesity/causes/health.html.

6. Roberts and Barnard, "Effects of Exercise and Diet," 3–30 (see note 1).

7. USDA and HHS, *Dietary Guidelines for Americans, 2010* (see note 3).

8. Ibid.

Institute of Medicine, Food and Nutrition Board, "Strategies to Reduce Sodium Intake in the United States," report (April 20, 2010), http://www.iom.edu/Reports/2010/Strategies-to-Reduce-Sodium-Intake-in-the-United-States.aspx.

9. Dario Giugliano, Antonio Ceriello, and Katherine Esposito, "The Effects of Diet on Inflammation," *Journal of the American College of Cardiology* 48, no. 4 (2006): 677–85.

10. Linda E. Cleveland, Alanna J. Moshfegh, Ann M. Albertson, and Joseph D. Goldman, "Dietary Intake of Whole Grains," (2010), http://www.am-coll-nutr.org/supplements/dietary-intake-of-whole-grains/.

11. Division of Nutrition and Physical Activity, *Research to Practice Series No. 2: Portion Size* (Atlanta: Centers for Disease Control and Prevention, 2006), http://www.cdc.gov/nccdphp/dnpa/nutrition/pdf/portion_size_research.pdf.

12. Carrie R. Daniel, Amanda J. Cross, Corinna Koebnick, and Rashmi Sinha, "Trends in Meat Consumption in the USA," *Public Health Nutrition* 14, no. 4 (2011): 575–83.

13. Andrew W. Speedy, "Global Production and Consumption of Animal Source Foods," *The Journal of Nutrition* 133, no. 11 (November 2003): 4048S–53S.

14. Daniel et al., "Trends in Meat Consumption," 575–83 (see note 12).

15. Renata Micha, Sarah K. Wallace, and Dariush Mozaffarian, "Red and Processed Meat Consumption and Risk of Incident Coronary Heart Disease, Stroke, and Diabetes Mellitus," *Circulation* 121, no. 21 (2010): 2271–83.

16. An Pan, Qi Sun, Adam M. Bernstein, Matthias B. Schulze, JoAnn E. Manson, Walter C. Willett, and Frank B. Hu, "Red Meat Consumption and Risk of Type 2 Diabetes: 3 Cohorts of U.S. Adults and an Updated Meta-Analysis," *American Journal of Clinical Nutrition* (August 10, 2011), http://www.ajcn.org/content/early/2011/08/10/ajcn.111.018978.abstract.

17. Leila Azadbakht and Ahmad Esmaillzadeh, "Red Meat Intake Is Associated with Metabolic Syndrome and the Plasma C-Reactive Protein Concentration in Women," *The Journal of Nutrition* 139, no. 2 (2009): 335–39.
Daniel et al., "Trends in Meat Consumption," 575–83 (see note 12).

18. Azadbakht and Esmaillzadeh, "Red Meat Intake," 335–39 (see note 17).

19. Paula Jakszyn, Antonio Agudo, Raquel Ibanez, Rena Garcia-Closas, Guillem Pera, Pilar Amiano, and Carlos A. Gonzalez, "Development of a Food Database of Nitrosamines, Heterocyclic Amines, and Polycyclic Aromatic Hydrocarbons," *The Journal of Nutrition* 134, no. 8 (2004): 2011–14.
Giuseppina Basta, Ann Marie Schmidt, and Raffaele De Caterina, "Advanced Glycation End Products and Vascular Inflammation: Implications for Accelerated Atherosclerosis in Diabetes," *Cardiovascular Research* 63, no. 4 (2004): 582–92.
Daniel et al., "Trends in Meat Consumption," 575–83 (see note 12).

20. American Cancer Society, "Learn about Cancer: Recombinant Bovine Growth Hormone," last modified February 18, 2011, http://www .cancer.org/cancer/cancercauses/othercarcinogens/athome/recombinant -bovine-growth-hormone.

21. Michael Barza, Sherwood Gorbach, and Stephen J. DeVincent, "The Need to Improve Antimicrobial Use in Agriculture," *Clinical Infectious Diseases* 34, suppl. 3 (2002), S71–S72, http://www.keepantibioticsworking.com/ new/KAWfiles/64_2_36922.pdf.

22. A. J. Cross, M. F. Leitzmann, M. H. Gail, A. R. Hollenbeck, A. Schatzkin, and R. Sinha, "A Prospective Study of Red and Processed Meat Intake in Relation to Cancer Risk," *PLoS Med* 4, no. 12 (2007): e325.

23. American Institute for Cancer Research, "Red and Processed Meats: The Cancer Connection," http://preventcancer.aicr.org/site/PageServer?page name=elements_red_processed_meat.

24. Y. Wang and M. A. Beydoun, "Meat Consumption Is Associated with Obesity and Central Obesity among U.S. Adults," *International Journal of Obesity* 33, no. 6 (2009): 621–28.

25. Rashmi Sinha, Amanda J. Cross, Barry I. Graubard, Michael F. Leitzmann, and Arthur Schatzkin, "Meat Intake and Mortality," *Archives of Internal Medicine* 169, no. 6 (2009): 562–71.

26. Kari Hamershlag, "What You Eat Matters," Environmental Working Group (July 2011), http://www.ewg.org/meateatersguide/a-meat-eaters-guide-to- climate-change-health-what-you-eat-matters.

27. Jonathan A. Foley, Navin Ramankutty, Kate A. Brauman, Emily S. Cassidy, James S. Gerber, Matt Johnston, Nathaniel D. Mueller, et al., "Solutions for a Cultivated Planet," *Nature* 478, no. 7369 (October 20, 2011): 337–42.

28. Environmental Working Group, *"Meat Eater's Guide to Climate Change and Health* At-a-Glance" brochure, last modified 2011, http://www.ewg.org/ meateatersguide/at-a-glance-brochure.

29. Daphne Miller, *The Jungle Effect* (New York: William Morrow, 2008).

30. Oldways Preservation Trust, "Characteristics of the Mediterranean Diet," http://www.oldwayspt.org/traditional-mediterranean-diet.

31. Shaw Watanabe, "Changes in Dietary Habits in Japan—Background of Shokuiku and Its Promotion," Government of Japan Shokuiku Promotion Council, http://www8.cao.go.jp/syokuiku/data/eng_pamph/pdf/pamph3 .pdf.

32. USDA and HHS, *Dietary Guidelines for Americans, 2010* (see note 3).

33. "Position of the American Dietetic Association: Vegetarian Diets," *Journal of the American Dietetic Association* 109, no. 7 (2009): 1266–1282.

34. Gary E. Fraser, "Vegetarian Diets: What Do We Know of Their Effects on Common Chronic Diseases?" *The American Journal of Clinical Nutrition* 89, no. 5 (2009): 1607S–12S.

35. C. Bamia, D. Trichopoulos, P. Ferrari, K. Overvad, L. Bjerregaard, A. Tjønneland, J. Halkjaer, "Dietary Patterns and Survival of Older Europeans: The EPIC-Elderly Study (European Prospective Investigation into Cancer and Nutrition)," *Public Health Nutrition* 10, no. 6 (2007): 590-98.

36. E. A. Spencer, P. N. Appleby, G. K. Davey, and T. J. Key, "Diet and Body Mass Index in 38,000 EPIC-Oxford Meat-Eaters, Fish-Eaters, Vegetarians and Vegans," *International Journal of Obesity* 27, no. 6 (2003): 728–34.

37. Serena Tonstad, Terry Butler, Ru Yan, and Gary E. Fraser, "Type of Vegetarian Diet, Body Weight, and Prevalence of Type 2 Diabetes," *Diabetes Care* 32, no. 5 (2009): 791–96.

38. T. Y. Szeto, T. C. Kwok, and I. F. Benzie, "Effects of a Long-Term Vegetarian Diet on Biomarkers of Antioxidant Status and Cardiovascular Disease Risk," *Nutrition* 20, no. 10 (2004): 863–66.

39. B. Burton-Freeman, A. Linares, D. Hyson, and T. Kappagoda, "Strawberry Modulates LDL Oxidation and Postprandial Lipemia in Response to High-Fat Meal in Overweight Hyperlipidemic Men and Women," *Journal of the American College of Nutrition* 29, no. 1 (2010): 46–54.

40. Fraser, "Vegetarian Diets," 1607S–12S (see note 34).

41. T. J. Key, G. E. Fraser, M. Thorogood, P. N. Appleby, V. Beral, G. Reeves, M. L. Burr, et al., "Mortality in Vegetarians and Nonvegetarians: Detailed Findings from a Collaborative Analysis of Five Prospective Studies," *American Journal of Clinical Nutrition* 70, no. 3 (199): 516S–24S.

42. Pan et al., "Red Meat Consumption and Risk of Type 2 Diabetes" (see note 16).

43. T. J. Key, P. N. Appleby, E. A. Spencer, R. C. Travis, N. E. Allen, M. Thorogood, and J. I. Mann, "Cancer Incidence in British Vegetarians," *British Journal of Cancer* 101, no. 1 (2009): 192–97.

44. American Institute for Cancer Research, "Recommendations for Cancer Prevention," http://preventcancer.aicr.org/site/PageServer?pagename= recommendations_04_plant_based.

45. T. T. Fung, F. B. Hu, S. E. Hankinson, W. C. Willett, and M. D. Holmes, "Low-Carbohydrate Diets, Dietary Approaches to Stop Hypertension-Style

Diets, and the Risk of Postmenopausal Breast Cancer," *American Journal of Epidemiology* 174, no. 6 (2011): 652–60.

46. Nikolaos Scarmeas, Yaakov Stern, Richard Mayeux, Jennifer J. Manly, Nicole Schupf, and Jose A. Luchsinger, "Mediterranean Diet and Mild Cognitive Impairment," *Archives of Neurology* 66, no. 2 (2009): 216–25.

47. Francesca L. Crowe, Paul N. Appleby, Naomi E. Allen, and Timothy J. Key, "Diet and Risk of Diverticular Disease in Oxford Cohort of European Prospective Investigation into Cancer and Nutrition (EPIC): Prospective Study of British Vegetarians and Non-Vegetarians," *BMJ* 343, no. 7817 (2011), http://www.bmj.com/content/343/bmj.d4131.full.

48. N. S. Rizzo, J. Sabate, K. Jaceldo-Siegl, and G. E. Fraser, "Vegetarian Dietary Patterns Are Associated with a Lower Risk of Metabolic Syndrome: The Adventist Health Study 2," *Diabetes Care* 34, no. 5 (2011), 1225–27.

49. L. Baroni, L. Cenci, M. Tettamanti, and M. Berati, "Evaluating the Environmental Impact of Various Dietary Patterns Combined with Different Food Production Systems." *European Journal of Clinical Nutrition* 61, no. 2 (2006): 279–286, http://www.personal.umich.edu/~choucc/environmental_impact_of_various_dietary_patterns.pdf.

CHAPTER 3

1. B. Farmer, B. T. Larson, V. L. Fulgoni, A. J. Rainville, and G. U. Liepa, "A Vegetarian Dietary Pattern as a Nutrient-Dense Approach to Weight Management: An Analysis of the National Health and Nutrition Examination Survey 1999–2004," *Journal of the American Dietetic Association* 111, no. 6 (2011): 819–27.

2. Institute of Medicine, *Dietary Reference Intakes: Macronutrients*, http://www.iom.edu/Global/News%20Announcements/~/media/C5CD2DD7840544979A549EC47E56A02B.ashx.

3. D. E. Sellmeyer, K. L. Stone, A. Sebastian, S. R. Cummings, "A High Ratio of Dietary Animal to Vegetable Protein Increases the Rate of Bone Loss and the Risk of Fracture in Postmenopausal Women," *The American Journal of Clinical Nutrition* 73, no. 1 (2001): 118–22.

E. L. Knight, M. J. Stampfer, S. E. Hankinson, D. Spiegelman, and G. C. Curhan, "The Impact of Protein Intake on Renal Function Decline in Women with Normal Renal Function or Mild Insufficiency," *Annals Internal Medicine* 138, no. 6 (2003): 460–67.

4. USDA and HHS, *Dietary Guidelines for Americans, 2010* (see Chapter 1, note 3).

5. Institute of Medicine, *Dietary Reference Intakes: Macronutrients* (see note 2).

6. Nutrition information based on national restaurant chain Web sites.

7. F. N. Mbagwu, V. U. Okafor, and J. Ekeanyanwu, "Phytochemical Screening on Four Edible Legumes (*Vigna subterranean, Glycine max, Arachis hypogea*, and *Vigna uniguiculata*) Found in Eastern Nigeria," *African Journal of Plant Science* 5, no. 6 (2011): 370–72.

8. P. B. Geil and J. W. Anderson, "Nutrition and Health Implications of Dry Beans: A Review," *Journal of the American College of Nutrition* 13, no. 6 (1994): 549–58.

9. M. Messina, "Insights Gained from 20 Years of Soy Research," *Journal of Nutrition* 140, no. 12 (2010): 2289S–95S.

10. American Institute of Cancer, "Foods That Fight Cancer: Soy," http://www.aicr.org/foods-that-fight-cancer/foodsthatfightcancer_soy.html.

    C. L. Rock, C. Doyle, W. Demark-Wahnefried, J. Meyerhardt, K. S. Courneya, A. L. Schwartz, E. V. Bandera, et. al., "Nutrition and physical activity guidelines for cancer survivors." *A Cancer Journal for Clinicians* (2012): Apr 26. http://www.ncbi.nlm.nih.gov/pubmed/22539238.

11. GMO Compass, "Soyabean," http://www.gmo-compass.org/eng/database/plants/67.soybean.html.

12. Bradley W. Bolling, Diane L. McKay, and Jeffrey B. Blumberg, "Review: The Phytochemical Composition and Antioxidant Actions of Tree Nuts," *Asia Pacific Journal of Clinical Nutrition* 19, no. 1 (2010): 117–23.

13. M. A. Martínez-González and M. Bes-Rastrollo, "Nut Consumption, Weight Gain and Obesity: Epidemiological Evidence," *Nutrition, Metabolism and Cardiovascular Diseases* 21, suppl. 1 (2011): S40-S45.

14. Hamershlag, "What You Eat Matters" (see Chapter 1, note 26).

15. Yuval Itan, Adam Powell, Mark A. Beaumont, Joachim Burger, and Mark G. Thomas, "The Origins of Lactase Persistence in Europe," *PLoS Computational Biology* 5, no. 8 (2009): e1000491.

16. Harvard Health Publications and Harvard School of Public Health, "Questions and Answers about the Healthy Eating Plate," http://www.health.harvard.edu/plate/questions-and-answers-about-the-healthy-eating-plate.

17. National Institute of Health, Office of Dietary Supplements, "Vitamin B12," http://ods.od.nih.gov/factsheets/vitaminb12.

    Institute of Medicine, *Dietary Reference Intakes for Calcium and Vitamin D, 2010.* http://www.iom.edu/Reports/2010/Dietary-Reference-Intakes-for-Calcium-and-Vitamin-D.aspx.

18. Loma Linda University, *The Vegetarian Food Pyramid*, http://www
.vegetariannutrition.org/food-pyramid.pdf.

U.S. Department of Health and Human Services, *Your Guide to Lowering
Your Blood Pressure with Dash* (2006). http://www.nhlbi.nih.gov/health/
public/heart/hbp/dash/new_dash.pdf.

U.S. Department of Health and Human Services, "MyPlate," http://www
.choosemyplate.gov.

CHAPTER 4

1. Satya S. Jonnalagadda, Lisa Harnack, Rui Hai Liu, Nicola McKeown, Chris
Seal, Simin Liu, and George C. Fahey, "Putting the Whole Grain Puzzle
Together: Health Benefits Associated with Whole Grains—Summary of
American Society for Nutrition 2010 Satellite Symposium," *The Journal
of Nutrition* 141, no. 5 (2011): 1011S–22S.

S. M. Virtanen, M. Kaila, J. Pekkanen, M. G. Kenward, U. Uusitalo, P.
Pietinen, C. Kronberg-Kippilä, et al., "Early Introduction of Oats Associated with Decreased Risk of Persistent Asthma and Early Introduction of
Fish with Decreased Risk of Allergic Rhinitis," *British Journal of Nutrition*
103, no. 2 (2010): 266–73.

A. T. Merchant, W. Pitiphat, M. Franz, and K. J. Joshipura, "Whole-Grain
and Fiber Intakes and Periodontitis Risk in Men," *American Journal of
Clinical Nutrition* 83, no. 6 (2006): 1395–400.

2. Jonnalagadda et al., "Putting the Whole Grain Puzzle Together," 1011S–22S
(see note 1, first source).

3. Rui Hai Liu, "Health Benefits of Fruit and Vegetables Are from Additive
and Synergistic Combinations of Phytochemicals," *American Journal of
Clinical Nutrition* 78, no. 3 (2003): 517S–20S.

4. E. A. Oelke, D. H. Putnam, T. M. Teynor, and E. S. Oplinger, "Quinoa,"
Alternative Field Crops Manual, last modified March 22, 2012, http://www
.hort.purdue.edu/newcrop/afcm/quinoa.html.

5. Lee S. Gross, Li Li, Earl S. Ford, and Simin Liu, "Increased Consumption of
Refined Carbohydrates and the Epidemic of Type 2 Diabetes in the United
States: An Ecologic Assessment," *The American Journal of Clinical Nutri-
tion* 79, no. 5 (2004): 774–79.

6. Ibid.

7. Brian Wansink, James E. Painter, and Jill North, "Bottomless Bowls: Why

Visual Cues of Portion Size May Influence Intake," *Obesity Research* 13, no. 1 (2005): 93–100.

8. B. Cholerton, L. D. Baker, and S. Craft, "Insulin Resistance and Pathological Brain Ageing," *Diabetic Medicine* 28, no. 12 (2011): 1463–75.

American Institute for Cancer Research, "The Diabetes-Cancer Connection," *AICR ScienceNow* 25 (Summer 2008), 1–2.

9. Kenneth W. Heaton, Samuel N. Marcus, Pauline M. Emmett, and Colin H. Bolton, "Particle Size of Wheat, Maize, and Oat Test Meals: Effects on Plasma Glucose and Insulin Responses and on the Rate of Starch Digestion in Vitro," *American Journal of Clinical Nutrition* 47, no. 4 (1988): 675–82.

10. J. Slavin and H. Green, "Dietary Fibre and Satiety," *British Nutrition Foundation Nutrition Bulletin* 32, suppl. 1 (2007): 32–42.

11. S. A. Bingham, N. E. Day, R. Luben, P. Ferrari, N. Slimani, T. Norat, F. Clavel-Chapelon, et al., "Dietary Fibre in Food and Protection against Colorectal Cancer in the European Prospective Investigation into Cancer and Nutrition (EPIC): An Observational Study," *Lancet* 361, no. 9368 (2003): 1496–1501.

12. USDA and HHS, Dietary *Guidelines for Americans, 2010* (see Chapter 1, note 3).

13. D. E. Thomas and E. J. Elliott, "The Use of Low-Glycaemic Index Diets in Diabetes Control," *British Journal of Nutrition* 104, no. 6 (2010): 797–802.

Amin Esfahani, Julia M. W. Wong, Arash Mirrahimi, Korbua Srichaikul, David J. A. Jenkins, and Cyril W. C. Kendall, "The Glycemic Index: Physiological Significance," *Journal of the American College of Nutrition* 28, no. 4 (2009): 439S–45S.

CHAPTER 5

1. National Center for Chronic Disease Prevention and Health Promotion, Division of Nutrition, Physical Activity, and Obesity, "Low-Energy-Dense Foods and Weight Management: Cutting Calories While Controlling Hunger," *Research to Practice Series, No. 5,* http://www.cdc.gov/nccdphp/dnpa/nutrition/pdf/r2p_energy_density.pdf.

2. C. L. Rock, S. W. Flatt, F. A. Wright, S. Faerber, V. Newman, S. Kealey, J. P. Pierce, "Responsiveness of Carotenoids to a High Vegetable Diet Intervention Designed to Prevent Breast Cancer Recurrence," *Cancer Epidemiology Biomarkers Prevention* 6, no. 8 (1997): 617–23.

Jennifer H. Cohen, Alan R. Kristal, and Janet L. Stanford, "Fruit and Vegetable Intakes and Prostate Cancer Risk," *Journal of the National Cancer Institute* 92, no. 1 (2000): 61–68.

3. Luc Dauchet, Philippe Amouyel, Serge Hercberg, and Jean Dallongeville, "Fruit and Vegetable Consumption and Risk of Coronary Heart Disease: A Meta-Analysis of Cohort Studies," *Journal of Nutrition* 136, no. 10 (2006): 2588–93.

4. Patrice Carter, Laura J. Gray, Jacqui Troughton, Kamlesh Khunti, and Melanie J. Davies, "Fruit and Vegetable Intake and Incidence of Type 2 Diabetes Mellitus: Systematic Review and Meta-Analysis, *BMJ* 341, no. 7772 (2010).

5. M. Cristina Polidori, Domenico Praticó, Francesca Mangialasche, Elena Mariani, Olivier Aust, Timur Anlasik, Ni Mang, et al., "High Fruit and Vegetable Intake Is Positively Correlated with Antioxidant Status and Cognitive Performance in Healthy Subjects," *Journal of Alzheimer's Disease* 17, no. 4 (2009): 921–27.

6. A. M. Moeller, N. Parekh, L. Tinker, C. Ritenbaugh, B. Blodi, R. B. Wallace, J. A. Mares, and CAREDS Research Study Group, "Associations between Intermediate Age-Related Macular Degeneration and Lutein and Zeaxanthin in the Carotenoids in Age-Related Eye Disease Study (CAREDS): Ancillary Study of the Women's Health Initiative," *Archives of Ophthalmology* 124, no. 8 (2006): 1151–62.

7. C. J. Prynne, G. D. Mishra, M. A. O'Connell, G. Muniz, M. A. Laskey, L. Yan, A. Prentice, and F. Ginry, "Fruit and Vegetable Intakes and Bone Mineral Status: A Cross Sectional Study in Five Age and Sex Cohorts," *American Journal of Clinical Nutrition* 83, no. 6 (2006): 1420–28.

8. I. Romieu and C. Trenga, "Diet and Obstructive Lung Diseases," *Epidemiologic Reviews* 23, no. 2 (2001): 268–87.

9. S. Goya Wannamethee, Gordon D. O. Lowe, Ann Rumley, K. Richard Bruckdorfer, and Peter H. Whincup, "Associations of Vitamin C Status, Fruit and Vegetable Intakes, and Markers of Inflammation and Hemostasis," *American Journal of Clinical of Nutrition* 83, no. 3 (2006): 567–74.

10. A. Esmaillzadeh, M. Kimiagar, Y. Mehrabi, L. Azadbakht, F. B. Hu, and W. C. Willett, "Fruit and Vegetable Intakes, C-Reactive Protein, and the Metabolic Syndrome," *American Journal of Clinical Nutrition* 84, no. 6 (2006): 1489–97.

11. Sanhong Yu, Veronika Weaver, Keith Martin, and Margherita T. Cantorna, "The Effects of Whole Mushrooms during Inflammation," *BMC Immunology* 10, no. 12 (February 2009): 1–13.

12. B. B. Freeman and K. Reimers, "Tomato Consumption and Health: Emerging Benefits," *American Journal of Lifestyle Medicine* 5, no. 2 (2010): 182–91.

13. Benedetta Bendinelli, Giovanna Masala, Calogero Saieva, Simonetta Salvini, Carmela Calonico, Carlotta Sacerdote, Claudia Agnoli, et al., "Fruit, Vegetables, and Olive Oil and Risk of Coronary Heart Disease in Italian Women: The EPICOR Study," *American Journal of Clinical Nutrition* 93, no. 2 (2011): 275–83.

Moeller et al., "Associations," 1151 (see note 6).

R. Edenharder, G. Keller, K. L. Platt, and K. K. Unger, "Isolation and Characterization of Structurally Novel Antimutagenic Flavonoids from Spinach (*Spinacia oleracea*)," *Journal of Agricultural and Food Chemistry* 49, no. 6 (2001): 2767–73.

H. Fujii, T. Noda, T. Sairenchi, and T. Muto, "Daily Intake of Green and Yellow Vegetables Is Effective for Maintaining Bone Mass in Young Women," *Tohoku Journal Experimental Medicine* 218, no. 12 (2009): 149–54.

Y. Wang, C. F. Chang, J. Chou, H. L. Chen, X. Deng, B. K. Harvey, J. L. Cadet, and P. C. Bickford, "Dietary Supplementation with Blueberries, Spinach, or Spirulina Reduces Ischemic Brain Damage," *Experimental Neurology* 193, no. 1 (2005): 75–84.

14. American Institute for Cancer Research, "AICR's Foods That Fight Cancer: Broccoli and Cruciferous Vegetables," http://www.aicr.org/foods-that-fight-cancer/broccoli-cruciferous.html#research.

15. N. Sithranga Boopathy and K. Kathiresan, "Anticancer Drugs from Marine Flora: An Overview," *Journal of Oncology* 9 (2010): 803–18.

16. Hunger and Environmental Nutrition Dietetic Practice Group, *Organic Food Production Talking Points* (May 2006), last modified April 2007, http://www.hendpg.org/docs/Resources%20-%20public/HEN_Organic_Talking_Points_April_2007.pdf.

17. Centers for Disease Control and Prevention, "State-Specific Trends in Fruit and Vegetable Consumption Among Adults—United States, 2000–2009," *Morbidity and Mortality Weekly Report* 59, no. 35 (2010): 1125–30.

CHAPTER 6

1. U.S. National Library of Medicine, "Vitamin C," MedlinePlus, last modified August 30, 2011, http://www.nlm.nih.gov/medlineplus/ency/article/002404.htm.

2. U.S. Department of Health and Human Services, *Health Facts: Sodium and Potassium*, http://www.csrees.usda.gov/nea/food/pdfs/hhs_facts_sodium.pdf.

3. F. M. Sacks, L. P. Svetkey, W. M. Vollmer, et al., "Effects on blood pressure of reduced dietary sodium and the Dietary Approaches to Stop Hypertension (DASH) diet," *New England Journal of Medicine* 344, no. 1 (2001): 3–10.

4. F. J. He, C. A. Nowson, M. Lucas, and G. A. MacGregor, "Increased Consumption of Fruit and Vegetables Is Related to a Reduced Risk of Coronary Heart Disease: Meta-Analysis of Cohort Studies," *Journal of Human Hypertension* 21, no. 9 (2007): 717–28.

5. Susanne Rautiainen, Susanna Larsson, Jarmo Virtamo, and Alicja Wolk, "Total Antioxidant Capacity of Diet and Risk of Stroke: A Population-Based Prospective Cohort of Women," *Stroke* 43, no. 2 (2012): 335–40.

6. World Cancer Research Fund, American Institute for Cancer Research, *Food, Nutrition, Physical Activity, and the Prevention of Cancer: A Global Perspective* (Washington DC: AICR, 2007).

7. E. Cho, J. M. Seddon, B. Rosner, W. C. Willett, and S. E. Hankinson, "Prospective Study of Intake of Fruits, Vegetables, Vitamins, and Carotenoids and Risk of Age-Related Maculopathy," *Archives of Ophthalmology* 122, no. 6 (2004): 883–92.

8. Lydia A. Bazzano, "Dietary Intake of Fruit and Vegetables and Risk of Diabetes Mellitus and Cardiovascular Disease," Joint FAO/WHO Workshop on Fruits and Vegetables for Health, September 2004, Kobe, Japan, http://whqlibdoc.who.int/publications/2005/9241592850_eng.pdf.

9. I. Tetens and S. Alini, "The Role of Fruit Consumption in the Prevention of Obesity," in "ISAFRUIT" special issue, *Journal of Horticultural Science and Biotechnology* (2009): 47–51.

10. Q. Dai, A. R. Borenstein, Y. Wu, J. C. Jackson, and E. B. Larson, "Fruit and Vegetable Juices and Alzheimer's Disease: The Kame Project," *American Journal of Medicine* 119, no. 9 (2006): 751–59.

11. W. H. Aldoori, E. L. Giovannucci, H. R. Rockett, L. Sampson, E. B. Rimm, and W. C. Willett, "A Prospective Study of Dietary Fiber Types and Symptomatic Diverticular Disease in Men," *Journal of Nutrition* 128, no. 4 (1998): 714–19.

12. M. A. Van Duyn and E. Pivonka, "Overview of the Health Benefits of Fruit and Vegetable Consumption for the Dieteics Professional: Selected Literature," *The Journal of American Dietetics Association* 100, no. 12 (2000): 1511–21.

13. A. C. Barbosa, M. D. Pinto, D. Sarkar, C. Ankolekar, D. Greene, and K. Shetty, "Varietal Influences on Antihyperglycemia Properties of Freshly Harvested Apples Using In Vitro Assay Models," *Journal of Medicinal Food* 13, no. 6 (2010): 1313–23.

14. O. Aprikian, V. Duclos, S. Guyot, C. Besson, C. Manach, A. Bernalier, C. Morand, C. Remesy, and C. Demigne, "Apple Pectin and a Polyphenol-Rich Apple Concentrate Are More Effective Together Than Separately on Cecal Fermentations and Plasma Lipids in Rats," *Journal of Nutrition* 133, no. 6 (2003): 1860–65.

15. Julie E. Flood-Obbagy and Barbara J. Rolls, "The Effect of Fruit in Different Forms on Energy Intake and Satiety at a Meal," *Appetite* 52, no. 2 (2009): 416–22.

16. Paul Knekt, Jorma Kumpulainen, Ritva Järvinen, Harri Rissanen, Markku Heliövaara, Antti Reunanen, Timo Hakulinen, and Arpo Aromaa, "Flavonoid Intake and Risk of Chronic Diseases," *American Journal of Clinical Nutrition* 76, no. 3 (2002): 560–68.

17. Francilene Gracieli, Kunradi Vieira, Graciele da Silva Campelo Borges, Cristiane Copetti, Luciano Valdemiro Gonzaga, Eduardo da Costa Nunes, and Roseane Fett, "Activity and Contents of Polyphenolic Antioxidants in the Whole Fruit, Flesh and Peel of Three Apple Cultivars," *Archivos Latino Americanos de Nutrition* 59, no. 1 (2009): 101–6.

18. Burton-Freeman et al.,"Strawberry Modulates LDL Oxidation," 46–54 (see Chapter 1, note 39).

19. R. G. Jepson and J. Craig, "Cranberries for Preventing Urinary Tract Infections," *Cochrane Database of Systematic Reviews* 1 (2008): CD001321.

20. Society for Neuroscience, "Diet of Walnuts, Blueberries Improve Cognition; May Help Maintain Brain Function," *ScienceDaily*, November 6, 2007, http://www.sciencedaily.com/releases/2007/11/071106122843.htm.

21. Katrine Baghurst, *The Health Benefits of Citrus Fruits* (Sydney, Australia: Horticultural Australia Ltd, 2003).

22. Flood-Obbagy and Rolls, "The Effect of Fruit," 416–22 (see note 15).

23. Christine Gartner, Wilhelm Stahl, and Helmut Sies, "Lycopene Is More Bioavailable from Tomato Paste Than from Fresh Tomatoes," *American Journal of Clinical Nutrition* 66, no. 1 (1997): 116–22.

24. USDA and HHS, *Dietary Guidelines for Americans, 2010* (see Chapter 1, note 3).

25. Rachel K. Johnson, Lawrence J. Appel, Michael Brands, Barbara V. Howard, Michael Lefevre, Robert H. Lustig, Frank Sacks, Lyn M. Steffen, and Judith Wylie-Rosett, "Dietary Sugars Intake and Cardiovascular Health. A Scientific Statement from the American Heart Association," *Circulation* 120, no. 11 (2009): 1011–20.

26. F. Bellisle and A. Drewnowski, "Intense Sweeteners, Energy Intake and the Control of Body Weight," *European Journal of Clinical Nutrition* 61, no. 6 (2007): 691–700.

27. Noori S. Al-Waili, Khelod Salom, Glenn Butler, and Ahmad A. Al Ghamdi, "Honey and Microbial Infections: A Review Supporting the Use of Honey for Microbial Control," *Journal of Medicinal Food* 14, no. 10 (2011): 1079–96.

28. University of Rhode Island, "54 Beneficial Compounds Discovered in Pure Maple Syrup," *ScienceDaily*, March 30, 2011, http://www.sciencedaily.com/releases/2011/03/110330131316.htm.

CHAPTER 7

1. USDA and HHS, *Dietary Guidelines for Americans, 2010* (see Chapter 1, note 3).

    Dietary Guidelines Advisory Committee. U.S. Department of Agriculture. "Report of the Dietary Guidelines Advisory Committee on the *Dietary Guidelines for Americans, 2010*," June 15, 2010, last modified March 14, 2012, http://www.cnpp.usda.gov/dgas2010-dgacreport.htm.

2. USDA and HHS, *Dietary Guidelines for Americans, 2010* (see Chapter 1, note 3).
    DGAC, "Report of the DGAC" (see note 1, second source).

3. USDA and HHS, *Dietary Guidelines for Americans, 2010* (see Chapter 1, note 3).
    DGAC, "Report of the DGAC" (see note 1, second source).

4. USDA and HHS, *Dietary Guidelines for Americans, 2010* (see Chapter 1, note 3).
    DGAC, "Report of the DGAC" (see note 1, second source).
    Penny M. Kris-Etherton, William S. Harris, and Lawrence J. Appel, "Fish Consumption, Fish Oil, Omega-3 Fatty Acids, and Cardiovascular Disease," *Circulation* 106, no. 21 (2002): 2747–57.

5. Alice H. Lichtenstein, Lawrence J. Appel, Michael Brands, Mercedes Carnethon, Stephen Daniels, Harold A. Franch, Barry Franklin, et al., "Diet and Lifestyle Recommendations Revision 2006, A Scientific Statement from the American Heart Association Nutrition Committee," *Circulation* 114, no. 1 (2006): 82–96.
    USDA and HHS, *Dietary Guidelines for Americans, 2010* (see Chapter 1, note 3).
    DGAC, "Report of the DGAC" (see note 1, second source).

6. National Cancer Institute, "Sources of Saturated Fat, Stearic Acid, and Cholesterol Raising Fat among the US Population, 2005–06," Risk Factor Monitoring Methods Branch Web site. http://riskfactor.cancer.gov/diet/foodsources/sat_fat.

7. USDA and HHS, *Dietary Guidelines for Americans, 2010* (see Chapter 1, note 3).
   DGAC, "Report of the DGAC" (see note 1, second source).

8. Q. Lu, Y. Zhang, Y. Wang, D. Wang, R. P. Lee, K. Gao, R. Byrns, and D. Heber, "California Hass Avocado: Profiling of Carotenoids, Tocopherol, Fatty Acid, and Fat Content during Maturation and from Different Growing Areas," *Journal of Agricultural and Food Chemistry* 57, no. 21 (2009): 10408–13.

9. Gary K. Beauchamp, Russell S. J. Keast, Diane Morel, Jianming Lin, Jana Pika, Qiang Han, Chi-Ho Lee, Amos B. Smith, and Paul A. S. Breslin, "Phytochemistry: Ibuprofen-like Activity in Extra-Virgin Olive Oil," *Nature* 437, no. 7055 (2005): 45–46.

10. Jeanette M. Fielding, Kevin G. Rowley, Pauline Cooper, and Kerin O'Dea, "Increases in Plasma Lycopene Concentration after Consumption of Tomatoes Cooked with Olive Oil," *Asia Pacific Journal of Clinical Nutrition* 14, no. 2 (2005): 131–36.

11. J. Van Rooyen, A. J. Esterhuyse, A. M. Engelbrecht, and E. F. du Toit, "Health Benefits of a Natural Carotenoid Rich Oil: A Proposed Mechanism of Protection against Ischaemia/Reperfusion Injury," *Asia Pacific Journal of Clinical Nutrition* 17, suppl. 1 (2008): 316–19.

12. Ellie Brown and Michael F. Jacobson, *Cruel Oil* (Washington, DC: Center for Science in the Public Interest, 2005), http://www.cspinet.org/palm/PalmOilReport.pdf.

CHAPTER 8

1. E. Langner, S. Greifenberg, and J. Gruenwald, "Ginger: History and Use," *Advanced Therapy* 15, no. 1 (1998): 25–44.

2. Al Mofleh, "Spices, Herbal Xenobiotics and the Stomach: Friends or Foes?" *World Journal of Gastroenterology* 16, no. 22 (2010): 2710–19.

3. B. Shan, Y. Z. Cai, M. Sun, and H. Corke, "Antioxidant Capacity of 26 Spice Extracts and Characterization of Their Phenolic Constituents," *Journal of Agricultural and Food Chemistry* 53, no. 20 (2005): 7749–59.

4. Monica H. Carlsen, Bente L. Halvorsen, Kari Holte, Siv K. Bøhn, Steinar

Dragland, Laura Sampson, Carol Willey, et al., "The Total Antioxidant Content of More Than 3,100 Foods, Beverages, Spices, Herbs, and Supplements Used Worldwide," *Nutrition Journal* 9, no. 3 (2010): 1–11.

5. P. Ninfali, G. Mea, S. Giorgini, M. Rocchi, and M. Bacchiocca, "Antioxidant Capacity of Vegetables, Spices, and Dressings Relevant to Nutrition, *British Journal of Nutrition* 93, no. 2 (2005): 257–66.

6. "UCLA-VA Study Names India Dietary Staple as Potential Alzheimer's Weapon," *EurekAlert!* December 28, 2004, http://www.eurekalert.org/pub_releases/2004-12/potn-usn122804.php.

7. Madhuri Kakarala, Dean E. Brenner, Hasan Khorkaya, Connie Cheng, Karim Tazi, Christophe Ginestier, Suling Liu, Gabriela Dontu, and Max S. Wicha, "Targeting Breast Stem Cells with the Cancer Preventive Compounds Curcumin and Piperine," *Breast Cancer Research and Treatment* 122, no. 3 (2010): 777–85.

8. Richard D. Mattes, "Spices and Energy Balance," *Physiology and Behavior* (2011), http://www.sciencedirect.com/science/article/pii/S0031938411005166.

9. B. Gout, C. Bourges, S. Paineau-Dubreuil, "Satiereal, a *Crocus sativus L.* Extract, Reduces Snacking and Increases Satiety in a Randomized Placebo-Controlled Study of Mildly Overweight, Healthy Women," *Nutrition Research* 30, no. 5 (2010): 305–13.

10. Tsz Ying A. Lee, Zhaoping Li, Alona Zerlin, and David Heber, "Effects of Dihydrocapsiate on Adaptive and Diet-Induced Thermogenesis with a High Protein Very Low Calorie Diet: A Randomized Control Trial," *Nutrition and Metabolism* 7, no. 78 (2010): 1–6.

11. Keith Singletary, "Turmeric: An Overview of Potential Health Benefits," *Nutrition Today* 45, no. 5 (2010): 216–25.

12. Fusheng Yang, Giselle P. Lim, Aynun N. Begum, Oliver J. Ubeda, Mychica R. Simmons, Surendra S. Ambegaokar, Pingping P. Chen, et al.,"Curcumin Inhibits Formation of Amyloid β Oligomers and Fibrils, Binds Plaques, and Reduces Amyloid *in Vivo*," *Journal of Biological Chemistry* 280, no. 7 (2005): 5892–5901.

13. G. Aviello, L. Abenavoli, F. Borrelli, R. Capasso, A. A. Izzo, F. Lembo, B. Romano, and F. Capasso, "Garlic: Empiricism or Science?" *Natural Product Communications* 4, no. 12 (2009): 1785–96.

14. Keith Singletary, "Red Pepper: Overview of Potential Health Benefits," *Nutrition Today* 46, no. 1 (2011): 33–47.

15. Keith Singletary, "Black Pepper: Overview of Health Benefits," *Nutrition Today* 45, no. 1 (2010): 33–47.

16. A. Q. Pham, H. Kourlas, and D. Q. Pham, "Cinnamon Supplementation in Patients with Type 2 Diabetes Mellitus," *Pharmacotherapy* 27, no. 4 (2007): 595–99.

17. Wei Zheng and Shiow Y. Wang, "Antioxidant Activity and Phenolic Compounds in Selected Herbs," *Journal of Agricultural and Food Chemistry* 49, no. 11 (2001): 5165–70.

18. C. C. Arcila-Lozano, G. Loarca-Pina, S. Lecona-Uribe, E. Gonzalez de Mejia, "Oregano: Properties, Composition and Biological Activity," *Archivos Latinoamericanos de Nutricion* 54, no. 1 (2004): 100–11.

19. Y. Shukla and M. Singh, "Cancer Preventive Properties of Ginger: A Brief Review," *Food and Chemical Toxicology* 45, no. 5 (2007): 683–90.

20. Langner et al., "Ginger," 25–44 (see note 1).

21. D. Dhingra and A. Sharma, "Antidepressant-like Activity of n-Hexane Extract of Nutmeg (*Myristica fragrans*) Seeds in Mice," *Journal of Medicinal Food Plants* 9, no. 1 (2006): 84–89.

22. M. A. Kelm, M. G. Nair, G. M. Strasburg, D. L. DeWitt, "Antioxidant and Cyclooxygenase Inhibitory Phenolic Compounds from *Ocimum sanctum Linn*," *Phytomedicine* 7, no. 1 (2000): 7–13.

    S. Moreno, T. Scheyer, C. S. Romano, and A. A. Vojnov, "Antioxidant and Antimicrobial Activities of Rosemary Extracts Linked to their Polyphenol Composition," *Free Radical Research* 40, no. 2 (2006): 223–31.

23. M. J. Kim, E. S. Nam, and S. I. Paik, "The Effects of Aromatherapy on Pain, Depression, and Life Satisfaction of Arthritis Patients," *Taehan Kanho Hakhoe Chi* 35, no. 1 (2005): 186–94.

24. S. M. Sharafi, I. Rasooli, P. Owlia, M. Taghizadeh, and S. D. Astaneh, "Protective Effects of Bioactive Phytochemicals from *Mentha piperita* with Multiple Health Potentials," *Pharmacology Magazine* 6, no. 23 (2010): 147–53.

    D. L. McKay and J. B. Blumberg, "A Review of the Bioactivity and Potential Health Benefits of Peppermint Tea," *Phytotherapy Research* 20, no. 8 (2006): 619–33.

25. S. Amrani, H. Harnafi, H. Bouanani Nel, M. Aziz, H. S. Caid, S. Manfredini, E. Besco, M. Napolitano, and E. Bravo, "Hypolipidaemic Activity of Aqueous *Ocimum basilicum* Extract in Acute Hyperlipidaemia Induced by Triton WR-1339 in Rats and Its Antioxidant Property," *Phytotherapy Research* 20, no. 12 (2006): 1040–45.

A. Hussain, K. Brahmbhatt, A. Priyani, M. Ahmed, T. A. Rizvi, and C. Sharma, "Eugenol Enhances the Chemotherapeutic Potential of Gemcitabine and Induces Anticarcinogenic and Anti-Inflammatory Activity in Human Cervical Cancer Cells," *Cancer Biotherapy and Radiopharmaceuticals* 26, no. 5 (2011): 519–27.

26. N. T. J. Tildesley, D. O. Kennedy, E. K. Perry, C. G. Ballard, S. Savelev, K. A. Wesnes, and A. B. Scholey, "*Salvia lavandulaefolia* (Spanish Sage) Enhances Memory in Healthy Young Volunteers," *Pharmacology Biochemistry & Behavior* 75, no. 3 (2003): 669–67.

27. M. Friedman, P. R. Henika, and R. E. Mandrell, "Bactericidal Activities of Plant Essential Oils and Some of Their Isolated Constituents against *Campylobacter jejuni, Escherichia coli, Listeria monocytogenes*, and *Salmonella enteric*," *Journal of Food Protection* 65, no. 10 (2002): 1545–60.

H. Carrasco A., L. Espinoza C., V. Cardile, C. Gallardo, W. Cardona, L. Lombardo, K. Catalán M., M. Cuellar F., and A. Russo, "Eugenol and Its Synthetic Analogues Inhibit Cell Growth of Human Cancer Cells," *Journal of the Brazilian Chemical Society* 19, no. 3 (2008).

28. B. N. Shyamala, M. M. Naidu, G. Sulochanamma, and P. Srinivas, "Studies on the Antioxidant Activities of Natural Vanilla Extract and Its Constituent Compounds through In Vitro Models," *Journal of Agricultural and Food Chemistry* 55, no. 19 (2007): 7738–43.

29. USDA and HHS, *Dietary Guidelines for Americans, 2010* (see Chapter 1, note 3).

30. Elizabeth Mostofsky, Emily B. Levitan, Alicja Wolk, and Murray A. Mittleman, "Chocolate Intake and Incidence of Heart Failure: A Population-Based Prospective Study of Middle-Aged and Elderly Women," *Circulation: Heart Failure* 3, no. 5 (2010): 612–16.

CHAPTER 9

1. J. Reedy and S. M. Krebs-Smith, "Dietary Sources of Energy, Solid Fats, and Added Sugars among Children and Adolescents in the United States," *Journal of the American Dietetic Association* 110, no. 10 (2010): 1477–84.

2. California Center for Public Health Advocacy, "Sugar-Sweetened Beverages: Extra Sugar, Extra Calories, and Extra Weight" (November 2009), http://www.publichealthadvocacy.org/PDFs/Soda_Fact_Sheet.pdf.

J. A. Nettleton, P. L. Lutsey, Y. Wang, J. A. Lima, E. D. Michos, and D. R. Jacobs, Jr., "Diet Soda Intake and Risk of Incident Metabolic Syndrome and Type 2 Diabetes in the Multi-Ethnic Study of Atherosclerosis (MESA)," *Diabetes Care* 32, no. 4 (2009): 688–94.

3. Natural Resources Defense Council, "Bottled Water," last modified April 25, 2008, http://www.nrdc.org/water/drinking/qbw.asp.

4. Sandra Bastin and Kim Henken, *Water Content of Fruits and Vegetables* (Lexington: University of Kentucky Cooperative Extension Service, December 1997), http://www.ca.uky.edu/enri/pubs/enri129.pdf.

5. Institute of Medicine, Food and Nutrition Board, *Dietary Reference Intakes: Water, Potassium, Sodium, Chloride, and Sulfate* (February 11, 2004), http://www.iom.edu/Reports/2004/Dietary-Reference-Intakes-Water-Potassium-Sodium-Chloride-and-Sulfate.aspx.

6. Kwang-Geun Lee and Takayuki Shibamoto, "Analysis of Volatile Components Isolated from Hawaiian Green Coffee Beans (*Coffea arabica L.*)," *Flavour and Fragrance Journal* 17, no. 5 (2002): 349–51.

7. Claudine Manach, Augustin Scalbert, Christine Morand, Christian Rémésy, and Liliana Jiménez, "Polyphenols: Food Sources and Bioavailability," *American Journal of Clinical Nutrition* 79, no. 5 (2004): 727–47.

8. Brian Keisler and Thomas Armsey, II, "Caffeine As an Ergogenic Aid," *Current Sports Medicine Reports* 5, no. 4 (2006): 215–19.

   T. A. Astorino and D. W. Roberson, "Efficacy of Acute Caffeine Ingestion for Short-Term High-Intensity Exercise Performance: A Systematic Review." *Journal of Strength and Conditioning Research* 24, no. 1 (2010): 257–65.

9. J. L. Góngora-Alfaro, "Caffeine as a Preventive Drug for Parkinson's Disease: Epidemiologic Evidence and Experimental Support." *Revista de Neurologia* 50, no. 4 (2010): 221–29.

10. M. Lucas, F. Mirzaei, A. Pan, O. I. Okereke, W. C. Willett, E. J. O'Reilly, K. Koenen, and A. Ascherio, "Coffee, Caffeine, and Risk of Depression among Women," *Archives of Internal Medicine* 171, no. 17 (2011): 1571.

11. Rachel Huxley, Crystal Man Ying Lee, Federica Barzi, Leif Timmermeister, Sebastien Czernichow, Vlado Perkovic, Diederick E. Grobbee, David Batty, and Mark Woodward, "Coffee, Decaffeinated Coffee, and Tea Consumption in Relation to Incident Type 2 Diabetes Mellitus: A Systematic Review with Meta-analysis," *Archives of Internal Medicine* 169, no. 2 (2009): 2053–63.

12. Gail Susana Masterton and Peter Hayes, "Coffee and the Liver: A Potential Treatment for Liver Disease?" *European Journal of Gastroenterology and Hepatology* 22, no. 11 (2010): 1277–83.

F. Bravi, C. Bosetti, A. Tavani, V. Bagnardi, S. Gallus, E. Negri, S. Franceschi, C. La Vecchia, "Coffee Drinking and Hepatocellular Carcinoma Risk: A Meta-Analysis," *Hepatology* 46, no. 2 (2007): 430–35.

13. Xiaofeng Yu, Zhijun Bao, Jian Zou, and Jie Dong, "Coffee Consumption and Risk of Cancers: A Meta-Analysis of Cohort Studies," *BMC Cancer* 11, no. 96 (2011): 1–11.

14. C. Lakenbrink, S. Lapczynski, B. Maiwald, and U. H. Engelhardt, "Flavonoids and Other Polyphenols in Consumer Brews of Tea and Other Caffeinated Beverages," *Journal of Agricultural and Food Chemistry* 48, no. 7 (2000): 2848–52.

    J. M. Hodgson and K. D. Croft, "Tea Flavonoids and Cardiovascular Health," *Molecular Aspects of Medicine* 31, no. 6 (2010): 495–502.

15. U.S. Department of Agriculture Agricultural Research Service, "Herbal Teas May Provide Health Benefits," *ScienceDaily*, March 1, 2011, http://www .sciencedaily.com/releases/2011/03/110301122055.htm.

16. Shinichi Kuriyama, Taichi Shimazu, Kaori Ohmori, Nobutaka Kikuchi, Naoki Nakaya, Yoshikazu Nishino, Yoshitaka Tsubono, and Ichiro Tsuji, "Green Tea Consumption and Mortality Due to Cardiovascular Disease, Cancer, and All Causes in Japan: The Ohsaki Study," *Journal of the American Medical Association* 296, no. 10 (2006): 1255–65.

17. U. Peters, C. Poole, and L. Arab, "Does Tea Affect Cardiovascular Disease? A Meta-Analysis," *American Journal of Epidemiology*, 154, no. 6 (2001): 495–503.

18. S. J. Duffy, J. F. Keaney, Jr., M. Holbrook, N. Gokce, P. L. Swerdloff, B. Frei, and J. A. Vita, "Short- and Long-Term Black Tea Consumption Reverses Endothelial Dysfunction in Patients with Coronary Artery Disease," *Circulation* 104, no. 2 (2001): 151–56.

    D. J. Maron, G. P. Lu, N. S. Cai, Z. G. Wu, Y. H. Li, H. Chen, J. Q. Zhu, X. J. Jin, B. C. Wouters, and J. Zhao, "Cholesterol-Lowering Effect of a Theaflavin-Enriched Green Tea Extract: A Randomized Controlled Trial," *Archives of Internal Medicine* 163, no. 12 (2003): 1448–53.

19. J. D. Lambert and C. S. Yang, "Mechanisms of Cancer Prevention by Tea Constituents," *Journal of Nutrition* 133, no. 10 (2003): 3262S–67S.

20. M. Monobe, A. Ogino, K. Ema, Y. Tokuda, and M. Maeda-Yamamoto, "A Crude Extract from Immature Green Tea (*Camellia sinesis*) Leaves Promotes Toll-like Receptor 7-Mediated Interferon-A Production In Human Macrophage-like Cells," *Cytotechnology* 64, no. 2 (2012): 145–48.

21. H. Yu, T. Oho, L. Xu, "Effects of Several Tea Components on Acid Resistance of Human Tooth Enamel," *American Journal of Dentistry* 23, no. 2 (1995): 101–5.

22. W. Rumpler, J. Seale, B. Clevidence, J. Judd, E. Wiley, S. Yamamoto, T. Komatsu, T. Sawaki, Y. Ishikura, and K. Hosoda, "Oolong Tea Increases Metabolic Rate and Fat Oxidation in Men," *Journal of Nutrition* 131, no. 11 (2001): 2848–52.

    P. Chantre and D. Lairon, "Recent Findings of Green Tea Extract AR25 (Exolise) and Its Activity for the Treatment of Obesity," *Phytomedicine* 9, no. 1 (2002): 3–8.

23. V. M. Hegarty, H. M. May, and K. T. Khaw, "Tea Drinking and Bone Mineral Density in Older Women," *American Journal of Clinical Nutrition* 71, no. 14 (2000): 1003–7.

24. Linus Pauling Institute, Micronutrient Research Center for Optimal Health, "Tea," http://lpi.oregonstate.edu/infocenter/phytochemicals/tea.

25. J. B. German and R. L. Walzem, "The Health Benefits of Wine," *Annual Review of Nutrition* 20 (2000): 561–93.

    W. Yu, Y. C. Fu, and W. Wang, "Cellular and Molecular Effects of Resveratrol in Health and Disease," *Journal of Cellular Biochemistry* 113, no. 3 (2012): 752–9.

26. Paul E. Szmitko and Subodh Verma, "Red Wine and Your Heart," *Circulation* 111, no. 2 (2005): e10–e11.

27. German and Walzem, "Health Benefits of Wine," 561–93 (see note 25, first source).

28. Northwestern University, "Red Wine's Health Benefits May Be Due in Part to 'Estrogen' in Grape Skin," *ScienceDaily*, December 19, 1997, http://www.sciencedaily.com/releases/1997/12/971219062019.htm.

    Joseph A. Baur and David A. Sinclair, "Therapeutic Potential of Resveratrol: The In Vivo Evidence," *Nature Reviews Drug Discovery* 5, no. 6 (2006): 493–506.

29. I. J. Goldberg, L. Mosca, M. R. Piano, and E. A. Fisher, "AHA Science Advisory: Wine and Your Heart: A Science Advisory for Healthcare Professionals from the Nutrition Committee, Council on Epidemiology and Prevention, and Council on Cardiovascular Nursing of the American Heart Association," *Circulation* 103, no. 3 (2001): 472–75.

    Y. Lin, S. Kikuchi, A. Tamakoshi, K. Wakai, T. Kawamura, H. Iso, I. Ogimoto, K. Yagyu, Y. Obata Y, and T. Ishibashi, "Alcohol Consumption and

Mortality among Middle-Aged and Elderly Japanese Men and Women." *Annals of Epidemiology* 15, no. 8 (2005): 590–97.

30. Centers for Disease Control and Prevention, "Alcohol Use and Health" fact sheet, last modified October 28, 2011, http://www.cdc.gov/alcohol/fact-sheets/alcohol-use.htm.

31. L. Baglietto, D. R. English, D. M. Gertig, J. L. Hopper, and G. G. Giles, "Does Dietary Folate Intake Modify Effect of Alcohol Consumption on Breast Cancer Risk? Prospective Cohort Study," *BMJ* 331, no. 7520 (2005): 807.

32. CDC, "Alcohol Use and Health" (see note 30).
    USDA National Nutrient Database for Standard Reference, http://ndb.nal.usda.gov.

33. Institute of Medicine, Food and Nutrition Board, "Dietary Reference Intakes: Water, Potassium, Sodium, Chloride, and Sulfate." February 11, 2004. http://www.iom.edu/Reports/2004/Dietary-Reference-Intakes-Water-Potassium-Sodium-Chlorideand-Sulfate.aspx.

CHAPTER 10

1. Mengmeng Du, Jennifer Prescott, Peter Kraft, Jiali Han, Edward Giovannucci, Susan E. Hankinson, and Immaculata De Vivo, "Physical Activity, Sedentary Behavior, and Leukocyte Telomere Length in Women," *American Journal of Epidemiology* 175, no. 5 (2012): 414–22.

2. American Heart Association, "The Price of Inactivity," last modified January 19, 2011, http://www.heart.org/HEARTORG/GettingHealthy/PhysicalActivity/StartWalking/The-Price-of-Inactivity_UCM_307974_Article.jsp#.TwUTjjWXQ2w.

3. Weight Control Information Network, "Overweight and Obesity Statistics," last modified February 2010, http://win.niddk.nih.gov/statistics.

4. Centers for Disease Control and Prevention, "Physical Activity and Health," last modified February 16, 2011, http://www.cdc.gov/physicalactivity/everyone/health/index.html.
    American Heart Association, "Physical Activity Improves Quality of Life," last modified January 26, 2011, http://www.heart.org/HEARTORG/GettingHealthy/PhysicalActivity/StartWalking/Physical-activity-improves-quality-of-life_UCM_307977_Article.jsp#.TwUT1jWXQ2w.

5. C. Friedenreich, "Observational and Experimental Evidence for the Role of Physical Activity in Cancer Risk," presented at 2011 AICR Research

Conference on Food, Nutrition, Physical Activity and Cancer, Washington, DC, November 2011, http://www.aicr.org/assets/docs/pdf/research/rescon2011/Friedenrich-2011-Approved.pdf.

6. AHA, "Physical Activity" (see note 3, second source).

7. National Institutes of Health Osteoporosis and Related Bone Diseases National Resource Center, "Exercise for Your Bone Health" (January 2009), http://www.niams.nih.gov/Health_Info/Bone/Bone_Health/Exercise/default.asp.

8. AHA, "Physical Activity" (see note 3, second source).

9. American Diabetes Association, "Top 10 Benefits of Being Active," http://www.diabetes.org/food-and-fitness/fitness/fitness-management/top-10-benefits-of-being.html.

10. Nikolaos Scarmeas, Jose A. Luchsinger, Nicole Schupf, Adam M. Brickman, Stephanie Cosentino, Ming X. Tang, and Yaakov Stern, "Physical Activity, Diet, and Risk of Alzheimer Disease," *Journal of the American Medical Association* 302, no. 6 (2009): 627–37.

11. Active Living Research, *Active Education: Physical Education, Physical Activity and Academic Performance* (San Diego: San Diego State University, 2007), http://www.activelivingresearch.org/files/Active_Ed.pdf.

12. Frank B. Hu, Walter C. Willett, Tricia Li, Meir J. Stampfer, Graham A. Colditz, and JoAnn E. Manson, "Adiposity as Compared with Physical Activity in Predicting Mortality Among Women," *New England Journal of Medicine* 351, no. 26 (2004): 2694–2703.

13. Patti Neighmond, "Impact of Childhood Obesity Goes beyond Health," *Morning Edition*, NPR, July 28, 2010.

14. G. N. Healy, C. E. Matthews, D. W. Dunstan, E. A. Winkler, and N. Owen, "Sedentary Time and Cardio-Metabolic Biomarkers in U.S. Adults: NHANES 2003–06," *European Heart Journal* 32, no. 5 (2011): 590–97.

15. U.S. Department of Health and Human Services, *2008 Physical Activity Guidelines for Americans*, http://www.health.gov/PAGuidelines/guidelines/default.aspx#toc.

American Heart Association, "Physical Activity Guidelines," last modified January 19, 2011, http://www.heart.org/HEARTORG/GettingHealthy/PhysicalActivity/StartWalking/American-Heart-Association-Guidelines_UCM_307976_Article.jsp#.T0Kia4cgc2w.

16. Rebecca A. Seguin, Jacqueline N. Epping, David Buchner, Rina Block, and Miriam E. Nelson, *Growing Stronger: Strength Training for Older Adults*

(Boston: Tufts University, 2002), http://www.cdc.gov/physicalactivity/ downloads/growing_stronger.pdf.

17. Center for Disease Control and Prevention, "Physical Activity for Everyone," last modified December 1, 2011, http://www.cdc.gov/physicalactivity/everyone/guidelines/adults.html#Musclestrengthening.

CHAPTER 11

1. M. Schmidt, S. G. Affenito, R. Striegel-Moore, P. R. Khoury, B. Barton, P. Crawford, S. Kronsberg, G. Schreiber, E. Obarzanek, and S. Daniels, "Fast-Food Intake and Diet Quality in Black and White Girls: The National Heart, Lung, and Blood Institute Growth and Health Study," *Archives of Pediatrics and Adolescent Medicine* 159, no. 7 (2005): 626–31.

   Sahasporn Paeratakul, Daphne Ferdinand, Catherine Champagne, Donna Ryan, and George Bray, "Fast-Food Consumption among U.S. Adults and Children: Dietary and Nutrient Intake Profile," *Journal of the American Dental Association* 103, no. 10 (2003): 1332–38.

2. Claim Jumper Restaurants, "Nutritional Information," http://www.claimjumper.com/menu_nutritional_information.aspx.

3. Nutrition information from various restaurant Web sites.

4. USDA National Nutrient Database for Standard Reference, http://ndb.nal.usda.gov.

5. Nutrition information from various restaurant Web sites.

6. USDA National Nutrient Database for Standard Reference, http://ndb.nal.usda.gov.

7. National Restaurant Association, *Chef's Survey: What's Hot in 2011*, http://www.restaurant.org/pdfs/research/whats_hot_2011.pdf.

CHAPTER 12

1. Brian Wansink, *Mindless Eating* (New York: Bantam, 2006).

2. U.S. Food and Drug Administration, "How to Understand and Use the Nutrition Facts Label," last modified November 2004, http://www.fda.gov/Food/ResourcesForYou/Consumers/NFLPM/ucm274593.htm.

3. V. A. Milsom, K. M. Middleton, and M. G. Perri, "Successful Long-Term Weight Loss Maintenance in a Rural Population," *Journal of Clinical Interventions in Aging* 6 (2011): 303–9.

Appendix

Nutrients in Action

NUTRIENTS	DAILY VALUE (DV)	FUNCTIONS
Biotin	300 mcg	Essential in the metabolism of fats, carbohydrates, and protein; plays a role in cell and DNA function
Calcium	1,000 mg*	Major structural element in bones and teeth with an important role in blood-clotting, blood vessel, and muscle functions
Chloride	3,400 mg	Maintains fluid volume outside of cells [endTB]
Chromium	120 mcg	Helps maintain normal blood glucose levels
Copper	2 mg	Functions as an antioxidant and plays a role in energy production, tissue formation, central nervous system activity, and melanin pigments in the skin, hair, and eyes
Folate	400 mcg	Required for the metabolism of DNA and amino acids
Iodine	150 mcg	Component of thyroid hormones
Iron	18 mg	Component of hemoglobin, which transports oxygen to body; functions as an antioxidant and plays a role in energy metabolism
Magnesium	400 mg	Necessary for energy production, DNA synthesis, bone structure, and cell functions

NUTRIENTS	DAILY VALUE (DV)	FUNCTIONS
Manganese	2 mg	Serves as an antioxidant and is involved in metabolism, bone development, and wound healing
Molybdenum	75 mcg	Play a role in production of proteins and enzymes needed for human health
Niacin	20 mg	Serves as an antioxidant and plays an important role in cell growth, DNA repair, and metabolism of foods into energy,
Pantothenic acid	10 mg	Necessary for conversion of food into energy; plays a role in cell and DNA function
Phosphorus	1,000 mg	Critical to the structure of bones and cells; energy production and storage; and DNA, hemoglobin, and hormone function.
Potassium	3,500 mg	Maintains fluid volume inside/outside of cells, prevents rise in blood pressure due to excess sodium intake, and decreases markers of bone turnover and recurrence of kidney stones
Riboflavin	1.7 mg	A component of enyzymes that serves as an antioxidant and is required for metabolism of foods
Selenium	70 mcg	Defends against oxidative stress, regulates thyroid hormone action, and functions in protein metabolism
Sodium	2,400 mg†	Regulates fluid in cell membranes and plays a role in nutrient transport, blood volume, and blood pressure
Thiamin	1.5 mg	The component of enzymes required for metabolism of foods into energy
Vitamin A	5,000 IU (international units)	Required for vision, gene expression, reproduction, embryonic development, and immune function
Vitamin B$_6$	2 mg	Plays important role in metabolism of foods into energy, nervous system function, red blood cell formation, and hormone function

NUTRIENTS	DAILY VALUE (DV)	FUNCTIONS
Vitamin B$_{12}$	6 mcg	An amino acid with an important role in DNA production and the synthesis of hemoglobin
Vitamin C	60 mg (milligrams)	Acts as an antioxidant, plays an important role in brain function, and is needed to create collagen, a structural component of blood vessels, tendons, ligaments, and bone
Vitamin D	400 IU‡	Plays an important role in calcium balance, bone development, cell growth, immunity, and blood pressure regulation
Vitamin E	30 IU	Important antioxidant with immune and anti-inflammatory functions
Vitamin K	80 mcg (micrograms)	Involved in blood clotting, cell growth, and bone metabolism
Zinc	15 mg	Important for metabolic chemical reactions and plays a role in structure and regulation of body cells

Sources: Information from *Dietary Reference Intakes for Calcium, Phosphorous, Magnesium, Vitamin D, and Fluoride* (1997); *Dietary Reference Intakes for Thiamin, Riboflavin, Niacin, Vitamin B$_6$, Folate, Vitamin B$_{12}$, Pantothenic Acid, Biotin, and Choline* (1998); *Dietary Reference Intakes for Vitamin C, Vitamin E, Selenium, and Carotenoids* (2000); *Dietary Reference Intakes for Vitamin A, Vitamin K, Arsenic, Boron, Chromium, Copper, Iodine, Iron, Manganese, Molybdenum, Nickel, Silicon, Vanadium, and Zinc* (2001); and *Dietary Reference Intakes for Water, Potassium, Sodium, Chloride, and Sulfate* (2004). These reports may be accessed via nap.edu.

Additional information from U.S. Food and Drug Administration, "Guidance for Industry: A Food Labeling Guide, Appendix F: Calculate the Percent Daily Value for the Appropriate Nutrients," last modified October 2009, fda.gov/Food/GuidanceComplianceRegulatory Information/GuidanceDocuments/FoodLabelingNutrition/FoodLabelingGuide/default.htm.

DV = Daily Value, nutritional requirements according to the Food and Drug Administration, based on 2,000 calories per day.

*In 2010 the IOM updated the RDA for calcium, with new recommendations according to age and sex: 1,000 mg for men 19 to 70 and women 19 to 50; 1,200 mg for women 51 and older and men 71 and older.

†Although the DV for sodium is set at 2,400 mg, in 2004 the IOM set the "Adequate Intake" level at 1,500 mg for ages 9 to 50.

‡Although the DV for vitamin D is set at 400 IU, in 2010 the Institute of Medicine (IOM) set the Recommended Daily Allowance (RDA) at 600 IU for ages 1 to 70.

Glossary

advanced glycation end products (AGEs) Compounds formed when animal proteins are cooked with sugars in the absence of water which are linked to inflammation, diabetes, kidney disease, and Alzheimer's disease

alkaloids A member of a large group of chemicals that are made by plants and contain nitrogen; they often appear in Chinese traditional herbs to treat conditions like asthma and pain, though not enough research has been performed on their health implications. Although excessive alkaloid intake is linked with promoting inflammation, cooking plants appears to lower alkaloid content

allicin The active ingredient in garlic that provides its known health benefits, such as antimicrobial action, as well as its distinctive odor

alpha-carotene A carotenoid found in plant foods that can be converted in the body into retinol, or vitamin A (see Nutrients in Action, page 394)

anthocyanin (also, related compounds **anthocyanidins, proanthocyanins**) Pigment producing blue and red colors in flowers and plants with antioxidant and anti-inflammatory abilities linked with health benefits, such as heart health, cancer protection, and brain protection

antioxidant A substance that may protect your cells against the effects of free radicals that can damage cells and that may play a role in heart disease, cancer, and other diseases

beta-amyloids The chief component of plaques that characterize the Alzheimer's brain; the pathogenesis has been related to inflammation

beta-carotene A yellow-orange compound found in various fruits and vegetables that serves as a precursor to vitamin A, or retinol (see Nutrients in Action, page 394)

beta-cryptoxanthin One of a group of carotenoids found in plant foods that can be made into vitamin A, or retinol, in the body (see Nutrients in Action, page 394)

beta-glucans Polysaccharides or fibers consisting of glucose units, found in grains such as barley and oats, linked with lowering blood cholesterol and boosting immune function

betalains Class of plant pigments that impart a red-violet or yellow-orange color and provide antioxidant and anti-inflammatory action

body mass index (BMI) A measure of body fat based on height and weight that applies to adult men and women

capsaicin A component of many types of hot peppers that provides their heat and other bioactive properties which are being investigated for treatment in pain relief and nerve disorders

carotenoids A large group of compounds found in fruits and vegetables, some that are converted to vitamin A or retinol, that promote antioxidant and immune-enhancing activity

catechin The major antioxidant flavonoid component in green tea, linked with protection against a variety of chronic diseases

cellulose A type of insoluble fiber that makes up most of the cell walls of plants and promotes good elimination and colon health

chlorophyll The green photosynthetic pigment found in plants that early research has associated with cancer protection

concentrated animal feeding operations (CAFOs) Agricultural operations where animals are raised in confined situations

Daily Value (DV) Nutrient levels developed by the U.S. Food and Drug Administration to help consumers determine the level of various nutrients in a standard serving of food in relation to their approximate requirements for the nutrients

dietary cholesterol A waxy substance found in animal tissues, that when eaten at high levels is linked with increasing blood lipids that may increase the risk for developing heart disease

dyslipidemia An abnormal condition, linked with increased risk for heart disease, characterized by either too high or too low amounts of lipids, such as total cholesterol, LDL cholesterol, or HDL cholesterol in the blood

ellagic acid/ellegitannin A phenolic compound found in nuts, berries, and fruits that appears to have anticancer effects

epigallocatechin gallate (EGCG) A catechin flavonoid found in green tea that may be at the root of health benefits linked with drinking tea

eugenol An active compound found in cloves linked with protection from cancer and inflammation

fermentable fibers Fibers found in fruits, vegetables, oats, and barley that are readily fermented by bacteria naturally found in the colon, thus increasing the numbers of friendly bacteria

ferulic acid A common plant antioxidant found in plant cell walls, leaves, and seeds that possesses antioxidant, anti-inflammatory, and anticancer action

flavonoids Flavonoids are ubiquitous in plants and include a wide variety of polyphenolic phytochemicals, with subclasses including **flavonols**, **flavones**, and **flavanones**. They offer antioxidant, anti-inflammatory, anticancer, antimicrobial, and antiviral effects which may protect against several diseases

free radicals A reactive atom or atoms produced in the body by natural biological processes or introduced from an outside source (such as tobacco smoke, toxins, or pollutants) that can damage cells, proteins, and DNA by altering their chemical structure

fucoidans A compound found in brown algae and brown seaweed that appears to offer antioxidant, anti-inflammatory, and anticancer effects

gamma-linolenic acid An essential omega-6 fatty acid found in some plant-based oils which preliminary research links with potential health attributes, such as lowering blood pressure and treating pain in arthritis and diabetic nerve damage

genetically modified Derived from an organism in which DNA has been intentionally altered for the purpose of improvement or correction of defects

gingerol An active constituent of ginger with anti-inflammatory properties that may help ease symptoms such as pain associated with arthritis

glycemic index (GI) A numerical index given to a carbohydrate-rich food that is based on the average increase in blood glucose levels after the food is eaten

glycemic load (GL) A ranking system for carbohydrate content in food portions based on their glycemic index (GI) and a standardized portion size of 100 grams

gut microflora Microorganisms that naturally occur in the digestive tract of animals and humans; a healthy population of friendly gut bacteria may promote health benefits, including digestive and immune support

HDL cholesterol The cholesterol in high-density lipoproteins; "good" cholesterol

hemicelluloses Type of insoluble fiber found in plant cell walls that promotes good digestive and colon health

heterocyclic amines (HCAs) Various carcinogenic compounds that are formed when meat is cooked at high temperature

inflammation A response to injury or infection characterized by redness, heat, swelling, and pain and involving a complex series of events that leads to the migration of white blood cells to the inflamed area

insoluble fiber Fiber that is not dispersible in water or digestible by humans and that provides bulk to the stool

insulin A hormone secreted by the beta-cells of the pancreas, required for normal glucose metabolism

insulin resistance A physiological condition where the natural hormone insulin becomes less effective at lowering blood sugars

ischemic heart disease Any of a group of acute or chronic cardiac disabilities resulting from insufficient supply of oxygenated blood to the heart

isoflavones One of a family of phytoestrogens found chiefly in soybeans that lowers blood cholesterol levels

LDL cholesterol The cholesterol in low-density lipoproteins; "bad" cholesterol

lignans A diverse group of plant-derived compounds that form the building blocks of plant cell walls and offer heart disease and diabetes protection

limonoids A class of phytochemicals abundant in citrus fruits that have anticancer action

lutein A yellow carotenoid pigment found widely in nature linked with protection against age-related eye disease

lycopene A red carotenoid pigment found primarily in tomatoes associated with heart health and prostate cancer protection

menthol/menthone Major compounds that give mint its aroma and cooling properties and have been linked with improvement of pain

metabolic syndrome A combination of medical conditions that places one at increased risk for cardiovascular disease and type 2 diabetes

monoterpenes Compounds found in the essential oils of plants, like herbs, fruits, and vegetables, and linked with cancer protection

monounsaturated fatty acids (MUFAs) Unsaturated fatty acids that contain a single double bond and are linked with lowering heart disease and diabetes risk

neurotransmitters A chemical substance that transmits nerve impulses across a synapse

nitroso compounds A class of organic compounds present in various foods and found to be carcinogenic in laboratory animals

nutrient dense Having a high nutrient-to-calorie ratio

nutritional yeast An inactive yeast grown on a nutrient-rich culture to produce a condiment that is naturally rich in vitamins and minerals and often enriched with others

oleocanthal A compound found in extra virgin olive oil that is responsible for the pungent, stinging sensation sometimes experienced in the throat when eating olive oil and that has been shown to decrease inflammation levels in the body

oleuropein A antioxidant polyphenolic compound found in olive oil

oligosaccharide A type of fiber found in some fruits, vegetables, seeds, and grains that resists digestion and feeds gut bacteria, thus promoting digestive and immune health

omega-3 fatty acids Any of several polyunsaturated fatty acids found in leafy green vegetables, vegetable oils, walnuts, flax, and cold-water fish linked with heart health

omega-6 fatty acids Essential fatty acids needed for normal growth and development, found in vegetable oils

oxidative stress A condition in which the effects of oxidation exceed the ability of antioxidant systems to neutralize them, resulting in damaging effects to cells and DNA

phlorotannins A type of tannin found in brown algae and kelp that possesses antioxidant activities

phenols/phenolic acids/phenolic compounds A large, diverse group of compounds found in plants, such as nuts, grains, fruits, and vegetables, that possess antioxidant properties and appear to impact human health in various ways

phytic acid/phytates The storage form of phosphate in plants that possesses antioxidant properties

phytochemicals Chemicals produced by plants that may affect health but are not essential nutrients

phytoestrogens Compounds with estrogenic activity that are derived from plants such as beans, grains, and seeds

phytosterols/plant sterols Plant-derived compounds that are similar in structure and function to cholesterol, thus may block the absorption of cholesterol in the body

polycyclic aromatic hydrocarbons (PAHs) Chemical pollutants formed during incomplete combustion of organic substances such as coal, oil, wood, and tobacco as well as food

polyunsaturated fatty acids (PUFAs) Fatty acids with more than one double bond between carbon atoms, linked with decreased risk of heart disease and diabetes

prebiotics Specialized plant fibers that beneficially nourish the good bacteria already in the large bowel or colon

protease inhibitors Compounds that treat or prevent infection by viruses by interfering with the protease enzyme

psyllium A fiber isolated from the husks of psyllium seeds that lowers cholesterol levels

quercetin A yellow flavonoid pigment found in fruits with antioxidant and anti-inflammatory abilities that may offer protection against heart disease and cancer

resistant starch A type of starch that resists digestion in the small intestine and may help lower glucose levels

resveratrol A polyphenolic compound found in grapes, red wine, purple grape juice, peanuts, and some berries linked with heart health

rosmarinic acid A polyphenol found in herbs of the mint family with antibacterial, antioxidant, and anti-inflammatory properties

salicylate An anti-inflammatory compound found naturally in plants; an active ingredient in many over-the-counter medications

saponins Compounds found naturally in plants that have a foaming characteristic when mixed with water and that appear to lower blood cholesterol levels

saturated fats Fatty acids with no double bonds between carbon atoms linked with raising total and LDL cholesterol levels

soluble fiber Type of fiber that is dispersible in water, forms a viscous gel, and is easily fermented by bacteria in the gut; linked with lowering blood cholesterol

stearidonic acid A naturally occurring PUFA with similar characteristics to omega-3 fatty acids

stone fruit A fruit with a fleshy outer part that surrounds a seed, such as apricots, cherries, and plums

sulfur compounds (e.g., glucosinolates, isothiocyanates, indoles) A group of sulfur-containing compounds found naturally in cruciferous vegetables, such as broccoli, Brussels sprouts, and cabbage, that have been linked with anticancer effects

tannins A large group of yellowish brown plant-derived compounds with antioxidant activity

terpenoids A large group of organic compounds found in almost all plants that show antioxidant activities

textured vegetable protein (TVP) A protein substance extracted from soy protein, soy flour or concentrate, cotton seeds, wheat, or oats and extruded into various shapes for use as a meat substitute

tocopherols/tocotrienols Compounds in the vitamin E family (see Nutrients in Action, page 393)

trans fats Fatty acids that are commonly produced by partially hydrogenating the unsaturated fatty acid in vegetable oils and are linked with poor blood lipid profiles

tyrosol A major phenolic antioxidant found in olives that may offer potential heart health benefits

vanillic acid A phenolic acid that is the oxidized form of vanillin

zeaxanthin A yellow carotenoid pigment found in many plant foods and important for eye health

Acknowledgments

I am deeply grateful to so many people for their contributions to this book. The first time I heard David L. Katz, MD, speak at a nutrition conference, he likened our current eating environment to transporting polar bears to the desert—we are no more adapted to our lifestyle of high-calorie foods and no physical activity than polar bears are to dry, hot climates. Since then, I have been completely inspired by his unique vision of how we can turn the tide of obesity and chronic diseases through diet and exercise. I am honored that he shared his eloquent words of nutrition wisdom in the foreword of my book.

My agent Linda Konner led me through the process of taking my book idea to fruition in the most professional and nurturing way possible. Matthew Lore, the editor and publisher at The Experiment, believed in my book from the start. It is an incredible experience for a dietitian-author to work with a publisher who, along with his whole team, is so firmly committed to health, nutrition, wellness, and plant-based diets. And my assistant and dietetic intern, Briana Austin, spent hours helping me review the nutritional information for my recipes.

My thanks goes out to thousands of registered dietitians working in the front lines every day, in clinics, hospitals, offices, schools, and research laboratories, helping to make a difference in the way people eat and live their lives. Every day, my colleagues inspire me to kick it up a notch as I write on nutrition and optimal health. In particular, there are several inspiring nutrition professionals sharing reliable information to the public on plant-based diets through programs like the Vegetarian Resource Group and the Loma Linda University School of Public Health, my alma mater.

The people who really made this book happen are my family. My sons Christian and Nicholas "suffered" through their childhood complaining, "How come we don't eat like 'normal' people?" Now at 15 and 14, they're proud of their "unusual" eating style. And they became my guinea pigs when our home kitchen turned into a test kitchen for researching healthy plant-based recipes. Most of all, I'd like to thank my husband, Peter, for his love and support throughout the creation of this book. He not only helped me to manage my ramped-up schedule during the book-writing process but has enthusiastically subscribed to a plant-powered omnivorous diet and looks and feels great as a result. This makes me feel especially hopeful that we will share a long, healthy life together.

Index

Note: Page numbers in *italics* refer to charts and lists.